Abolishing State Violence

A World Beyond Bombs, Borders, and Cages

Ray Acheson

Haymarket Books

Chicago, Illinois

Published in 2022 by
Haymarket Books
P.O. Box 180165
Chicago, IL 60618
773-583-7884
www.haymarketbooks.org
info@haymarketbooks.org

ISBN: 978-1-64259-693-9

Distributed to the trade in the US through Consortium Book Sales and Distribution (www.cbsd.com) and internationally through Ingram Publisher Services International (www.ingramcontent.com).

This book was published with the generous support of Lannan Foundation and Wallace Action Fund.

Special discounts are available for bulk purchases by organizations and institutions. Please email orders@haymarketbooks.org for more information.

Cover design by David Gee.

Printed in Canada by union labor.

Library of Congress Cataloging-in-Publication data is available.

10 9 8 7 6 5 4 3 2 1

Abolishing State Violence

for all the abolitionists,
past, present, and future

and for tim and nela,
for solidarity and laughter

Contents

Introduction

In the sizzling northern hemisphere summer of 2020, demands for police abolition burst into mainstream public consciousness. As people around the world took to the streets in revolt against police brutality in the wake of George Floyd's murder in Minneapolis, among the principal rallying cries were Defund the Police and Abolish the Police. These demands took many people by surprise, yet were a clarion call built from decades, even centuries, of abolitionist organizing. Just as Floyd's murder was the latest in a long bloodied and bruised history of police brutality against Black lives and the lives of other people of color, LGBTQ+ people, and other marginalized and criminalized people, the call for abolition also has a long and storied past.

Throughout history, people have demanded the abolition of structures and systems that cause harm. Activists, organizers, and inspired people around the world have demanded the abolition of slavery and segregation; of restrictions and discrimination based on sex, gender, sexual orientation, race, or religion; of weapons and of war; of the death penalty and unlawful detention; of economic inequalities and the capitalist system; and of so much more. Each of these demands were, or continue to be, met with derision. Structures or systems that have now been abolished were once considered instrumental to economics or politics, the calls to dismantle them treated as naïve, irrational, or irresponsible. For the struggles still underway, the obstacles are similar—ridicule and deliberate spread of misinformation; massive investments in "reforms" instead of real change; and, fundamentally, failure of imagination that keeps people's minds locked

1

into believing that systems of oppression are the best chance we have for survival, even as the evidence mounts that these same systems are responsible for our pain—and now, increasingly, for our extinction.

Nevertheless, abolitionist organizers persist. People agitating for change have worked for generations to open the minds of naysayers to the possibilities of alternative ways of living and organizing our societies. They have sought to change the economic, political, and social costs and benefits of these structures. They have altered, disrupted, and undone the pursuits of power and profit that have been forged by the few at the expense of the very, very many. Strikes, walkouts, sit-ins, boycotts, marches, rallies, petitions, letter writing, phone calls, direct action, street theater, public debates, media engagement, and so much more—these are but some of the tools devised and employed by those working for change.

Much of this work has taken place within the framework of abolitionism. Evoking a historical continuity, the language and practice of abolition provides context and clarity to our efforts for social transformation. "Many abolitionists root this work in W.E.B. Du Bois' classic analysis of abolition democracy," note scholars Dan Berger and David Stein. This includes "the political struggle led by formerly enslaved people in the wake of the Civil War to construct new institutions while also eradicating violent ones."[1] The simultaneous pursuit of tearing down violent structures while building up systems for equality, justice, and well-being is the crux of abolitionism. This dual effort is also rooted in the earliest days of the tradition. While some antislavery activists worked just for the abolition of slavery, others recognized "that slavery could not be comprehensively eradicated simply by disestablishing the institution itself, leaving intact the economic, political, and cultural conditions within which slavery flourished," organizer Angela Davis explains. "They understood that abolition would require a thorough reorganization of U.S. society—economically, politically, and socially—in order to guarantee the incorporation of formerly enslaved Black people into a new democratic order."[2]

That this process never occurred is why the United States continues to face issues of systemic and structural racism in 2020 that should have been addressed more than one hundred years ago, Davis argues. Thus, the project of the "radical reconstruction" of US society, called for by Martin Luther King Jr., is ongoing.[3] But since the abolition of slavery, the framework of abolitionism has been instrumental in guiding work against other structures of state violence, from the capitalist system to nuclear bombs. Multitudes of people across a myriad of identities, experiences, and geographies have been part of abolitionist projects. Black organizers, Chicanx and Latinx activists, Muslim groups, Indigenous nations, Quakers, pacifists, disarmament and anti-war activists, veterans, feminists, LGBTQ+ communities, communists, socialists and others on the radical Left, workers, people on the move, faith and interfaith groups, disability rights groups, and many, many others have agitated and organized for social transformation through abolition of weapons, wars, borders, police, prisons, capitalism, and many other structures that serve oppression and inequality.

The frame of abolition speaks directly to the need not only to put an end to a particular source of harm but to fundamentally transform the political, economic, and social relations that allowed that source of harm to grow and persist. It's about looking at the root causes of harm and violence and working to build alternatives that prevent this harm, rather than relying on existing structures that only create more harm. Abolition seeks not the destruction, but the *transformation* of our current world order, including through the disarming, demilitarizing, defunding, and disbanding of entities of coercive state power that work against peace and freedom. Abolition is not just about tearing down the system, but also about building anew, based on cooperation, equity, and justice for all. Abolition is a political project of "promiscuous care"—of living in a more expansive way than our current capitalist, racist, patriarchal society tells us we can.[4]

Systems abolition

Abolition is about more than one aspect of injustice or harm. The forces and philosophies that stand against justice, peace, equality, and care are pervasive, enmeshed within and throughout multiple structures of violence. Patriarchy, for example, is an overarching system of power embedded in all the structures discussed in this book. Patriarchy is, in the barest sense, a hierarchical social order that not only insists men "are inherently dominating, superior to everything and everyone deemed weak," as bell hooks explains, but that also endows the hegemonic male "with the right to dominate and rule over the weak and to maintain that dominance through various forms of psychological terrorism and violence."[5]

Patriarchy shapes and entrenches gender as a cultural construction. It insists upon norms, roles, and conditions of being a "man" and a "woman." It thus oppresses not just women but anyone who does not conform to norms of their prescribed gender or to the gender binary. This includes men who do not abide by the cultural expectations of "masculinity," as well as gender nonconforming, nonbinary, intersex, and trans people. It is important to note that such norms are constructed—they are neither inherent nor universal. Gender norms are produced in various sites, including through the policies of states, security discourses, education, media debates, popular culture, and family relations.[6]

Patriarchy is also about more than gender or sex. It is a philosophy of domination not just of men and masculinity but also of whiteness and wealth, of able-bodiedness and heteronormativity. It derives from the capitalist prioritization of profit over people, and helps sustain the militarism that accumulates wealth through war. Together with racism, colonialism, and imperialism, patriarchy permeates the systems that oppress us and must be confronted within each, abolished as part of the abolition of the systems it sustains, informs, feeds. Decolonization, gender and racial justice, ecological well-being, and global equality are thus imperative for the abolition of each of the structures of violence we confront in these pages.

The book starts with policing and prisons as related structures of violence that are (largely) internal to the state. It then turns to surveillance as apparatus and technique deployed within these structures and also beyond them, including at borders, which is the fourth structure of violence considered. As we move beyond the state, we look at wars and nuclear weapons as global manifestations of state violence, and finally capitalism—and its colonial, militarist, and racist machinations—as a system of violence underpinning the rest.

Capitalism is at the core of all of these structures, an overarching system that generates and sustains exploitation and oppression, as well as the state institutions that enforce them. Black thinkers and organizers have traced the lines from economic privilege to social control—lines marked on bodies and drawn as borders, between countries, between "us" and "them," north and south, poor and rich, white and Black. As Ruth Wilson Gilmore, Angela Davis, and others have shown, the US capitalist state uses police and prisons as a racialized system for class control. Similarly, the state turns to surveillance to monitor exploited and oppressed people and control their resistance. It thereby protects the rule of the capitalist class and its ability to make profit through exploitation of workers and land, plants, animals, water, and air.

The same systemic forces shape states' border regimes. As Harsha Walia, Justin Akers Chacón, and others argue, states use their borders to criminalize racialized migrant labor, suppress those workers' wages, intimidate them, and thereby prevent them from organizing resistance. This enables the capitalist class to drive down the wages of all workers and politically divide them between citizen and migrant, undermining the capacity of the labor movement to effectively challenge the capitalist system.

The system also drives capitalist states into competition with one another to protect their corporations' market share, access to resources, and ability to accumulate wealth. It sets states up to compete for geopolitical hegemony. This can trigger arms races, including nuclear ones, and even war. This inter-state competition shaped the whole of the twentieth century and its impact continues today. We are now immersed in yet another arms race, with global military spending on the rise and with all the nuclear-armed states investing billions into "modernizing" and expanding their nuclear arsenals. The blatant attempts by the so-called great power rivals to resurrect the Cold War is clearly a response to capitalist crises and global uprisings. Their answer to unrest is more weapons, more war, requiring investments in the military machine, expansions of "spheres of influence," and oppressions of populations at home and abroad in the name of stability and security. As the world burns, of course, this stability and security is only for the small subset of humanity holding the box of matches and the lighter fluid.

The Red Nation, a coalition of Native and non-Native organizers working for Indigenous resistance and liberation in the United States, has clearly mapped these cogs in the US capitalist wheel. "The military it uses to enforce its global domination and steal natural resources from the Global South; the police it empowers to repress domestic resistance to occupation; and the prisons it funds to warehouse and punish those who do not adhere to settler capitalist social norms" have been coalesced into "an occupying force on stolen land that operates by reinforcing settler dominance, white supremacy, and global imperialism."[7] This system is replicated and modified globally, with many other countries adapting these forms of violence to suit their capitalist needs. Violence is upon us, in so many ways from so many places. *I can't breathe* is no metaphor; it is daily life in the Anthropocene.

The structures of violence do not live in isolation, they grow from and strengthen each other, like vines crawling a trellis for support. The war on terror's architecture, Darakshan Raja of the Justice for Muslims Collective argues, is dependent on the infrastructure and the politics of the prison industrial complex, including the apparatus of surveillance and incarceration.[8] The systemic anti-Black racism in the United States helped shape the development of the Patriot Act and the construction of Muslims as a criminal threat, while the framework of national security and militarization, utilized in wars against brown people around the world, did not need to be created in 2001, only inflated. The Black Power movement recognized the US war against Viet Nam as a form of policing that had to be contested along with policing at home, as law professor Aziz Rana notes.[9] The structures of racist, imperialist violence spilling blood across Southeast Asian rice fields were the same as those tearing apart communities in US cities.

They are also the same as those tearing apart families at the border and constructing a Latinx and other "non-white" other and simultaneously ensuring those "others" engage in essential work under circumstances in which they have no rights or any kind of political voice. Border politics, Rana argues, are a direct successor to the logics that generated Jim Crow in the past. Along with the prison industrial complex and war, he explains, borders are specific spaces that highlight the foundational dichotomy of US society, which is that freedom for some is predicated on the exclusion of others. Furthermore, all three share the operative framework of policing and all are defined by systemic state impunity.

Settler colonialism, nuclear weapons, and surveillance also fit into this framework. Each relies on the construction of "the other" to be controlled, surveilled, or exterminated in order to provide for the freedom and the "security" of those privileged on the basis of race or wealth within US society. To this end, the concept of inherent criminality is essential. Whether it's Indigenous people to be massacred, Black people to be enslaved or incarcerated, Muslims or Arabs or those perceived to be from the Middle East to be surveilled, rendered, tortured, or drone striked, or the Russians or Chinese or North Koreans or <insert perceived enemy here> to be bombed with nuclear weapons, or the Latinx or Caribbean or African asylum seekers, migrants, or refugees to be detained or deported, or LGBTQ+ people to be criminalized or kept from having equal rights and access—each of these constructions relies on the idea that there is something intrinsic to particular peoples that precludes them from enjoying the same rights and freedoms as others. Each of these constructions also necessitates and facilitates the processing of human beings as objects, of systematically dehumanizing people as categories and identities to be sorted into those that will be accepted, tolerated, or rejected.

All of this is done in the name of so-called safety and security. Police and prisons, we are told, are necessary to maintain law and order. Borders are necessary to ensure countries of the North are not "overrun" with people wanting access to "our" resources and well-being. Surveillance is necessary to prevent terrorist attacks. Wars are necessary to maintain international law and order, and nuclear weapons are necessary to prevent wars. All of the posturing and fearmongering and chest thumping from our political leaders, the military, the police, the media, and all the government and many nongovernment entities is blasting us all day every day with the message that all of this violence and all of these weapons and all of the discriminations and inequalities are necessary to "keep us safe." We are told and taught that this is the way the world is and there is no way to change it. Tweak it, maybe, but change it—not a chance. There's an age-old saying that it's easier to imagine the end of the world than the end of capitalism—well, that is also true for most when it comes to prisons, police, borders, nuclear bombs, or war.

This framing of the inevitability of it all, the disorientations and the deceptions necessary to lull us into acceptance of the oppression of the majority to retain vast inequitable privileges and freedoms of a minority, is very, very lucrative for some. The corporate profiteers of occupying forces are as entwined as their projects of oppression. Many of the same companies are involved in manufacturing weapons, building surveillance technologies, and militarizing borders; others profit both from incarcerating US citizens and detaining asylum seekers and migrants. Some are involved in both bombing and then rebuilding other countries, while others extract minerals and fossil fuels from the earth while lobbying against freedom of movement for the people displaced by their devastation. This is war, and they are the profiteers.

Just as entangled as the corporate threads are the strategies and policies that enable them. Take deterrence, for example. The idea that if you inflict enough pain, you can prevent others from undertaking certain actions runs like a river through nuclear weapon policy, imperial war-making, border enforcement, and the prison industrial complex. Deterrence is not really about dissuasion; it's about death. Callous and cruel, deterrence practices incarcerate or kill in an attempt to prevent any action that threatens the power of the state. Deterrence requires endless investments in the occupying forces, because deterrence Does. Not. Work. Prisons don't deter "crime," borders don't deter migration, nuclear weapons don't deter conflict.

But they are, nevertheless, productive. Whether in relation to policing, prisons, borders, bombs, or war, the harms caused by the state apparatus in service of capitalism generate the "structural distribution of vulnerability"[10] that is necessary for the system to continue. "Capitalism does not just produce a universal relation of waged labor," writes border abolitionist Harsha Walia. "Capitalism actually requires and reproduces the racial hierarchies that underpin all the processes of territorial expansion, dispossession, enslavement, ownership, proletarianization, surveillance, and border rule."[11]

Each of these, in turn, tries to render invisible the people who suffer from this "productive violence." From offshore detention and the use of deserts and oceans as deterrents and death traps, to the incarceration of Black, queer, poor, and other criminalized communities, to remote-controlled warfare targeting "killable bodies" from afar, to erasing Indigeneity and Native realities from US history and current life, the "occupying forces" operate through "the creation of distance and concealment" in order to inform and enforce "our understandings of 'progress' and 'civilization.'"[12] What we can't see, we won't object to; what we don't know, we can't fight. "Certain images do not appear in the media," explains philosopher Judith Butler, "certain names of the dead are not utterable, certain losses are not avowed as losses, and violence is derealized and diffused.... The violence that we inflict on others is only—and always—selectively brought into public view."[13] But the violence is there, and the bodies are piling up. "The dead live in our backyard," writes border violence researcher Jason De León. "They are the human grist for the sovereignty machine."[14]

Yet the grinds and gears of institutionalized abuse and misery are not infallible. They are not invincible. They are not magic. They churn through human life and chew up the lives of animal, land, and water relations— they need us. Not our consent but our participation—through our jobs and purchases, through our choice to ignore wars, drone strikes, and police brutality, through our tacit acceptance of budgets for violence instead of care. The capitalist machine and its tools of violence can be gummed up, broken down, thrown out. New things can be built in their place. We can build them. It is not impossible, only incredibly difficult. But it is also incredibly difficult—and soon, impossible—to survive in the world of death and despair emerging as a great sinkhole beneath our feet. We have a choice: to do nothing, to acquiesce to the fates foretold by the capitalist gods, or revolt and build anew, across all the borders that seem insurmountable now, but can come crumbling down as we create a new democratic society that serves the interests of people and planet. To do this, as Ruth Wilson Gilmore says, "we need to change one thing: everything."[15]

Transform, not reform

> We will never have a complete definition of fascism, because it is in constant motion, showing a new face to fit any particular set of problems that arise to threaten the predominance of the traditionalist, capitalist ruling class. But if one were forced for the sake of clarity to define it in a word simple enough for all to understand, that word would be "reform."
> —**George Jackson**, *Blood in My Eye*[16]

Why abolition instead of reform? Because reform of systems built on discrimination and violence is not just insufficient, it's counterproductive. Reform leaves the underpinning rationales and philosophies intact and tinkers at the edges to make the harm less visible or more palatable. It doesn't eliminate the source of the harms or give space to building and investing in alternative approaches.

Reformism is counterinsurgency, abolitionist Dylan Rodríguez argues. Adjusting isolated aspects of a system's operation to protect that system from total collapse is "bad faith incrementalism" that rests "on the fundamental assumption that these systems must remain intact—even as they consistently produce asymmetrical misery, suffering, premature death, and violent life conditions for certain people and places."[17]

Those working for the abolition of slavery in the United States in the nineteenth century did not call for reforms to this system—for mere changes that would make slavery more "humanitarian." They rightfully demanded its outright abolition. But the structures of segregation, policing, and incarceration were established in slavery's place, leading to continuous repression and criminalization of Black lives. With this, together with the repression and genocide of Indigenous nations and the surveillance and criminalization of other people of color and LGBTQ+ people, came the increasing militarization of the police and borders, the building of the prison industrial complex, the growth of surveillance capitalism, and the endless expansion of the war machine.

This is where reform has gotten us. Body cameras so we can watch police brutalize Black people. Diversity in the military so that women, queer, and trans folks can now kill people with impunity, just like the straight boys do! Less family separation at the border, but more deportation. Fossil fuel companies planting trees to "offset" their destruction of the climate. "Reformism limits the horizon of political possibility to what is seen as achievable within the limits of existing institutional structures," writes Rodríguez, whether in relation to electoral politics, racial capitalism, heteronormativity, the nation-state, or whatever. Not only does it limit our imaginations, reformism "defers, avoids, and even criminalizes peoples' efforts to catalyze fundamental change to an existing order."[18] It makes it *more* difficult to achieve the real transformations we need in our societies—both because the act of reform legitimizes the overall system, but also because it takes away energy, resources, and people power from more meaningful changes.

Organizer Dean Spade notes that abolitionism "helps us discern what kinds of advocacy we will not take up."[19] While reformists work for narrower, shorter-term victories, at best they will leave the most vulnerable people behind, and at worst become active participants in reinforcing the violent structures they ostensibly oppose. "If my focus is on ending harm, then I can't be pro death-making and harmful institutions," says Mariame Kaba, one of the foremost feminist thinkers and organizers for abolition. "I'm actually trying to eradicate harm, not reproduce it, not reinforce it, not maintain it."[20]

This isn't to say that all reform is bad. There is a difference between reforms that strengthen the status quo and reforms that fundamentally challenge and change the existing structure of violent power. Ruth Wilson Gilmore and other abolitionists describe these as "non-reformist reforms." Reforms that reinvest in the system (e.g., bias training for police officers) are fundamentally different from reforms that divest from the system (e.g., reduction of police budgets). Reducing funding is reform, but it is reform toward abolition. It is reform that moves us away from reliance on a system of violence and instead gives us freedom to invest in alternatives that might offer a better chance at well-being and justice.

"The long arc of abolition does not have to be abstract," writes journalist Todd Miller. "It can be constructed in small steps, based on direct community needs, of a practical political project."[21] Abolition is not just a goal, it's a practical organizing strategy.[22] There are hundreds of ideas, actions, and organizing efforts for abolition already underway throughout the United States and in many other countries. As can be seen throughout these pages, creative, courageous efforts are being made to deconstruct and reconstruct a society that fits all our needs, a society that offers peace instead of profit, well-being instead of warfare, and safety instead of surveillance.

Dismantle, change, build

In this work, it's important that we're building as much as we're taking apart. "Abolition is not primarily a negative strategy," Angela Davis has said. "It's not primarily about dismantling, getting rid of, but it's about re-envisioning, it's about building anew." And in this, she argues, "abolition is a feminist strategy."[23]

Feminism is a methodological approach and practice that, among other things, helps us to understand the intersectionality of oppressions, struggles, and identities, and to challenge systems of oppression such as patriarchy and white supremacy. Intersectional feminism is about centering the voices of those experiencing overlapping, concurrent forms of oppression in order to understand the depths of the inequalities and the relationships among them.[24] As theory and practice it can help us recognize that the threats to our safety and security "come not primarily from what is defined as 'crime,'" explains Davis, but rather from the failure of institutions to address issues of health, violence, education, and so forth. In this sense, "abolition is really about rethinking the kind of future we want, the social future, the economic future, the political future. It's about revolution."[25]

Abolition is about rejecting the current structures as a source of, rather than a solution to, violence. It's about building alternatives. In place of police and prisons, we must build a system of community-based mechanisms to respond to harms caused, as well as invest in education, jobs, housing, healthcare, mental health, food security, and more to prevent the conditions that lead to this harm. In place of discrimination and violence against Indigenous communities, we must initiate processes of decolonization and restoration of Indigenous lands and governance. In place of borders, we must enable freedom of movement and instill respect for the human right to live, while also providing reparations for the destruction wrought in so many countries from colonialism, capitalism, conflict, and climate change.

Indeed, redressing harms caused is important for all projects of abolition, whether for survivors of nuclear weapons or police brutality or colonial genocide or sexual violence. It is within spaces of atonement and remedy that we can learn the lessons of post-conflict transformation and projects of transformative justice. Securing a ceasefire, undergoing a peace process, and engaging in disarmament, demilitarization, reintegration, and restoration of the community, including through truth and reconciliation processes, are all part of the work necessary to achieve lasting peace and redirect communities from conflict and punishment toward personal and collective restorative justice. This is an essential part of the abolition process: the rebuilding of community through accountability and commitment to change.

"Abolition is a movement to end systemic violence including the interpersonal vulnerabilities and displacements that keep the system going," writes Ruth Wilson Gilmore. "In other words, the goal is to change how we interact with each other and the planet by putting people before profits, welfare before warfare, and life over death."[26]

We are often told that abolition is naïve. That we are inviting chaos into our world by thinking of dismantling any of these structures of violence. For each project of abolition, there is the same refrain: "But what about those who would seek to do us harm!?!" We are told that we must have police, we must have prisons, we must have borders, and above all else, we must have weapons!

But why must we? Our current world order has been built, by and large, by capitalist, racist, militarist patriarchs. We are conditioned to believe that police, prisons, and nuclear weapons are the "necessary evils" of our world—but they are only "necessary" in a construct built to value and profit from violence instead of peace, the hoarding of fortunes instead of sharing and equitable distribution, the privileges of patriarchy, heteronormativity, and white supremacy, and on and on. Abolition is about rejecting and tearing down the structures that sustain this world order of inequity and horror. But it is also so much more. In Critical Resistance's book *Abolition Now!*, scholar and activist Alexis Pauline Gumbs asks:

> What if abolition isn't a shattering thing, not a crashing thing, not a wrecking ball event? What if abolition is something that sprouts out of the wet places in our eyes, the broken places in our skin, the waiting places in our palms, the tremble holding in my mouth when I turn to you? What if abolition is something that grows? What if [abolition] is the fruit of our diligent gardening, building and deepening of a movement to respond to the violence of the state and the violence of our communities with sustainable, transformative love?[27]

This is the nature of the work ahead for those willing to decarcerate their minds from the restrictions of our current system and work with others for the creation of a new world. A world based in promiscuous care for each other instead of a world ordered by state violence through the tools of oppression and violence. A world that prioritizes decolonization and investments in the well-being of people, animals, land, and water rather than the destructive forces of capitalism, colonialism, racism, and patriarchy. A world without states, without borders, without bombs and cages.

The work for peace, freedom, equality, and well-being of people and planet is intertwined, connected branch and vine through our movements for justice and transformation. We all come to this work from different spaces and experiences, and we each have something different to offer. In that spirit, this book is not meant to offer a definitive account of abolitionist projects. It seeks to convey and connect some of the current critical thinking about and action against certain structures of violence, including police, prisons, surveillance, borders, war, nuclear weapons, and capitalism. Much more than what can be described in these pages is out there. People around our planet have been working for decades, collectively and independently, with faith that others are out there with them, sharing in the struggle. Hopefully, some may find each other in the work described here.

While most of the chapters offer international perspectives, the focus is on the United States because its behavior and policies affect so many other countries, including through its wars, occupations, and military bases; its training of soldiers, police, and border officials in other countries; and the export of its weapons and systems of militarism around the world. The United States is exceptional—though not in the way it thinks it is.

Yet the structures and stories in these pages are globally present, manifesting in various ways in various contexts. Capitalist violence is universal; we just experience it differently depending on where in the machine we currently live. The more we can see, of the system and of each other, the better chance we have of weaving our hands together through the cogs of the machine, to grasp each other and take hold of the radical idea that we can build a world of peace, freedom, justice, and solidarity for us all.

Chapter 1

Disbanding Police

At the end of May 2020, protests erupted across the United States following the murder of George Floyd by police in Minneapolis. In response, heavily militarized police forces cracked down violently against people in the streets. As one commentator noted on May 30, "The police are rioting across America tonight—shooting and mowing down protestors, assaulting journalists, terrorising neighbourhoods, gleefully brutalising and arresting civilians en masse."[1] Another highlighted that "police all over the country teargassed protestors, drove vehicles through crowds, opened fire with non-lethal rounds on journalists or people on their own property, and in at least one instance, pushed over an elderly man who was walking away with a cane."[2] The violence continued for weeks, with police kettling, beating, and arresting protestors, deploying tear gas, and breaking bones.

The show of overwhelming and violent force from police, backed by the National Guard and threats by the US president to deploy the military[3] and shoot protestors,[4] may have appeared shocking to some, but is rooted in long-standing and ongoing patterns of racist police brutality. This brutality is a fixture of the US carceral, militarist, and imperialist systems. The "band of brothers" in blue, much like the military, is part of the apparatus of coercive state power designed and deployed to maintain the privileges of the elite. Borne through the enclosure of the commons,[5] shaped by settler colonialism, raised by slavery and segregation, trained by military operations abroad, and reinforced through the rise of the prison industrial complex and border imperialism, US policing is a key node in the network of the "national security state," which relies on perpetual war abroad and oppression at home to sustain itself. This is not an issue of individual police officers, good or bad. This is an issue of structure: of systemic racism and a culture of militarism within policing *as a whole*.

Police violence and racism are not, of course, limited to the United States. But examining the particular history of US policing is important for understanding a broader trajectory of structural violence both within the United States and the violence it has exported abroad. The United States plays an outsized role in training police in other countries and in exporting weapons and militarism abroad; the material and conceptual approaches of the US government to domestic control and global domination are intimately related. Thus, so too are the movements and demands to effect change. Defunding, demilitarizing, disarming, and disbanding the police, and instead investing in care and transformative justice to prevent and address harms, are relevant not just to opposing the carceral system in the United States. They're also material to ending the structures and violences of war, militarism, and border imperialism in which the US government engages and perpetuates abroad. And while the historical dynamics may differ in other countries, the problems of carcerality as the solution to social, political, and economic inequalities are similar across landscapes—and thus the organizing for and building up of alternatives are relevant globally.

Structural racism in policing

The roots of policing as a whole are tied to the enclosure of the commons and the establishment of private property that took place throughout Europe over two hundred years ago. Karl Marx, Friedrich Engels, Michel Foucault, and other philosophers situate the rise of the "police state" in this process as the method devised by governments to create what scholar Mark Neocleous describes as a "peaceful and secure order of lawful obedience"[6] in the face of dispossession and rising poverty created by capitalism. "A divided world was being engineered by enclosure," writes political geographer Ian G. R. Shaw, "and an industrializing civilization had to forcibly subdue its alienated denizens."[7]

The enclosure of commons, dispossession of those living on the land, and the "forcible subduing" of people also became a key component of settler colonialism. As white settlers moved across the United States beginning in the sixteenth century, they cleared the land by force and took as private property what had been the territorial land and waters of Indigenous nations. The roots of policing in the United States are thus tied, as The Red Nation describes, to the volunteer militias composed of settlers that "slaughtered Indigenous people to clear the land for more plantations."[8]

These plantations were worked by enslaved Africans, forming another node in the origins of US policing. Militias of the state and of plantation owners hunted and captured anyone attempting to escape bondage. But this practice did not end with the abolition of slavery. The police continued to be the main tool the state used to control, monitor, and incarcerate Black people, including in order to ensure the continuation of a cheap labor pool through the bondage of imprisonment. Police were also used to control and suppress Mexicans after the southern border was established through force; East Asians with the Chinese Exclusion Act and Japanese-American internment; and Muslims, particularly after 9/11. As abolitionist Angela Davis writes, "The evolution and expansion of the police and the prisons are constant reminders that capitalism has always fundamentally relied on racism to sustain itself."[9]

In 1967, Black radicals Stokely Carmichael and Charles V. Hamilton coined the term "institutional racism," describing how it worked systematically to keep Black communities down economically and socially.[10] Successive US governments actively constructed racialized inequalities while simultaneously perpetuating notions of racialized "crime," depicting Black poverty and Black resistance to systemic racism as "lawless disorder" that required more and more policing.[11] Keeanga-Yamahtta Taylor explains:

> The political fusion of race and crime plays a critical role in manufacturing racist ideology here and abroad. The overwhelming presence of police in presumed Black spaces—from typical police patrols in neighborhoods to officers' menacing and intimidating role in public schools to their offices in public housing—mark these places as sites of disorder and therefore in need of the hard hand of the law. This hyper-surveillance of Black communities then produces a disproportionate number of arrests, which legitimize calls for even more aggressive policing and more punishment. These are the daily policing practices that conflate race and crime, thereby criminalizing African-Americans. This is what makes policing institutionally racist in the United States.[12]

As explored in books such as *Policing the Planet* and *The End of Policing*, many police tactics have been designed specifically for communities of color, particularly Black communities: broken windows policing,[13] so-called community policing, and stop-and-frisk practices, for example, have all been designed and directed toward surveillance and oppression of people of color, leading to their effective criminalization. LGBTQ+ people, the poor and houseless, sex workers, and others have also been subjected to the same scrutiny and criminalization.

Maintenance of the "order" established between the bourgeois and the landless peasant, settlers and Indigenous nations, white landowners and Black enslaved people, white upper- and middle-class communities and everyone else, has been the main charge of US police forces. Challenges to this order have thus always been met with violence. The brutality in the streets seen in 2020 mirrors the violent response to the civil rights movement, ACT UP's direct actions against HIV/AIDS policies, anti-globalization protests, Occupy Wall Street, or any other social justice efforts in the recent or distant past. The violence isn't new, but as it plays out across our television screens, many are waking up to it for the first time. "Maintaining order" is not about preventing "crime"; it is about maintaining the order of privilege and inequality necessary to sustain capitalism as a system, in which the few accumulate wealth while the majority suffer for it. Institutional racism and militarized police brutality are key tools in this operation.

Building the capacity to maintain this economic and social "order" has required a lot of investment. Between 1977 and 2017, state and local spending on police increased from $42 billion to $115 billion a year, adjusted for inflation. During this period, police spending remained fairly consistent as a share of budgets, while spending on social services has decreased.[14]

Today, some cities spend from 30 to 60 percent of their entire annual budgets on their police forces.[15] The New York Police Department (NYPD), the biggest police force in the United States, has an annual budget of about $5.5 billion. Comparing this amount to global military budgets, the NYPD clocks in as the thirty-sixth largest military in the world. It has about fifty-five thousand employees, nine thousand vehicles, and its own navy, global intelligence agency, and special operations units.[16]

All of this comes at the expense of social services. New York City currently spends "more on policing than on health, homeless services, youth development, and workforce development combined."[17] During the COVID-19 pandemic, most cities increased or maintained their policing budgets while proposing cuts to virtually every other department—jobs, housing, health care, and more. The choices driving these investments clearly demonstrate the lengths to which governments are willing to go in order to maintain the capitalist "order."

International police violence

Globally, similar investment choices are being made, leading to police brutality around the world. The brutal violence of Colombian police in May 2021 against people protesting austerity measures and lack of support during the COVID pandemic resulted in scores of deaths and injuries, sexual violence, and incarceration.[18] During the same month, Israeli police viciously attacked the Al-Aqsa Mosque in East Jerusalem, firing tear gas, stun grenades, and rubber bullets at Palestinians worshipping there during Ramadan. This violence was initiated in the midst of announcements about forced evictions of Palestinians from the city's Sheikh Jarrah neighborhood by the Israeli settler colonial state. In commenting on the attacks, which are part of a broader program of ethnic cleansing, Israel Police Commissioner Kobi Shabtai said the police had been too restrained in their response to the violence.[19] Nigerian police forces responded to protests against police abuse in 2020 with tear gas, water cannons, and live ammunition, killing several people.[20] In France, police cracked down on the Yellow Vests movement in 2018 and 2019, exponentially increasing their use of so-called less-lethal weapons such as "defensive ball launchers," which caused severe head and eye injuries and at least two deaths.[21] The examples are endless. Police brutality is transnational.

The systemic racism of US policing is also present in other countries. As protests were ongoing throughout US cities in May and June of 2020, in Toronto people were demanding answers about the death of Regis Korchinski-Paquet, a Black woman who fell from her apartment balcony while police were in her home.[22] The Ontario Human Rights Commission has reported that a Black person in Toronto is nearly twenty times more likely than a white person to be shot and killed by police.[23]

Police violence in Canada is also disproportionately directed against Indigenous people. The federal police force, the Royal Canadian Mounted Police (RCMP), was created in 1872 "to extend Canada's colonial control over Indigenous territories in what would become Western Canada," explains Sean Carleton.[24] Since then, it has engaged in wars and relocations against many First Nations, the objectives of which were to "serve and protect the interests of capital, settler colonialism, and Canadian nation-building." The RCMP is still deployed today to serve these interests. According to documents obtained by *The Guardian*, RCMP commanders strategizing for a militarized raid on the Wet'suwet'en First Nations in early 2020 instructed officers to "use as much violence toward the gate as you want" ahead of the operation to remove a roadblock that the Wet'suwet'en had set up to prevent construction of a gas pipeline on their unceded land.[25]

In Australia, another settler colonial state, police brutality is likewise disproportionately directed toward Indigenous communities. There are high rates of incarceration and detention of Indigenous adults and youth, high rates of Indigenous deaths in custody and murder by police, and targeted surveillance against Indigenous youth deemed to be "at risk of committing crimes."[26] Countless cases of police violence against Indigenous people are recorded every year, but as Indigenous Australians note, it is "a practice that has occurred since colonisation."[27]

Across Europe, racial profiling and police brutality against individuals and communities of color abound.[28] In Sweden, for example, police have targeted Muslims, Roma, and Afro-Swedes with discrimination and violence. In 2013, Swedish police established a "Roma register," a secret—and unlawful—database to track Roma people living in the country; the state was found guilty of ethnic discrimination by the courts in 2016.[29] Swedish police have also discussed the possibility of bringing the military into certain neighborhoods profiled as "problematic" suburbs to increase surveillance and support them in "battling crime."[30]

These are again but a few examples among many. While each of these cases, and scores of others, have their own internal and historical dynamics that have shaped the structure and culture of policing, they share a disdain for human life. Across the world, people who have been deliberately marginalized by the state—disenfranchised, dispossessed, discriminated against on the basis of race, color, caste, ethnicity, religion, gender, sexual orientation, ability, immigration status, and more—experience police as an oppressive force, the primary task of which is to maintain the political, economic, and social order.

Uprising against police brutality

It was because of these kinds of countless experiences across the world that the protests in response to the murders of George Floyd and Breonna Taylor in 2020, and police brutality against Black lives more generally, went global. Solidarity marches were held around the world, many in recognition that systemic racism and police brutality are not unique to the United States but also cost the lives and well-being of Black, Indigenous, and other people of color in many countries.

Protestors and officials in many US cities also began tearing down racist monuments.[31] Statues celebrating white supremacists, particularly Confederate soldiers and slave owners, were removed in the states of Alabama, Kentucky, Louisiana, Pennsylvania, Tennessee, and Virginia.[32] This, too, spread across the pond, where activists in Bristol, England, pulled down a statue of a slave trader and rolled it into a river.[33] Statues of Columbus in Massachusetts, Minnesota, and Virginia were torn down or beheaded.[34] As the people and groups tearing down these statues have stated clearly, the intention isn't to "rewrite history"; the history of racism and oppression must be remembered. But it must not be honored.

Policing in itself is a monument to slavery[35]—and must likewise be dismantled. This is made abundantly clear when the shooting of unarmed Black people continues even in the wake of public outrage. In the days after George Floyd's murder, the killing continued. On June 2, 2020, in Vallejo, California, Sean Monterrosa, twenty-two, was on his knees with his hands raised when he was fired at five times and killed by a police officer. On June 6, California state police shot and killed twenty-three-year-old Erik Salgado and injured his pregnant girlfriend, Brianna Colombo. Since then, there have been countless more attacks on Black lives across the country and around the world. While the trial of George Floyd's murderer was ongoing in March and April 2021, more than three people a day were killed by police, including children.[36]

In the United States, police kill over a thousand people a year.[37] In 2021, the website Mapping Police Violence found that 1,134 people were killed by police, more than any other year in recent history.[38] Black people make up 28 percent of those killed, despite constituting only 13 percent of the population.[39] Mapping Police Violence also found that in all of 2019 there were only *twenty-seven days* when US police did not kill someone.[40] "What we're talking about here is a worldview that says that police are the only force capable of holding society together," explained Alex S. Vitale, author of *The End of Policing*, in an interview with the Intercept. The view turns on the notion that "without the constant threat of violent coercive intervention, society will unravel into a war of all against all." In this context, "authoritarian solutions are not just necessary, they're almost preferable."[41]

Militarization of police

The "warrior mentality," like structural racism, has been embedded in US policing since its inception. Historian Alfred McCoy traces this phenomenon back to 1898, when the US military annexed the Philippines and imposed a police state over the country. In the early 1900s, the US repatriated this policy to build a system of surveillance, informants, and "counterintelligence" agencies at home.[42] Police forces across the country began to be "professionalized" through bureaucratic management, explains Ian G. R. Shaw, transforming the police into a more hierarchical, and authoritarian, agency.[43]

The militarization of the US police really took off in the 1960s, in response to the civil rights movement. The Special Weapons and Tactics (SWAT) police units were created in 1969, setting in motion what Shaw describes as "a ruinous lurch toward a machismo-infused military policing in the United States."[44] This was followed in the 1980s by the Military Cooperation with Civilian Law Enforcement Agencies Act. Coupled with the decision to name the drug trade a "national security threat," this act set the stage for the total militarization of the police forces.

Since 1987, when Congress began allowing the US military to transfer "surplus equipment" to US police forces across the country, billions of dollars of military weapons, vehicles, and other gear have been transferred to state and local police departments.[45] These have included assault weapons, ammunition, grenade launchers, armored vehicles, helicopters, battle armor, night-vision equipment, and more. Most of this equipment has been transferred under the 1033 Program, established in 1997 as part of the "War on Drugs."[46] This program was further amplified after September 11, 2001, with the "War on Terror"—which transferred not only equipment but also tactics from the military to the police.

US police forces also receive direct training from the US military and from private military and security companies. Alex S. Vitale notes that the police have been trained to respond to uncertainty or fear with deadly force. "Part of this emphasis on the use of deadly force comes from the rise of independent training companies that specialize in in-service training, staffed by former police and military personnel," he explains. "Some of these groups serve both military and police clients and emphasize military-style approaches."[47]

The equipment and training aren't just for show. "Departments use these wartime weapons in everyday policing, especially to fight the wasteful and failed drug war, which has unfairly targeted people of color," notes the American Civil Liberties Union.[48] They are also used, as we have seen time and again, to suppress protest. In Seattle in 1999, nonviolent activists protesting globalization were attacked by police armed with pepper spray, tear gas, stun grenades, and rubber bullets. In Ferguson, Missouri, where protests erupted over the police killing of Michael Brown in 2014, people on the streets "were met with armored vehicles, noise-based crowd-control devices, shotguns, M4 rifles like those used by forces in Iraq and Afghanistan, rubber-coated pellets, and tear gas."[49]

As is explored further in chapter 3, the rising use of technology to "fight crime" is also a key feature of the militarization of police. While surveillance and control of Black, Indigenous, Muslim, Asian, Latinx, and also LGBTQ+ people has been persistent throughout US history, new technologies such as facial recognition, biometric technologies, data mining, and "predictive policing" tools are massively exacerbating the structural racism of surveillance.

Militarization of police also has implications for the border. As described in chapter 4, the framing of the transnational movement of human beings as a crisis has led to the expansion of budgets and the weaponization of the border in a "War on Migration," leading to horrific human rights violations, abuse, and the deaths of thousands of people. Furthermore, the US and Israeli governments have initiated "exchange programs" that bring together US police officers, US Immigration and Customs Enforcement and

Border Patrol agents, and the Federal Bureau of Investigation with soldiers, police, and border agents from Israel. This "exchange of worst practices," as the Jewish Voice for Peace describes the program, promotes and extends "discriminatory and repressive policing practices that already exist in both countries, including racial profiling, massive spying and surveillance, deportation and detention, and attacks on human rights defenders."[50]

While the militarization of police in the United States has led to much more violence, and its apparatus has become increasingly entrenched in our daily lives, it has not led to less "crime." A report released in 2018 found that police militarization "neither reduces rates of violent crime nor changes the number of officers assaulted or killed."[51] Instead, as other studies have found, the transfer of military equipment to police increases not just the material militarization of police departments but also militarizes their cultural, organizational, and operational practices and leads to more violent behavior.[52] Militarism celebrates, promotes, and facilitates a culture of violence. The weapons and strategies deployed to oppress and kill abroad, which are being integrated into domestic policing, inevitably carry that violence with them. Thus, the militarization of the police only leads to one thing: violence. There is no room for militarization to lead to de-escalation of conflict or resolution of grievances. When governments and police forces decide to go down this road, they take an active stance for violence.

The failures of reform

These realities demand a fundamental shift in our thinking about security. We need to stop looking to the apparatus of coercive state power to keep us "safe" and start looking at alternatives to those structures. This is true of borders, police, prisons, militaries, and all the other structures through which this power manifests and sustains itself at the expense of human life and well-being. An essential part of making this shift in thinking is recognizing that the current structures are past the point of reform.

Police reform has been tried. Bias training, body cameras, anti-racist courses. Minneapolis, for example, was one of the pilot cities for the

Obama administration's response to the national call for police account-ability. Its police force underwent a multiyear, multibillion dollar training project, yet police officers still murdered George Floyd in broad daylight. Alex S. Vitale argues that police reforms implemented in the wake of Michael Brown's death in Ferguson in 2014—from diversity initiatives to community policing to body cameras—"fail to acknowledge that policing as an institution reinforces race and class inequalities by design."[53] Individual accountability of officers, when it comes, likewise feeds into the idea that there are just some "bad seeds" at work and they are not representative of policing as a whole.

Yet as one former police officer reports, there are no bad seeds, only bad structures. "Police officers do not protect and serve people, they protect and serve the status quo, 'polite society,' and private property," he writes. "Using the incremental mechanisms of the status quo will never reform the police because the status quo relies on police violence to exist. Capitalism requires a permanent underclass to exploit for cheap labor and it requires the cops to bring that underclass to heel."[54]

The prison abolition organization Critical Resistance argues that reform only seeks to improve policing's war against people.[55] Reform does not address structural racism or the "warrior mentality" deliberately infused and embedded within US policing; it leaves intact the size, composition, and nature of police forces, and it can actually lead to increasing police budgets. For example, in the midst of the 2020 actions and demands to defund police in many cities, then-US presidential candidate Joe Biden proposed *increasing* budgets for police so they can "institute real reform."[56]

At the end of the day, "police cannot be reformed," notes abolitionist organizer and educator Mariame Kaba, "because the essence of their power is their discretion to use violence."[57] This is what enables them to beat protestors, murder Black people, harass queer communities, sexually assault women, and escape any accountability. "The system was designed to perpetuate harm, not to prevent it," says organizer Micah Herskind, "so if we want to undo harm, we have to undo the system."[58]

Rethinking harm and "crime"

Demands for the abolition of police and the creation of new forms of community-based security and safety mechanisms and tools, rooted in the pursuit of equitable human security, are increasingly recognized as the only chance for real change. Yet when abolitionists advocate for the deconstruction of the current structure, the public tends to push back, posing questions like, How will you eliminate crime? How will you prevent harm? The idea of police abolition is alarming to many who fear a descent into chaos and crime. Many people, particularly those raised in largely white middle- and upper-class neighborhoods, are taught that they can trust the police, that the police keep people safe from murder, rape, theft, and other harms. Television shows relentlessly bombard the airwaves with what abolitionists have termed "copaganda"—the portrayal of police as fundamentally valiant and just, taking on criminals and the few "bad apples" within the force alike. It seems like a given to many that without police, our lives would be much worse. "The political leaders of our country have spent the better part of fifty years trying to convince the public that the biggest threat to their lives is the possibility that they might become the victim of a violent crime," explains Keeanga-Yamahtta Taylor. "Those ideas will not just melt away in a matter of weeks."[59]

Concerns about calls to defund and abolish police come not just from wealthy white communities, but also from some who live in so-called high crime neighborhoods, who see the loss of a police presence as enabling even further harm within those communities. As Angela Davis notes, many people living in communities with gangs, cartels, or armed individuals see these as threats at least as great as the police. Such people may wonder how, in a world of defunded and dismantled police forces, they could "survive at the mercy of malevolent groups who hardly care about the trajectory of stray bullets that have taken the lives of children and other bystanders." These are real concerns, Davis notes, but they also provide the opportunity for "the kind of educational activism that might help to encourage all of us, especially those of us who live in the most vulnerable neighborhoods, to purposefully rethink the meaning of safety and security."[60]

The counterquestion to those who want to know what will happen without police is, What is the current system doing to eliminate crime or prevent harm? The answer is that the current system is massively exacerbating both.

It's important to remember that, as abolitionist organizer and lawyer Andrea Ritchie explains, "We are not proposing to abandon our communities to violence. We are naming policing as a form of violence that we all experience."[61] Along with recognizing the failure of reforms to the current carceral system, shifting people's perspectives about who is dangerous and what constitutes "crime" is an important aspect of the work to build true human security. Right now, as activist and writer Dean Spade explains, in the United States, the police, the military, and agencies like ICE are purveyors of violence and are in possession of the most dangerous weapons.[62] Yet their violence is deliberately made invisible. Further, not all violent or criminal acts are considered either violent or criminal; these categories are political. Pollution and contamination of water and land, war profiteering and the military-industrial complex, corporate greed and the oppression of labor—these are not considered criminal or violent acts despite the incredible harm they generate for billions of people and the planet.[63]

Secondly, we need to recognize that the current carceral system of police and prisons does not prevent crime. It does not prevent harms from being committed. That is not what police do. Police respond to harms already committed. Thus, for those who respond to calls for police abolition with comments such as, "But how are you going to stop murder? Or school shootings? Or rape?" the first thing to recognize is that *our current system is not stopping these crimes.* It is a false equivalence, then, to demand that abolitionists offer a guaranteed roadmap to stop them. But what abolition does offer is a chance to try something else that *is* preventative. Unlike the police system, which only responds to the aftermath of harm, abolitionists seek to build structures, services, and systems that could actually prevent violence and harm.

As an initial step on the path to abolition, we need to ask, Why are violence and harm being committed in the first place? The former police officer referenced previously explains:

Every single second of my training, I was told that criminals were not a legitimate part of their community, that they were individual bad actors, and that their bad actions were solely the result of their inherent criminality. Any concept of systemic trauma, generational poverty, or white supremacist oppression was either never mentioned or simply dismissed. After all, most people don't steal, so anyone who does isn't "most people," right? To us, anyone committing a crime deserved anything that happened to them because they broke the "social contract." And yet, it was never even a question as to whether the power structure above them was honoring any sort of contract back.[64]

As Dean Spade points out, the United States is a highly militarized, patriarchal, and white supremacist culture.[65] This environment produces the kind of violence of which we are all so rightly terrified. Thus, we need to shift our society away from the idea that the way to be powerful is by wielding weapons and exercising violence. But the carceral system *facilitates* a culture of violence, glorification of weapons, white supremacy, and toxic masculinity—all of which actively facilitate the commission of harms. What abolition can offer instead is a chance to reduce the context for harm by making our world safer, by expanding care for people, by creating a different context in which people live and work and go to school. "An abolitionist vision means that we must build models today that can represent how we want to live in the future," explains Critical Resistance. "It means developing practical strategies for taking small steps that move us toward making our dreams real and that lead us all to believe that things really could be different. It means living this vision in our daily lives."[66]

Abolition is not just about dismantling or disbanding existing structures—it's also about building alternatives in their place. As explains Angela Davis,

Defunding the police is part of the abolition demand, but reflects only one aspect of the process represented by the demand. Defunding the police is not simply about withdrawing funding for law enforcement and doing nothing else. . . . It's about shifting public funds to new services and new institutions, mental health counsellors who can respond to people in crisis without arms. It's about shifting funding to education, to housing, to recreation. All of these things help to create security and safety. It's about learning that safety safeguarded by violence is not really safety.[67]

Ultimately, "people want guarantees," says Mariame Kaba, "but there are none."[68] We have to try, and fail, and try again. But trying something other than what we *know* is failing, what we *know* is creating harm, is essential. As Alex S. Vitale says, "There is no perfect world, there's no perfect solution. What we have now is far from perfect. People get killed all the time, even though our society is filled with police. Can we come up with a situation where there are fewer killings, and fewer collateral consequences?"[69]

To reflect on our current reality and possible alternative futures, we need to ask ourselves and each other questions such as, What is our current system doing about people who commit harm? What do our current systems do to protect people? Do they actually protect people? Do they harm certain people in the process of protecting others? Do they produce more harm than protection? Whose protection and safety should be valued, accounted for? Everyone's, or just a few? Who is protected the most, and from whom are they protected?

We also need to ask ourselves, Who profits from the current system? Who is making money from militarizing the police and from incarcerating millions of people? What happens to those who are incarcerated and the economic and social futures of these individuals and their communities?

What if everyone had food, shelter, employment, care, community? What if everyone had access to healthcare and mental health support? What if we had recreational opportunities? What "crime" would manifest from such a society?

What do we even consider crime? Right now, most of those who create and enforce the systems of inequality that generate poverty, unemployment, and lack of food security, housing, and healthcare are not considered criminals; in fact, they are the ones the state apparatus seeks to protect at the expense of everyone else's safety and security.

So then we also need to ask, What violence does the system itself generate? Is our system of policing, incarceration, and so-called justice producing more violence than it prevents? Is there something else we could try that might produce less harm while still obtaining accountability and justice for harms caused? What processes might result in accountability for those causing harms to entire societies and communities through the imposition and generation of inequalities and poverty?

Answering these questions, depending on who you are and what your experiences have been, might require that you think beyond your current beliefs or thoughts and listen to what others are describing about their experiences. Doing the work of critical thinking, listening, and reflecting is essential to understanding the range of harms that are caused by our current carceral system.

The road to abolition

Fortunately, decades of work by abolitionists can provide plenty of material for that reflection. While it may seem remarkable that the call for police abolition has entered into the mainstream discourse so quickly, the reality is that the theorizing and organizing for police abolition has been going on for decades. Black and other activists of color, in particular Black feminists such as Angela Davis, Ruth Wilson Gilmore, Mariame Kaba, Andrea Ritchie, and many others, have long theorized about and organized for the abolition of police. These activists have founded organizations, written books, given interviews and podcasts, and created online resources for years. Groups like Critical Resistance, Incite!, Survived and Punished, Black Visions Collective, Project NIA, and others have long been advocating for the abolition of prisons and the establishment of alternative systems of care and community well-being. We can also trace the calls to defund and abolish the police back to incarcerated organizers and thinkers such as George Jackson in the 1970s and James Yaki Sayles in the

1980s, as well as to the Black Radical Congress and the Prison Moratorium Project through to the Movement for Black Lives.[70]

The shift of these ideas and concepts into the mainstream represents an excellent example of people "picking up the ideas that are lying around" in times of crisis. As Naomi Klein says, "During moments of cataclysmic change, the previously unthinkable suddenly becomes reality."[71] In the context of the recent uprisings against white supremacy and police brutality against Black lives, in the midst of a pandemic that has also disproportionately affected Black, Indigenous, and Latinx communities and resulted in a tailspin of unemployment, the idea of defunding the police and redirecting that money to invest in communities started to be recognized by many as not only necessary but also as the only real solution available.

Work to defund, demilitarize, and disband police forces is already underway in many US cities. In Minneapolis, the city council voted to dismantle and abolish the police department and replace it with a new system of community-led safety mechanisms—though this decision was later overruled by a city charter commission.[72] In Oakland, San Francisco, Los Angeles, New York City, and other cities across the US, mayors and city councilors have started looking at ways to reduce police budgets. The New York State Legislature voted to repeal section 50-a of the New York Civil Rights Law, which for forty-four years has kept police disciplinary records secret from the public. Draft legislation in Maine sought to shut down its fusion center—an "intelligence sharing" partnership between local, state, and federal law enforcement agencies.[73] Public school systems in Denver, Minneapolis, Oakland, Portland, Seattle, and others have announced the termination or suspension of contracts with their city police departments.

These are just a few examples. Much more is happening—but resistance to these kinds of changes is fierce, and at the same time, much more still needs to happen. From May 2020 to April 2021, more than thirty states passed more than 140 new police oversight and reform laws,[74] organizers have secured the divestment of over $840 million from police departments and investments of at least $160 million in communities, and chemical weapons or military-grade weapons have been banned in six cities.[75] Yet, in this same time period, police brutality has continued across the country. Change is desperately needed.

In order to effectively prioritize human well-being, as abolitionists articulate well, there is not just "one thing" that can replace the current system. We will need a collection of mechanisms, tools, and structures to prevent the conditions that lead to the commission of harm and to respond to harm that does occur. Building on the theorizing and organizing of Black feminists and other activists who have long championed prison and police abolition, several organizers set up a website in 2020, 8toabolition.com, to help break down the essentials of what police abolition would look like. Key recommendations include:

Defund the police, including by ending contracts with private companies, rejecting increases to police budgets and demanding budget cuts each year until funding for police departments reaches zero, and reducing the power of police unions, among other things.

Demilitarize communities, including by disarming police; ending the 1033 Program that acts as a pipeline for military equipment to police forces; prohibiting training exercises between police and the military; ending broken windows, community policing, and other strategies that target Black and brown communities; removing cops from hospitals; ending and preventing police use of surveillance technologies and "predictive policing" tools; and more.

Remove police from schools, including by ending contracts between schools and universities and police departments, removing surveillance technologies from schools, and more.

Free people from prisons, jails, and detention centers, which is not just about freeing those currently in those facilities but also establishing alternative transformative justice mechanisms, ending immigration detention and family separation, and rejecting "alternatives to incarceration" that are still carceral in nature.

Repeal laws that criminalize survival, which includes decriminalizing houselessness and sex work, and decriminalizing survivors of gendered violence.

Invest in community self-governance, including by promoting neighborhood councils as representatives in municipal decision-making; investing in multilingual resources for immigrant and asylum-seeking communities; assessing community needs and investing in community-based resources, such as groups from tenant unions to local shop owners and street vendors, prioritizing those from marginalized groups; and investing in community-based public safety approaches, including non-carceral violence prevention and intervention programs and skills-based education on bystander intervention, consent and boundaries, and healthy relationships.

Provide safe housing for everyone, including by repurposing empty buildings to house people experiencing houselessness, removing cops from shelters, prohibiting evictions, providing support to refugees and asylum seekers, and more.

Invest in care, not cops, including by allocating city funding toward healthcare, wellness resources, neighborhood-based trauma centers, non-coercive drug and alcohol treatment, peer support networks, and training; investing in teachers and counselors, universal childcare, and support for all family structures; building free and accessible public transit; investing in food banks, grocery cooperatives, gardens, and farms; and investing in youth programs that promote learning, safety, and community care.

As the above makes clear, there is not one thing that will replace the police. There are many things, each of which requires building and investing in community-based mechanisms for safety, support, and prevention rather than relying on the state's system of militarized coercive power and discipline to control, confine, and kill those it deems problematic. There are steps, as organizer Rachel Herzing sets out, that we can undertake today, tomorrow, next month, next year, and beyond to reduce our reliance on police, defund and dismantle the structures of the violent carceral state, and build alternative resources, responses, and networks.[76]

It is also important to recognize and accept that there is no checklist with dates, deliverables, or measurables. A common reaction to the call for the abolition of police is to demand that abolitionists show exactly what will happen if we make changes like the ones proposed by 8toabolition.com, to demonstrate exactly how it will work. But as Mariame Kaba said in an interview with MSNBC's Chris Hayes, this isn't possible.[77] For hundreds of years, our societies have invested in the carceral state, we have lived under white supremacy and patriarchy, we have been ruled by capitalism. To demand that people wanting to try something else—people who've never received the resourcing or funding or the opportunity to try a different way—must draw a guaranteed roadmap of how to make it all work is not realistic or fair.

If we had investments, resources, and willingness within our cities and communities to try alternatives, then we could start establishing some of the "roadmaps" that people are looking for. We can already learn from local and contextual practices—from organizers working on alternative mental health responses, from groups of survivors of sexual violence, and so on. But we also need to imagine, together, what alternatives we need to invest in and how to build a different system.

The imperative of now

Abolition is inevitably a long-term, ongoing project of change. But abolition is not just about the future: it needs to start now.

In this moment that we are currently experiencing, an extended moment of profound shifts in thinking and in action happening around the world, it is important to recognize that people are *already doing abolitionist work*. Throughout the COVID-19 pandemic and during the Black Lives Matter protests of 2020, collectives around the country built and enriched mutual aid networks—models of community support learned from Indigenous, Black, and queer communities, among others. People from all walks of life came together to care for each other physically and emotionally. Many of these acts of solidarity and support were documented through independent media; many of them will never be recorded. But they are happening, and they show what more we can do.

Yet, the police continue to kill Black people in the streets and in their own homes. Meanwhile, our tax dollars continue to go toward funding police instead of investing in initiatives that would help prevent the conditions that lead to "crime" and violence. Even in the midst of a global pandemic, while healthcare workers did not have access to adequate protective gear and there were vast shortages of intensive care unit beds, it seems that US cities somehow had enough money to pay cops overtime and fly helicopters over protests nonstop for weeks.

We also need to be aware that there have already been pushbacks against the efforts to defund and abolish police. Police departments in some of the cities where actions are underway have denounced mayoral or city council decisions to reduce police budgets, with the LAPD union even accusing the LA mayor of "losing his mind."[78] Meanwhile, other cities have announced budget increases for police: Chicago, for example, has announced it will invest $1.2 million in taxpayer dollars into private security companies.[79] In the midst and aftermath of COVID-19, cities across the world are facing big budget cuts. This is a moment to demand changes to what we collectively prioritize; to ask, Do we want to fund the well-being of all people, or the profits of a privileged few?

The momentum for police abolition is growing, but it must be supported and sustained. This is an unprecedented opportunity to finally undertake decisions and actions that will support real structural change, rather than tinkering around the edges of a system of violence and oppression. Activist Kenyon Farrow, who was a staff member of Critical Resistance in the early 2000s, notes that back then, "most ppl thought we were delusional at best. At worst ppl said we were destructive provocateurs for questioning the validity of police and the prison industrial complex. The lesson? Dream big. Keep working."[80]

Keep working we must. Because the bottom line is, *what we have now is not working for the majority of people.* What we have now is creating and reinforcing inequalities, violence, and harm. If we are serious about building a world that works for all, disarming, demilitarizing, and disbanding the "brothers in blue" by defunding and abolishing the police is an urgent imperative. So too is the dismantling of an intimately related part of the carceral system: the prison.

Chapter 2

Dismantling Prisons

From afar, a prison looks like a fortress. Bricks, steel, barbed wire. Towers for surveillance, populated with armed guards. The sounds of the gates and the doors lend further to the fortress-like atmosphere, as do the uniforms and the weapons. Within these gates and walls are sites of extreme violence, built to confine and dehumanize. They are not just places where people are "put" once they have been arrested or convicted. Prisons themselves arrest: they arrest development—of those locked away inside them, of those charged with "guarding" them, of the communities from which the incarcerated are drawn, and the communities within which the facilities are based. Prisons arrest all our minds: they stunt our ability to seriously consider alternative forms of accountability and reparation, even when we know full well the extent to which the current system has failed and harmed all of us.

As French philosopher Michel Foucault wrote in *Discipline and Punish*, his foundational text on prisons, the carceral system is, above all else, about power.[1] It is comprised of discourses, architectures, regulations, programs, and more, all determined to control, coerce, and surveil. It is ostensibly, of course, about "correction" or rehabilitation, but in reality, prisons are about retribution, not restitution. Certainly not restoration.

Incarceration is directly related to the same racist, sexist, homophobic, capitalist, militarized systems and structures of policing. The dominant narrative around safety and security that purports the "necessity" of prisons is constructed and perpetuated by those commissioned to maintain a social order at home and abroad that ensures that the accumulation of wealth by the few is not disrupted or interrupted by the needs of the many. Deconstructing the dominant narrative requires us to ask questions about safety. To this end, we can learn from not just police abolitionists, but also nuclear weapon abolitionists, who encourage us to ask, Who is made "safe" by atomic bombs and this threat of genocidal violence—and who is being harmed by them? Also: Who constructs the narrative around safety? Who tells us that nuclear weapons "keep us safe"? Who tells us that killing hundreds of thousands of people in other countries keeps us safe? In the context of prisons: From whom are prisons keeping us safe? Who are they keeping safe? Who are they harming? What even *is* safety? Do victims of harm feel any safer because of prisons? And: Who tells us that mass incarceration keeps our communities safe? What is this approach costing us—all of us? Who is it helping? Who is profiting from it?

As with policing, the United States may appear to be in a "unique" situation given that it is a site of extreme mass incarceration as well as particular historical and modern dynamics of structural racism and capitalist accumulation. However, the analysis is applicable to other contexts and countries, particularly other settler colonial states, and the work for prison abolition is not—and must not be—limited to the United States alone. In addition, the work to abolish the carceral system includes not just efforts to dismantle police, prisons, and surveillance, but is also deeply tied to the material and conceptual structures of border imperialism, war and occupation, and the capitalist state itself.

The structural racism of incarceration and criminalization of "the other"

There are currently more than 2.3 million incarcerated people in the United States.[2] This means that while the US is home to about 5 percent of the world's population, it has 21 percent of the world's incarcerated people. This astonishing figure does not account for the additional 4.6 million people living under the carceral system in the form of parole or probation. And these are just those currently ensnared. Nineteen million people have been convicted of felonies. Seventy-seven million have criminal records. One hundred and thirteen million adults in the US have an immediate family member who has been to jail or prison.[3] That's nearly a third of the US population whose lives have been corroded by the politics of incarceration.

These numbers alone, however, do not tell the whole story. Racism and white supremacy are deeply embedded within the US carceral system, as are anti-queerness and gender normativity.

Racial incarceration

People of color make up 37 percent of the US population but 67 percent of the prison population. African Americans constitute 34 percent of those incarcerated, even though they make up only about 12.7 percent of the US population. They are incarcerated at a rate five times greater than whites.[4]

Indigenous peoples are the only group incarcerated at a higher rate. Native Americans are incarcerated at a rate 38 percent higher than the national average.[5] Indigenous youth are the most affected: representing just 1 percent of the US youth population, they constitute 70 percent of incarcerated youth.[6]

Meanwhile, migration detention centers are sites of incarceration of predominantly Latinx people in the United States. Migrant detention, notes Harsha Walia, comprises "one of the fastest-growing prison populations with over two hundred detention facilities, representing an 85 percent increase in detention spaces."[7] On any given day in the United States, there are approximately fifty thousand migrants and asylum seekers in detention centers. The context and violence of migrant detention and border imperialism is explored in chapter 4. For now, it is important to highlight the intention of power, coercion, and control that migrant detention serves, including through the criminalization of migration, which is a human right.

As explored in chapters 1 and 3, entire communities of color, in particular Black, Latinx, and Indigenous people, are subjected to surveillance and scrutiny and are targeted with particular strategies that lead to higher rates of arrest and conviction for "crimes" than white populations. As Angela Davis explains, many people "are sent to prison, not so much because of the crimes they may have indeed committed but largely because their communities have been criminalized."[8]

US prisons, like the police, are rooted in slavery. Building on the work of Angela Davis and Ruth Wilson Gilmore, civil rights advocate Michelle Alexander demonstrates how incarceration was used as a way to control Black labor and lives after the abolition of slavery.[9] Incarceration was also, as Naomi Murakawa outlines, a response to the advances of the civil rights movement in the 1960s. "The United States did not face a crime problem that was racialized," she argues. "It faced a race problem that was criminalized."[10] By which she means, the race "problem" of the 1960s—marked by gains made for Black communities through the advances of the civil rights movement—"was answered with pledges of carceral state development."[11]

Going back even further, incarceration in the United States is also linked to colonialism. "The extension of criminal jurisdiction has long been central to the subjugation and displacement of indigenous polities," writes Robert Nichols.[12] From the commission of genocide to the dispossession of people from their land to the establishment of reserves and residential schools, state violence has been essential to the formation of the United States—and other settler colonial states, such as Australia and Canada. In this way, the carceral system can be seen as serving the continuation of settler colonialism: "criminal control" of Indigenous populations is an extension of the "conquest" that came before.

This background is not just historical context. These injustices are the reason that prison populations in the United States today are disproportionately Black and Indigenous. But this truth is made invisible by the official narrative of the state, which places racialized blame on entire communities for "criminal behavior." Government officials, police officers, the mainstream media—all would have us believe in the "inherent criminality" of certain groups of people, marked by skin color or ethnicity; they would have us believe in the inevitability that certain people will either fill the prisons or roam free to wreck havoc on the "innocent" white communities.

Queer incarceration

This framing doesn't stop with race. In much the same way that migrants and people of color are criminalized and disproportionately incarcerated in the United States, so too are LGBTQ+ people—particularly trans people of color and other gender nonconforming queer people. In fact, the criminalization and incarceration of those who do not conform to sexual or gender norms, argues Queer (In)Justice, was instrumental to the colonization of the United States, the maintenance of slavery, and violence against people at the country's borders.[13] Policing and punishment of queer and nonconforming bodies has been and remains part of how the state has exerted its control over racialized others throughout its history and in modern times. Enforcing gender conformity and heteronormativity remains a central feature of the carceral state, scholar Eric A. Stanley explains.[14] The reinforcement and reproduction of binary gender is part of the deliberate work of prisons, including through violence against and repression of queer identities.

As a result, as several queer activists have argued, laws ostensibly designed to "protect" LGBTQ+ people are insufficient to actually prevent violence or inequality against queer lives. Much like the idea that police brutality is the product of a few "bad apples" in law enforcement, laws extending "protections" to LGBTQ+ lives "frame the problem of violence in our communities as one of individual 'hateful' people," argue Morgan Bassichis, Alexander Lee, and Dean Spade.[15] In reality, queer and trans people "face short life-spans because of the enormous systemic violence in welfare systems, shelters, prisons, jails, foster care, juvenile punishment systems, and immigration, and the inability to access basic survival resources."[16] Looking to systems of "law and order" and punishment through incarceration as an answer to violence against LGBTQ+ people only expands and enriches the carceral system, which itself is a site of anti-queer violence.

The political economy of incarceration

This feat of finding ways to draw more resources into itself to address problems that it itself facilitates or exacerbates is a feature of the prison industrial complex—much like the military-industrial complex.

In his farewell address in 1961, US President Eisenhower warned against the growing power of the military-industrial complex—the system comprised of weapons manufacturers, various branches of the US military, and the country's political and economic elite. The manifestations of the military-industrial complex, which will be explored in further detail in chapter 5, can be seen clearly today: decades of war in Iraq and Afghanistan; proxy wars and coups against democratically elected leaders around the world; a current annual military budget of $778 billion, accounting for 39 percent of the global total;[17] an arsenal of about 3,800 nuclear warheads[18] and an ever-growing budget for nuclear weapon maintenance and modernization;[19] a growing private military and security company sector; and a cartel of powerful arms contractors who make billions in the design, production, and sale of weapons.

The term "prison industrial complex" borrows this concept of an economic and political system that perpetuates itself. "Prison industrial complex" seems to have first been used by incarcerated people when, in 1974, the North Carolina Prisoners' Labor Union called for an end to "the judicial-prison-parole-industrial complex."[20] The term later came to prominence in 1995 after the publication in *The Nation* of an article written by geographer Mike Davis in which he deliberately drew upon the concept of the military-industrial complex to describe the system of mass incarceration in the United States. "It has become a monster that threatens to overpower and devour its creators, and its uncontrollable growth ought to rattle a national consciousness now complacent at the thought of a permanent prison class," he warned.[21]

As of 2020, the prison industrial complex includes "1,833 state prisons, 110 federal prisons, 1,772 juvenile correctional facilities, 3,134 local jails, 218 immigration detention facilities, and 80 Indian Country jails as well as military prisons, civil commitment centers, state psychiatric hospitals, and prisons in the U.S. territories."[22] It employs hundreds of thousands of guards, parole officers, and administrative and caretaking staff. The prison industrial complex has sunk its claws deep into the communities where it sets up shop, providing direct employment as well as jobs in nearby service industries, in particular in rural communities where the industrial or farming base has been decimated by globalization and neoliberal economic reforms.[23]

The rise of the neoliberal agenda

The timing of the rise of the prison industrial complex in the 1980s coincides directly with the rise of the US neoliberal agenda. Free trade agreements and globalization meant economic downturn for farming and manufacturing in the United States. Growing levels of unemployment were met with cuts in social service provision including education, healthcare, housing, and more. This meant a surplus of people employable by the prison industrial complex, but also a surplus of people living in poverty. As jobs were cut and the working class social safety net was dismantled, more people became marginally employed and housed and were forced into criminalized economies.[24]

The number of people incarcerated in the United States has gone up more than 700 percent in the last fifty years.[25] Angela Davis wrote about the prison industrial complex as performing "a feat of magic"—seemingly constructed to "disappear" social problems. In reality, she argued, prisons disappear human beings, mostly from poor, immigrant, and racially marginalized communities.[26] This is deliberate: as Christian Parenti has suggested, the main function of prison is to displace, demoralize, and criminalize the poor, thus working to justify, in the minds of the middle and upper classes, state repression, militarization, and incarceration, while simultaneously making it more difficult for the working class and poor to organize against it.[27] In this sense, incarceration is in large part about management of poverty—management of the vast social and economic inequalities that define the United States.

Incarceration as class warfare

Even in the 1970s, before the prison industrial complex began to reproduce itself with gusto, Marxists like George Jackson—who was later killed
by prison guards—saw how incarceration is a deliberate response to unemployment and poverty. Law itself, he argued, is a political construction
designed to manage the poor and the unemployed. "Crime is simply the
result of grossly disproportionate distribution of wealth and privilege, a
reflection of the present state of property relations," he wrote.[28] Class determines the way the law is applied and implemented, and what kinds of
activities are counted as "criminal."

In this vein, Ruth Wilson Gilmore locates the rise of the prison industrial complex as originating in 1967 and 1968, which marked the "close
of the golden age of U.S. capitalism" and the transformation of the US
political economy into a permanent war economy, as well as the explosion
of revolutionary movements against the US wars in Southeast Asia and
for Black Power, and the development of anti-capitalist, anti-racist, and
internationalist solidarity.[29] As the state entrenched its political economy
in the production of weapons and violence, it simultaneously sought to
crush worker militancy and solidarity, ensuring the unequal distribution
of wealth and power along racial and gender lines. In this context, Gilmore argues, prisons became partial solutions to political economic crises—
the place to put people disenfranchised by the state's economic choices.[30]
Poverty was criminalized, Keeanga-Yamahtta Taylor notes, with many
consequences of poverty being turned into arrestable offenses, such as
"sleeping in cars or public places, panhandling for money or food, public
urination, shoplifting, and many other things that poor people do when
they do not have the privacy and discretion of their own residence."[31] At
its core, "crime is a manifestation of social deprivation and the reverberating effects of racial discrimination, which locks poor and working-class
communities of color out of schooling, meaningful jobs, and other means
to keep up with the ever-escalating costs of life in the United States."[32]

Today, people living in poverty are vastly overrepresented among the
incarcerated population. In 2015, the median annual income of incarcerated

people was less than $20,000. About 57 percent of those made less than $22,500 at the time of their incarceration, meaning that more than half of those incarcerated lived in poverty or in very low-income situations prior to their arrest.[33] Incarceration also contributes to poverty by "creating employment barriers; reducing earnings and decreasing economic security through criminal debt, fees and fines; making access to public benefits difficult or impossible; and disrupting communities where formerly incarcerated people reside."[34] Once released, people are thrown into or kept in poverty. The 4.5 million people in the United States on parole or probation[35] live under conditions that make it difficult for them to secure employment and end up channeling them back into prisons and jails.

Incarceration is a choice

This cycle of political and economic choices creating poverty and inequality, the criminalization of certain communities and segments of the population, and the violence and harms generated by the prison industrial complex mean that it has become a self-reproducing system. Much like the military-industrial complex, the prison industrial complex is a force unto itself within the economic and political fabric of the United States. It is, as scholar Julia Sudbury characterizes, "a symbiotic and profitable relationship between politicians, corporations, the media, and state correctional institutions that generates the racialized use of incarceration as a response to social problems rooted in the globalization of capital."[36] Or, as investigative journalist Eric Schlosser describes it, the prison industrial complex is "a set of bureaucratic, political, and economic interests that encourage increased spending on imprisonment, regardless of the actual need."[37]

This, if nothing else, should be a key takeaway from all the investigations and writings about the prison industrial complex: *incarceration is a political and economic choice, not an inevitability.* Eisenhower cautioned that with the military-industrial complex, "the potential for the disastrous rise of misplaced power exists and will persist," which had implications for "the very structure of our society."[38] The rise of both the military- and prison industrial complexes has served to reinforce and reconfigure in the most violent of ways the "order" upon which the United States was built: white supremacy, dispossession, repression of those deemed "other," and the pursuit of private profit above human well-being.

Carceral profiteering

Indeed, as the number of prisons has grown, so has the budget for incarceration. The official budget for incarceration in the United States today is $81 billion. But that figure only includes "the cost of operating prisons, jails, parole, and probation."[39] There are other hidden costs of incarceration, including those related to phone calls, commissaries, court fees, and more. Overall, according to a 2017 report by the Prison Policy Initiative, the annual total cost of incarceration is about $182 billion.[40]

Part of this money goes to private companies. "As the U.S. prison system expanded, so did corporate involvement in construction, provision of goods and services, and use of prison labor," explains Angela Davis.[41] CoreCivic (formerly the Corrections Corporation of America) and GEO Group (formerly Wackenhut Corrections Corporation) are the two largest companies running private prisons and detention centers in the United States. Like military corporations, they also operate abroad, running prisons in Australia, South Africa, and the United Kingdom.

Other elements of private industry are also profiting from the prison industrial complex. As Eric Schlosser found in 1998, the complex had already become a multibillion-dollar industry with trade shows and conventions, mail-order catalogues, and marketing campaigns. "The prison-industrial complex now includes some of the nation's largest architecture and construction firms, Wall Street investment banks that handle prison bond issues and invest in private prisons, plumbing-supply companies, food-service companies, health-care companies, companies that sell everything from bullet-resistant security cameras to padded cells available in a 'vast color selection,'" he wrote.[42]

However, unlike the military-industrial complex, the overall prison industrial complex is primarily a public enterprise, with private industry making up only a relatively small part of the system. Most prisons and jails are publicly operated state, federal, and local facilities. The Prison Policy Initiative finds that the government payroll for prison employees is more than one hundred times higher than the private prison industry's profits.[43] Still, where prisons and detention centers are privatized, those with capital have yet another way to make money off those without, in a very literal manifestation of the domination of rich over poor. As Ruth Wilson Gilmore says, mass incarceration is class warfare.[44]

Federal and state governments could have chosen alternative investments and thus alternative employment in industries and sectors that would not be reliant on caging people for generating income and would, in fact, diminish all forms of harms rather than exacerbating them. Investments in, for example, education instead of incarceration would create jobs for teachers, support faculty, and staff, and would simultaneously create new opportunities and engagements for young people. This would be an investment in the prevention of "crime" or harms.

Yet, as a 2016 report from the US Department of Education notes, "Over the past three decades state and local government expenditures on prisons and jails have increased about three times as fast as spending on elementary and secondary education."[45] At the level of university and college, the contrast is even starker: from 1989 to 2013, the report notes, "state and local spending on corrections rose by 89 percent while state and local appropriations for higher education remained flat."[46] As Jackie Wang says, "The United States chose the path of *divestment* in social entitlements and *investment* in prisons and police. There was nothing inevitable about this policy path."[47]

Militarization of incarceration

While there was nothing inevitable about choosing the path of incarceration to deal with the racialized "socioeconomic challenges" produced by capitalism, once that path was chosen, militarization of it may have been inevitable. When the choice is made to lock up as many people as possible in order to control and confine the "surplus populations" created by neoliberal economic policies that eliminate jobs while simultaneously destroying the social safety net, the state has already decided to weaponize itself. The physical manifestations of that weaponization include figurative weapons of prosecutors and prisons, and the literal weaponization of guards.

To help illuminate the political and economic dynamics of the militarization of incarceration, it may be useful to consider again how these dynamics play out in terms of weapons and war. There are similarities, for example, in the certainty of authority exuded by prison guards and that of nuclear war planners, police officers, and military commanders. This certainty is bound up in the systems of power, privilege, and profit they are charged with protecting. They are certain in their perspectives, in their theories, in their actions. They impose power over others, dismissing alternative experiences—especially those rooted more deeply in lived reality than their own. They yield weapons and violence as the tools to assert the "rightness" of their approach to the world and their vision of "peace," "justice," and "security." They make the rules and the laws and then they break them at will, all while forcing the rest of the world to abide, regardless of circumstance. Whether a treaty against nuclear weapon proliferation or laws against unlawful search and seizure or against cruel and unusual punishment—it is those with the biggest weapons and an outsized perception of being the rightful master of one's (and all others') domain who dictate the terms to the rest of us. And we are all made less safe as a result.

We are all less safe with the existence of nuclear weapons, designed to incinerate entire cities and melt the skin from people's bodies. We are all less safe thanks to the wars waged around the world, costing billions of dollars in bullets and bombs and costing the lives and the futures of generations of people. We are all less safe because of the violence imposed by police and prisons, which reinforce and perpetuate violence, coercion, and domination as the solution to poverty and inequality. As Keeanga-Yamahtta Taylor notes, "These problems are not solved by armed agents of the state or by prisons, which sow the seeds of more poverty and alienation, while absorbing billions of dollars that might otherwise be spent on public welfare. The police and prisons aren't solving these problems: they are a part of the problem."[48]

Then there are the similarities in terms of literal weaponization. Both the military-industrial complex and the prison industrial complex design the policies and make the machinery of industrialized killing abroad or incarceration at home. Often, technologies developed for the military are then marketed for use by police and in prisons. Tear gas is a case in point. Outlawed as a chemical weapon in warfare, it is used liberally in the United States and many other countries by police forces as a "crowd control weapon."[49] Tear gas has been used against incarcerated people in prisons, as have pepper spray, tasers, beanbag rounds, and Sting-Ball grenades.[50]

Most of these weapons were designed by the military for use in the military, but that is a limited market, notes Dr. Rohini Haar, a medical expert with Physicians for Human Rights. "So the next step for companies that are trying to make a profit off these weapons that they design is to sell them to one, law enforcement and police, and two, to prisons."[51] As more attention is paid to police militarization and brutality, prisons are becoming a bigger market for these weapons. Meanwhile, though guards are not supposed to carry guns inside of prisons, shotguns loaded with birdshot, as well as lethal semiautomatic rifles, have been used inside some facilities.[52]

Militarization as a culture

More than the weapons themselves, in prison the militarization is about culture. The "warrior mentality" infused in police forces is also taught to so-called corrections officers. On paper, guards are not supposed to suppress fights or respond to perceived threats with lethal force. But violence by guards against those incarcerated is endemic, including beatings, sexual assaults, humiliation, cruel and unusual punishment, and torture, including through solitary confinement.[53] Qualified immunity, a legal loophole, protects guards against prosecution, as it does for police officers.

The violence that the incarcerated perpetrate against each other is also part of the militarized, toxic masculinity infused in the life breath of prisons. Violence is a primary form of communication, socialization, and order of life behind bars, reinforced and reproduced by the entire carceral system.[54] One does not need to be part of the military or have access to military-grade weapons to be militarized. One just needs to see violence as the solution to perceived threats and to see this violence as the source of one's power—or survival.

State of surveillance

Surveillance is also a crucial part of the militarized carceral state. The idea of constructing the prison as a "panopticon," developed in the eighteenth century by English philosopher Jeremy Bentham, was about asserting and maintaining physical and psychological control over those incarcerated at all times. The panopticon was a theoretical prison in which cells ring a central tower, from which those incarcerated could be observed at any time, without knowing whether they are being watched at any given moment.

Even though Bentham's panopticon was never built, notes Ian G. R. Shaw, it generated a blueprint that could be endlessly replicated.[55] Projecting the perception that one is monitored at all times is a hallmark of the prison as a physical facility. As Shaw warns, the technologies of this kind of control are already bleeding into larger society. Technologies developed by the carceral system for the monitoring and control over incarcerated populations at home, or by the US military for surveillance of "enemy combatants" abroad, are used increasingly by police forces, border patrols, and federal investigators. As explored further in chapter 4, technologies developed by Israel to confine and control Palestinians and enforce settler developments on Palestinian territory have also been exported around the world for use at other borders and in other police states.

As this surveillance trend continues, society becomes increasingly enclosed "under a generalizable mechanism of panopticonism," cautions

Shaw.[56] The state seeks to impose constant surveillance over its subjects, using technologies to form an open prison with the objective of pacifying and controlling the population.

Thinking beyond bars

This future, however, is not inevitable. Just like mass incarceration is a political choice—made by successive US governments to avoid having to provide for all citizens of the country and instead protect the wealth of the privileged—the dystopian nightmare of a digital surveillance state is not set in stone. We can choose a different path.

This starts with abolishing the prisons we already have. The demand for prison abolition has been ongoing for as long as prisons have existed. Those working for jail and prison closures have contributed to an abolitionist discourse and practice. The political work of incarcerated people, including through uprisings, writings, and teaching groups, has been instrumental in advancing the goals of abolition. Black feminists and organizers, LGBTQ+ activists, survivors of sexual violence and other harms, the housing insecure, and many others have over decades built the case for prison abolition, pathways to achieve it, and alternative systems of harm prevention and community care.

All of this organizing, thinking, and building means that in this moment of public reckoning with the failures of policing and the impacts of a global pandemic on incarcerated people, these ideas are ready to go. For example, as COVID-19 spread like wildfire throughout jails, prisons, and detention centers around the world, abolitionists called on governments to release all pretrial detainees, anyone over the age of sixty, all pregnant people, any immunocompromised person, and anyone with less than eighteen months remaining on their sentence; abolish bail; commute the sentences of those serving life without parole; and ensure that all people released from prisons and jails have the resources to socially distance and be fed and housed.[57]

Decarceration for all

Beyond the immediate actions necessary in the context of the pandemic, the process of abolishing prison will also require further steps, such as those set out by the activists behind 8toabolition.com. This includes measures to free all people from involuntary confinement; permanently close local jails; grant clemency to criminalized survivors; pressure state legislatures to end mandatory arrest and failure-to-protect laws that lead to the criminalization of survivors of gendered violence; reject "alternatives to incarceration" that are carceral in nature, including problem-solving courts and electronic monitoring and coercive restorative justice programs; reduce jail churn by reducing arrests; cut funding to prosecutor offices; end pretrial detention and civil commitment; release all people held pretrial and on parole violations; make all communication to and from prisoners free; and end immigration detention and family separation, and let undocumented community members come home.

Decarceration will also require the decriminalization of many activities that currently result in imprisonment—drug use, sex work, migration, and survival of gender-based violence among them. It will require decriminalization of people of color, LGBTQ+ people, and poor people, which are over-policed and targeted by various forms of surveillance.

Of crucial importance to the process of immediate decarceration is that we do not legitimize incarceration for some people while advocating for the release of others. For example, it may seem strategic or practical to call for the release of all "nonviolent criminals" or those who have committed "nonviolent" "crime." But each of these words needs to be contested, as does the approach that suggests some incarcerated people need to remain behind bars or are more inherently "risky" to release than others. As organizer Micah Herskind explains, structural racism is at play across these "crime categories"; the idea that risk resides within people is problematic and damaging; the contexts of "violent" and "nonviolent" are neither static nor necessarily accurate; and differentiating between these categories means that we are accepting that incarceration is necessary for some people.[58] If we accept, as the political project of abolition requires, that incarceration is a source of violence and generates more harm than it prevents or resolves, then we cannot perpetuate these distinctions—as well-intentioned as they may be.

Decarcerating our minds

But decarceration isn't just about minimizing the number of people being sent to prison; it's also about preventing "crime" by building more equitable societies, as described above, and about building alternatives to dealing with people who do commit acts of violence against others.

Embarking on this path obligates us first and foremost to decarcerate our own minds. We need to think beyond police and prison and imagine a different system for community and social safety, security, and care, a different way to prevent harm and to ensure accountability and justice.

As with the abolition of police, the abolition of prisons requires the realization that the most dangerous and violent people in our society are not in prison, but, as Eric Stanley notes, are actually running our government, militaries, prisons, police forces, and financial institutions.[59] Once we recognize "that prisons promote order and security for a few at the cost of generating violence, inequality, and social disruption for the many," writes Julia Sudbury, we can "go beyond arguing for the release of those incarcerated for nonviolent or drug offenses, or the reform of penal regimes, and demand a radical restructuring of the way in which we deal with the social conditions that generate 'crime.'"[60]

This is similar to the process required of those opposed to war. Can we credibly oppose only certain military actions? Can we differentiate between armed conflicts by this or that state, or that are conducted within the "laws of war," or that only use certain types of weapons? Can we distinguish between "wars of aggression" or "just wars," especially when we know full well that those determining these categories are also creating the narrative of justification or excuse, are also the ones producing the weapons and profiting off the violence, and are also claiming total immunity from the consequences of these actions?

We are either for the system of war, or we oppose it on the grounds that the entire system is a flawed approach to mediating human conflict, that it creates more harm than it prevents or resolves. That violence, punishment, and retribution are not the answer to harms committed or threatened. When we oppose war as a system, we do not say, but in the case of X, Y, or Z, war is acceptable. When we advocate for the abolition of nuclear weapons, we do not say, but it is fine and necessary for X government to possess, just not anyone else. Instead, we offer alternative systems to govern international relations. We promote accountability, justice, and peace through processes such as disarmament, demilitarization, dialogue, non-violent conflict resolution, and peaceful settlement of disputes through arbitration and mediation, and more.

The same must hold true for the abolition of the carceral system. But, as with police, many of us are taught that incarceration is the only way to make our communities and societies "safe" or to hold "criminals" accountable. Many people see prison as a more humane alternative to the bodily punishment—much of it public—that was enacted on people in the past, despite the fact that such punishment "nevertheless endures in the death penalty and many torturous conditions of confinement," as Ruth Wilson Gilmore notes.[61] Meanwhile, none of the standard justifications for incarceration—retribution, deterrence, rehabilitation, or incapacitation—have delivered their stated objectives, she argues, as the prisons just keep on filling up regardless of external factors like "crime rates."[62]

Yet the question, "But what do you do with all the criminals!?!" is the first thing one hears when advocating from an abolitionist position—just as those advocating for the abolition of war or nuclear weapons are asked, "What do you do with all the 'bad actors'!?!" While it is rational for people to fear alternatives they have been taught are naïve or dangerous, the answer to these questions is the same: *the current system is not working.* That must be the starting point—encouraging people, before they can become frantic about "chaos and criminality," to stop and think about what incarceration is really doing to our collective society and to the individuals living within it.

The current system is not preventing harm or conflict or violence. In fact, the current system is generating more harm. It is investing resources into social destruction rather than human well-being and real, equitable safety for all. "Harm is a basic fact of human reality," argues Amanda Aguilar Shank. "We can't avoid being harmed and harming others. It's just that current systems we have in place perpetuate harm and increase suffering, while claiming to do the opposite."[63] Expanding our thinking to include others beyond our own lived experience is important, but also recognizing what the system does to our society as a whole is crucial here, too. We need to think about the money spent on caging people by the millions, we need to think about the harm and violence that is generated within those cages and whether or not it actually keeps people outside the cages safe or whether it provides "justice" to the victims of harm. But also, we need to think about what this massive, machine-like production of violence does to all of us, what it says about how we are willing to treat other people, how we think about other human beings.

Undoing criminality as a concept

Before we can think through these matters, the question of what to do about the "criminals" needs further unpacking. Criminality is not a state of being. It is not inherent to a person. Who determines what constitutes a crime is important—sex work and drug use are crimes while devastating the global economy through a few wrong moves on the trading room floor is just a bad day at the office, or while manufacturing weapons and profiting from war is celebrated and encouraged. Crime, to a large degree, is relative, determined by the most privileged in our societies.

This is why many prison abolitionists prefer to speak about "harm" than "crime," and to focus on why harm—particularly the kinds of harm that tend to result in incarceration—is committed in the first place. As noted above, the answer has a lot to do with political economy—access to education, jobs, housing, food, care, love, recreation, safety, and freedom from surveillance and harassment of the carceral state. It has to do with where you live, how much money you have, whether you have access to employment and healthcare and recreation and peace and books and food. "Crime" and harm come from the toxic structures and cultures embedded in all aspects of our societies: white supremacy and racism, patriarchy and toxic masculinities, militarization and violence, capitalism and neoliberal exclusionary agendas. "People who harm are not individuals," says activist Eli Dru. "They are created in a context."[64]

Thinking about why harm is committed helps open up space to think about how we could respond to harm committed. The articulation of alternatives to the carceral system is important. As Arthur Waskow has noted, "First, having no alternative at all would create less crime than the present criminal training centers"—meaning prisons with their high rates of violence, oppression, and recidivism. But beyond that, he argues, "the only full alternative is building the kind of society that does not need prisons: A decent redistribution of power and income" and "a decent sense of community that can help support, reintegrate, and truly rehabilitate those who suddenly become filled with fury or despair, and that can face them not as objects—'criminals'—but as people who have committed illegal acts, as have almost all of us."[65] This is a crucial aspect of prison abolition: being able to see those who have committed harm as human beings. Not as monsters who need to be locked away, not as disposable objects that can be imprisoned, put out of sight and mind from the rest of society.

Building communities of care, not cops and incarceration

Understanding all of these dynamics is key to preventing harms being committed. Prevention means investing in care, not cops. It means putting resources toward equal opportunities for education, jobs, housing, healthcare, food security, youth services, recreation programs. It means providing more opportunities for people to live well, to live equitably to one another, to build safe communities for all. It means allocating municipal funding toward healthcare infrastructure, including wellness resources, neighborhood-based trauma centers, noncoercive drug and alcohol treatment programming, peer support networks, and training for healthcare professionals. It means making these services available for free to low-income residents. In some cities, residents and organizations have started building a "care not cops" model that others can adapt to their local contexts.[66]

The process of building new forms of care also means investing in teachers and counselors, universal childcare, and support for all family structures; providing free and accessible public transit, especially servicing marginalized and lower-income communities; ensuring investments in community-based food banks, grocery cooperatives, gardens, and farms; and investing in youth programs that promote learning, safety, and community care. Research shows that urban greening and improved built environments dramatically increase community safety, including creating livable communities where the local landscape affirms people's dignity and humanity.[67]

The provision of safe housing for all is another important aspect of building communities of care.[68] As set out by #8toabolition, this will require steps such as cancelling rent without burden of repayment during COVID-19; repurposing empty buildings, houses, apartments, and hotels to house people experiencing homelessness; prohibiting evictions; removing cops from all reentry and shelter institutions; providing unequivocal support and resources to refugee and asylum-seeking communities; allowing community benefits agreements to be a community-governed means of urban planning; making public housing accessible to everyone, including by repealing discriminatory laws barring people from accessing resources based on income, race, gender, sexuality, immigration status, or history of incarceration; supporting and promoting the existence of community land trusts for Black and historically displaced communities; ensuring that survivors of gendered violence have access to alternative housing options in the event their primary housing becomes unsafe; and providing noncoercive housing options for young people experiencing abuse or family rejection of their queer or trans identities.

All of these steps will require cities, towns, and neighborhoods to build or expand mechanisms and cultures of community self-governance,[69] for example by promoting neighborhood councils as representative bodies within municipal decision making; investing in multilingual resources for immigrant and asylum-seeking communities; assessing community needs and investing in community-based resources, including groups from tenant unions to local shop owners and street vendors, prioritizing those from marginalized groups; investing in land stewardship councils to oversee return of land to Indigenous communities; and investing in community-based public safety approaches, including noncarceral violence prevention and intervention programs and skills-based education on bystander intervention, consent and boundaries, and healthy relationships.

These will be some of the investments and changes necessary to build the infrastructure, policies, and cultures of equity, peace, safety, and nonviolence that can begin to offer alternatives to the carceral state. All will require further elaboration and brainstorming, and will be broadly context-dependent, changing based on the needs of the communities engaged.

Decarceral and abolitionist feminism

In addition to preventing the commission of harm by building a culture of care, shifting away from the carceral state also requires that we change expectations and understandings of concepts such as accountability, justice, and safety. In the pursuit of decarcerating our minds from the assumption that locking people up is the best, or only, way to deal with "crime," Angela Davis asks us to imagine, among other things, a society "in which punishment itself is no longer the central concern in the making of justice."[70] To this end, in addition to the investments in education, health, and community-based structures described above, we also need what Davis describes as "a justice system based on reparation and reconciliation rather than retribution and vengeance."[71]

Restorative and transformative justice programs and mechanisms are critical for dealing with harms that are committed. Decarceral and abolitionist feminists have done the most thinking about this, including in the context of sexual and domestic violence. Reports such as *Because She's Powerful* document the overwhelmingly negative effect mass incarceration has on women, including the financial and emotional costs, especially chronic loneliness and depression.[72] The *Crime Survivors Speak* report, one of very few reports conducted with survivors to find out what response they wanted to address violent crimes committed against them, found that most generally do not want punitive criminal law responses and instead want restorative justice approaches.[73]

The carceral system, as survivors well know, is stacked against survivors of gender-based violence, including sexual and domestic violence. This system does not create accountability or lasting change; it does not deal with patriarchy, misogyny, and structural sexism. It focuses on individual behavior rather than the cultures of toxic masculinity that lead to the systemic and structural nature of gender-based violence. The carceral system in reality *disincentivizes* accountability, argues abolitionist organizer Mariame Kaba. Under threat of incarceration, the inclination of perpetrators of harm is to deny the harm, thus putting the survivor on trial to prove that harm was committed.[74]

In those rare cases when someone who does commit sexual violence or engages in police brutality is prosecuted and found guilty, this cannot be taken as an indication that "the system works." The infrequency with which the perpetrators of these kinds of harms become ensnared in the carceral system clearly shows that the system does not effectively work as a mechanism of "accountability" or "justice" for gender-based violence or police brutality. But even more importantly, as Mariame Kaba and Andrea Ritchie argue, "We can't claim the system must be dismantled because it is a danger to Black lives and at the same time legitimize it by turning to it for justice."[75] While we may find a sense of relief in the conviction of someone we believe must be held accountable for wrongdoings, we must not assume the conviction means that the system is changing.

"While there is something satisfying about knowing Hollywood mogul Harry Weinstein's ankle is finally chafing under an ankle monitor the same way the ankles of immigrants and POC parolees have been for years, we also know how this story ends," notes activist Amanda Aguilar Shank. "Any time the state steps in to deliver safety, it is always a white suprem-acist model of safety that sees our communities as the threats to be pro-tected against. We never win when we expand the powers and resources of the state to control and punish."[76] For every Weinstein behind bars, there are thousands of other abusers walking free, living with impunity in our patriarchal world order. The vast majority of perpetrators of sexual assault are not arrested, convicted, or incarcerated.[77] The failures of the current system are so widespread and well known that many survivors of sexual violence don't even bother reporting cases at all, understanding that it is more likely that their reputations and lives will be damaged, that they will be further traumatized, than it is that those who caused them harm will ever be held accountable. Yet framing the carceral state as the best or only form of "protection" against sexual and gender-based violence sets us to invest even more in a failed system and teaches us to celebrate the few convictions that are handed down while true justice, accountability, and prevention remain elusive.

Further, the carceral system itself is a site of sexual and gender-based violence. Police themselves have been known to rape people in custody[78] and commit acts of domestic violence[79] within their families. Sexual vi-olence is rife within prisons, committed by guards and by those incar-cerated. There is no safety or protection from sexual and gendered harm within the existing system. "Prison isn't feminist, because it recreates the same sexual violence and the same fear, the same kinds of oppression," ex-plains organizer Shira Hassan. "It is the pin on the head of the racist and sexist system that we live in."[80]

Understanding how incarceration is gender violence, rather than an answer to it, "helps us get out of the false idea that we can have a govern-ment that promotes 'gender equality' while we still have imprisonment, and helps clear up the fantasy that we could have some kind of prison system that is safe for queer or trans people or women," explains Dean Spade.[81] Rejecting policing and prisons, however, does not mean turn-ing away from accountability. Instead, Kaba and Ritchie argue, it "means we stop setting the value of a life by how much time another person does in a cage for violating or taking it—particularly when the criminal punishment system has consistently made clear whose lives it will value, and whose lives it will cage."[82]

Thinking through this morass is challenging—it requires critically thinking about terms and concepts we use all the time, like criminal justice and accountability, and interrogating what they really mean. The current system is neither about accountability nor justice; it is about punishment, retribution, revenge. Kaba often says, "This isn't about your feelings!" As much as the desire for revenge is human, it doesn't help us achieve safety or justice. In fact, as Kaba argues, "punishment actually undermines safety." The act of punishment, of "inflicting suffering on others in response to an experience of harm/violence/wrongdoing," is harmful and counterproductive, attests Kaba. "We cannot effectively teach people not to harm others by harming them."[83] Looking for and building mechanisms for real accountability and justice, as well as for prevention of future harm, requires us to let go of our instincts for retribution and, as Kandace Montgomery of Black Visions Collective says, end the culture of punishment and instead step into addressing conflict with each other and within community in nonviolent ways.[84]

Toward transformative justice

In the quest to establish alternative forms of accountability and justice that do not rely on punishment, confinement, surveillance, and violence, decarceral and abolitionist feminists advocate for transformative justice (TJ) processes and mechanisms. This type of process is survivor-led, designed to support and facilitate the healing of the survivor through holding the perpetrator of harm responsible and accountable, but without "punishment" at the center of that accountability. TJ recognizes that "many survivors do not necessarily want harm to be done in response to the harm caused," explains Ann Russo. "Instead, they want the person to take responsibility for their behaviour and its impact, to feel remorse, to offer a genuine apology, to address the survivor's needs, and to commit to individual change and transformation."[85]

As generationFIVE writes in *A Transformative Justice Handbook,* many of those who have experienced harm report that they need to tell their own stories about their own experiences, within a context of trust and safety; experience validation that the harm they experienced was and is real; observe that the person who abused or harmed them feels remorse and is accountable for their actions; receive support that counteracts isolation and self-blame; have choice and input in the resolution of the harm they experienced; and be accepted and encouraged, not shamed and blamed, for coming forward by their families, peers, and communities.[86]

While survivors' experiences, needs, and goals must be at the center of any TJ process, this "does not mean that people who may have been deeply wounded are suddenly handed full responsibility for a community dialogue and rehabilitation process," writer and artist Kai Cheng Thom makes clear. "Survivor-led does not mean that the community gets to abdicate its responsibility for providing support, safety, expertise, and leadership in making healing happen."[87] It is also not meant to place a burden on the person harmed to lead a process or reach out to their perpetrators. On the contrary, it means organized support for survivors is made available throughout a process that is designed with the survivor's needs and goals leading the way.

TJ processes can take many forms. In *Beyond Survival,* Ejeris Dixon explains, "Some groups support survivors by helping them identify their needs and boundaries while ensuring their attackers agree to these boundaries and atone for the harm they caused," while others "create safe spaces and sanctuaries to support people escaping from violence. There are also community campaigns that educate community members on the specific dynamics of violence, how to prevent it, and what community-based programs are available."[88]

Another key goal of any TJ process is preventing future harm. To this end, TJ processes are meant to facilitate transformation in the behavior of those who have committed harm and, where possible, restoration in communities and relationships where harms have been committed. This means providing space for the transformation of "the individual perpetrator, the abusive relationship, and the culture and power dynamics of the community," explains Janaé E. Bonsu of Black Youth Project 100, "rather than a process in which revenge, retribution, or punishment is enacted."[89]

Because "as much as we try to 'throw away' people—through the prison industrial complex, through deportation, through violence—people do not simply 'go away' when it is convenient or desired," says Amanda Aguilar Shank. When we exile people for their "crimes," she argues, "there is very little possibility of reconciliation, transformation, or healing."[90] Offering people an opportunity to understand and name their behavior and the impact of their actions, to issue an apology, and to take specific steps toward reconciliation or restitution can provide a way to prevent future harm, create a culture against harm, *and* offer justice to survivors.

For perpetrators, as the Philly Stands Up collective outlines, key steps in the TJ process might include recognizing the harm they have done, even if it wasn't intentional; acknowledging that harm's impact on individuals and the community; making appropriate restitution to the individual and community; and developing solid skills for transforming attitudes and behavior to prevent further harm.[91]

Accountability can take different forms. It can include "stopping harmful behavior, naming harmful behavior, giving sincere apologies, stepping down from leadership roles, developing daily healing and reflection practices to address root causes of harmful behavior,"[92] as well building systems for support, providing material repair, and contributing to community efforts to prevent the types of harms in which the perpetrator engaged. But key to an abolitionist conception of accountability is that it isn't carceral or punitive.[93] That doesn't mean there are no consequences—there should indeed be material and emotional consequences for harm caused—but these "should be determined in direct relation to the harm done and should involve input from people impacted by the harm."[94]

There are many models for TJ processes, developed largely by Black, feminist, queer, disabled, and other marginalized communities that have never been able to rely on the carceral system to provide for justice, accountability, or safety. As any TJ practitioner will report, these processes are not perfect. They can be messy, they can retraumatize or cause new trauma, and they do not always satisfy the survivor or result in transformation of the perpetrator. But, just as with the alternatives to policing and other aspects of the carceral system, TJ offers a different approach that by and large produces much less violence and harm in responding to violence and harm. And, just like the alternatives to policing, the long-term transformative effects cannot be felt until real investments are made into these alternatives. Right now, people engaged in TJ work usually operate on shoestring budgets without wider community, city, or state support. If the billions spent every year on policing and incarceration were instead invested in building up TJ systems on a larger, more resilient scale, we could see meaningful change.[95]

"We simply do not know, and cannot know, what the occurrence, prevention, or resolution of harm could look like in our society under more just conditions," note Mariame Kaba and Kelly Hayes. "There is no road map for justice, because under [the carceral] system we have never seen it. But the current system has been thoroughly mapped, and it has already failed."[96]

Breaking the cage

While many people may see "criminal activity" and "criminal behavior" as the main obstacles to pursuing the abolition of police and prisons, it is really the carceral state itself that is the impediment. It is the profits made by the prison industry, the benefits gained by the capitalist class, the privileges accrued by the white supremacist, neoliberal state that continues to choose to make more investments in locking people up than in providing a livable world. And as our states make these choices and investments, our minds become increasingly trapped in the same buildings and systems designed to control the "surplus population," of which the state seeks to dispose.

Due to its very nature as an institution that confines and hides away those the state rejects, prisons are easily taken for granted. "It is difficult to imagine life without them," Angela Davis acknowledges. "At the same time, there is reluctance to face the realities hidden within them, a fear of thinking about what happens inside them. Thus, the prison is present in our lives and at the same time, it is absent from our lives."[97]

For those who have worked for the abolition of nuclear weapons, this contradiction may sound familiar. Objects designed to inflict massive violence against entire cities, the lived reality of which is horrific, intergenerational pain, trauma, and suffering, seemingly exist in most people's minds as abstract objects that "keep us safe." Many people can acknowledge nuclear weapons are horrible, yet claim their necessity as tools of security. In order to reconcile this ghastly incongruity and live with the cognitive dissonance it inevitably buries in our minds, most people put the atomic bomb out of sight, out of mind. They exist, but they are meant to never be used. Except, they are used. Every day, nuclear weapons shape the way our world operates, waste precious human and economic resources, and put our entire planet in danger.

It is the same with prisons. For those who have never had to interact with the carceral system, it can seem to be a necessary evil. To those who have had that displeasure, in any shape or form, it is simply evil. Prisons are not abstractions that "keep us safe," they are physical manifestations of brutality, cruelty, and the reproduction of harm, over and over and over.

The insistence on continuing to invest in the broken systems that operate "to exile, cage, and torture immigrants, poor people, people of color, and people with disabilities always seem to rely on an idea that we need these systems, we just need to clean them up or fix them up somehow," says Dean Spade. "Abolitionists are asking, in a variety of ways, if we can imagine letting go of the idea that some people need to be caged, exiled, or kept out."[98] This requires us, first and foremost, to "unlearn what is possible," as Derecka Purnell suggests.[99] Deconstructing and reconstructing what is achievable or feasible is essential for the abolition not just of the prisons, but of the whole carceral system, and of other systems of violence that keep us all caged in the global hell of inequality and violence of our own making. One such system, which has existed throughout history but is increasingly facilitated by emerging technologies, is surveillance. Monitoring, scrutinizing, and cataloguing people is a crucial element of the prison system, and is essential to several of the other structures of violence discussed in this book—including policing, border "enforcement," and war.

Chapter 3

|||||||||||||||||||||||||||||||||||||||||||||||||||||||

Decoding Surveillance

When many of us think of surveillance, we may think of science fiction dystopias. Of stories like *1984* or *Minority Report*, where our movements, activities, and even our thoughts are monitored, regulated, or predicted by governments or private corporations. But surveillance is not science fiction. It is not the future. It is our reality, now.

From CCTV cameras installed in many major cities to facial recognition to online data collection to drones, governments around the world are increasingly monitoring, tracking, and controlling human beings. Tech corporations are making billions from the surveillance boom, helping police forces and government agencies spy on or hunt down certain people or groups, facilitating the criminalization of entire populations. Often, governments present these tools as necessary for fighting or deterring crime. Other technologies, which people willingly install in their own homes, are presented as making life easier—our "smart" phones, refrigerators, doorbells, and televisions help normalize technology like voice and facial recognition as well as the idea of being electronically monitored at all times—ostensibly for our own "comfort."

We are accepting this at our own peril. The surveillance industry is not only increasingly pervasive, but also increasingly violent. Ultimately, all of these technologies—from Ring doorbells to Reaper drones—are about monitoring, categorizing, and processing human beings as objects. Whether or not they are weaponized with bombs or bullets, they are all used as weapons—to control, incarcerate, or kill.

Surveillance is about gathering information and data points about people in order to sort them and classify them.[1] It is also about curtailing freedom—of movement, of expression, of existence. States and corporations use surveillance to monitor, censor, regulate, and monetize the behavior of workers and oppressed peoples. Not only can surveillance enable the placement of specific restrictions on individuals or groups, but it can also shape behavior by incentivizing certain actions or expressions and discouraging others. As Jasbir Puar, professor at Rutgers University, has said, surveillance is preemptive: it seeks to control now so that it can avoid having to repress later.[2]

This has serious implications for the exercise of civil liberties. Academic Neil M. Richards notes that surveillance erodes privacy, makes people less likely to engage in protest or with ideas considered "controversial," and creates a power dynamic between the watcher and the watched that results in coercion and censorship.[3] It enables governments to track dissidents or opponents, justifying broad spectrum surveillance against those deemed threats to "national security."[4]

Anja Kovacs of the Internet Democracy Project argues that, as governments engage increasingly in mass surveillance, they are criminalizing everyone. Even people who are not suspected of a crime now fall under the gaze of the state, which is contrary to international human rights law. Surveillance has nothing to do with the behavior of the individual being surveilled. "Today, your mere presence in a place, or simply having provided one or more data points, is enough for you to be brought into yet another network of control," cautions Kovacs. "Unless you stop participating in modern public life, it will be hard to escape surveillance right now."[5]

The protection of human rights and dignity is why activists and organizers around the world are working to shut down surveillance. Fighting for bans on facial recognition and predictive policing software and campaigning to end the use of drones or prevent the development of autonomous weapons, people are actively seeking to abolish the apparatus and practice of surveillance. These efforts are also a critical part of challenging other forms of state violence, as the ability of governments, police, militaries, and corporations to monitor, track, and categorize human beings lies at the heart of their ability to oppress, control, incarcerate, and kill.

The panopticon of our discontents: a brief sketch of surveillance

Surveillance has existed throughout history. Espionage has long been part of international relations; spying on citizens and immigrants has long been an activity of most governments. Federal officials have surveilled and at times embedded themselves in social movements to spy or to even steer the direction of activities. Racialized communities have been monitored and tracked; women and LGBTQ+ people have been watched, harassed, abused, and controlled; incarcerated people are surveilled constantly.

Surveillance is also a key part of the capitalist system. Throughout history, ruling classes and states have surveilled the laborers they exploited and peoples they oppressed. Capitalism's enclosure of the commons (described elsewhere in this book) forced people off the land and into cities and brought them together into massive workplaces to make products and provide services. The logic of competition drove corporations to squeeze more out of workers, compelling them to monitor their behavior on the job to make sure they were working as hard and as fast as possible and as efficiently as possible. The state played a central role in this process of primitive accumulation and dispossession, and it continues to defend private ownership and control and oppression of workers. Capital also depends on the state to discipline workers outside of the workplace, ensuring "law and order," which has entailed the development of surveillance of workers on and off the job as a central feature of the capitalist state.

The same logic of surveillance to control is horrifically concentrated on oppressed groups within and beyond the boundaries of the colonialist states. Settler colonial states mapped the land and surveilled the people they dispossessed. Other colonial states had to enforce minority rule over the land and Indigenous communities to extract resources, exploit labor, and preempt resistance. This took extreme and barbaric form with the exploitation of slave labor on the capitalist plantations of colonies.[6]

Thus, capitalism has created a terrifying symbiosis of state and capital in surveilling human lives. Above all else, surveillance is about control and power. As the technologies of surveillance spread, as they become more sophisticated and ubiquitous, the distinction between the inside and the outside of a "panopticon" becomes blurrier, cautions Jackie Wang. "It is even possible to imagine a future where the prison as a physical structure is superseded by total surveillance without physical confinement."[7] As a result of the high-tech revolution over the last few decades, surveillance has already metastasized into Big Brother structures that Orwell could not have imagined. In the workplace, industries, services, and logistics have turned surveillance into a brutal regime; police are using sophisticated surveillance and software to not only locate those they deem "criminals" but to "predict" crime; state-sanctioned hackers are operating inside each other's networks with the capacity not just to collect information but to disrupt and destroy critical infrastructure.

Our awareness of this panopticon style of surveillance has not always kept up with reality. But organizers have always pushed back against it, denouncing the ways in which governments and corporations have deployed the most basic to the most sophisticated technologies to surveil, sort, and oppress populations. Much of this work depends on those impacted by surveillance and other concerned activists and organizers exposing the means of surveillance. Earlier this century, revelations enabled by courageous whistleblowers have meant we have at least some idea of how we are being watched and tracked, and how that information is being used.

Along with the war crimes it revealed, WikiLeaks' publication of diplomatic cables leaked by Chelsea Manning in 2010 unmasked new cases and forms of international espionage around the world—including that the US and UK governments had eavesdropped on UN Secretary-General

Kofi Annan in the lead-up to the US-led invasion of Iraq.[8] In 2013, Edward Snowden exposed the breadth and depth of the US surveillance network run by the National Security Agency (NSA). Among other things, the NSA has engaged in a program of warrantless wiretapping of telephone conversations of US citizens and noncitizens alike, and built a massive supercomputing facility in Utah "with the goal of capturing and archiving much of the world's Internet traffic, with a view to decrypting and searching it as decryption technologies inevitably advance."[9]

The Snowden files also revealed new information about the NSA's collusion with or coercion of tech firms and foreign governments, including through the Five Eyes network, consisting of the intelligence agencies of the United States, United Kingdom, Canada, Australia, and New Zealand. Under the Five Eyes agreement, each country surveils and collects and analyzes information from a different part of the globe.[10] Since the Snowden revelations, global surveillance has increased while those revealing its scope have been criminalized, chased, and confined. The development of new technologies is enabling government agencies around the world to continue to monitor, track, control, confine, and kill individual human beings and entire groups at unprecedented rates.

Modern advanced technologies—and our own voluntary use of much of this technology—has enabled exponentially more surveillance, both in terms of volume and distance. Snowden's leaks revealed the multiple and simultaneous technical and commercial programs that place backdoors into software and hardware, rendering much online infrastructure vulnerable to attack, explains technology and surveillance researcher Felicity Ruby. Cell phones, server stacks, email clients, payment mechanisms, browsers, fiber-optic cables, encryption technology—all have been compromised by the US government. "According to Snowden, the entire Internet is 'owned' by the NSA and its Five Eyes partners, including all the networked devices in the hands of individuals, heads of state and their spouses included, and the corporations are along for the ride, willingly or unwittingly."[11]

Surveillance capitalism

In many cases, corporations both build and profit from surveillance technologies that are then tapped into, subpoenaed, or otherwise used by governments. Surveillance is a capitalist enterprise as much as anything else, as outlined above. Shoshana Zuboff, an author and academic focusing on technology, describes surveillance capitalism as claiming "human experience as free raw material for translation into behavioural data."[12] Information about human beings, collected digitally, is "fed into advanced manufacturing processes known as 'machine intelligence,' and fabricated into *prediction products* that anticipate what you will do now, soon, and later." Data profiteers trade these prediction products in a new kind of marketplace she labels *behavioral futures markets*. "Surveillance capitalists have grown immensely wealthy from these trading operations, for many companies are willing to lay bets on our future behaviour."[13]

Many people invite this form of surveillance into their lives, mostly on the grounds of convenience or efficiency. Surveillance technology is increasingly being normalized in our homes and places of work, through our smartphones, our computers, and the "Internet of things" that many people rely on for convenience and connection in their daily lives.[14] More and more points of data about our daily lives are made available through the "sensor-based society" we have developed, including through wearables (smart watches and fitness trackers), smart home devices, connected toys, and automated travel. "Sensors such as microphones, cameras, accelerometers, and temperature and motion sensors add to an ever-expanding list of our activities (data) that can be collected and commodified."[15]

All of the networked devices we operate, and the Internet itself, may appear to make our lives better or easier, but they are not cost-free. In reality, they are "funded by billions of transactions where advertisements are individually targeted at Internet users based upon detailed profiles of their reading and consumer habits," explains law professor Neil M. Richards.[16] This has given a number of companies "a window into most of our movements online,"[17] and also into our physical lives.

"Every minute of every day, everywhere on the planet, dozens of companies—largely unregulated, little scrutinized—are logging the movements of tens of millions of people with mobile phones and storing the information in gigantic data files," reported the *New York Times* in 2019.[18] Using software slipped into smartphone apps, companies large and small are collecting and selling data that grants anyone with access the ability to see where you go every moment of the day. The *Times's* investigation found that although the companies claim they are not associating location data with specific people, it is "child's play" to connect real people to any given phone.

In addition to tracking our movements, other technologies spy on us in our homes. Across the United States, Amazon has sold more than 100 million Alexa-enabled devices. Alexa was preceded by Apple's phone-based voice assistant, Siri. These devices have recorded conversations, accidentally released them, communicated with each other, and stored data about user behavior and patterns. Amazon Echo is fully integrated into people's homes, always waiting to listen in. "Some Echo devices already have cameras," notes Garfield Benjamin, "and if facial recognition capabilities were added we could enter a world of pervasive monitoring in our most private spaces, even tracked as we move between locations."[19]

The companies developing these technologies are actively "building an infrastructure that can be later co-opted in undesirable ways by large multinationals and state surveillance apparatus, and compromised by malicious hackers," says Dr. Michael Veale.[20] Even without voice assistance turned on, smartphones—especially those made by Google and Apple, which control the hardware, software, and cloud services related to the phones—collect data on what we search, listen to, or send in our messages.[21]

Facebook and Google both engage in persistent and pervasive surveillance of billions of people around the world. Amnesty International has argued this poses a systemic threat to human rights, including the right to privacy, freedom of opinion and expression, freedom of thought, and the right to equality and nondiscrimination. All of the companies' platforms, such as Facebook, Instagram, Google Search, YouTube, and WhatsApp, use exploitative algorithms "that process huge volumes of data to infer incredibly detailed characteristics about people and shape their online experience. Advertisers then pay Facebook and Google to be able to target people with advertising or specific messages."[22]

The Cambridge Analytica scandal exposed how easily people's data can be used in this way to manipulate and influence them, both politically and for financial gain.[23] But there is a much bigger, largely invisible, proliferation of data tracking, brokerage, and exchange between multiple tech companies, in which third-party developers and data analytics companies take the data harvested by the "frontline" company (the app or platform) and sell it further, or sell their analysis. Privacy International has found, for example, that at least 61 percent of the apps it tested "automatically transfer data to Facebook the moment a user opens the app. This happens whether people have a Facebook account or not, or whether they are logged into Facebook or not."[24]

The surveillance, sale of data, and manipulation of tech users all indicate a growing threat to human rights. Indeed, "human rights abuses might be embedded in the business model that has evolved for social media companies," writes Sarah Joseph of the Castan Centre for Human Rights Law at Monash University.[25] These models profile and target people based on every aspect of their lives, from political opinions to online shopping preferences. This gives political and commercial power to anyone with access to this data, and enables the facilitation of "fake news" and fomenting violence.

As the models for social media platforms are fundamentally about keeping users engaged, they seek to amplify content that gets attention, which is often content that contains conspiracy theories or violence. Algorithms "actively funnel users from the mainstream to the fringe, subjecting users to more extreme content, all to maintain user engagement," pointed out US Congressperson Robin Kelly during a congressional hearing on social media's role in promoting extremism and misinformation. "This is a fundamental flaw in your business model," she argued, "that mere warning labels on posts, temporary suspensions of some accounts, and even content moderation cannot address. And your companies' insatiable desire to maintain user engagement will continue to give such content a safe haven if doing so improves your bottom line."[26]

The bottom line is showcased by the billions of social media users who continue to engage with these platforms. Journalism professor Jack Linchuan Qui explores the sheer volume of people who voluntarily use surveillance technologies through smartphones and social media, comparing the scale of the "free labor" performed by users to the transatlantic slave trade. Drawing a connection between past slavery with the conditions faced by workers at the notorious Foxconn company in China, where Apple phones are made, Qui draws a line from the sweatshops to "servile consumerism," in which labor is provided through addiction to devices and services. In 1800, he notes, the British Empire had one million slaves, or 2.5 billion hours of labor. In 2014, Foxconn had 1.4 million workers, or 4.8 billion hours. In the same year, Facebook had 1.4 billion users, or 652 billion hours of labor. That is, he argues, Facebook has 261 British Empires or 137 Foxconns of labor at its disposal.[27]

Of course, the labor we provide that enables companies to track, monitor, and manipulate us is not used just for corporate profit. It is also largely made accessible to governments, usually without our knowledge or consent. Public- and private-sector surveillance use the same technologies and techniques and operate through partnerships. The "surveillant symbiosis" between companies and governments "means that no analysis of surveillance can be strictly limited to just the government or the market in isolation. Surveillance must instead be understood in its aggregated and complex social context."[28]

The implications of both corporate and governmental surveillance for our lives are grave and unprecedented. The coupling or networking of vast government agencies interested in our political lives and companies interested in our consumer lives is becoming increasingly entangled. This means that our physical movements, our purchases, our political opinions, our affiliations and associations can be tracked, monitored, and scrutinized for purposes of profit or power.

Technology-facilitated gender-based violence and discrimination

This caution is particularly relevant when it comes to those facing gender-based violence. Even without high-tech surveillance technologies, surveillance practices have long been tied to systemic forms of discrimination that facilitate violence against people based on sex, gender, and sexual orientation. The growing architecture of surveillance apparatus only exacerbates this.

Tracking devices used to locate individuals have been used by abusive partners to track and find women. In Saudi Arabia, for example, the Google app Absher, which is owned and operated by the interior ministry of Saudi Arabia, allows men to track women's movements, including across borders.[29]

In April 2011, Apple came under media fire for invading user privacy after it was revealed that iPhone is able to transmit information assumed by consumers to be private. Multiple applications transmit the phones' unique device identifier along with detailed location data and time stamps. As Corrine Mason and Shoshana Magnet explain, the methods that Apple uses to place its customers under surveillance "are identical to some of the new technological strategies that abusers use to stalk their intimate partners, including screen shots and the use of GPS [Global Positioning Systems] technology to track individual location."[30]

According to the YWCA, more than one in four stalking survivors report that some form of cyberstalking was used against them, while electronic monitoring of some kind is used to stalk one out of every thirteen stalking survivors. A 2020 survey found that 52 percent of young women and girls have experienced online abuse, 68 percent of which took place on social media platforms.[31] Abusers are increasingly using GPS to track the physical location of their targets, including through vehicles and smartphones.[32] In the United States, a survey of women's shelters indicated that 85 percent of shelters said they were "working directly with victims whose abusers tracked them using GPS."[33] Other commercially available technologies are also used in tech-related gender-based violence, such as small, wireless cameras that can be "placed or purchased pre-installed in a variety of common household items, including smoke detectors, children's toys, and lamps, many of which can be activated remotely."[34]

Spyware and surveillance technologies can be used to monitor and intercept an individual's communications, including emails, phone calls, text messages, and social media activity; send fake messages on behalf of the target; remotely activate device microphones and cameras; access photos and videos; steal application passwords; duplicate call and message logs; and notify a monitoring party if the device is turned off.[35] Software with the same capabilities as tools used to covertly monitor state actors or abused to target human rights activists can be affordably purchased for the purpose of monitoring a spouse or ex-partner.[36]

"Existing forms of violence are replicated online in many of the same ways as they are present offline; the same patriarchal norms, exclusions and violence form a link into the digital age," writes Shmyla Khan of the Digital Rights Foundation. In many countries, "the presence of women online, or transgressions from societal norms in the cyber realm, has direct and immediate repercussions offline and has resulted in instances of honour killings, violence, social ostracism and application of discriminatory laws to regulate speech of marginalised communities."[37]

Khan notes that women's experiences of surveillance is different than the dominant cisgendered male experience. "Many women experience, and are conscious of, the 'male gaze' when they enter physical spaces that are traditionally male-dominated, such as public streets," she writes. Feminist perspectives on surveillance connect being "leered at" by men to that of being "watched" by the surveillance state. In this context, "the feeling of being *watched*, an experience shared by many in online spaces, is an essentially *female* experience. The male gaze, lurking on the female body, is not dissimilar to online users feeling like they have to modify their behaviour under the gaze of surveillance."[38] The anonymity and impunity offered online can also make the experience of digital violence more intense or embolden aggressions, which can then manifest into physical violence.[39]

Queer surveillance

The continuum of online to physical violence also relates to LGBTQ+ people, who can face the same kinds of harassment and aggression that women do online. Again, the harms in the digital space can also spill over into the physical space, such as, for example, cases in which police in Egypt exploited dating apps and messaging platforms to identify and locate LGBTQ+ users, creating fake profiles to arrange meetups, and then arresting, detaining, and torturing people.[40]

Surveillance technologies can also be used in ways that normalize maleness, heterosexuality, and able-bodiedness.[41] "Modern surveillance systems operate upon masculine logics of disembodied control at a distance," writes communications professor Torin Monahan.[42] Surveillance is objectifying. Regardless of who is being surveilled, "these systems enforce masculinized representations of social experience and value."[43]

Surveillance can be used to monitor "transgressive" gender identities and sexual orientations. Trans people have been marked for surveillance on the basis of the clothing they wear.[44] Biometric technologies, such as facial recognition, are "calibrated upon binary assumptions of gender embodiment and compulsory heterosexuality," so people who do not conform to these "standards" do not register.[45]

As Anja Kovacs writes, all of this results in "discrimination by abstraction." Human beings are reduced to data points, "disembodied and denuded from our social context, abstract representations of the world— or at least of what those who are in control of the data consider important in it." Understood from this perspective, the fact that surveillance is about power is clearly reinforced. Surveillance reinscribes existing power equations, "because it generally aims to control, even eliminate, those who 'deviate' from the norm."[46]

Technology is usually presented as being "gender neutral"—but the way it is developed and used is not. Surveillance is itself a tool of patriarchy that controls and limits the exercise of fundamental freedoms of people. While it may be presented as "gender neutral" or "race neutral" it is not—it reinforces and amplifies existing inequalities.[47] In addition, access to and use of technology is also gendered. If there is one mobile phone per household, who owns it? Are public internet cafes accessible to all people? Are LGBTQ+-focused apps or sites blocked by the government?

Concerns about gender-based surveillance are about more than just the harms that are enacted against people based on sex, gender, or sexual orientation. This kind of patriarchal and discriminatory surveillance is rooted in the objectification of human beings by the capitalist state and corporations, as described above. Monitoring, controlling, and oppressing people who are deemed to be a "threat" to the "normative" behavior of "good citizens" is a crucial part of the surveillance state's activities to suppress potential dissent and resistance. Surveillance tools are thus an essential element of the carceral system's approach to determining criminality and caging those it deems threatening to the "stability" of law and order, as well as to the projects of border imperialism and capitalist accumulation.

Colonial and racist surveillance

Understanding the patriarchal control offered by surveillance is important for exploring how surveillance technologies are exploited—and even created—as instruments of colonialism, racism, and white supremacy. As Shmyla Khan of the Digital Rights Foundation argues, the colonial state built mechanisms to "control the colonial subject in the form of documentation, classification and criminalization of certain races and tribes."[48] Surveillance apparatus was used to target and control certain communities while patronizing others, applying particular legal regimes to some groups and a wholly different set of laws and logics of control to others.

As elaborated further in the next chapter, surveillance technologies are also used at borders, reinforcing colonial projects of border imperialism and racialized notions of who is a threat to "national security."

Today, a new form of corporate colonization is taking place through surveillance and digitalization of knowledge and control. Just as in past European colonial undertakings, when private corporations helped dispossess, murder, and enslave Indigenous populations in the "pathological pursuit of profit and power,"[49] sociologist Michael Kwet argues that now, instead of the conquest of land, Big Tech corporations are colonizing digital technology. A handful of US multinational corporations control everything from smartphones to search engines to business and social networking platforms to online advertising, and so much more. As Big Tech products are integrated into societies around the world, the companies—and the United States—"obtain enormous power over their economy and create technological dependencies that will lead to perpetual resource extraction."[50]

As these companies come to dominate the landscape of transportation (e.g., Uber) or media advertising (e.g., Google), they undermine local development, dominate the market, and extract revenue from the local economy to feed foreign coffers. Kwet argues that the structural domination over digital architecture created by these companies facilitates further imperial control: "Under digital colonialism, foreign powers, led by the United States, are planting infrastructure in the Global South engineered for its own needs, enabling economic and cultural domination while imposing privatized forms of governance."[51]

The control of code also facilitates surveillance: it allows Big Tech corporations to control the flow of information, social activities, and even military functions that are mediated by Big Tech architecture. It allows them to extract data while they control and filter what people can access or share online. This new form of colonization mirrors the structures of extraction, surveillance, and control of colonial projects of the past, leaving in its wake populations both oppressed by and dependent on the architecture created by corporate profiteers.

In settler colonial states, surveillance has long been used to silence Indigenous voices and eliminate Indigenous populations.[52] From the first time Europeans set foot onto the shores of land that was not their own, they monitored Indigenous populations with the location-tracking devices of their time. For example, the Surveillance Technology Oversight Project (S.T.O.P.) explains that in the United States in the 1700s, "this meant citywide 'lantern laws,' requiring Indigenous and enslaved Black people to carry lamps" and deputized white citizens to confront them.[53]

More recently, the Federal Bureau of Investigation (FBI) spied on the American Indian Movement, planting informants, bugging reservations, and jailing the group's leaders.

Today, states use social media monitoring, mobile phone interception and hacking, and a range of more visible technologies and techniques to surveil Indigenous activists and organizers, including evidence-gathering teams, body cameras, drones and helicopters, automated license plate readers, and mobile surveillance vehicles.[54] Many of these were used by US police and private contractors to surveil Indigenous water protectors and other opponents to the Dakota Access Pipeline (DAPL) in 2016 at Standing Rock. While the police used helicopters and drones, private security firm TigerSwan—hired by Dakota Access parent company Energy Transfer—surveilled "activists through aerial technology, social media monitoring, and direct infiltration," as well as infrared cameras and "listening posts."[55]

The Intercept, which obtained documents about TigerSwan's surveillance operations, notes that the company is largely made up of special operations military veterans. It "was formed during the war in Iraq and incorporated its counterinsurgency tactics into its effort to suppress an indigenous-led movement centered around protection of water."[56] As the Oceti Sakowin Dakota Access Pipeline resistance camp disbanded, Tiger-Swan actively sought new targets for its operations. It began monitoring anti-Trump protests and other Indigenous activists, regardless of their relationship to the #NoDAPL movement.[57]

The US government and police forces also, of course, surveil Black activists and organizers. The US Department of Homeland Security has been monitoring the Black Lives Matter movement since protests erupted in Ferguson, Missouri, in 2014. Documents obtained by the Intercept "indicate that the department frequently collects information, including location data, on Black Lives Matter activities from public social media accounts, including on Facebook, Twitter, and Vine" across the United States.[58]

The US government has also long been engaged in global racialized surveillance. As noted in chapter 1, the US military undertook surveillance in the Philippines in the 1800s to suppress resistance to occupation, identifying, recording, and analyzing networks of organizers and their fi-nances.[59] In South Africa under the apartheid regime, US mining officials carried out surveillance over Black miners, while IBM supplied the punch card system to establish and monitor the four "categories of race" deployed by the government. Today, the NSA works with Big Tech companies to carry out surveillance on South African economic agencies and human rights activists.[60]

With the war on terror, which the US government initiated in 2001 in Afghanistan and Iraq before expanding its extrajudicial killings and extraordinary renditions around the world, a global surveillance machine against Muslims and those perceived to be Muslim expanded as well. US "intelligence agencies" and military operations spied on foreign govern-ments and citizens abroad and built an enormous surveillance apparatus within the United States that to this day monitors, collects data on, and seeks to entrap Muslims based on their religion.[61]

From the PATRIOT Act to the Countering Violent Extremism and the Targeted Violence and Terrorism Prevention programs, anti-Muslim legislation propelled a buildup of surveillance architecture that is also de-ployed against other targeted groups in the United States and globally. In New York City, the police department actively engages in religious profil-ing and suspicionless and pervasive surveillance of Muslims throughout the city, including through mapping of Muslim communities, photo and video surveillance, police informants, undercover agents, tracking indi-viduals, and generating daily reports from intelligence databases.[62] Mean-while, the US military monitors Muslims around the world by purchasing location data from third-party data collectors that store information on users of a private Muslim prayer app downloaded to smartphones.[63]

Criminalization through surveillance

These are but a few examples of racialized and discriminatory surveillance. But the common thread, as critical race scholars and Black rights advo-cates have argued, is that surveillance is an important means by which the state enhances its control over Black, Indigenous, and other people of color.[64] New technologies, such as facial recognition, biometric technologies, data mining, and "predictive policing" tools are massively exacerbating the structural racism of surveillance.

Facial recognition

Along with digital colonialism's extractivism and surveillance, other technologies are geared toward facilitating the identification, sorting, and control of people based on specific characteristics. Voice and facial recognition technology fall into this category. As noted in chapter 1, not only is the origin of facial recognition racist itself,[65] but this technology is leading to further incarceration, harassment, and battery of Black people and other people of color.[66] The algorithms used in facial recognition software have consistently been shown to be racist, resulting in much higher rates of false positives for Black, Asian, and Indigenous faces than for whites. The system's worst failings were with African American women.[67]

"Since many of these systems have demonstrated racial bias with lower performance on darker skin," warns the Algorithmic Justice League, "the burden of these harms will once again fall disproportionately on Black people."[68] Recent studies, including one by Inioluwa Deborah Raji, Joy Buolamwini, and Timnit Gebru, show how facial recognition software exhibits gender and racial bias for gender classification.[69] A key problem is that many "benchmark datasets" are biased—they are composed predominantly of male and lighter-skinned faces.[70] When used by police or military, these types of technologies risk leading to the arrest, incarceration, detainment, or death of individuals on the basis of mistaken identity.

Video surveillance

Meanwhile, doorbell cameras, video surveillance systems, and crime-reporting platforms "are playing a role in people of color being reported as 'suspicious' while they are simply going about their daily lives."[71] Amazon

Ring produces "home security" cameras, one of which allows you to see who rings your doorbell, or the doorbell of your neighbors. The company has cultivated a surveillance network around the United States "with the help of dozens of taxpayer-funded camera discount programs and more than 600 police partnerships," a *VICE* exposé found.[72] Ring has, *VICE* explains, helped organize police package-theft sting operations, coached police on how to obtain footage without a warrant, and promised people free cameras in exchange for testifying against their neighbors.[73]

This kind of technology is advertised to residents as "crime prevention" and enhancing neighborhood safety, but in reality is used by police to surveil already criminalized communities. As MediaJustice argues, Ring "offers the police unprecedented access to data recorded by its video doorbell devices, effectively bringing police surveillance to our front doors. This technology digitizes racial profiling while perpetuating the routine criminalization and over-policing that communities of color already face."[74] In some cases, starting in Jackson, Mississippi, police will be able to receive livestream feeds from Ring owners.[75] It has also enabled people to spy on their neighbors and report "suspicious behavior" to police.[76]

Video camera surveillance systems have also been installed in many lower-income housing units, some of them equipped with facial recognition or heat mapping sensors to track who enters and exits buildings. Coupled with increasingly automated scoring systems, surveillance is used by landlords to flush out "undesirable" tenants as part of the gentrification process in many urban areas. This becomes a basis for algorithmic redlining for loan and apartment applications.[77]

Higher education is also getting into the video surveillance business. As *Democracy Now!* reported, the University of Miami used a network of surveillance cameras and facial recognition software to track down students involved in a protest against the university's decision to resume in-person classes during the COVID-19 pandemic.[78] Students and faculty have actively opposed the use of facial recognition software on campuses,[79] as well as "geo-fencing"—a form of GPS and Wi-Fi-based surveillance that records data from smartphones and other wireless devices within a set vicinity.[80] Off-campus, students and educators have been pushing back against online proctoring spyware such as the tools developed by Proctorio, which forces students to accept being recorded during classes and tests in their own homes and being reviewed for "suspicious behavior."[81]

Predictive policing

As introduced in chapter 1, the use of "predictive policing" technology also has grave implications for criminalized communities and individuals considered to be "undesirable" or "risky."[82] The technology relies on data sets of past "crime" to determine where and when future crime will occur. Police are given maps of neighborhoods to patrol in order to deter or stumble upon criminal acts. As Jackie Wang argues in *Carceral Capitalism*, "Even when it does not use race to make predictions," predictive policing technologies "can facilitate racial profiling by calculating proxies for race, such as neighborhood and location." This type of technology does not benignly "interpret data," it actively *constructs reality*. It constructs the future "through the present management of subjects categorized as threats or risks."[83]

But, abolitionist Micah Herskind points out, risk is not an identity. "The risk assessment paradigm tells us that risk, or dangerousness, is something that resides within a person—and that risk categorizations can tell us the likelihood of one's inner dangerousness manifesting externally."[84] Predictive policing frames human beings as inherently "risky," when in reality it is the conditions in which people live that produce risk and create the potential for harm.

Tools such as predictive policing do not look at root causes of harms caused. Instead, they construct the future based on the past, amplifying existing inequalities. If white supremacy has guided past police work, those patterns of harassment and arrest become part of the training set that is codified into the technology. As Liz O'Sullivan, an expert in algorithms and director of Parity Technologies, says, there's no way to build a predictive policing algorithm that is more than simply an extension of the status quo—it's a matter of "mathwashing," where people hide behind algorithms as not being racist when in fact racism is baked into the algorithm.[85] Organizers against carceral technologies agree that arguments about being able to "de-bias" technologies are flawed. "Carceral technologies are racist because the institutions that develop and use them are intended to manage populations in a country that has a white supremacist inheritance," notes Sarah T. Hamid. "These technologies are not *incidentally* racist. They are racist because they're doing the work of policing—which, in this country, is a racist job."[86]

As part of the growing militarized surveillance state, predictive policing algorithms only serve to provide the state with yet another way to control and confine populations ascribed with characteristics determined by that state. And once this kind of "digital carceral infrastructure" is built up, Wang warns, "it will be nearly impossible to undo, and the automated carceral surveillance state will spread out across the terrain, making greater and greater intrusions into our everyday lives."[87]

US police are not alone in their use of this technology. Marseille, France, has been experimenting with a combination of artificial intelligence, citizen data, and government surveillance networks to conduct predictive policing and to aid in police investigations.[88] In the Netherlands, Amnesty International documents predictive policing projects that "use mathematical models to assess the risk that a crime will be committed by a certain person or at a certain location, with law enforcement efforts then directed towards those individuals or locations deemed 'high risk.'" One such project deliberately engages in ethnic profiling of Eastern Europeans. It monitors people driving in certain areas and collects data to process using an algorithmic model that calculates a "risk score" for each vehicle. One of the indicators used to make this assessment is whether people in a vehicle are from Eastern Europe.[89]

In November 2020, the UN Committee on the Elimination of Racial Discrimination published guidance to combat racial profiling, emphasizing, among other issues, the serious risk of algorithmic bias when artificial intelligence (AI) is used by police and other law enforcement agencies. The report notes that the increased use by police of data, AI, facial recognition, and other new technology risks deepening racism, racial discrimination, xenophobia, and consequently the violation of many human rights. "We are deeply concerned with the particular risks when algorithmic profiling is used for determining the likelihood of criminal activity," said Committee member Verene Shepherd, who led the drafting of the general recommendation. "For example, historical arrest data about a neighborhood may reflect racially biased policing practices; and such data will deepen the risk of over-policing in the same neighborhood, which in turn may lead to more arrests, creating a dangerous feedback loop," she explained.[90]

Data collection and sharing

Private tech corporations are increasingly contracting their services and software to police forces and government agencies around the world, profiting directly from enabling the surveillance of activists and suppression of human rights.

Palantir, a secretive data analytics company with ties to the defense and intelligence communities, allows the Los Angeles Police Department to use its Palantir Gotham database to indiscriminately document "the names, addresses, phone numbers, license plates, friendships, romances, jobs of Angelenos," regardless of whether or not they are suspected or convicted of committing any harm.[91] As tech worker Laura Nolan points out, "This is effectively targeted police harassment, and is punitive in itself, but the most significant harm here is that the individuals on the chronic offenders list are more likely to be arrested and incarcerated due to this additional monitoring (or to be deported, if they are immigrants)."[92]

Meanwhile, the Intercept has reported that artificial intelligence startup Dataminr helped police across the United States "digitally monitor the protests that swept the country following the killing of George Floyd, tipping off police to social media posts with the latest whereabouts and actions of demonstrators."[93] Using privileged access to Twitter data, Dataminr sent tweets directly to police forces across the United States, converting the data into "tidy police intelligence packages." Much of this material is allegedly based on "prejudice-prone tropes and hunches to determine who, where, and what looks dangerous."[94] Both Dataminr and Twitter have denied that this kind of "protest monitoring" constitutes surveillance.

Clearview AI, which amassed an enormous database of more than three billion images "scraped" from websites such as Facebook and Twitter, has freely shared and also sold its facial recognition software to police forces and other government agencies across the United States.[95] BuzzFeed has found that more than seven thousand employees from at least 1,803 publicly funded agencies used or tested the software before February 2020, including "local and state police, US Immigration and Customs Enforcement, the Air Force, state healthcare organizations, offices of state attorneys general, and even public schools."[96] Twitter has demanded Clearview stop scraping data from its site,[97] and a coalition of civil liberties activists have filed a lawsuit against Clearview, noting that automatic scraping of people's images and extraction of unique biometric information without notice or consent "violate privacy and chill protected political speech and activity."[98]

Global surveillance for oppression

These are but a few examples of how the US government, police, and private contractors are using surveillance to suppress dissidence and human rights. There are too many to account for in the space of this chapter. But it is also important to note that of course, surveillance is by no means just a US phenomenon.

Law professor Neil M. Richards points out that the United Kingdom is one of the most heavily surveilled countries in the world, with a network of public and private surveillance cameras, traffic enforcement cameras, and broad government powers to examine Internet traffic.[99] Meanwhile, governments resisting the Arab Spring uprisings have sought social media data to track dissidents.[100] Israel, which has an extensive surveillance network monitoring in particular Palestinians in Israel and the occupied territories, also uses tech to directly threaten dissidents—the Israeli intelligence agency Shin Bet, for example, sent threatening text messages to Palestinians protesting Israeli's ongoing apartheid colonial efforts.[101] Some activists suspect that the Vietnamese government may have used computer viruses to monitor the Internet activity and private data of those protesting government mining policies,[102] while Thailand is ramping up its repression of activists and critics who share information online.[103]

Digital censorship, content control, and restrictions that prevent people from speaking freely with one another online or connecting, or are criminalized for what they post, are connected to surveillance. This is true in many places around the world, but China and other parts of Asia are especially notorious.[104]

China is well known for its use of Internet activity to detect and censor dissidents. WeChat, China's "super app" used by 1.1 billion users globally, is subject to "real-time, automatic censorship of text and images" by the Chinese government to exert control and censorship over political discussion on a wide range of issues.[105] China's so-called Great Firewall prevents Chinese citizens from viewing websites outside of the country. It also has a "Great Cannon," which injects JavaScript code into users' insecure requests. "This code weaponizes the millions of mainland Chinese Internet connections that pass through" Internet service providers based in China, explains Danny O'Brien of the Electronic Frontier Foundation. "When users visit insecure websites, their browsers will also download and run the government's malicious javascript—which will cause them to send additional traffic to sites outside the Great Firewall, potentially slowing these websites down for other users, or overloading them entirely."[106]

Pervasive online surveillance is common throughout China, but particularly for its Uyghur and Tibetan populations. In Xinjiang, China, Uyghurs live under mass surveillance.[107] The Chinese government has invested billions of dollars into making Xinjiang "an incubator for increasingly intrusive policing systems," particularly against its Muslim population.[108] The "virtual cage" created by the surveillance system complements the indoctrination camps in which police have detained a million or more Muslims.[109] The system helps identify people to be sent to the camps or investigated and tracks them after they are released. (The company that built the system, the China Electronics Technology Group Corporation, also helped build China's first nuclear weapons.) China is also actively surveilling Uyghurs abroad, targeting users on Android and Windows devices that access websites with primarily Uyghur readership.[110]

The Australian government has spied on environmental activists, including by utilizing private security companies.[111] Under metadata laws passed in 2015, the Australian Federal Police can view, without a warrant, the metadata for the past two years of citizens "deemed a risk to national security."[112] This type of data can inform where a person is located, what apps they are using, and who they are calling.

The Canadian Security Intelligence Service has spied on and surveilled nonviolent pipeline protestors, using everything from "open sources" such as newspapers to undercover agents to collect information on people and groups whose activities are suspected of constituting a threat to national security.[113] The Tactical Internet Intelligence Unit of the Royal Canadian Mounted Police, Canada's federal police force, uses social media and facial recognition to track protestors.[114] Provincial privacy commissioners have also found that Clearview AI violated Canadian privacy laws when it collected more than three billion images of Canadians without their knowledge or consent and then allowed law enforcement groups and companies to compare photos to this database.[115]

A great deal of surveillance, of course, transcends borders. Surveillance technologies are manufactured by private companies, many of which are based in Europe or Israel; their "products" circumvent trade restrictions and are sold directly to governments for them to spy on activists, organizers, and other elements of civil society, with dire human rights impacts.

For example, The Citizen Lab at the University of Toronto has identified forty-five countries[116] in which operators of spyware called Pegasus, developed by Israeli firm NSO Group, may be conducting operations. At least ten Pegasus operators appeared to be actively engaged in cross-border surveillance; "at least six countries with significant Pegasus operations have previously been linked to abusive use of spyware to target civil society"; and it "appears to be in use by countries with dubious human rights records and histories of abusive behavior by state security services."[117] The Citizen Lab also found that Israel's Cyberbit, a wholly owned subsidary of the infamous weapons and surveillance corporation Elbit Systems, developed spyware for conducting targeted malware attacks. It has sold this technology to other countries, including Ethiopia, which has used it against Ethiopian dissidents in the United States, United Kingdom, and other countries.[118]

Meanwhile, Italian firm Hacking Team has been found to have sold malware and vulnerabilities to security services in a range of countries including those with poor human rights records, including Azerbaijan, Kazakhstan, Uzbekistan, Russia, Bahrain, Saudi Arabia, and the United Arab Emirates. In 2013, Reporters Without Borders named the company one of the "corporate enemies of the internet" for its role as a "digital mercenary."[119]

Biometric surveillance is also proliferating globally, in no small part due to a mandate from the United Nations Security Council. Primarily at the behest of the US government, UN Security Council Resolution 2396 requires that states "develop and implement systems to collect biometric data" in order to "responsibly and properly identify terrorists, including foreign terrorist fighters."[120] This mandates that all 193 UN member states acquire and use biometric surveillance technologies. As the UN special rapporteurs on human rights and on counterterrorism have argued, Resolution 2396 has serious human rights implications. Given that implementation of human rights laws regarding the collection and use of biometric data is inadequate and uneven globally, and that private corporations rather than governments are often employed to collect and store this data, a requirement for all countries to engage in this kind of surveillance as part of "counterterrorism" operations risks facilitating human rights violations.[121]

Surveillance and death

Biometrics are by no means the only surveillance technologies utilized in "counterterrorism." The most notorious instrument for such operations in the past two decades has perhaps become the drone. Built to survey "enemy combatants" in far-flung battlefields—or, civilians going about their daily lives—drones have been weaponized with Hellfire missiles to turn search and monitor operations into search and destroy, with operators safely ensconced at mission control stations thousands of miles away.

Drones and other aerial devices are also increasingly being used in the context of policing protests, leading writer Ian G. R. Shaw to warn about the installation of "a system of ubiquitous air policing across major US cities," which would establish "a permanent police presence in the skies."[122] The expanding use of surveillance planes and drones during the 2020 protests for Black lives and against police brutality, at the US-Mexican border, and during the Standing Rock protests in 2016[123] shows another tactic for police to monitor and enact violence against anyone they consider a threat, be they immigrants, Indigenous Water Protectors, or Black rights activists. The city of Baltimore approved the use of "surveillance planes" to conduct persistent monitoring of the city under the guise of aiding investigations of "violent crimes."[124] The LA County Sheriff's Department has also tested an airplane-mounted surveillance kit to monitor the entire city of Compton, with equipment similar to the US military's Gorgon Stare technology.[125]

The FBI has flown drones for surveillance operations; US Customs and Border Protection (CBP) operates a fleet of Predator drones along the US-Mexico and US-Canada borders; and CBP has "loaned" its drones to local law enforcement agencies hundreds of times.[126] Intercepted data can be stored indefinitely and there have been proposals to modify drones so they can track cell phones. The Los Angeles Police Department began recording and storing footage of protests from its helicopters in 2020, using cameras that can identify individuals in crowds.[127] As journalist Ali Winston notes, examples like this demonstrate the ways in which protests are treated with counterinsurgency tactics.[128]

The application of "counterterrorism" tactics against people on the move or people exercising their human right to assembly, coupled with the use of surveillance technologies to categorize and control people, raises serious concerns about the trajectory of state violence. "Counterterrorism surveillance" is carried out globally. This can include surveillance leading to the detention, rendition, torture, or extrajudicial killing (murder) of "terrorist" suspects, or the hacking and tracking of journalists, dissidents, political leaders, or defenders of human rights, land, or water.[129] This application of counterterrorism and counterinsurgency tactics and frameworks in surveillance only leads in one direction: to detention or death.

Drone strikes and metadata

Already, there are connections between the techniques of surveillance and extrajudicial killing in war and surveillance tactics used in policing contexts. For example, the policies and practices of "signature strikes" used in US drone strikes determine "threats" from various signifiers and patterns.[130] People are attacked on the basis of observed characteristics with no substantial intelligence regarding actual identity or affiliations.[131] Algorithms have been used to "predict enemies" based on assumptions about the "inherent risk" of certain categories of people.[132] In this way, "packages of information" become "icons for killable bodies on the basis of behavior analysis and a logic of preemption."[133]

This practice resembles racial profiling by US police forces, as activists have noted. "Much like the Obama administration's policy of signature strikes—lethal drone attacks on young men who might be terrorists or may one day commit acts of terrorism—the presumption of guilt based on racial profiling is an essential component of broken windows policing," writes Robin D. G. Kelley.[134] The concept of "inherent criminality" and the idea that risk resides within people is as necessary to predictive policing at home as it is to signature strikes abroad—and just as dangerous.[135]

But it is not just the techniques of profiling and targeting people that are shifted from battlefield to city streets. It's also the technologies. Surveillance equipment developed and used by militaries is increasingly used by governments against their own populations. And as the surveillance technology develops in sophistication and spreads in geography, it lends itself to the project of not just watching people but also deciding who should live and who should die.

"Surveillance, a technology of racial sorting and subjugation, structures drone technology and its dehumanizing tendencies," writes Jennifer Rhee.[136] The concept of "remote warfare"—identifying and tracking targets and launching missiles from the sky from the safety of half a world away—is an abstraction of violence, a disembodiment for both attacker and attacked. Scholar Thomas Gregory notes that drone violence completely ignores the people that are harmed—both their bodies and their embodied experiences.[137] It distances and sanitizes the violence, which in turn makes it easier to "justify" to the public. The dehumanizing "eyes in the sky" of surveillance—of watching, categorizing, and processing people as ones and zeroes—goes hand in hand with the executions it enables.

Once human beings are rendered into objects, traceable through the identities prescribed by those conducting this kind of processing, categorizing, sorting, and surveillance, then it becomes even easier to choose who should be subjected to harm. The trend toward processing, identifying, and targeting human beings through metadata and algorithms is creating a world in which people are being seen and treated as objects to be categorized, controlled, incarcerated, and, when deemed necessary, killed as disposable objects. As this world further develops, more and more people will be pushed into this category of "surplus population," marked for incarceration or death.

In 2014, it became clear that the National Security Agency was using electronic surveillance to locate targets for drone strikes. It would use signals intelligence, or SIGINT—such as cell phone records, metadata of who is called and when, as well as the content of phone and online communications—to determine the owner of a phone. It also used geolocation to track the SIM card in order to locate the phone. "Rather than confirming a target's identity with operatives or informants on the ground," the Intercept reported, "the CIA or the U.S. military then orders a strike based on the activity and location of the mobile phone a person is believed to be using."[138] But this type of data is difficult to confirm and is often misattributed, leading to the execution of civilians.[139] Thousands of civilians have been killed in US drone strikes in Afghanistan, Pakistan, Somalia, and Yemen.[140]

Automating violence

It's not difficult to imagine drones eventually being used in a similar fashion by police forces, especially given the well-known patterns of white supremacy and police brutality already beating through the hearts of existing law enforcement institutions. Some police departments have already started to experiment with robots and remote-controlled devices, which is facing opposition by the public and politicians.[141] But the trajectory from surveillance to increasingly automated tools of violence is clear, which makes the development of autonomous weapon systems incredibly alarming.

Unlike drones, which are piloted remotely, a fully autonomous weapon would be programmed so that once it is deployed, it operates on its own. It would be able to identify, select, and fire upon targets all on its own, based upon its algorithms and data analysis programming.[142] An autonomous weapon, using sensors to determine and engage targets without human analysis or control, goes further in dehumanizing human beings than any previous weapon technology. Operating without meaningful human control, such weapons will rely on "target profiles" to establish "the set of conditions under which such a system will apply force."[143] A target profile could include infrared emissions, shape, or biometric information. It will actively reduce human beings to objects—into ones and zeroes—marked by sensors and software for death or detainment on the basis of their sex, race, age, or other physiological or sociological characteristics.[144]

With drone strikes, there are indications that the United States uses "maleness" as a signifier of militancy. According to a *New York Times* report from May 2012, in counting casualties from armed drone strikes, the US government reportedly records "all military-age males in a strike zone as combatants . . . unless there is explicit intelligence posthumously proving them innocent."[145] Targeting people, or considering them to be militants when proximate to other targets, on the basis of their sex or gender constitutes a form of gender-based violence. It also sets a dangerous precedent for such associations in the future, particularly in relation to the development and use of increasingly autonomous weapon systems.[146]

Already, more than 380 partly autonomous weapon systems have been deployed or are being developed in at least twelve countries, including China, France, Israel, South Korea, Russia, the United Kingdom, and the United States.[147] Major tech companies like Microsoft and Google have been commissioned to create or adapt technologies for military use, such as Microsoft's HoloLens headset that soldiers are using "to detect, decide and engage before the enemy,"[148] or its JEDI cloud computing contract with the Pentagon that would have involved developing and running applications that are part of the drone kill chain.[149]

If this trend continues unconstrained, humans will eventually be cut out of crucial decision-making over the use of force and over the control of weapon systems. There is grave risk that the tools used now for mass surveillance, controlling populations, or dispersing goods may be weaponized in the future. The "permanent police presence" predicted by Shaw is likely to include not just the "eyes in the sky" provided by surveillance drones, but also the suite of biometrics, facial recognition, predictive policing and precrime reporting, and weaponized autonomous or artificial intelligence systems that operate together to monitor and control populations.

As such weapons will rely on sensors and software to determine "targets" without meaningful human control, they will inevitably reflect the innate bias and racism within the system that produces them.[150] As New School professor Peter Asaro notes, "It would be easy to intentionally design a robocop to be racist, and quite difficult to design one that is not, given the existing standards, norms, and policing strategies."[151] We can imagine the ways in which such biases built into technologies like facial recognition—which already have led to people being held without bail before their trial,[152] or have misidentified members of Congress as people who have been arrested,[153] or claimed to be able to determine sexual orientation based on faces[154]—will be catastrophic when these algorithms are weaponized.

But beyond the horrifying problem that the bias embedded in programming will translate into mistakes in identifying targets, there is also the risk that the machine's bias would not be a mistake at all. It could be deliberately programmed to target people bearing certain "markers" or identities. The construct of target profiles for people will reduce human beings to ones and zeroes—targeted for their sex or gender identity, their race or ethnicity, their religious clothing, their disability, or other physical markers that the machine determines as "correct" for killing. This will exacerbate racial profiling in war, policing, border surveillance, and other activities; it will result in gender- and race-based violence.

Digital dehumanization

Algorithms would create a perfect killing machine, stripped of the empathy, conscience, or emotion that might hold a human soldier back. Robots programmed to kill might also accidentally kill civilians by misinterpreting data. They would lack the human judgment necessary to evaluate the proportionality of an attack, distinguish civilian from combatant, and abide by other core principles of the laws of war. They would also be susceptible to cyberattacks and hacking. And they would be unaccountable for their mistakes or misuse.

Autonomous weapons will be weapons of power and inequity: countries of the Global South may not be the ones to develop and use killer robots, but they will likely become the battlegrounds for the testing and deployment of these weapons. It will be the rich countries using these weapons against the poor—and the rich within countries using it against their own poor, through policing and internal oppression.

Autonomous weapons thus pose a particularly egregious threat to human rights, justice, and peace. Marking certain populations as threats and enabling technology to kill them without any human intervention, simply because they exhibit characteristics or behavior deemed by algorithms to be suspicious or to fit a target profile, has implications for the normalization and abstraction of violence beyond that to which our world is already subjected.

Spy versus spy

Meanwhile, several governments are leading us all down a path toward dark destruction with their surveillance not just of people, but of each other. Government-to-government and government-to-corporate surveillance are both ongoing, pervasive, and increasing. Many states around the world are actively spying on and, in some cases, using collected information to disrupt or destroy each other's functions—including by targeting critical civilian and government infrastructure. Many of these incidents make international headlines: the US and Israel's Stuxnet attack on Iran's nuclear facilities; Russia's attack on Ukraine's power supply and the US elections; North Korea's attack against Sony; China's espionage against US corporations. But the scope and volume of these attacks is much broader and more entrenched than most of us realize.

As Nicole Perlroth investigates in *This Is How They Tell Me the World Ends*, there is an elaborate black market for what are known as zero-days—software or hardware flaws for which there is no existing patch.[155] Zero-days are the "invisible backdoors" into an operating system or an application or code that hackers can use to infiltrate phones, computers, and other devices. Zero-days can fetch millions on the market; governments pay hackers for their finds and use them against each other or against corporations to extract information, reveal secrets, delete or disrupt websites, or destroy infrastructure. Some governments also employ hackers directly or coerce them to hack on their behalf. The more sophisticated spy operations are usually run by advanced persistent threat groups (APTs), which are technically nongovernmental but are financed by and linked to governments. These groups usually spy over a long period of time, cause some minor nuisances or disruption, and steal data. But states have been clever in employing proxies to do the dirty work, which raises serious questions about legal accountability.

The governments engaged in cyber espionage are constantly poking around in each others' systems and the systems of their corporations. There has been a strange "gray zone" of toleration for this. But some aggressive hacks have shown the potential for catastrophe—either because the actor doing the hacking might shut down or destroy a critical system, or at some point, the threshold might be crossed in which the state that is hacked uses the attack to justify a kinetic (non-cyber) response. There are not yet any clear "rules to the road" delimiting what is considered "off limits," or what constitutes an appropriate response. The SolarWinds operation, for example, included hacking into and spying on the Pentagon, the Department of Homeland Security, the State Department, the Department of Energy, and the National Nuclear Security Administration. US President Biden placed individuals linked to Russia, which is believed to be responsible, under sanction in response, which seems to be a growing response to cyberattacks.[156]

Cyberattacks are an important part of any discussion on surveillance, and on the broader militarization and weaponization of cyberspace. The militarization of cyberspace and cyberattacks are being addressed through ongoing work at the United Nations on "information and communications technology." Governments have convened for many years to discuss the options for ensuring "state security" as well as human rights online. When it comes specifically to zero-days, in 2015 a UN group agreed that all countries should report tech vulnerabilities and share remedies.[157] Some governments have expressed concern about government stockpiling of zero-days, which the United States, China, and Russia, among others, do—building their cyber arsenal alongside their conventional and nuclear arsenals. But these concerns have not yet been reflected in any UN agreements.

Some countries and activists would like to see the development of a kind of "Geneva Conventions" for the online world, in which restrictions on attacks, particularly those that harm civilians, would be universally agreed upon. All countries have already agreed that international law applies online. But the governments dominating these discussions are not that interested in developing legal commitments or obligations regarding their cyber operations. Russia does want a cyber treaty, but its vision of what it would include makes many other governments nervous—including in relation to human rights implications. Other countries oppose any kind of legally binding agreement, preferring to maintain their "freedom of movement" online, but also politically motivated to thwart Russia's efforts.[158]

Anti-surveillance organizing

The inability or unwillingness thus far of governments to address the growing threat of cyber warfare speaks loudly to the need for action against cyber violence along with action against surveillance in all its aspects. "There are many ways to solve social problems," notes law professor Frank Pasquale. "Not all require constant surveillance coupled with the mechanised threat of force."[159] This is true for government-to-government relations as well as government-to-people. There is already incredible ongoing organizing aimed at preventing and prohibiting surveillance technologies as well as armed drones, autonomous weapons, and other violent technologies that will further automate harm.

The Surveillance Technology Oversight Project (S.T.O.P.) seeks to litigate, legislate, educate, and advocate against discriminatory surveillance, including on Muslim Americans, immigrants, the LGBTQ+ community, Indigenous peoples, and communities of color, particularly in relation to anti-Black policing. It provides services to those who have been harmed by surveillance and works to ensure that future laws protect people.[160]

The Stop LAPD Spying Coalition is a community coalition in Los Angeles working to expose and abolish surveillance, including government-sanctioned spying and intelligence gathering and other forms of racial and social control.[161]

Fight for the Future is a group of artists, engineers, activists, and technologists who seek to promote technologies that help people rather than harm them. Among other things, it works for net neutrality, banning facial recognition, and canceling partnerships between Amazon and police.[162]

The Tech Workers Coalition organizes workers in the tech community to work in solidarity with existing movements toward social justice, workers' rights, and economic inclusion. Among other things, they believe that technology should be used for good, and have been behind some of the powerful challenges within tech corporations against military contracts.[163]

The Electronic Frontier Foundation is a network of community and campus organizations across the United States working for user privacy, free expression, and innovation through impact litigation, policy analysis, grassroots activism, and technology development. Its mission is to ensure that technology supports freedom, justice, and innovation for all people of the world.[164]

The Campaign to Stop Killer Robots is a coalition of hundreds of activist groups globally working with governments to develop an international ban on autonomous weapon systems and to ensure that meaningful human control is always retained over the use of weapons and force.[165]

The Women's International League for Peace and Freedom advocates for cyber peace at the United Nations, working with concerned governments and activists to advance norms and laws that would prevent cyber war and stop the militarization of the online world.[166]

Amnesty International urges governments to adopt and enforce robust data protection laws and effective regulation of Big Tech in line with human rights law. As a first step, Amnesty Tech has argued, governments must enact laws to ensure companies like Google and Facebook are prevented from making access to their service conditional on individuals "consenting" to the collection, processing, or sharing of their personal data for marketing or advertising.[167] In addition, Amnesty Decoders is a platform for volunteers to help with research on surveillance technology, online harassment, and a variety of other tech-related issues.[168]

The American Civil Liberties Union (ACLU) has been at the forefront of the struggle to prevent the entrenchment of a surveillance state by challenging the secrecy of the government's surveillance and watchlisting practices; its violations of the rights to privacy, free speech, due process, and association; and its stigmatization of minority communities and activists.[169]

A coalition of groups in Oakland, California, are working to stop Big Tech platforms from tracking and categorizing people for advertising purposes, seeking a ban on "surveillance advertising."[170]

The Open Observatory of Network Interference is a free software project that aims to empower decentralized efforts in increasing transparency of Internet censorship around the world.[171]

The Coalition Against Stalkerware works to fight against technology-facilitated abuse, including by uniting organizations that work to end domestic violence with the IT security community.[172]

Surveillance abolition

These are but a few examples of resistance to surveillance; there are countless more. Banning the use of surveillance technologies by police and other government agencies—especially technologies that facilitate the processing, categorizing, identifying, and tracking of people, such as facial recognition—is imperative for preventing racialized harms. Technologies like spyware that facilitate gender-based violence should not be sold on the consumer market. Companies developing apps should not be collecting location or other data, especially not without informed consent.

Technologies that attempt to predict people's behavior or judge "inherent risk" must be outlawed. Technologies that destroy privacy; collect, store, and process data on humans; and can be used to facilitate spying on each other must not be allowed. Military and police use of data to identify, track, and kill people must be prohibited—which will also require the prohibition of new types of weapon systems such as autonomous and artificial intelligence–based weapons.

We also must not accept a digital architecture built by Big Tech in the interests of a corporate–state surveillance state. "Digital technology can be owned and controlled by the popular classes," argues Michael Kwet, but a paradigm shift from privacy and discrimination to "structural power at the technical architectural level within a global context" is necessary.[173] Free software, free hardware, net neutrality and equal bandwidth, and Internet decentralization can help us push back against the dispossession by corporations and states that own and operate digital architecture.[174]

If we allow corporate, military, and policing interests to dictate and drive the development of technology, we face an increasingly dystopian future depicted in science fiction lore. The current state of surveillance calls for an abolitionist framework: one in which we are not simply seeking to prevent governments, militaries, cops, corporations, or other people from spying on us, but in which we are actively working to build a world that upholds principles of privacy, prevention of harm, and equality. If we work now to ban and disrupt technologies that create inequalities or cause harm, we can instead build a world where we hold on to the fundamentals of humanity. A world in which we respect each other's inherent dignity and prevent dehumanization. Where technology is developed and used to promote peace, equality, and life in greater freedom for all.

This approach is also necessary when it comes to dealing with borders. Built to exclude and contain, borders rely on surveillance and are materially and philosophically tied to all the structures of violence that seek to sort, process, and profit from human beings. Contesting not just the physical manifestation of borders, but also the concepts of exclusion borne through notions of nationality and inscribed through conditions of citizenship, is important for the work of justice, equality, and peace pursued through abolition.

Chapter 4

‖‖

Deconstructing Borders

Writing about the 1918 influenza pandemic, historian Esyllt W. Jones notes that "an epidemic represents a moment of marginality between life and death, between chaos and order; it is a border region where the meaning and membership in the community is imagined and re-imagined."[1] This feeling of being between life and death, between chaos and order, has dominated during the COVID-19 pandemic. It was certainly felt in the United States, where police brutality, structural racism, the violence of neoliberal capitalism, and the material realities of militarism coalesced on the streets of US cities in 2020, giving rise to and simultaneously repressing protests for racial justice, for housing, freedom, and dignity, for life itself. The questions about meaning and membership in the community were—and remain—starkly present in every move and every breath.

In the "moment of marginality" described by Jones, we the people are meant to feel marginalized—yet we are the majority. In moments of what can feel like chaos, the structures of coercive state violence want to restore "order"—but what order? An order that controls and presses those who seek justice, that suffocates and shoots Black people with impunity. An order that has the one percent looting wealth and preventing equality and justice. *An order that reinforces the borders that are designed and deployed to keep the majority marginalized.*

The concept of the nation-state is a modern invention, the lines drawn by the most privileged in society and imposed upon the rest. It is maintained through violence, cruelty, and military technologies meant to restrict the mobility of certain people, reflecting and entrenching systems of white supremacy and racism. Abolishing borders would mean actively rejecting the cultural othering of people and conceiving differently of migration and belonging. It would require not just the disarmament and demilitarization of border control but also eliminating our conception of borders in order to build instead a connected world of solidarity, care, and justice.

The pandemic of borders

If the pandemic itself is a border, as Jones suggests, what can it show us about the borders we have drawn in our world? Does the border between life and death of the pandemic match, for example, the borders we have constructed around our countries, or the borders within our communities, borders based on race, class, sex, gender, sexuality, ability? What can the border of the pandemic teach us about the violence of our borders? The pandemic created dispossession—of our lives, our communities and families, our livelihoods. It displaced people through economic hardship, physical separation, social isolation. Physically, the virus made it difficult for people to breathe; metaphorically, it did the same to many—people felt cut off, suffocated, confined, marginalized through social distancing and financial struggle.

The borders between people within our countries also make it hard to breathe. "I can't breathe" were the last words of many Black people killed by police in the United States. The divisions deliberately constructed through the systems of slavery persist today, upheld by those who benefit from the privileges and power these divisions grant them. These systems also inform and instruct the ways in which the United States—as well as other countries built on white supremacy, the genocide of Indigenous nations, and the enslavement of Black and other people of color—operates to keep out those deemed "other" in defiance of international law, human rights, and morality.

In this sense, the borders of our nation-states make it hard to breathe. They dispossess and displace. Whether lines on maps, or systems of walls and checkpoints, borders separate people physically, socially, politically, economically. They demarcate lines of privilege and oppression. They are mechanisms of extraction, exclusion, and exploitation. They determine fates of countless human beings based on random geographic location— based on where you were born, how much money you have, if you can get a passport, if you can get a visa, if you can afford to travel, if you are allowed to travel, if you can find work, if you can get asylum. These conditions are based on historic and ongoing acts of physical and structural violence, starting with colonialism.

Colonialism

In many of our minds, borders are fixed and clear. We have grown up in a world with borders, with set demarcations between countries, with ideas about the sanctity of national sovereignty, patriotism, and nationalism. But borders are relatively new, especially in the form we think of them now. Europe's modern-day borders only really began to emerge in the decades after the Peace of Westphalia in 1648.[2] With the construction of countries in Europe throughout the seventeenth and eighteenth centuries, colonization of territories abroad massively expanded. Many borders around the world were not established by the people who live within them, but by colonial forces who paid no attention to ethnicity, language, history, or needs of local populations and environments. "Borders are not fixed or static lines," argues organizer Harsha Walia, "they are productive regimes concurrently generated by and producing social relations of dominance."[3]

In the nineteenth century, the Europeans got together and carved up the continent of Africa, deciding who could pillage and plunder which population, which lands.[4] The UK government decided the borders of South Asian countries. Some borders, such as that between the United States and Mexico, were set by force, through war against Mexicans and genocide of Indigenous populations. Those establishing settler colonial states, like Australia, Canada, and the United States, paid no heed to the multiplicity of nations already living on the land. The Europeans arriving took what they wanted, established systems of private property, land enclosure, and extraction, and displaced and murdered Indigenous communities along the way.

Capitalism

The economic, political, and cultural privileges that colonialists and imperialists have accrued over the past few hundred years are now protected by borders, which as Reece Jones exposes in *Violent Borders*, create and exacerbate inequalities and serve to maintain dominance by the wealthy few.[5] As economic inequality between states, and between people within states, has skyrocketed, borders have become essential tools to secure not individual nations, but the international class of wealthy people, Jeff Halper explains in *War Against the People*.[6] The ratio of gross domestic product between the richest and poorest nations went from 22:1 at the beginning of the twentieth century to 267:1 by the year 2000. In this situation, the experience of most people worldwide is impoverishment, marginality, exploitation, dislocation, and violence.[7]

Colonialism has served well the interests of capitalism, enabling imperialist forces to extract and exploit their way to the pursuit of endless accumulation of wealth, privilege, and power. Thus, it is no surprise that the establishment and entrenchment of the concept of borders has been structured to serve the capitalist system. This system allows the free flow of money and corporations between borders while constricting the movement of people, creating the perfect conditions for exploiting workers and the environment with impunity. The effects of this exploitation are felt globally, but they are carried out unevenly across the planet. Borders, writes journalist Todd Miller, "largely serve as a neocolonial scaffolding for a planet divided into exploiting and exploitable countries and people."[8]

Trade agreements between states, such as the North American Free Trade Agreement and the US-Mexico-Canada Agreement, are part of the system whereby borders are "open" for capital but closed for people. The method of capitalist accumulation enshrined in these trade agreements ensures the maintenance of low wages and dangerous working conditions in the Global South and the exploitation and repression of undocumented workers in the Global North.[9] As Reece Jones documents, various countries have different wages, environmental regulations, taxes, and working conditions. "While corporations are able to operate in many countries in order to take advantage of these differences, workers are usually contained by these borders and regulators are unable to enforce rules outside their jurisdiction. The problem crosses borders, but the solutions are contained by them."[10]

Or as sociologist William Robinson puts it, "Global capitalism exerts a structural violence over whole populations and makes it impossible for them to survive in their homeland."[11]

Climate change

The same countries doing the extracting and exploiting are also disproportionately responsible for the pollution that has led to our current climate crisis, burning carbon at greater rates and being more energy-intensive per capita than the countries that now suffer the most from rising sea levels, droughts, and increasing disastrous weather events. Wealthy countries extract fossil fuels and minerals for consumer goods from around the world, despoiling forests, plains, rivers, lakes, oceans—much of it land and water protected by Indigenous nations. Toxic substances used in mining, oil production and transportation, dams, and other measures of resource extraction contaminate and destroy land and water, putting the environment as well as people and animals in harm's way. Usually there is no compensation or remediation by the corporations or governments responsible for the harm.

Millions of people will be driven from their homes by environmental degradation and the climate crisis over the coming decades—many already have been. "Climate disasters displace an average of 25.3 million people annually," reports Walia, "representing an astounding 86 percent of all internal displacement."[12] This has led the UN Human Rights Committee to rule that countries cannot deport people who seek asylum for climate-related threats violating the right to life.[13] Yet the countries and corporations that have led us to this crisis hide behind their borders, shirking their responsibility for climate change and for the people displaced by it.

Conflict

The same dynamics of inequity can be seen in armed conflict, another driver of migration. Many wealthy, industrialized countries produce and sell weapons for profit—weapons that fuel conflicts and violence around the world. In Libya, for example, warring factions are supported by various governments that are supplying weapons despite the arms embargo.[14] The acting UN envoy in Libya warned, "From what we are witnessing in terms of the massive influx of weaponry, equipment and mercenaries to the two sides, the only conclusion that we can draw is that this war will intensify, broaden and deepen—with devastating consequences for the Libyan people."[15] More than 370,000 people have been displaced by the conflict in recent years.[16] In Yemen, which a coalition led by Saudi Arabia has been bombing since 2015 with weapons supplied by the United States, United Kingdom, and other major arms exporters, over 24 million people are in need of humanitarian aid and more than 4 million are displaced.[17] In Syria, there are about 6 million internally displaced people and another 5.6 million refugees.[18] The intentional bombing of towns and cities, particularly by Russia and the Syrian state, have destroyed countless hospitals, homes, schools, water and sanitation facilities, and other critical infrastructure.[19] The statistics go on and on.

A steady stream of US guns has been flowing into Mexico and Central America since the early 2000s, contributing to rising paramilitary, gang, and cartel violence, as well as gender-based violence.[20] In Mexico, ten women a day are killed, at least 60 percent with guns. The United States also trains officials throughout Latin America in violence and oppression. Many of the soldiers and other state personnel who have graduated from the Western Hemisphere Institute for Security Cooperation, for example, have gone on to lead genocides against Indigenous and local populations, often with weapons also provided by the United States through military aid packages.[21] The learned violence is then deployed against civilian populations disposed by climate change or capitalism, leading to displacement and the pursuit of a new life farther north.

The failure to provide refuge

The brutal impacts of colonialism, capitalism, climate change, and conflict work in tandem to create vast numbers of people on the move. Right now, around the world, about seventy million people are unroofed and on the run. By 2050, predictions are that number will rise to 250–500 million. Possibly half a billion people will be migrants, refugees, and asylum seekers in just thirty years.[22]

This crisis is not, however, about migration itself, but the global response to it. The crisis is caused by the militarization of borders, the incarceration and brutalization of those seeking refuge, and the denial of fundamental human rights to life and movement. It is about "the systems of power that create migrants yet criminalize migration."[23]

This "unprecedented crisis of uprootedness," explains writer John Washington, is caused by people being pushed from their homes by violence, upheaval, hunger, and poverty, and then being denied a new home.

> When we take those two actors into account—first all the elements that push people out of their homes and then the politics of nativism or cold-heartedness . . . that denies them a new home, that erects borders around nations and communities and hounds people within those communities, that throws them into detention centers, to modern gulags—combines to create another unprecedented crisis, an amalgamated crisis of global apartheid.[24]

This denial of refuge, of dignity, of life—that is where the real crisis lies. And it is where the concept of borders becomes most hardened, with a proliferation of walls, weapons, and other violent apparatus to keep people "out" and othered.

The rise and militarization of La Migra

"Border enforcement" and "border security" are terms that account for the migrant-repressive state apparatus, surveillance technologies, networks of checkpoints and patrols, databases, detention centers, and local police. *La Migra*, Spanish slang for immigration officials, is becoming synonymous with entire countries. Determined to keep out migrants, refugees, and asylum seekers—often in violation of international law—these countries are working together to not just build and enforce walls but to make the entire process of movement more difficult for most people in the world. "Without such an iron fist, there is no other way the yawning gaps of global inequalities can persist," writes Todd Miller. "Wars are no longer about the animosity between nation states, the new long war is rather 'pacification in the name of enforcing the hegemony of transnational capital.'"[25]

The pursuit of capitalist accumulation has required vast investments in militarism: in weapons, soldiers, and wars to protect the wealthy elite interests in extraction and exploitation around the world. The "enforcement of borders" is no exception. The militarization of border apparatus is about securing investments for resource extraction while criminalizing opposition and controlling mobility, as anthropologist Rebecca Galemba documents.[26]

It is in this context that the US government enforces its borders not only along US territorial borders but also throughout Latin America, the Caribbean, the Middle East, and Asia, as Todd Miller shows in *Empire of Borders*.[27] US Border Patrol operates in dozens of countries around the world and equips and trains immigration officials in many others. Geographers Jenna Loyd and Alison Mountz have documented how the network of the eight hundred US military bases around the world, both active and decommissioned, have become locations for refugee and migration-control operations. The colonial bases on these edges of US empire, they write, provided the foundation for the construction of today's detention, deportation, and border apparatus.[28]

Border militarization reflects the influence of military strategies, culture, technologies, and hardware, and deploys many former military personnel as border agents.[29] It means that the use of force and preparation for armed conflict are used as the guiding principles for "protecting" and securing the border. The rise of *La Migra* reflects a process through which "police and military combine into an all-encompassing logic of perpetual war, surveillance, and security," notes Reece Jones. "The historic distinction between the internal and external roles of the police and military has blurred, and the border is a key site where the emerging security state is visible and where privileges are maintained by restricting movement through violence."[30]

Border walls

In 1989, when the Berlin Wall fell, there were fifteen border walls around the world. Today, there are more than seventy—and that number is rising.[31] In some situations, borders are marked by electric fences and razor wires, in others tall walls, in others high-tech systems known as "smart walls" that include systems of cameras, drones, sensors, and radar.

While the Trump administration was notorious for its building of a border wall, the expansion of surveillance at the US-Mexico border began years ago. President George H. W. Bush initiated the Secure Border Initiative (SBI) in 2005, over which US Customs and Border Protection (CBP) had the lead role in implementation. Due to the vast terrain, it decided to build a "virtual fence"—a surveillance system along the US, Mexican, and Canadian borders. Military contractors saw the virtual fence as a new theater of war and pushed for the installation of security systems deployed in Iraq and Afghanistan. Boeing won a $1 billion contract to develop and manage SBI. The proving ground was in Arizona, where eighteen towers with technology arrays along fifty-three miles would utilize "detection, identification, and surveillance tools such as unattended ground sensors, radar, and cameras for comprehensive awareness of the surrounding environment."[32] But it was "a billion-dollar boondoggle," notes John Carlos Frey.[33] The transmission of information is slow, the camera resolution is poor, and the system has reportedly been declared by its operators to be useless.

But it isn't useless to the contractors that developed the technology. Much of the SBI technology was built by the Israel company Elbit Systems and tested in Israel's apartheid laboratory of the Gaza Strip.[34] In the United States, this system is not used only to monitor the US-Mexico border; it's also used to persistently surveil the Tohono O'odham Nation's reservation that is roughly one mile from the border.[35]

Google is also profiting from the "virtual border wall." In 2020, it signed a contract with CBP for use of Google Cloud technology to facilitate the use of an artificial intelligence system at the border. Research by former Google employee Jack Poulson uncovered that CBP's work with Google is being carried out through a third-party federal contracting firm, ThunderCat Technology, and that Google's technology will be used in conjunction with Anduril Industries, which already operates sentry towers along the US-Mexico border that are used by CBP for surveillance and apprehension of people entering the country, facilitating the arrest and detention of migrants and asylum seekers.[36]

Drones, biometrics, and other tools of surveillance and control

A growing tool of enforcement of border surveillance and "security" are drones. Drones are not used only on the US-Mexico or US-Canada borders. The European Border Surveillance system deploys surveillance drones in the Mediterranean Sea to help facilitate migrant pushbacks. In addition, the European ROBORDER project, a "fully functional, autonomous border surveillance system," serves to exacerbate "the decentralization of the border zone into various vertical and horizontal layers of surveillance, suspending state power from the skies, and extend the border visually and virtually, turning people into security objects and data points to be analysed, stored, collected, and rendered intelligible."[37]

Tendayi Achiume, the UN special rapporteur on contemporary forms of racism, racial discrimination, xenophobia, and related intolerance, argues that the use of drones for so-called border security "bolsters the nexus between immigration, national security, and the increasing push towards the criminalization of migration and using risk-based taxonomies to demarcate and flag cases."[38] As a whole the surveillance of people on the move is aimed at the "bureaucratic production of knowledge about suspect populations."[39] This includes the utilization of "advance passenger processing, the compilation of databases of 'high risk' travelers, the biometric identification of asylum seekers and biometric passports," among other things.[40]

In her November 2020 report, Achiume outlined how governments and even UN agencies "are developing and using emerging digital technologies in ways that are uniquely experimental, dangerous, and discriminatory in the border and immigration enforcement context."[41] Through the use of such technologies, governments and the United Nations "are subjecting refugees, migrants, stateless persons and others to human rights violations, and extracting large quantities of data from them on exploitative terms that strip these groups of fundamental human agency and dignity." Surveillance and other digital technologies are being used, she argued, "to advance the xenophobic and racially discriminatory ideologies that have become so prevalent, in part due to widespread perceptions of refugees and migrants as *per se* threats to national security," and highlights "that vast economic profits associated with border securitization and digitization are a significant part of the problem."[42]

Governments are increasingly using extraction tools to download data from migrants' smartphones, including contacts, call data, text messages, stored files, and location information. In Austria, Belgium, Denmark, Germany, Norway, and the United Kingdom, the report notes, "laws allow for the seizure of mobile phones from asylum or migration applicants from which data are then extracted and used as part of asylum procedures."[43] As of April 2019, the United States requires visa applicants to disclose their social media account information in the past five years from the time of application.

Biometric data collection at borders is also an increasing problem. The collection of biometric data from refugees and asylum seekers is often sold to private contractors likely to surveil and track them—for example, the UN World Food Programme has sold data to Palantir, a data analytics company that also has contracts with US Immigration and Customs Enforcement (ICE). As Achiume's report describes, in most cases refugees in humanitarian aid settings need to consent to the collection of biometrics, but "conditioning food access on data collection removes any semblance of choice or autonomy on the part of refugees—consent cannot freely be given where the alternative is starvation."[44] Meanwhile, since January 2020, the US government has been collecting DNA from any person in immigration custody, moving toward the construction of a "genetic panopticon"—a "dystopian tool of genetic surveillance" encompassing anyone within US borders.[45]

Palantir, in the meantime, asserts that its software and biometric collection does not facilitate immigration enforcement. But Amnesty International and others have shown that ICE has used Palantir technology to arrest parents and caregivers of unaccompanied children, leading to detentions and harming children's welfare; that it has also used Palantir technology to plan mass raids, such as those ICE carried out in Mississippi in August 2019, "which led to the separation of children from their parents and caregivers, causing irreparable harm to families and communities."[46] Amnesty notes that these raids have led to cases of prolonged detention and deportations, and that Palantir's technology "facilitated these operations by enabling DHS/ICE to identify, share information on, investigate, and track migrants and asylum-seekers to effect arrests and workplace raids."

Some countries are also starting to experiment with artificial intelligence to automate decision-making at their borders. The tasks given to this technology in Canada, for example, include assessing whether an application is complete, whether a marriage is "genuine," or whether someone should be designated as a "risk." The Citizen Lab highlights the "intimate relationship between these emerging technologies and 'big data' surveillance,"[47] especially given the "mass and untargeted 'bulk collection' of electronic data" collected by the Canadian Security Intelligence Service and Canada's signals intelligence agency, the Communications Security Establishment. "This practice of mass data collection is crucial to understanding the risks of algorithmic decision-making in public policy, as it illustrates that the potential sources of 'input data' for automated decision systems may be vast, open-ended, and deeply problematic from a human rights perspective," warns The Citizen Lab.[48] Immigrants and refugees are "at particular risk of disproportionate surveillance of their electronic communications, and also face more serious potential consequences as a result"; even for Canadians, there are allowances for the collection of any and all "publicly available information," which could include "anything from social media posts, information sold by data brokers, and data obtained through hacks, leaks, and breaches."[49]

In Australia, where migrants and asylum seekers are often detained and incarcerated for years, surveillance technologies "are integral to strategies of punitive preemption based on 'social sorting'—the filtering of individuals in relation to coded categories of high or low risk."[50] As Dean Wilson and Leanne Weber argue, while its patterns of border securitization match those of the United States and European Union (EU), Australia's history as a British colony situated in the Asia Pacific region feeds much of its white population with an "invasion anxiety fired by xenophobic narratives which envisage the white Australian nation being overrun by Asiatic multitudes descending from the north." They note that these racialized narratives "have informed and intensified the contemporary politicization and securitization of border control in Australian public debate" and accelerated its deployment of surveillance technologies.[51]

This is also true in "Fortress Europe." The EU is investing billions in surveillance technologies for border enforcement, focusing on various sites, especially where migrants are crossing from North Africa and the Middle East. Among other systems, it's building an automated surveillance network on the Greek-Turkish border aimed at detecting migrants and "deterring" them from crossing. Universities have partnered with private corporations to develop surveillance tech and test it at Greek borders, including AI-powered lie detectors, virtual border-guard interview bots, the integration of satellite data with footage from drones on land, air, sea and under water, palm scanners that record the unique vein pattern in a person's hand to use as a biometric identifier, and live camera reconstruction technology to erase foliage virtually, exposing people hiding near border areas.[52]

Costs of La Migra

Building the border battlescape, of course, costs money. The US government has spent over $324 billion on border and immigration enforcement since 2003 and employs about fifty thousand people in various border enforcement and immigration control roles.[53] The industry is predicted in the 2020s to exceed more than $700 billion,[54] with multiple corporations profiting from this boon. The Transnational Institute reports that thirteen companies play a pivotal role in the US border industry: CoreCivic, Deloitte, Elbit Systems, GEO Group, General Atomics, General Dynamics, G4S, IBM, Leidos, Lockheed Martin, L3Harris, Northrop Grumman, and Palantir.[55] Several of these are the largest military contractors in the United States, manufacturing weapons for the US arsenal and for sale abroad. Several are also involved in the US nuclear weapon complex; others are deeply embedded with the US prison industrial complex, providing surveillance technologies or detention facilities.

It's important to note that while the investments in *La Migra* in the United States came under public scrutiny under the Trump regime, in particular due to the "Muslim bans," the separation of children from families, and the growing visible violence of ICE, this system was built over years by various Democratic and Republican administrations. The Biden administration, while stating its opposition to some of Trump's policies and to the border wall, received three times more campaign contributions from the "border security" industry during the 2020 election cycle than the Trump administration did.[56] Biden has also indicated his support for continuing construction of the "virtual wall" and deployment of surveillance technologies.

While there is much more to say about the militarization of US borders, one particular irony is that "the factories that will produce the border fortresses" designed by US and Israeli companies "could end up mainly located in Mexico," as Todd Miller warns. "Ill-paid Mexican blue-collar workers will manufacture the components of a future surveillance regime . . . all of which may well help locate, detain, arrest, incarcerate, expel, or even kill those same workers if they try to cross into the United States."[57]

Meanwhile in Europe, Thales, Airbus, and Leonardo are among the companies benefiting most from "border security" spending. According to a report from the Transnational Institute, Thales, which produces radar and sensor equipment, is currently developing border surveillance infrastructure for the European Border Surveillance system. Italian arms firm Leonardo was awarded a $73.7 million contract by the European Maritime Safety Agency to supply drones for EU coast guard agencies.[58] These companies are also involved in the manufacture and modernization of nuclear weapon systems and other armaments.

The EU, which has already spent billions on "border security," plans to spend another $38.4 billion over the next six years.[59] Frontex, the EU's border and coast guard agency, "is turning into a €10bn super-agency" with a ten-thousand-person standing corps.[60] It "connects surveillance data from all EU member states, and beyond the external borders."[61] In early June 2020, the EU signed a contract for a massive biometric database, while police forces across the EU are looking to establish a facial recognition database network.[62]

Military budgets in several European countries including Poland, Romania, Finland, and Sweden are growing, while the United Kingdom, France, Germany, Italy, and Spain maintain already high levels of spending on militarism. This spending is not just about national militaries but also border control: as reported in *The Guardian*, "An integrated border management fund and an internal security fund will make more billions available for national police and border guards, forces that look increasingly militarised." The EU is "investing billions in infrastructure and hardware produced by military and hi-tech corporations, including drones and surveillance technology."[63]

The failure of "deterrence"

This global battlescape of border security is part of the effort of wealthy Western governments to work together make sure that migrants, refugees, and asylum seekers have as difficult a time as possible entering their countries or even making it to their shores. Many of the efforts to prevent those seeking a new life abroad from obtaining entry are based on policies of "deterrence." Make it as hard as possible for anyone to get in, the theory goes, and others won't even try.

But deterring migration simply does not work. People desperate to survive gang violence or armed conflict or climate change or economic despair will undertake dangerous actions to try to secure a better life—any life—for themselves and their families.

The migration deterrence policies of the United States—such as shutting down border crossings near urban areas, for example—have driven people to cross instead through the desert, where many die of thirst, hunger, or exposure.[64] The US government, researcher Jason De León writes, has turned the desert "into a killing field, a massive open grave."[65] The deterrence policies in Europe have driven many to make dangerous crossings of the Mediterranean Sea, at the bottom of which many bodies of refugees now lie. Some European governments have tried to prevent and even criminalize attempts by nongovernmental organizations and activists to rescue people at sea, while the Italian government has deployed its anti-Mafia task force against migration networks.[66] The deterrence policies of Australia, known as the "Pacific Solution," have likewise drowned many migrants coming from Southeast Asia and have left the rest in perpetual internment in squalid conditions in "off-shore" prisons.[67] Globally, over seventy-five thousand migrants are known to have died since the mid-1990s.[68] Many more have disappeared, or the deaths simply haven't been recorded.

"As well as forcing migrants to take more perilous routes and put their lives in the hands of smugglers," notes researcher Charlotte Gifford, "increased security increases the risk of human rights abuses at the borders themselves."[69] Officials in countries from the United States to Slovenia often don't allow people to even ask for asylum, in violation of international law. Officials lie on the forms they fill out for applications, and don't ask the right questions or give proper information, including legally mandated information.[70]

Violence against refugees, asylum seekers, and migrants is also extreme. Along the Balkan Route in Europe, for example, it includes violence by border guards, police, and private security, and terrible conditions at camps that are run by the UN International Organization for Migration and funded by the EU.[71] Many of these camps are places where people who have tried to make it to Western Europe have been "pushed back" to—a process by which authorities prevent people from seeking protection on their territory "by forcibly returning them to another country. By pushing back those seeking safety and dignity over a border, states abdicate responsibility for examining their individual cases."[72]

Pushbacks are in violation of international and EU law, human rights groups explain, "because they undermine people's right to seek asylum, deny people of the right to due process before a decision to expel them is taken, and may eventually risk sending refugees and others in need of international protection back into danger."[73] According to the reports collected and collated by the Border Violence Monitoring Network as of November 2020, of nearly nine hundred documented illegal pushbacks against migrants, refugees, and asylum seekers since 2016, over 90 percent involved some form of violence by officials.[74] In May 2020, for example, Greek police were found rounding up asylum seekers living in the country and forcibly expelling them to Turkey.[75] Greece has also been using tear gas against migrants at the Turkish-Greek border.[76] In some cases, people on the move are being subjected to enforced disappearances by immigration authorities. They are rounded up, their identifications are confiscated, and then they are transported to and dumped in Turkey, without any proper procedure or legal acknowledgement.[77]

For people on the move, gender-based violence, particularly sexual violence, is also rampant. The UN Development Fund for Women reports that at least 60 to 70 percent of women migrants who cross the border alone experience sexual abuse. While this is the case everywhere, the danger is greater "for migrants from Central American countries, who must pass through two militarized borders—between Guatemala and Mexico and between Mexico and the US," where "sexual violence often occurs while being robbed, as 'payment,' or in exchange for not being apprehended or detained by immigration authorities."[78]

Trying to prevent migration through deterrence does not change the root causes of migration. It only endangers the lives of endangered people even more and punishes those trying to flee unlivable conditions. Then, when people are not deterred, and are instead captured by *La Migra* while on the move, they are subject to detention and incarceration.

Detention and deportation

Integral to the militarization of borders are efforts to criminalize the people who try to cross them. Thus, an essential part of the "bureaucratic razor wire" of borders is detention. If people survive the deserts, seas, bullets, and beatings, and manage to make it to a country of possible refuge, many are then arrested and incarcerated—sometimes for days, sometimes for years. The conditions in detention centers from Australia to the United States are like concentration camps due to the overwhelming violence, abuse, and degradation.

On any given day, there are about fifty thousand asylum seekers and migrants in detention in the United States.[79] Even more are detained across Europe, with the highest numbers currently in France.[80] Australia is currently detaining nearly ten thousand migrants, mostly in "off-shore" detention facilities.[81] "It's not always clear who learned how to inflict this brutality from whom," writes John Washington in *The Dispossessed*, "but the United States, Mexico, Australia, and Greece, among other countries, all consign asylum seekers to prolonged or indefinite detention, solitary confinement, physical abuse, unsanitary conditions, death threats, racist, homophobic, and gender-based hate from guards, and deadly neglect."[82]

While not a detention center, the migrant camp in Moria, Greece, hosts nearly twenty thousand people in an area about one square mile.[83] In January of 2020, the group Are You Syrious? reports, "field researchers counted 90 toilets and 90 showers inside of Moria, and another 30 sanitation units in the adjacent overflow camps. Food rations distributed fall short of caloric needs, compromising the growth and immune systems of its residents."[84] For years, doctors in Moria have struggled to contain a host of environmentally driven health issues such as respiratory illnesses, scabies, and lice.[85] At the camp in Velika Kladuša, Bosnia and Herzegovina, Bosnian police have entered the camp and beaten migrants.[86]

In Australia, the Human Rights Commission has found that the government has actively tried to make its detention centers more like prisons, including constructing walls and using restraints on detainees, and continues to detain people without justification and for far longer than any other country.[87] There have been many instances of violence, deaths, and suicides of detainees in the off-shore camps,[88] where among other things incarcerated people live in small tents, have limited access to hygiene, and suffer extreme medical neglect.[89]

In the United States, children are separated from their parents and put in cages without care; people are crammed into confined spaces surrounded by razor wire, some of which are open-air; people have to share foil blankets and tarps; they are denied showers, a change of clothes, diapers, soap, sanitary products, and toothbrushes for weeks at a time.[90] Family separations at the border amount to torture, according to medical and human rights experts performing psychological evaluations of asylum seekers in the United States.[91] Meanwhile, women detained in an immigration detention center in Georgia were subjected to forced hysterectomies.[92] In Louisiana, ICE agents threatened to expose asylum seekers to COVID-19 if they didn't accept deportation.[93] More broadly, ICE mismanagement resulted in coronavirus outbreaks across the country, with Detention Watch Network blaming the agency for nearly a quarter-million cases.[94]

In all countries, but particularly in the US and Australia, detainees are held for long periods of time before, in most cases, being deported. During this time, as documented by John Washington in relation to asylum seekers in the United States, they are often misinformed about their situation, not given proper legal counsel or interpretation at hearings, and pressured to consent to deportation before ever having their case for asylum even heard.[95] People who have lived in the countries where they have made their homes for years or decades are sent back to violent situations, to instability and insecurity, to uncertainty about how they will live or if they will ever be able to see their families again. With the US and European deportation machines, the practice of deporting people to border towns or the shores of other countries exposes migrants and asylum seekers to many of the threats they were trying to escape.

Profiting from detention

Of course, since we live in a capitalist system, many corporations are profiting from all this violence. In the United States, where the "zero tolerance policy" introduced by the Trump administration in violation of the Refugee Convention has resulted in separation of families, many of the administration's corporate friends have benefited financially. The migrant detention industry in the United States is mostly privatized. ICE contracts out 70 percent of its two hundred detention facilities, which are spread around the country, to GEO Group and CoreCivic.[96] When the zero tolerance policy was announced, the stocks of these groups increased by 5.9 percent and 8.3 percent, respectively, documents John Washington.[97]

Private companies also run detention centers in Australia[98]—where the government has tried to conceal the identities of its contractors[99]— and in the United Kingdom[100] and Italy.[101] Other countries vary: the Netherlands and Sweden operate their own facilities; in Germany they are managed by regional governments that contract some services to private companies; in France the regional and local authorities operate the centers but contract nongovernment organizations to provide services.[102]

The EU made a deal with Libya, providing the Libyan coast guard with equipment and training worth millions of dollars in exchange for its help preventing migration to Europe. Libya's detention centers, operated by the International Organization for Migration (IOM) and the UN High Commissioner for Refugees (UNHCR), are known sites of grave human rights abuses. Several former and current officials of the IOM and the UNHCR have accused these agencies "of ignoring or downplaying systemic abuse and exploitation in migrant detention centers in order to safeguard tens of millions of dollars of funding from the EU." In turn, they argue, the EU uses the UN agencies "to sanitize a brutal system of abuse that its policies are funneling tens of thousands of vulnerable people directly into."[103] Volunteers and activists along the Balkan Route have made similar claims.[104]

Detention and COVID-19

People in detention have been made even more vulnerable by the COVID-19 pandemic. In Europe, the Border Violence Monitoring Network found that the public health measures enacted at camps and detention centers have been militarized and have exacerbated human rights violations at borders. Military forces were deployed at borders and camps in Slovenia and Serbia; pushbacks, removals, and deportations persisted and even increased, using COVID-19 as a justification for not letting people in or expelling those already there. This marking of people as "public health risks" also meant the movements of those in camps were further constrained and access to soap, hand sanitizer, and masks was limited or nonexistent. "Within the context of the viral pandemic, the physical rights of people-on-the-move have been suspended in both settlement and transit," warns the Network. "Protections against inhumane accommodation and detention have been cast aside with the mass confinement of tens of thousands of people in the Western Balkans and Greece."[105]

Others found that security measures like lockdowns, isolation, and surveillance disproportionately impacted migrants. In France, for example, people had to carry documents proving their address if they left their house, which is impossible for homeless asylum-seekers. As journalists Iida Käyhkö and Laura Schack note, "Failure to produce these documents results in a significant fine, denying refugees access to supermarkets and other shops where they could obtain necessary food and hygiene items."[106]

In Bosnia, the government used the opportunity of COVID-19 to forbid movement of migrants and refugees, who were placed in lockdown in camps run by the IOM where they are subject to violence by both police and security contractors along with scarce food and tight spaces.[107] In Serbia, the government issued a temporary halt to asylum, which means people cannot initiate or resolve their asylum procedures. The army, as noted earlier, has been deployed at the camps to ostensibly "protect migrants from getting infected," but this has trapped people inside.[108] "These securitized responses to COVID-19 bode ill for the future, as reactive policy soon establishes itself as an enduring mechanism of control," warns the Border Violence Monitoring Network. "In the aftermath of COVID-19, whether and how such unlawful treatment will be lifted is an open ended question."[109]

In the United States, this question seems less open-ended. The treatment of migrants in detention is already closely connected to the treatment of all incarcerated peoples. High rates of infection have spread across the country's detention centers, jails, and prisons during the pandemic. Campaigns to "Free Them All," which are seeking the release of all people from detention and incarceration, have been launched across the United States; some cities have responded while others have refused.[110]

Thus, many migrants, asylum seekers, and refugees who have made it to the shores of other countries find themselves not only fighting for a new life but for life itself. This is a strategic plan of the governments that crafted the policies and built the apparatus of a killing machine. The governments that designed and fund this system, argues Jason De León, mobilize "a combination of sterilized discourse, redirected blame, and 'natural' environmental processes that erase evidence of what happened . . . in order to render invisible the innumberable consequences this sociopolitical phenomenon has for the lives and bodies" of people on the move.[111]

Undoing border imperialism

This "sociopolitical phenomenon" is far from inevitable. It is a political and economic choice. We can change it, by imagining alternatives and working to build them. To return to the comment from Esyllt W. Jones that an epidemic "is a border region where the meaning and membership in the community is imagined and re-imagined," we should use the COVID-19 pandemic as an opportunity to undertake this vital work. Not just because the spread of the virus raged out of control in detention centers and camps, but because what the pandemic revealed to us about our national and global inequities must not be ignored or forgotten. These inequities must instead be undone, deconstructed through urgent action, and replaced by something new.

There are urgent actions that national governments need to undertake immediately: demilitarizing and disarming borders, ending the cruelty at detention centers and ending detention altogether, abolishing agencies like ICE, stopping pushbacks and unlawful refusals of entry, protecting and upholding the rights of refugees and asylum seekers, decriminalizing labor migration, facilitating safe and humane border crossings, and providing housing, healthcare, and necessities for everyone within their territories regardless of nationality, immigration status, or criminal conviction.

This comprehensive disarmament of borders is essential. But we can't just disarm the apparatus of borders. *We need to also disarm the system of borders.*

Ultimately, appeals to make the migration, asylum, refugee, and immigration processes more "humanitarian" or "humane" still rely on the state as being the site of protection and well-being for migrants. But, as Bridget Anderson, Nandita Sharma, and Cynthia Wright argue, "migrants are not naturally vulnerable; rather the state is deeply implicated in constructing vulnerability through immigration controls and practices."[112]

Furthermore, this approach continues to treat certain migrants as objects of control and rescue rather than as human beings. It also treats their migration as the problem, something that needs to be fixed: "Consequently, people's mobility is seen as only ever caused by crisis and as crisis producing."[113] It also reinforces the construction of a migrant—who counts as a migrant, who is determining that? The migration of people from the Global North within Western countries, or even to the Global South, is not problematized in the same way. Referred to as "expats" instead of immigrants, their movement is largely unimpeded by borders.

All of this means that border control and immigration policies, even if humane, continue to produce inequalities between people. They continue to demark between here and there, between those people and our people. "Borders are not only ways of dividing nations, cities, and land," writes Todd Miller, "they are also ways of dividing people, corralling people, organizing people, producing compliance in people, extracting profit from people."[114] Borders are prisons, confining people and forcing them to live in conflict, in camps, in poverty, amidst rising seas and expanding deserts.

Thus the demand of those calling for the abolition of borders is instead for every person to have *the freedom to move or not to move*. This would involve establishing equitable human rights globally—the rights of being a person. In contrast to rights of property, consisting of the right to exclude others from enjoying that which has been privatized, the rights of persons consist of the right to not be excluded. Joseph Nevins also describes this in his appeal for "the right to the world"—a right to mobility and to share our planet's resources sustainably.[115]

Mutuality and "promiscuous care"

Beyond the responses of racists and nationalists, a typical reaction to this kind of "no borders" politics is that it will lead to people flooding "liberal democratic states," which will impact the most disadvantaged within those countries by overwhelming social services and well-being. But this reaction needs to be deconstructed. These states right now are prominently reliant on the violence of the capitalist system, on the division of people, the exploitation of labor, and the destruction of the environment. Borders are not designed to keep people safe; they are designed to maintain vast economic inequalities and assure the provision of cheap labor, lax regulations, and a hoarding of wealth.

Opening borders means opening them for labor, which will strengthen protections for people and planet, and it means opening them for human rights, which will improve the lives of all. This approach would dismantle the differentiated systems of labor and environmental regulations that currently create the necessity of migration in so many parts of the world and that oppress so many within certain countries in order to generate wealth for the few in other countries. While people would have equitable rights, the environment and labor would also be treated equally. In this sense, a "no borders" politics calls into question not just the legitimacy of the global system of nation-states but also of capitalism, especially neoliberal extractivism and exploitation of workers. "Anything else means we remain subservient to a capitalist system that banks on its ability to divide and exploit us all," as Justin Akers Chacón notes.[116]

Which brings us to another important point raised in the introduction. Abolition doesn't just mean eliminating one thing and then having a vacuum. It also means building something in its stead. Abolition is a positive approach that highlights not just what needs to change but also the possibilities of alternatives. It also means looking not to "reform" systems, but to dismantle them. Almost all reforms suggested for immigration are aimed at whitewashing and maintaining the status quo. We must break free from the idea that tweaking the system can bring justice, security, or equality, and instead think about what new systems are needed to achieve real change.

This, of course, requires a willingness to seriously consider and construct alternatives. It requires imagination and determination. It requires us to think beyond what we have been taught about what to fear, who to love, and how to care.

More than a century ago anarchist Gustav Landauer asserted, "The state is a social relationship; a certain way of people relating to one another.

It can be destroyed by creating new social relationships; i.e., by people relating to one another differently."[117] Organizer Harsha Walia suggests we can do this through collective solidarities with and responsibilities to each other, rather than to the state. An open borders politics necessitates the nurturing of relationships of mutuality with others. It requires "the collective and public recognition of all bodies, all abilities, all genders, all experiences, and all expressions as inherently valuable, and by virtue of their very existence, as distinctly human," explains Walia.[118]

It also means valuing nurturing, love, healing, transformative justice, connections to each other and the earth. It means, as Washington suggests, building communities "that are willing and able to receive those in need, not merely incarcerate or expel them. Practically, this means boldly and emphatically resisting federal law. It means building on ICE-out-of-community efforts, and it means taking immediate, active steps toward offering sanctuary, offering love and welcome to people."[119]

This approach also supports feminist and Indigenous environmental and ecological demands for political economy, including degrowth politics—downscaling resource and energy demands in our societies and ending the plundering of the environment and oppression of those providing underpaid or unpaid labor, including women. It also supports calls for a culture and practice of "promiscuous care"[120]—the proliferation of our circles of care beyond immediate kinship in expansive and nongendered ways.

Undoing the borders of our imaginations

If all of this sounds impossible or fanciful, keep in mind a few things.

The main limitations on how we "order" our societies and how we pursue "safety" and "security" are set by those who benefit the most from the systems within which we currently operate. This is not the majority of people in the world. These systems are undeniably skewed toward privileges for white people of a certain class living in Western states. When we think about "protecting our communities" from "mass immigration," or when we think about what the purposes of our borders are, we need to keep this in mind. Who are we protecting ourselves from? Who are we harming in pursuing "security" through borders, in particular through the global system of militarized border regimes that exist today?

Are we protecting the social services of our "welfare states," which have failed to prevent mass inequality and poverty within the countries utilizing borders to keep "others" out? Or are we really protecting the systems that produced the inequality, poverty, conflict, and climate crisis in the first place?

As we rise up against systemic racism, white supremacy, and police brutality, we must also ask ourselves how the racism we may reject within police forces and other institutions of state power manifests itself in and through borders: through the agencies that enforce them, through the military equipment and training that guard them, through the biometric and surveillance technologies that monitor them, through the camps and detention centers that constrain and degrade human beings. These systems are connected. They are rooted in a presumption that some lives matter and others don't. That some people count and others are expendable, disposable. "The binaries produced by borders," writes Todd Miller, such as "us versus them, exceptional versus inferior, good versus bad, innocent versus criminal, legal versus illegal," are "reinforced by the gun, the camera, the wall, and the law."[121] We can disarm and deconstruct all of these.

Ultimately, we need to wrap our heads around this political project of care, of peace, and of justice in a comprehensive way. Not only justice for *this* community or care for *that* state, but for everyone, everywhere, all the time. This is what the abolition of borders can bring to us, metaphorically and literally. The concept of comprehensive care and justice is also fundamental to mobilizing against and ending war, a system of violence that is intimately bound up in the construction, enforcement, and militarization of borders and the other structures discussed in this book.

Chapter 5

||||||||||||||||||||||||||||||||||||||||||||||||||||||||||||||||||||

Demobilizing War

S ome people see war as an inevitable consequence of the mass of humanity sharing the same planet, but it is not. States go to war for hegemony over each other within the imperialist nation-state system, and to ensure control over access to markets, resources, and cheap labor within the capitalist system of exploitation. For the United States, war is more than something it engages in regularly. The US is a country born of war—a war of conquest and dispossession to establish a settler colony and expand it westward. War was baked into the United States' DNA even before it became an imperial power at the end of the nineteenth century and then a world hegemon in the twentieth century, a hegemon it established through two world wars and the "cold war." War has become the United States' key industry, its political culture, its constant state of being.

The pursuit by successive US governments of "full spectrum dominance"—the ability to monitor, control, and deploy weapons at a moment's notice to anywhere on the planet—has ravaged our world. We are all forced to live with the implications of this constant of war, trying to survive under the threat of nuclear annihilation, drone strikes, disappearance, detention; the threat of our cities being vaporized, incinerated, exploded; of bullets or bombs tearing apart everything and everyone we love.

War, like all the other structures of violence explored in this book, is by no means exclusive to the United States. But US wars abroad and at home have shaped the world, tarnishing and imprinting irreparably upon history and lives; spreading the culture, technologies, and techniques of killing, coercion, and control across the globe. US wars inspire the world toward violence, fear, and hate. The idea that "security" can be achieved by weaponizing and militarizing as many aspects of life as possible is perpetuated by US wars and its colossal levels of military spending. This has led, among other things, to horrifying levels of internal gun violence, police brutality, mass incarceration, and abuses at the border; has led to endless war, invasion, and occupation abroad; and has led countless allies and enemies alike to spend more on bombs and guns than on the well-being of people or preservation of our planet.

Questions about whether or not armed conflict is ever justifiable, i.e., in terms of resistance or liberation, or within the context of "responsibility to protect," are outside of the considerations undertaken here. Hannah Arendt observed that "the practice of violence, like all action, changes the world, but the most probable change is to a more violent world."[1] From this perspective, looking at war as a structure and exploring the material realities that come with the creation and maintenance of a state that is based on war—a state that relies on war at home and abroad to preserve the "law and order" that benefit its political and economic elite—is important for understanding "why things are the way they are" in today's world. The United States, again, is not alone in this reliance on war. We can see it elsewhere, from Israel to Russia to any other state that derives its "stability" from violence and projects its power with force, internally and externally. But with a 39 percent share of global military spending, the United States merits a specific focus.

There is not one particular place from which the war machine manifests; a complex web of institutions within the United States makes its wars in all their aspects possible. Political, economic, social, academic, entertainment, and industrial institutions are complicit. They derive power from and perpetuate patriarchy and racism. There are intimate connections between the use of violence for control and coercion abroad and within countries. The structural fascism built into the policies and practices of US wars abroad, for example, are implicated in its structures of violence "at home," including those related to police, prisons, and borders. But it is possible to buck this trend, to break the cycle of violence, to divest from weapons and war-making and invest instead in people and the preservation of our planet. With all the converging crises beset upon us, from COVID-19 to climate change, we must look not just to solving or mitigating these emergencies, but to ending the crisis underlying them all: the dominance of war and the war mentality.

Impacts of war

War is a declaration of power through death; of violence over peace; conflict over cooperation. It has marred generations, begetting only war and more war. The cost of war can, and should, be measured in blood or bodies. The human cost of US wars has been unconscionable. Millions killed; millions more injured, tortured, disappeared; millions more displaced, driven from their homes made unlivable by raging conflict, environmental devastation, destruction of civilian infrastructure, or all of the above.

Since September 11, 2001, US-led wars in the Middle East and Asia have directly killed over 800,000 people;[2] another twenty-one million have been displaced and hundreds of thousands have been detained and tortured.[3] Millions were killed in the US wars in Viet Nam and Korea; hundreds of thousands killed, detained, or disappeared at the hands of US-trained soldiers and paramilitaries across Latin America. US drone strikes, special forces operations, and other extrajudicial, "unofficial" acts of war have killed thousands more.

These are just a few examples, and the numbers alone do not capture the horrors these wars have inflicted upon human bodies and lives, or on the natural world. The following is an extremely brief overview of but a few of the humanitarian and environmental consequences of war and armed conflict.

Blood and bones

War devastates. Whether fought with guns, bombs, or drones, armed conflict leads to death and destruction. Examining all the human impacts of war is not possible for a chapter of this nature or length, but even a cursory look at impacts on human life and dignity provides a horrifying snapshot.

The use of everything from guns, cluster bombs, landmines, armed drones, depleted uranium weapons, and nuclear weapons have all had catastrophic impacts on human life and health. From loss of limbs to radiation poisoning, the direct impacts of these weapons as well as their remnants have caused intergenerational harm across the world.

Explosive violence can be particularly egregious. In many US-led or -supported wars, bombing and shelling of villages, towns, and cities has become increasingly commonplace. While the practice of firebombing or carpet-bombing cities seen in World War II or the so-called Vietnam War has waned, the use of explosive weapons in populated areas has continued.[4] When mortars, rockets, artillery shells, aircraft bombs, and improvised explosive devices are used in towns and cities, civilians account for 90 percent of the casualties.[5] Reverberating effects, caused by damage to housing, places of work, health and sanitation facilities, and more, impact people's access to food, water, housing, and healthcare long after the conflict has ended.[6]

Examples of these tragedies abound. Since a Saudi-led coalition, armed primarily by the United States and other Western governments, began bombing Yemen in March 2015, the country has spiralled into the world's worst humanitarian crisis. The relentless bombing has destroyed homes, hospitals, schools, markets, and other vital civilian infrastructure, displacing over 3.65 million people. More than ten million people face food shortages and millions of children are suffering from acute malnutrition.[7] In Mosul, Iraq, where US-led forces mounted a military operation against Daesh in 2016 and 2017, thousands of civilians were killed and 1.8 million displaced. The western part of the city was largely destroyed, mostly because of US airstrikes, which increased from four hundred a month at the beginning of the operation to about eight hundred a month toward the end.[8]

Overall, the United States and its allies have dropped more than 326,000 bombs and missiles on people in other countries since 2001. "That's an average of 46 bombs and missiles per day, day in day out, year in year out, for nearly 20 years," note Medea Benjamin and Nicolas J.S. Davies, who compiled the research.[9] When we add in Israel's regularized and horrific bombardments of Gaza, and the Russian and Syrian shelling of Syrian towns and cities since 2011, and the bombs, rockets, mortars, and missiles used in all the other armed conflicts around the world, the explosive violence is completely overwhelming.

In addition to the destruction of infrastructure, death, injury, and displacement, the psychological harm caused by armed conflict is devastating. High numbers of those who have experienced armed conflict, particularly the use of explosive weapons in populated areas, report anxiety, depression, and post-traumatic stress disorder.[10] Many children growing up in Gaza, Syria, Yemen, and other places where the bombing of homes, schools, and hospitals is part of daily life have been experiencing extreme and chronic trauma from a young age—some their entire lives.[11]

Poisoning the planet

War also has a devastating and lasting impact on the environment.[12] Direct environmental impacts of armed conflict can include damage to industrial sites, deforestation, toxic and hazardous war remnants, and the destruction of water, sanitation, and health infrastructure.[13] Explosive weapons that destroy buildings can result in the fragmentation and projection into the air of toxic building materials. Certain weapons made with heavy metals can cause toxicity. The targeting of oil refineries, chemical facilities, or other industrial sites can cause toxic substances to leak into soil and water. Even guns have environmental and health impacts: residual lead from bullets can cause lead poisoning in those who have been shot and can contaminate soil and water.[14]

Arms production, testing, and storage can also lead to environmental destruction. The manufacturing of depleted uranium munitions, comprised of radioactive and chemically toxic heavy metals, has contaminated nearby communities.[15] Uranium mining and milling for nuclear weapons have contaminated land and water around the world, from Canada to the Democratic Republic of the Congo.[16] The thousands of atmospheric nuclear weapon tests conducted by a handful of states around the world—mostly on the lands of Indigenous nations—have had grave and lasting environmental impacts.[17] As discussed further in chapter 6, the US government exploded about a thousand nuclear weapons at the Nevada Test Site (now called the Nevada National Security Site) with predictable and preventable costs to people and the planet: radioactive soil, increased rates of cancers in the downwind areas, early death for uranium miners, and the destruction of sacred Native lands. Its use of nuclear weapons on Japan and its nuclear tests on the Marshall Islands and other Pacific countries were likewise based on white supremacy resulting in radioactive racism.[18]

Through military operations, construction of bases, destruction of infrastructure, land, and water, and the production, use, testing, transportation, and storage of weapons, militarism is devastating to the environment. Furthermore, the consumption of fossil fuels by militaries is astronomical. The US military is one of the world's biggest polluters. It consumes more hydrocarbons than most countries; in fact, if it were a country, it would be the world's fifty-fifth largest emitter of carbon dioxide.[19] Since it began the "Global War on Terror" in 2001, the US military has produced at least 1.2 billion metric tonnes of greenhouse gas.[20] The Intercept has highlighted the "grim irony" that the heavy US military footprint in the Middle East has largely been about preserving access to the region's oil—the industrial extraction of which has been one of the major drivers of global carbon dioxide emissions—while consuming enormous levels of fossil fuels itself. "In other words," writes Murtaza Hussein, "we have been killing, dying, and polluting to ensure our access to the same toxic resource most responsible for our climate disruption."[21]

War everywhere

Despite all the devastation wrought by war, the United States has, as a country, consistently and relentlessly turned to armed aggression throughout its history. Since before it was a country, the United States has been at war. The settlers warred with Indigenous nations and with the state of Mexico. Landowners warred against enslaved Africans. Since then, the political and economic elite of the United States have waged wars abroad—fighting wars of economic and political imperialism meant to secure resources and geopolitical influence; supporting coups and dictatorships that benefited US interests; training militaries and shipping weapons to conflict zones. Scholar Elizabeth Cook-Lynn links contemporary US wars directly to its origins, which derive from a policy of imperial dominance. "Trampling on the sovereignty of other nations for most of its several centuries of nationhood has been the legacy of the American Republic's power."[22]

Currently the United States is "officially" involved to some degree in seven wars—in Afghanistan, Iraq, Libya, Niger, Somalia, and Yemen—and it is unofficially involved in conflicts in many countries.[23] It launches strikes or conducts military training and exercises, stations weapons, and accompanies forces in conflict zones across Africa.[24] It has at least eight hundred military bases around the world.[25] It participates in joint military exercises with various allies and rotates special forces as "advisors" around the world. In fact, US special forces are deployed in up to 134 countries at any one time.[26]

Simultaneously, the US state and its apparatus has waged war at home—against women, against Black, brown, and Indigenous people, against Asian Americans, against Muslims, against migrants and asylum seekers, and now, in an increasingly visible way, against anyone who demonstrates against state violence. The wars "at home" and "abroad" are increasingly entangled, in terms of tactics, weapons, and even, at times, troops.

War abroad → War at home → War abroad → War at home . . .

When the Trump administration first threatened to deploy the US military against protestors in US cities,[27] which led to the actual deployment of US Customs and Border Protection (CBP) and US Immigration and Customs Enforcement (ICE) agents in Portland in early July 2020, many politicians, journalists, and citizens expressed outrage about this situation as well as the levels of violence being perpetrated by police and other state agents. But despite their outrage, many commentators seemed indifferent to or unaware of the fact that for decades, people in countries around the world have been experiencing US-sanctioned or US-influenced violence. Setting ICE and CBP agents loose on Portland to pull protestors off the streets into unmarked vehicles, for example, wreaks of the same playbook of "low-intensity warfare, death squads, forced disappearances, and massacres" the US military has been exporting for many years.[28]

For many peace groups, the similarities have been clear. About Face, a group of anti-war veterans of the post-9/11 era, tweeted, "People are so stressed about some smashed windows. How much 'private property damage' would you estimate is caused by 7,423 bombs? That's how many the U.S. dropped on Afghans last year. . . ."[29] And Los Angeles Chargers football player Justin Jackson quipped, "Now that we've all come to the agreement that we don't like an occupying force on our streets, can we normalize being against that for foreign people we don't know in other countries?"[30]

While the outrage against police brutality in the United States was absolutely justified, some of the commentary served to signal that the use of this type of violence abroad by the military is acceptable. As activist Zoé Samudzi noted, it is perverse that "there is this acceptance of this violence overseas whereas 'Americans' shouldn't be subjected to that kind of violence—and I say Americans with caveats because there are so many people [in the US] that *are* subjected to that violence."[31]

Yet many of the reactions also appeared indifferent to or unaware of the fact that many Black, Indigenous, and other people of color in the United States consistently experience this kind of violence from the US government, too. Comments that US war has "come home" overlook the fact that it never left. The tactics used by ICE and CBP in Portland have been used against migrants, asylum seekers, and refugees for decades. There are similarities between tactics and weapons used by the military around the world and those used in US cities against people of color, queer people, and people whose poverty has been criminalized. As a case in point, the recent situation in Portland is reminiscent of the "small army" that occupied Ferguson, Missouri, in the wake of Black Lives Matter protests over the police murder of Michael Brown in 2014.[32]

"The war has always been home," academic and activist Nick Estes points out. "It has traveled abroad, but it never quite left our homelands."[33]

Institutionalization of war

To oppose war, in this context, cannot be just to oppose this or that war, or to "bring the troops home" from Afghanistan or Iraq. It is not just about ending US material and political support for coups or dictatorships in Latin America or the Middle East or Southeast Asia, nor just about preventing the next war—with Iran, or China, or whomever else is manufactured as the next enemy. Given the embeddedness of war in the politics and economics of the United States, and the lived reality of violence experienced by many around the world and within the USA, *opposing war must be about opposing the institutions that make war possible*, at home and abroad.

These institutions include the various branches of the military and the government agencies that "hunt, capture, or kill" the state's perceived or constructed "enemies" from the deserts of Afghanistan to the streets of Portland; local police forces and agencies of the Department of Homeland Security, such as CBP and ICE; the weapon manufacturers that profit from blood spilled, mostly from people of color; the private corporations and public entities running migrant detention centers and prisons; the policies and practices that criminalize Black, Indigenous, and other people of color, that criminalize migrants and migration and put "border enforcement" above human lives, and that criminalize poverty; and the decisions by Congress and other decision-makers to invest in war instead of well-being, in weapons instead of healthcare, education, or housing.

These institutions—or rather, those who establish, operate, and fund these institutions—choose to invest in violence rather than peace, in weapons rather than houses or hospitals or books. These choices have costs: humanitarian costs, environmental costs, and economic costs. These costs, in turn, set up the world we live within. Understanding the costs is necessary to challenge the institutions and their choices. In addition to the humanitarian and environmental costs of war described above, the economic costs have been steep: trillions of dollars spent on violence over decades; billions spent on violence every single year.

Military spending

In 2020, US military spending amounted to $778 billion, which accounts for 39 percent of the global total.[34] The US spends more than the next ten largest military spenders *combined*—and that doesn't even include the nearly $200 billion earmarked for veterans' affairs. Yet the US military budget is on the rise: it spent 5.3 percent more in 2019 than in 2018, and 4.4 percent more in 2020 than 2019. As the Stockholm International Peace Research Institute noted, "The increase in US spending in 2019 alone was equivalent to the entirety of Germany's military expenditure for that year."[35]

Since 2001, the US government has spent about $6.4 trillion on war in the Middle East and Asia.[36] The US maintains about eight hundred foreign military bases around the world, to the tune of $25 billion to $150 billion per year, depending on what is being included in the calculation.[37] It spends billions on weapons research and development, on purchasing bullets and bombs from corporations, and, increasingly, on contracting out work to private military and security companies.

Nuclear weapon spending

Also, the United States has nuclear weapons. The budget for nuclear bombs is held by the US Department of Energy rather than the Department of Defense. The US currently has an arsenal of about 3,800 nuclear warheads as well an extensive fleet of nuclear bombers, missiles, and submarines, and an extensive network of nuclear weapon production facilities across the country.[38]

The money going toward nuclear weapon maintenance and modernization is also on the rise. In 2019, the US spent $41.4 billion on nuclear weapons[39]—which on its own is larger than the *total military spending in all but nine other countries.*

"Intelligence" spending

The US government also devotes billions to sixteen "intelligence agencies," many of which engage in war activities abroad and/or surveillance at home. In 2020, $23.1 billion went to agencies that are part of the Military Intelligence Program—which includes the intelligence arm of each of the armed forces branches, as well as Special Operations Command. Another $62.7 billion went to the National Intelligence Program, which includes the Central Intelligence Agency, Federal Bureau of Investigation, and others. Some agencies, such as the National Security Agency, are cross-appointed.[40]

This money doesn't go through the Pentagon and isn't calculated as being part of US military spending. It's a black budget, and it grows every year.[41] Many of the agencies receiving this money are infamous for their roles in spying on US citizens and the leaders of foreign countries, establishing and operating "black sites" where suspected "terrorists" are tortured and indefinitely detained, launching covert operations in countries with which the United States is not officially at war, and carrying out extrajudicial killing with armed drones.

"Homeland security" spending

About $50 billion a year goes to the US Department of Homeland Security (DHS), which was created in 2003. Among other activities, DHS houses the agencies that police the border—and, more recently, the streets of Portland. US CBP currently receives $18.2 billion and ICE gets $8.8

billion.[42] Both are seeing their budgets and mandates rise, despite the well-documented accounts of horrific abuses committed by their officers.

Prison industrial complex

Which brings us to the police. With many police forces taking up between 30 and 60 percent of each US city's budget, the United States as a whole spends about $100 billion annually on policing.[43] Incidentally, the New York Police Department's current budget of nearly $6 billion—the largest in the United States—would make it the thirty-third largest military spender on the planet.[44]

Meanwhile, the official budget for incarceration in the United States today is $81 billion. But as noted in chapter 2, there are other, hidden, costs, leading the Prison Policy Initiative to calculate that the annual total cost of incarceration is about $182 billion.[45]

War profiteering and the merchants of death

Together, all of this means that the United States spent somewhere around $1.4 trillion on war and militarism in all its aspects in 2020. War is, simply put, big business. And that means certain people are profiting from it.

Private military and security companies are making a (financial and literal) killing from war. In 2019, there were fifty-three thousand US contractors operating in the Middle East, compared to thirty-five thousand US soldiers. A recent study by Brown University shows that much of the growth in US military budgets since 2001 is due to payments to military contractors.[46] Some contractors are infamous for their commission of human rights abuses, from DynCorp in Bosnia to Blackwater in Iraq. Others handle laundry, food services, transportation, and construction, employing foreign nationals and paying them less than US employees.[47]

Many private military and security companies have their hooks in multiple industries. G4S, for example, has contracts with Israeli prisons in the West Bank, South African prisons, and the Guantánamo Bay detention camp—all of which have engaged in torture; provides transportation for ICE—including van rides that the American Civil Liberties Union has found to be inhumane; and guards nuclear weapon and nuclear power facilities throughout the United States—where it has been implicated in security breaches and lapses.[48] These private firms are profiteering not just from war abroad, but from the entire global carceral system.

An even more essential piece of the war industry is the weapon manufacturers. More than a century ago, the founders of the Women's International League for Peace and Freedom (WILPF) saw that those who made weapons were at the heart of a grave, deeply gendered racket, in which myths such as "security through violence" and "peace through war" are peddled in order to justify ever-increasing extravagant military budgets and profits. In the midst of World War I, WILPF located "in the private profits accruing from the great armament factories a powerful hindrance to the abolition of war."[49] Writing years later during World War II, British anti-war activists Fenner Brockway and Frederic Mullally similarly warned that the interests of the military-industrial complex cannot "coincide with the interest of the nation and the world, which is security." Investment in weapons and war "must of necessity continue just so long as the interest of profit is allowed to run counter to the best interests of the community at large."[50]

The global war economy has only deepened and expanded since the armed conflicts of twentieth century, as is explored further in chapter 7. The fusion of capitalist accumulation with state militarization has been facilitated by the US government's "expansion of opportunities for private capital to accumulate through militarization, such as by facilitating global weapons sales by military-industrial-security firms," sociologist William I. Robinson writes, which in turn requires the "conjuring up" of external enemies.[51] For the United States, this may be immigrants, or Muslims, or China or Russia, but the mission is to turn to militarization and war to ensure continued valorization of capital and the perceived "legitimacy" of the state, while simultaneously repressing opposition and reinforcing social control at home.

Today, the production of war remains big business. The top five US weapon manufacturers—Boeing, Lockheed Martin, General Dynamics, Northrop Grumman, and Raytheon—each made between $21 and $48 billion in revenue in 2018.[52] Their executives and board members receive millions of dollars a year, at taxpayers' expense. US corporations also continue to dominate the international arms market, accounting for 37 percent of global arms exports for the last five years.[53] During this period, the United States sold weapons to at least ninety-six countries, far more than any other supplier.[54]

Even in the midst of the COVID-19 pandemic, the military-industrial complex has done well for itself. In many countries, arms producers were deemed essential services at the onset of the crisis. Boeing, a major US military contractor, successfully pushed for billions in aid to the arms industry in the $2 trillion US stimulus bill.[55] Despite risks to workers and the urgent need for medical equipment and protective gear, war profiteers continued to pump out bombs and bullets. US officials in charge of military acquisition even announced plans to accelerate contract awards during the COVID-19 crisis in order to protect the profit margins of weapons companies.[56]

Meanwhile, despite the UN Secretary-General's appeal for a global ceasefire during the COVID-19 pandemic,[57] the international arms trade also continued. Some countries even used the chaos of the moment to conduct controversial arms sales that would otherwise face public opposition, in a classic demonstration of disaster capitalism.[58]

The profits to be made from the destruction of countries where war is fought is a key part of war profiteering. In her book *The Shock Doctrine: The Rise of Disaster Capitalism*, Naomi Klein documents how neoliberal ideologues work with big corporations and other segments of the capitalist elite to use moments of crisis to ram through political and economic changes that benefit their accumulation of capital.[59] In the midst and aftermath of war, often working hand in hand with so-called peace facilitators, they encourage legal reforms to enable privatization of national industries, "flexibilization" of labor laws, and other structural reforms that will allow them easy access to markets and cheap labor. They also "rebuild" destroyed infrastructure in ways that suit the interests of capital and private profit at the expense of those who lived in the affected communities before the conflict.

Social destruction

All the billions of dollars that go toward war, violence, and "security" ultimately end up in the pockets of those who benefit from the destruction and chaos, at the expense of everything and everyone else. The war machine sucks up public funds, leaving mere breadcrumbs and table scraps for social safety nets, education and housing, and environmental preservation.

While military spending, the "intelligence" black budgets, "homeland security," and carceral system investments continue to rise, all other US budget lines are being cut. The US government's budget for 2020 saw a 31 percent cut to the Environmental Protection Agency (EPA), a 16 percent cut for housing, and 12 percent cuts to each of health and education, among others.[60] Its budget for 2021 further cut these departments, including, for example, another 26 percent cut from the EPA. The 2021 budget cuts Medicare by about $500 billion, Medicaid by nearly $1 trillion. It also cuts $182 billion from the food stamp program and $2.5 billion from the nutrition program.[61]

In 2019, the Pentagon spent $55.9 billion on weapon research and development.[62] This included research and design of high-tech armaments such as autonomous and artificial intelligence weapon systems, drone swarms, and hypersonic missiles capable of reaching anywhere in the world at five times the speed of sound. *Scientific American* compared this amount of money to spending on research on health ($38.9 billion), energy ($4.4 billion), and the environment ($2.8 billion).[63] "For the majority of the past two decades, the U.S. government has equated Americans' national security with military supremacy," write political scientists Neta C. Crawford and Catherine Lutz, codirectors of the Costs of War Project. "Instead of investing in programs and supplies that would have saved thousands of lives, our leaders were investing trillions in new weapons and continuing old wars."[64]

War poverty

The investors in weapons and war have not just spent trillions on death and violence, but have actively plundered from the institutions, programs, and mechanisms designed to save lives, protect the environment, and provide for human well-being. This has resulted in catastrophic levels of hunger, houselessness, and poverty within the United States and around the world.

In 2019, about 12 percent of the US population—around 43.5 million people—lived below the poverty line.[65] This number is expected to increase dramatically due to the extraordinary rates of job loss because of the COVID-19 pandemic.

When it comes to jobs, the military industry portrays itself as a great employer, from soldiering to weapons manufacturing to base building—even though as veterans and economists have pointed out, this is not the case. In fact, federal spending on healthcare, education, clean energy, and infrastructure creates more jobs than military spending by 21–28 percent.[66] Investments in elementary and secondary education create nearly *three times* as many jobs as military spending.[67]

Yet military investments continue to be prioritized, lining the pockets of the privileged and producing more weapons and more war for the entire world. The result is not just unemployment, but a culture that invests in militarism while its population staggers under the crushing weight of economic crisis.

After his official visit to the United States in 2017, UN Special Rapporteur on extreme poverty and human rights Philip Alston noted that the concept of "American exceptionalism" was a steady theme in his conversations, while in reality, "today's United States has proved itself to be exceptional in far more problematic ways that are shockingly at odds with its immense wealth and its founding commitment to human rights. As a result, contrasts between private wealth and public squalor abound."[68]

Alston found levels of inequality, incarceration, and houselessness disproportionate to the country's wealth. Compared to other wealthy countries, the US has fewer doctors and hospital beds, less access to water and sanitation, higher rates of disease and infections, and much lower economic mobility. His report also described how poverty in the United States is racialized and gendered, with Indigenous communities, people of color, and women facing the brunt of poverty's impacts; and how economic hardship is criminalized as a deliberate effort to conceal the problem. "At the end of the day," Alston wrote, "particularly in a rich country like the USA, the persistence of extreme poverty is a political choice made by those in power."[69]

It is also a choice that results in extreme poverty abroad. The armed conflict that the United States perpetuates or facilitates abroad has spun the economies of countries and entire regions into disastrous disarray. In Iraq, for example, one in five people live in poverty and one in four youth are unemployed.[70] In Afghanistan, about 55 percent of the population lives below the poverty line and food insecurity is on the rise.[71] These are just a couple of examples.

Rising militarism, rising violence

US militarism doesn't only affect the countries it bombs. It also impacts the spending choices of its allies and its perceived "enemies." China, which is targeted by the US as a major rival in military power, has increased its military spending by 76 percent over the past decade in line with its stated desire to "catch up with other leading military powers."[72] The US government's badgering of the North Atlantic Treaty Organization to contribute more of their budgets to militarism is leading to increased military investments among members: in 2020, twelve NATO members spent 2 percent or more of their GDPs on their militaries.[73] Other major US allies, including Australia, India, Japan, and South Korea, many of which participate in joint military exercises with the United States, increased their military spending in 2020.[74]

Another factor leading to rising military expenditure in Europe, also encouraged by the United States, is the increasing militarization of borders, which is described in chapter 4. The weaponization and militarization of borders has resulted in social destruction of migrant and immigrant lives. Violence against refugees, asylum seekers, and migrants is as extreme in Europe as it is in the United States. Along the Balkan Route in Europe, for example, there is rampant violence by border guards, police, and private security, and terrible conditions at camps run by the UN International Organization for Migration and funded by the European Union. The militarization of borders, through investments in weapons, surveillance apparatus, and military personnel, is steadily reinforcing a fortress against those who are fleeing war and violence—much of it caused or facilitated by the very governments now denying these populations entry.

The militarism of "development assistance" and "international economic cooperation"

Meanwhile, countries grappling with "development" agendas to ostensibly improve living conditions for people face increasing militarism, too. Bilateral and multilateral development assistance, as well as the role of international financial institutions (IFIs), often incentivizes or directly contributes to increases in military spending. The US government frequently stipulates that recipients of its "foreign aid" must use part of the funds to purchase military equipment or invest in training. The European Union also gives "support" to countries for weapons, surveillance technologies, and other equipment for police. In Bosnia and Herzegovina, for example, some of the funding made available by the European Union for the country's response to the increase in migration flows has gone into purchasing surveillance and other equipment for the police forces. Even funds earmarked for "humanitarian assistance" are given to private security companies operating within the concentration camp–like migrant detention centers, which are rife with human rights violations, as described in chapter 4.[75]

  Indirectly, conditionalities attached to IFI loans and grants that require, among other things, privatization of public works, weakening of labor laws, and cuts in social spending lead to increasing inequality and poverty. This often prompts governments to spend more on militarism, including by equipping police forces with army-grade weapons to protect private interests and resist opposition.[76]

Disappearance and destruction

All these investments in militarism instead of social well-being result in more violence and more harm. The investment in war does not bring security. Weapons do not prevent or deter conflict. Police do not deter "crime." Prisons do not disappear problems. Instead, these structures of violence disappear human beings.

"The practice of disappearing vast numbers of people from poor, immigrant, and racially marginalized communities has literally become big business" in the United States, wrote Angela Davis in 1998 in relation to the prison industrial complex.[77] This practice of disappearing people, whether at home through policing and prisons or abroad through war and occupation, amounts to what Davis describes as social destruction. The structures of violence devour social wealth, decimating the public sector and breeding even more violence and harm.

As much as some US citizens might like to believe that the US war machine is there to "protect them," the reality is that the war machine protects no one but those directly profiting from it. It turns public funds into private prosperity; it profits from social destruction. And that social destruction feeds both wars and prisons with bodies, particularly those of Black and brown people. It creates more targets for drone strikes abroad, more targets for incarceration at home.

The economic investments that the wars abroad help to protect for the capitalist elite—the extraction of oil, gas, minerals; the ability to build McDonalds in Baghdad or pay workers in Bangladesh $1 per day to sew clothing sold for $100 per item in the United States—all ensure poverty and violence abroad as well as the bleeding of jobs from the United States, leading to increasing unemployment, precarity and poverty at home, and the continued dominance of the capitalist class.

Structural violence

All of this—mass incarceration, war and occupations, arms exports to conflict zones, social and economic devastation of so many people—requires a process of dehumanization and "othering." It requires the idea that some human beings are worth less; that, by the nature of the color of their skin, their sex, gender, or sexuality, their dis/ability or religion or place of birth, they are inherently more dangerous, less deserving of care and love and protection.

Power relations, as Michel Foucault explains, are embedded in processes of categorization and differentiation.[78] These processes produce hegemonic norms and hierarchies between identities, categorizing people based on sex, gender, sexual orientation, race, class, ability, religion, and any other "marker of difference" between people. This categorization and hierarchization among people enables—and even requires—violence against certain groups in order to maintain the established "order." Patriarchy and racism are two such systems of ordering that simultaneously demand and reinforce power relations.

Structural patriarchy

Patriarchy, as described in the introduction, is a system of power that celebrates a certain form of masculinity, namely a "particular idealized image of masculinity in relation to which images of femininity and other masculinities are marginalized and subordinated."[79] In most cultures today, this "hegemonic masculinity" is represented by a heterosexual cisgender man who makes claims to being independent, risk-taking, aggressive, rational, physically tough, courageous, and unemotional. This hegemonic gender norm also has implications for weapons culture and possession. Weapons—from small arms to nuclear bombs—are seen from this perspective as being essential to power.[80] Whether the concern is having the biggest stockpile or the most high-tech capabilities, weapon possession and proliferation are treated as indicative of status: of being ready to "defend," of being able to oppress and control—and in particular, of being "a real man."

The military plays a primary role in shaping images of masculinity in the larger society, to the point where "the dominant adult male role model could largely be the product of the military."[81] As Judy Wajcman notes, "War provides the ultimate test of manliness and is the legitimate expression of male violence."[82] Primacy in the military was, and still is, awarded to "toughness, skilled use of violence, presumption of an enemy, male camaraderie, submerging one's emotions, and discipline (being disciplined and demanding it of others)," writes feminist scholar Cynthia Enloe.[83] The shaping of this dominant expression of masculinity requires the gender binary to thrive: the idea of a masculine "warrior hero," the infusion of honor into violence, needs to be positioned or contrasted with an opposite—with women needing and wanting protection. It requires a complicit "other"—women—and no option for alternative realities: of gender nonconforming, nonbinary, genderqueer, or trans people; or of cisgender men and women refusing to buy into the prescribed gender roles and norms.[84]

Militarized masculinities, and the preference for weaponized violence over dialogue and cooperation, are embedded within institutions of violence like the military, and perpetuate that culture beyond these institutions. From police to prison guards to border patrol agents, those trained in the tradition of militarized masculinities reproduce the processes of differentiating and "othering" that reinforces the ideal of gendered and racialized hierarchies.

Turning people into warfighters or border guards requires breaking down their sense of ethics and morals and building up a violent masculinity that is lacking in empathy and glorifies strength as violence and physical domination over others portrayed as weaker. Hierarchy is fundamental to this training. Teaching human beings to kill, incarcerate, or repress other human beings "requires dehumanizing others by promoting the belief that another human is somehow a 'lesser' creature," Cynthia Enloe explains. "One of the central forms of dehumanization promoted by military training and the culture of daily life in the military has been the supposed inferiority of women—that women are less than men."[85]

These norms and power dynamics are what lead to a culture of sexual violence and to impunity for perpetrators. Violence toward and degradation of women, or others considered to not fit with dominant gender norms, are part of the military's purposeful development of violent masculinities. One immediate consequence of this culture is that women in the military are often subject to sexual assault[86] and that LGBTQ+ servicemembers experience discrimination, threats and intimidation, sexual harassment, and physical and sexual assault, even after the repeal of "Don't Ask, Don't Tell"—the policy that barred asking military personnel whether they were LGBTQ+, but prohibited "openly gay" personnel.[87]

The push for a "woke" military, seen in efforts of diversity and inclusion, celebration of "girlboss" missileers,[88] and promotion of women and people of color within the military and national security complexes,[89] does not address the patriarchal norms at the heart of militarism. Diversifying the empire doesn't undo it, it mostly just risks further legitimizing the institutions, practices, and policies that many seeking "gender equality" would arguably like to change.[90] As feminist scholar Cynthia Enloe says, "You can militarize anything, including equality."[91]

Within the US "national security" field, women have found themselves having to conform to the orthodoxy of thought within the field in order to be taken seriously.[92] Most women who do "make it" into these circles, who climb the ranks in militarized jobs, tend to embrace and uphold the normative framework of thought and practice rather than challenge it. As of January 2019, for example, the chief executive officers of four of the United States' biggest weapon-producing companies—Northrop Grumman, Lockheed Martin, General Dynamics, and the weapons wing of Boeing—were women.[93] These women are not challenging the patriarchal structures and systems that have created the militarized world order—they are actively maintaining it and profiting from it.

Liberal feminism is "dedicated to enabling a privileged few to climb the corporate ladder or the ranks of the military," through which it "subscribes to a market-centred view of equality that dovetails with corporate enthusiasm for 'diversity,'" write feminist scholars Nancy Fraser, Cinzia Arruzza, and Tithi Bhattacharya.[94] Rather than abolish social hierarchy, liberal feminism "aims to feminize it, ensuring women at the top can attain parity with the men of their own class."

The same is true for military "pinkwashing"—the efforts of the US (and Israeli) militaries to portray themselves as friendly to LGBTQ+

servicemembers. Military personnel march in Pride parades, while recruiters design advertisements meant to lure LGBTQ+ people toward a career in the military. Activist Dean Spade describes this as a makeover for "the most violent and harmful institutions in our society," in which they are now being "cast as sites of liberation and inclusion for gay and lesbian people."[95] If diversifying institutions led to their fundamental change, that would be one thing. But if the institution itself is at its core about violence, domination, and death, adding people of different genders, sexual orientations, or skin color is not sufficient in itself to change them. This is true of the military just as it is of police. "I have very little faith that winning legal changes toward inclusion and recognition results in material changes for those facing the worst conditions of maldistribution and violence," argues Spade. "I do, however, observe that winning inclusion 'victories' provides a makeover for dominant systems and bolsters narratives that we are in a 'postracial' or otherwise equal society."[96]

Structural racism

It's clear from the descriptions of all the structures of violence explored in this book that we are definitely not in a "post-racial" society, and that the process of othering and dehumanization is not only gendered. As discussed in chapters 1, 2, and 4, white supremacy manifests in structural racism that targets Black, Indigenous, Latinx, Arab, Asian, and other racialized communities for violence, oppression, and exclusion. From the origins of policing to mass incarceration and migrant detention to criminalization of queer people, poor people, and people of color, racism is endemic to institutions of the US war at home, as it is with US war abroad.

US military bases from Japan to Djibouti have resulted in extensive sexual and gender-based violence against local populations, including by establishing and entrenching racialized structures of forced prostitution and trafficking. The US military's use of napalm in Viet Nam, depleted uranium in Iraq, cluster bombs in Laos, drone strikes in Afghanistan, as well as all the bullets and bombs it has deployed across the world, have left a long trail of lasting, grave, and incredibly discriminatory suffering and environmental degradation that will scar the planet in perpetuity.

War at home and abroad both require the generation of fear of "the other"—fear of categories of people based on race, religion, immigration status, or another marker. Racist fearmongering is necessary to normalize violence against people, to foment support for military action or immigration raids or police crackdowns. "Once a people become a 'calamity,'" notes Ta-Nehisi Coates, "all means of dealing with them are acceptable."[97]

Structural fascism

The fates of these "calamities" at home and abroad are intimately linked. Violence against people in other countries helps embolden discriminatory violence and human rights violations of non-US citizens at home. The US Department of Homeland Security (DHS) agencies responsible for abuses at migrant detention centers, for example—including Customs and Border Protection (CBP) and Immigration and Customs Enforcement (ICE)—have not just been allowed, but encouraged, to oppress and even kill.

DHS was created in the wake of 9/11—though plans for it were drawn up earlier. It comprises "the largest law-enforcement body in the country, with the biggest budget and the fewest mechanisms of public oversight and accountability."[98] This has led to unconstitutional raids, in-custody deaths, and widespread abuse. In a 2018 article for the Intercept, journalist John Washington describes the culture of abuse inherent to these agencies through accounts of whistleblowers and those who have suffered their wrath.[99] In addition to humiliating, degrading, and enacting violence upon the bodies of migrants directly, these officials also have a habit of destroying any lifesaving mechanisms deployed by humanitarian activists.[100] Documentarians embedded with ICE even found that the agency "evaluated the success of its border policies based not only on the number of migrants apprehended, but on the number who died while crossing."[101]

The agencies of the DHS have always been used to exert fascist power—the department has been a "Trojan Horse for state-sponsored violence since the day it was written into existence," argues Elie Mystal at *The Nation*. "It's just that, up until now, brown people have borne the brunt of the violence."[102] Under the Trump administration, these agencies were weaponized against everyone. But the potential for abuse at the scale we saw in 2020 was there from the beginning, "baked into these federal agencies and the systems that allow them to operate with impunity," notes journalist Tina Vasquez.[103]

Not surprisingly, DHS has also targeted activists working to protect human rights. A 2019 report from Amnesty International documented how DHS engaged in a sweeping, multiyear campaign targeting human rights defenders, attorneys, and journalists working on the border.[104] In early August 2020, US Border Patrol raided No More Deaths' humanitarian aid station, detaining over thirty people who were receiving medical care, food, water, and shelter from the scorching heat.[105]

More broadly, resistance to the US war machine is increasingly being criminalized, from resistance to US occupation and invasion abroad to resistance to white supremacy and institutionalized violence at home. From Water Protectors to the Movement for Black Lives to Abolish ICE and Free Them All campaigners, those opposing state power have been monitored, surveilled, shot at, and now, disappeared into unmarked vans by unidentified "law enforcement officers."

The increasingly visible violence against protestors, activists, and journalists feels like a warning, perhaps even a foreshadowing of things to come. It is not difficult for one's mind to wander to the US "black sites" and military bases used as detention centers around the world, where those who challenge US violence are disappeared, detained, tortured, murdered.

The local and the global of racialized war

Indeed, the policies and practices of surveilling, criminalizing, incarcerating, and, in many instances, killing people in the US based on the color of their skin, religion, or sexual orientation are like those applied in US wars abroad. There are also direct connections between the wars "at home" and "abroad," making many military and police actions inseparable. The "war on drugs," the "war on migration," and the "war on terror" each have domestic and international aspects.

Military interventions in Latin America to ostensibly stop the supply of drugs (or, in some cases, facilitate it) are directly related to the policing and incarceration of communities of color for drug-related offenses in the United States. The "Global War on Terror," meant to bring hellfire to the Middle East, also brings brutality to the United States' Arab and Muslim populations—and many others whose skin color is such that they get caught up in the backlash. As for the war on migration: US wars and sales of weapons, the US military's disproportionate contributions to climate chaos, and the US neoliberal economic agenda violently imposed abroad have all contributed to unprecedented levels of displacement around the world. And if those migrants attempt to reach US shores, surviving deserts, jungles, sexual violence, and kidnapping, they are most likely imprisoned, degraded, and deported by the US government.

A coalition of US-based peace and justice organizations that have put forward a grassroots policy agenda for abolishing the "Global War on Terror" have traced the clear interconnections among criminalization structures in the United States, showing how the entanglement of border controls and immigration "enforcement" structures comingle with the country's national security and war-making structures. The groups point out how structural Islamophobia and the dehumanization of Muslims (and anyone perceived as Muslim) are built upon broader structures of anti-Black racism, white supremacy, settler colonialism, and imperialism. They also recognize how these structures, sustained through the carceral system in the United States, paved the way to the war on terror and how the war itself is now "being deployed to expand the carceral and police state domestically and globally."[106]

The connections between labor and these militarized industries are also interesting to reflect upon. For example, veterans of US wars make up about one-third of Border Patrol agents.[107] Migrant workers are frequently hired by private military companies as cooks, cleaners, and construction workers—for example, by Halliburton in Iraq.[108] Just as the major US weapons contractors are also engaged in building border walls, as described in chapter 4, private military security companies are entangled in multiple sites of violence. They inflict or enable harm against racialized populations while also frequently hiring those populations to perform dangerous work at low wages or employing veterans of one war abroad to wage another war at home.

Successive US governments have maintained this reinforcing system of violence, through financial investments and by waging deadly warfare in dozens of countries, operating an archipelago of secretive black sites, torturing and sexually assaulting prisoners from Abu Ghraib to Guantánamo Bay, expanding immigration detention and deportation, and laying the basis for a strengthened military-security state that simultaneously creates imperialist displacement while criminalizing subjugated citizens and immigrants alike through imperial racist logics," as organizer Harsha Walia describes.[109] Each of these aspects of the war machine reinforces the others, always prioritizing the profits of the weapon makers and the incarcerators over the well-being of human lives and justifying this on the basis of "national security."

The casting of weapons, war, police, prisons, and borders as essential to security operates as what scholar Amira Jarmakani describes as a "technology of imperialism." Organizing the political economy of a state around the "anticipation of threat" requires "training resources away from basic needs (food, shelter, etc.) and toward the defense of industry (at all levels—from gated communities to the military)."[110] This both ensures that the war machine emerges as an engine of capitalist expansion and produces the conditions for perpetual war, while simultaneously displacing "the violence of neoliberal capitalism (dispossession) and imperialism (militarized defense) onto racialized others."[111]

US citizens (in particular, its white citizens) seem to be taught—through history textbooks, political speeches, television shows, and films—that war keeps them safe. That having more weapons than anyone else in the world is what ensures US sovereignty and hegemony. The military-industrial complex, lobbyists, the state, and everyone else profiteering from war invest heavily in fearmongering, constantly designing "others" for US citizens to fear in order to justify the vast expenditure on militarism and carcerality. US citizens are also largely taught that the United States is a force for good in the world—that it uses its weapons wisely, to protect and defend against despots and dictators. That it spreads democracy and decency. The reality, of course, is quite the opposite. To much of the world, the US government is a despot and dictator; it is what needs defending against. But throughout its history, particularly with the rise of the military-industrial complex in the post-World War II landscape, the United States has composed a narrative of "peace through war" and "justice through violence," a deceitfully composed Orwellian narrative that is written in the blood of all those who do or might stand in its way.

This doesn't mean the world isn't "dangerous" or that other governments don't engage in similar behavior. But the United States is pathological in its pursuit of peace through perpetual war and in its presentation of—and massive investments in—violence as the cure to all threats, whether real, perceived, or imagined. Landscaping the world as an endless pit filled with existing and potential enemies, the United States creates the world it fears—it manifests violence through its own militarism and its militarization of everything around it, including its relationships with enemies and allies, and its relationships with the people within its own borders, anyone who crosses those borders, and people on the other side of the world.

Predators, the panopticon, and the processing of human beings

All of this violence is about more than creating carnage and chaos from which its corporate investors and political backers profit. It is also about control. Through its investments in the culture and matériel of militarism, the US government has been actively building what Ian G. R. Shaw describes as a "Predator Empire"—a state that unabashedly pursues "full spectrum dominance" over the entire world through war-making, economic coercion, and persistent surveillance.[112]

The patriarchal propensity for total control of others, especially those it deems inferior, is brilliantly manifested in the concept of full spectrum dominance.[113] Patriarchy and racism underwrite the mainstream US conception of "national security," which is executed through transnational monitoring, policing, incarceration, sanction, and execution, asserting its authority regardless of geography or legality.

In this way, the United States—and other governments of military and economic power—are creating a world in which the majority of people are being seen and treated as objects to be categorized, controlled, confined, and, when deemed necessary, killed as disposable objects that are in the way of the profit-making of the elite, wealthy few. As this world further develops, more and more people will be pushed into this category of "surplus population," marked for incarceration or death.

Objectifying and processing the "surplus population"

This processing of people doesn't just segregate and hierarchize people, it also suggests that some people inherently pose a "threat" to state security because of their race, location, or other identifying factor. As Harsha Walia writes, "The social control and criminalization that delineates the carceral network and disappears undesirables is the frequently invisible yet entrenched racist colonial belief that incarceration is a legitimate response to communities that are constructed and characterized *innately* as being illegals, deviants, criminals, terrorists, or threats."[114]

As noted in chapter 1, this concept of "inherent criminality"—that risk resides within people—is problematic and damaging. Criminality, risk, or threat is not a state of being. Categorizing people as such is done by the most privileged in our societies, by those who have something to lose materially from equality and peace. Yet it is used as a justification for both mass incarceration and extrajudicial killing. It has led the US military to develop policies and practices for "hunting" individual people designated "terrorists," with the entire globe as its hunting ground. Shaw describes how many domestic policing strategies are used by the United States in what has become "preemptive planetary policing," through which individuals are targeted on the basis of what they could potentially become. In this way, the US state seeks to "protect" or "immunize" itself "against not only actualized forms of danger, then, but also potential threats, those patterns of life that *may* become threats in the future."[115]

Weaponizing against "inherent criminality"

Through this process, state-sanctioned violence becomes infused with moral language. Think of the terminology used by representatives of nuclear-armed states or within mainstream "national security" discourses, which bear the mark of moral righteousness when it comes to justifying violence, militarism, and weaponization to "protect the homeland" or ensure "strategic stability." As scholar Elke Schwarz describes, this is about establishing a notion of "productive violence"—of violence that is "necessary" to secure life or liberty.[116] This framing of acts of political violence as "necessary technical acts" for security and survival perpetuates and normalizes the idea that security must be achieved through violence, and that this violence is facilitated best by weapons that are, as Schwarz describes, "rendered as inherently ethical."[117]

In reality, intersectional oppressions of people are amplified by the weaponization of technologies that are designed to process people as objects, to categorize and compartmentalize human beings and mark them for surveillance, incarceration, or death. The technologies deployed by this system include weapons and apparatus used by police, border patrols, and the military, as well as the equipment needed to cage and incarcerate. They also include the rising "panopticon" provided by technologies of surveillance, biometrics, facial recognition, predictive policing, precrime reporting, drones, and the development of autonomous weapon systems, as described in chapter 3.

Just as the carceral system is constructed as the solution to harm, as discussed in chapter 2, war and weapons are constructed as the solution to all threats—perceived, imagined, manufactured, or real. "Prison is simply a bad and ineffective way to address violence and crime," write abolitionists Mariame Kaba and Kelly Hayes. "Our failure to build a culture of care that nurtures human growth and potential, rather than incubating desperation, ensures that more 'criminals' will be created and subsequently punished, to the great benefit of those who profit from industries associated with incarceration."[118] Similarly, war is a bad way to address violence and "terrorism"—and the investment in the tools of more harm and oppression will only further "incubate desperation," leading not to peace and justice but more violence and more war—which, as with prisons, is to the great benefit of those who profit from related industries.

Abolishing the war machine

The breadth of the project of full spectrum dominance, the deep entanglement of war apparatus across so many US agencies and corporations, and the growth of war profiteering through new, more advanced technologies of violence require that opposition to war be more encompassing and inclusive than ever before. As we confront rising authoritarianism across the world, we must recognize its roots in US wars, occupations, and coups abroad, as well as in the carceral and anti-immigration policies and practices at home.

For centuries, those working against the power and profit of war in all its aspects have been called naïve, irrational, or irresponsible. Nevertheless, they persisted. While far from perfect in process or achievement, social movements for political and economic change—women's suffrage, civil rights, LGBTQ+ equality, debt cancellation, anti-war action—have advanced change inch by inch. Any progress in our world that we have seen has come from the relentless work of organizers, activists, and others who stand up for justice and equality.

As the COVID-19 pandemic wreaked further havoc on those suffering from war and armed conflict, as well as those who are impoverished, incarcerated, and criminalized, the stranglehold that militarism and its material realities have over US economics and politics may be finally shifting. Even while militarism remains deeply embedded in US culture and expenditure, more and more people are starting to ask, How could the government have been so unprepared for this crisis? Many are looking at where their tax dollars have been going: toward weapons, war, and militarized "security." They are asking, What else could this money have been spent on?

Activist groups have those numbers. The Global Campaign on Military Spending, for example, has shown that one F-35 Joint Strike Fighter aircraft could pay for 3,244 intensive care unit beds, or that one submarine could pay for over nine thousand fully equipped ambulances.[119] The International Campaign to Abolish Nuclear Weapons has shown that a year's worth of current investments in nuclear weapons in each country that has them could pay for hundreds of thousands of medical workers, ventilators, protective gear, and more.[120] These staggering numbers make it clear that we are a world prepared to fight wars, not pandemics—and for many, this moment has been a turning point in their thinking about our priorities.

A portal to a new world order

The time for reimagining—and establishing—a new world order is upon us. With war serving as both cause and consequence of our ugly baggage of patriarchy, racism, and capitalism, undoing the institutions, culture, and economics of war must be at the heart of our efforts.

In April 2020, Mikhail Gorbachev, former premier of the Soviet Union, called for an emergency special session of the UN General Assembly to revise the "entire global agenda," including by committing states to cut military spending by 10–15 percent.[121] Fifteen percent of the $1.9 trillion spent globally on militarism is $285 billion. While this could be a start, it must not be the end. Defunding and abolishing war must go beyond partial trimmings or half measures. Our work to spare future generations from the "scourge of war" the way the United Nations promised in 1945 must recognize the ways in which armed violence insidiously infects and destroys all human and planetary potential. It must move away from the traditional discourses of security and stability and the minor reforms that current mandates permit.

The harms caused by war are inflicted indifferently and devastatingly upon those who have the least to do with creating this system, including women, Indigenous groups, LGBTQ+ people, racialized and religious minorities, and the poor and disenfranchised. Such populations tend to have no or little role in shaping the discourse on military spending, let alone establishing the limits or creating the budgets. To ensure real rather than cosmetic change, we need to center in our work those whose lives have been harmed by the weaponization of our world. This means privileging an intersectional feminist practice and policy that exposes the dominant militaristic narrative as *a* perspective, not the only credible perspective, and dismantling systems that give advantage to the militarized voices in our midst.

Dismantle, change, build

The connections between military spending, human rights, and the health of people and planet have never been clearer. We are what we spend our money on. Right now, we are armed to our teeth without a ventilator to spare. If we are to survive this crisis, and the next one—crises of our own making because of our choices in investment in militarism, fossil fuels, and the capitalist economy—we absolutely must learn and adapt. In this case, adaptation means divestment, demilitarization, and disarmament. This is entirely possible, if we choose to act now. Among other things, we should:

End participation in current wars and end the war on terror, dismantle foreign military bases and black sites, stop the deployment of special forces in hundreds of countries, eliminate nuclear weapons, stop the use of explosive weapons in populated areas, prohibit autonomous weapons, and cut the military.

End policies and practices related to full spectrum dominance, including extrajudicial killing and drone strikes, and ban the development and use of technologies of control, coercion, and violence including carceral technologies like surveillance apparatus, facial recognition, and predictive policing, as well as drones, hypersonic missiles, and autonomous weapons.

Redirect military spending—and other related spending identified above—toward education, housing, food security, healthcare, social services, environmental protection, and renewable energy.

Divest—as individuals, financial institutions, city councils, governments—from weapon producers, companies that develop or produce carceral technologies, and other aspects of the war machine.

Outlaw the privatization of military production and the influence of corporate interest over national policies that perpetuate war, undermine disarmament, and preclude a rational analysis of spending priorities.

End the international arms trade, starting by stopping arms transfers and "military aid" to countries violating international law, committing war crimes, or engaged in occupation and oppression. Establish an international system that deals directly with the production of weapons, as well as their sale, trade, and trafficking, and with war profiteering. While we have an international Arms Trade Treaty, it is not living up to its promise or potential to prevent human suffering. We need an international program for general and complete disarmament, building on the prohibitions, divestments, and elimination of specific weapon systems that we already have, taking the economic and political incentives out of arms manufacturing, and ensuring the reduction of global military spending.

Challenge the culture of militarism and its embeddedness in patriarchy and gendered norms of violent masculinity, including through the entertainment industry such as films, television, and video games.

Throughout all these efforts for disarmament, divestment, and demilitarization, we should pursue and promote principles of promiscuous care, nonviolent and degrowth political economies, decolonization, and solidarity, as outlined below in chapter 7.

This is not a comprehensive list, but rather the beginnings of what we can imagine, together, for a world without war. As one of Critical Resistance's slogans says, we need to "Dismantle, Change, Build." Opposing war means embracing peace; to move from one system to another we must invest in ourselves and each other, and in the belief that what we live with now is not our only possible world. Part of this process must involve eliminating the most violent technology yet created: the nuclear weapons. The bomb is embedded in our imaginations much the same way that police, prisons, and borders are: it is seen by many as a "necessary evil," as something that "keeps us safe." But this, too, is a failure of imagination. And it is deadly one, because nuclear weapons can, in a single moment, destroy entire cities, countries, regions, or the world. Eliminating nuclear weapons is imperative not just for our survival, however, but also for uncaging our minds from the reliance on violence to save us.

Chapter 6

██

Decommissioning Nuclear Weapons

J ust over seventy-five years ago, the United States detonated the first-ever nuclear weapon in a New Mexico desert, Jornada del Muerto, or Journey of the Dead. The test marked the culmination of years of secretive work to develop an atomic bomb, a collaborative project of scientists and government officials in the United States, United Kingdom, and Canada. On July 16, 1945, the light, heat, and shock wave of the Trinity test blast could be seen and felt for miles. J. Robert Oppenheimer, one of the lead designers of the bomb, later remarked that it brought to mind words from the Bhagavad Gita: "Now I am become Death, the destroyer of worlds."[1]

Three weeks after this test, the US government dropped two atomic bombs on Japanese cities: one on Hiroshima, the other on Nagasaki. These two detonations unleashed hell on earth for those within both cities, incinerating hundreds of thousands of people along with plants, animals, and buildings. The heat and fire from the blasts melted objects and turned living beings into shadows. The burns and the radiation poisoning killed many more in the days, months, and years after the bombings.

As testimony from the survivors, the *hibakusha*, tells us, the terror of the bombs impacted forever the lives of those who survived.[2]

For seventy-five years, the world has lived under the threat of radioactive blast and firestorm, the effects of which are immediately devastating and punishingly intergenerational.[3] For seventy-five years, from production to testing to use to storage of radioactive waste, nuclear weapon activities have contaminated land and water—and will continue to do so for thousands of years to come. For seventy-five years, some of our governments have spent billions of dollars building and deploying these weapons of terror, putting all of our lives at risk and stealing much-needed money from the things we need to be safe and secure.

Those who possess or desire nuclear weapons argue that the mere possession of the bomb prevents conflict and deters attack. They insist on talking about nuclear weapons in the abstract, as magical tools that keep us safe and maintain stability in the world. But nuclear weapons are not abstract. They are made of radioactive materials. They are made to destroy flesh and bone. They are designed to turn human beings into shadows. To melt the skin from our bodies. To reduce entire cities to ashes.

Nuclear weapons are arguably the most extreme expression of violence and control of the patriarchal, racist, and capitalist world order. To most people struggling daily under this oppressive order, the abolition of nuclear weapons may not seem like a priority. When faced with the grinding unemployment, chronic poverty and food insecurity, displacement, climate catastrophes, war and occupation, violence of settler colonialism, racist police brutality, mass incarceration, border imperialism, and violence in our homes and communities, nuclear weapons may seem like an abstraction. But these weapons are part of the spectrum of institutionalized violence. Even without being launched, they are used to project the power and invincibility of their possessor. They are the pinnacle of a state's monopoly on violence, which has been described in some of its other forms in earlier chapters. The bomb is the ultimate signifier of domination, irrevocably tying national violence to the possibility of human extinction.[4]

Yet, there is hope. The movement for the abolition of nuclear weapons has persisted for these same seventy-five years. While it has undergone ebbs and flows of its numbers and reach, the antinuclear movement is as alive now as it ever was. It is alive in the efforts of activists and diplomats to ban the bomb at the United Nations; it is alive in work undertaken in cities and parliaments and financial institutions to stigmatize and divest from nuclear weapons and demand their elimination; it is alive in the testimony of the *hibakusha*, in the music and art of those who have survived, and in the eagerness of younger generations to take up the work.

But the hope for nuclear abolition lies more broadly in the efforts of all social justice organizers. Everyone demanding disarmament and abolition of police forces; everyone calling for a redirection of military spending toward collective care; everyone envisioning a more equitable, just, and peaceful world order—all their efforts are collaborative with the efforts for nuclear abolition. Whether deliberate or not, our work for peace, social and economic justice, decolonization, and environmental protection is entangled. Our fates are woven together: the world we seek to build—a world of solidarity, health, and well-being across peoples and our shared planet—is not compatible with a world in which nuclear weapons and the other technologies of violence are stockpiled in the arsenals of hate built and viciously safeguarded by our so-called leaders. There is not an order in which things must be dismantled or eliminated or changed; there is no set playbook we can follow. But the systems of hate and hierarchy, and the structures of violence through which they manifest and solidify their control over our lives, they will all be torn down—including the nuclear bomb.

Nuclearism and its profiteers

As of mid-2021, there are an estimated 13,150 nuclear weapons in the world.[5] Over 90 percent of these belong to Russia and the United States. The rest are in the arsenals of China, Democratic People's Republic of Korea (North Korea), France, India, Israel, Pakistan, and the United Kingdom.

This number is much smaller than at the height of the Cold War. In the 1980s, peak global nuclear arsenal reached around 70,300 weapons. But the drawdown since then has not resulted in elimination. In fact, investments in nuclear weapons are reaching some of their highest levels. In 2020, the nine nuclear-armed states spent nearly $72.6 billion on their nuclear weapon systems.[6] This comes to $137,666 spent on nuclear weapons *per minute*. Each of the nuclear-armed states is currently investing not just in the maintenance but also the "modernization"—the upgrading, updating, and life-extending—of nuclear weapons.[7]

Who is profiting from all this? Corporations. It is private companies like Lockheed Martin, Boeing, and Bechtel that build nuclear weapons and their delivery systems and manage nuclear weapon laboratories. Most of these companies also produce other goods and are open to public investment. Right now, over three hundred financial institutions from around the world are investing hundreds of billions of dollars into the companies that generate and sustain nuclear arsenals.[8]

In addition, certain academics, politicians, and bureaucrats have risen through the ranks of think tanks or government administrations in positions bankrolled by the nuclear profiteers, spinning theories of "nuclear deterrence" and "strategic stability" to justify this massive, unconscionable investment in technologies of massive violence.

For the past seventy-five years, the people who benefit institutionally and financially from nuclear weapons have told the rest of us that the bomb is absolutely necessary for (a select few) governments to possess. Eliminating nuclear weapons, they argue, will lead directly to another global conflict (as if the globe is not embroiled, right now, in conflicts of mass slaughter and destruction), or to "nuclear blackmail," or to whatever other perceived threat they can conjure. US officials justified their use of nuclear weapons against Japan as "necessary" to end World War II—though as an ever-growing mountain of literature reveals, this was not the case.[9] Since then, the primary justification for nuclear weapons has been that they *prevent* war. This, too, has been proven fallacious. Countless conflicts between nuclear-armed states, even if not fought on their own territories in a traditional land war, coupled with the acquisition of nuclear weapons by additional states and the hundreds of incidents of near-use of nuclear weapons, have shown that as deterrents, nuclear weapons do not live up to the hype.[10]

But it's interesting how a weapon designed for use in conflict has since taken on the mythology of a weapon meant never to be used. A weapon by its very nature is meant to be used. Weapons are tools of violence, the very purpose of which are to kill, injure, and destroy. Yet the dogma of "nuclear deterrence" has been so engrained in politics and popular culture alike that many people have been trained to believe that this weapon will never be used. *Nuclear weapons are not the droids you're looking for.*

Of course, nuclear weapons are used, every day, in an exercise of power. They have been used thousands of times through nuclear weapon tests. They are deployed and targeted every second of the day. And they have cost the world billions of dollars in their development, testing, use, deployment, maintenance, and modernization—and will cost billions more if not abolished. But the theory of deterrence insists that all of this is necessary to ensure national, and even global, security.

This is what Robert J. Lifton and Richard Falk describe as nuclearism: "a political and psychological dependence on nuclear weapons to provide an impossible security."[11] Nuclearism is an epic feat of gaslighting that insists weapons capable of killing everyone on the planet many times over are the only things keeping us safe.

As theory and myth, nuclear deterrence has likely been so successful because it provides a solution to the problem of what to do with nuclear weapons. Economies and careers are bound up in sustaining a rationale for the maintenance of nuclear weapons. These weapons are catastrophic to use, so their existence needs to be justified. In short, "deterrence" provides an easy answer to an impossible question—that is, how can the money and privilege and prestige they offer and entail and supply and absorb be justified? One way to justify nuclear weapons is to create a theory that we need them in order to never use them. That we need them to prevent war. That by reinvesting in them regularly, making new kinds, building more facilities—we are ensuring security, stability, and safety for all.

To sell an object that the public knows is catastrophic—a public that lived in fear of nuclear war and radioactive fallout for decades—is no small feat. Constructing the idea that they exist to not be used was a deliberate answer to this problem: possessing these weapons was portrayed as the best way to ensure that people would never have to experience the use of these weapons. Nuclear war was presented in language dripping with Orwellian doublespeak, simultaneously described as something that could never happen and "as phantasmagoria, a spectral fascination," to distract from the ongoing daily machinations of the US nuclear complex. "The constant end game articulation of nuclear discourse has," researcher Joseph Masco argues, "enabled two of the most profound cultural achievements of the nuclear age: the near erasure of the nuclear economy from public view, and the banalization of the U.S. nuclear weapons in everyday American life."[12]

Through a process of what Joseph Masco describes as "radioactive nation-building," so much US technology and infrastructure originated in the Manhattan Project and the extended nuclear complex built throughout the Cold War, including roads, emergency evacuation plans, power stations, and much more.[13] The nuclear complex itself has hundreds of sites around the country, from uranium mines to fuel fabrication plants, bomb construction and dismantling facilities, nuclear reactors, radioactive waste storge sites, and more.

The process of radioactive nation-building is not just toxic in and of itself—its contaminating effect is reflected in the construction of toxic politics of race and class in the United States. "We can see in the logistics of the nuclear complex not only a peculiar evaluation of risk and security in the name of an imagined national culture, but also a powerful display of the state's evaluation of citizenship."[14] The US nuclear weapon complex has dug into, blown up, poisoned, and otherwise destroyed Indigenous land across the country. The Los Alamos National Laboratory in New Mexico, where the first nuclear bombs were constructed, was built on a sacred Tewa Pueblo mesa; the damage to Native land expanded from there, as is further explored below. The atomic age, notes The Red Nation, was "made possible by settler colonialism and Indigenous genocide."[15]

In this same vein, radioactive nation-building also helped orient the United States toward a political economy of war and violence. The Cold War rivalry with the Soviet nuclear arsenal "created the image of an ever-present threat, a condition that facilitated the orientation toward national security as the dominant paradigm, both domestically and internationally," explains scholar Amira Jarmakani.[16] The nuclear arms race and the "ruse of imminent foreign threat" also helped conceal the social impact of neoliberal economic policies, in particular the shifting of public resources from social services to the military- and prison industrial complexes, as described in earlier chapters. "Under the guise of privatization, personal responsibility, and national security, the defense industry replaced people as the recipients of social welfare."[17]

This social welfare also included the use of underpaid migrant workers and African Americans to construct nuclear facilities, working on contaminated ground without proper safety equipment or training, or even knowledge of the risks. Inside the plant, women were often assigned the most dangerous work, again without information about the materials they were handling or what to do in case of accidents. Corporate contractors "privatized the tremendous profits from nuclear weapon production while socializing the risks to health and environment," historian Kate Brown reveals in her research on plutonium plants in the United States and Soviet Union.[18]

Another element of the radioactive nation-building process was making nuclear weapons themselves as invisible as possible. This was facilitated by the switch from aboveground to underground nuclear testing, which helped the bomb become "a philosophical project increasingly linked not to mass destruction or war but to complexity, safety, and deterrence within the laboratory, allowing new generations of scientists increasingly to invest in nuclear weapons as a patriotic intellectual enterprise to produce machines that could only prevent conflict."[19] The bomb ceased to be a bomb; it became a "security technology," thought about and dealt with almost exclusively by those with appropriate "expertise."

The removal of nuclear explosions from the public eye helped move nuclear weapons from a subject of national debate into the hands of select scientists and military personnel. This helped achieve a cultural and social normalization of the bomb of "living in a world where the everyday has been so thoroughly colonized by the possibility of annihilation that, for most, it has become simply banal."[20] This is reflected in the abstract, "technostrategic" ways in which "defense intellectuals" talk about nuclear weapons and plan for nuclear war, which is discussed later in this chapter.[21]

This element of radioactive nation-building—the abstraction of the atomic bomb and the constant potential for annihilation—has arguably helped enable or facilitate the normalization of other harms the state inflicts upon people, such as steadily increasing surveillance, encroachment upon human rights and civil liberties, the devastation to water, land, and climate through resource extraction and armed conflict. It has also helped numb people to the fact that the country's entire political economy came to center on the nuclear weapon complex. Not just financially, but also culturally, in terms of the propensity for extreme violence as the norm rather than the exception, particularly in reaction to any perceived or real international or national "threat" or experience of harm. Through the institutionalization of nuclear weapons, the violence of the Second World War became the norm. While presenting World War II as the "war to end all wars," the United States instead invested economically, politically, and socially to ensure that perpetual war, coupled with the persistent possibility of destroying the planet, became its leitmotif.

"Weapons, to be sure, are things," wrote Edward (E. P.) Thompson during the Cold War. "Their increment is not independent of political decisions. But politics itself may be militarized: and decisions about weaponry now impose the political choices of tomorrow. Weapons, it turns out, are political agents also."[22]

Fetishizing the bomb

While nuclear weapons were being deliberately normalized for the US public, they were also being increasingly fetishized by the US elite. Over time, through relentless political and academic repetition, the value assigned to nuclear weapons as "deterrents" has come to be treated as intrinsic to the weapon itself. They have become what Marx would describe as "fetish objects." They are the physical embodiment of power, argues scholar Anne Harrington de Santana, similar to how money is the physical embodiment of social value and wealth. "Just as access to wealth in the form of money determines an individual's opportunities and place in a social hierarchy, access to power in the form of nuclear weapons determines a state's opportunities and place in the international order," she writes. "In both cases, the physical form of the fetish object is valuable because it serves as a carrier of social value. In other words, the power of nuclear weapons is not reducible to their explosive capability. Nuclear weapons are powerful because we treat them as powerful."[23]

This fetishization occurs through a process. Nuclear deterrence is not an inherent quality of nuclear weapons. It is a concept that we ascribe to nuclear weapons. That is why it can be helpful, academic Nick Ritchie suggests, to look at and talk about nuclear weapons as "social objects"— objects that are embedded in a network of relationships, interests, and identities.[24]

Those of us listening to governments talk about nuclear weapons at the United Nations and other international spaces can see very clearly that nuclear weapons are social objects. It sometimes feels as if the diplomats representing nuclear-armed or other nuclear-supporting countries believe that if they say the same thing over and over again, they can make it true, even if the majority of other governments believe the opposite. The nuclear-armed assert that nuclear weapons make us safe, while nearly everyone else says they increase insecurity and put our whole world in peril.

Meanwhile, within the nuclear-armed states, academics and policymakers are churning out rhetoric and war planning that asserts nuclear deterrence as fact and nuclear weapons as the golden ticket to national security. Nuclear weapons themselves "don't provide material protection or security; indeed the weapons may make one more vulnerable and insecure," explains scholar Shampa Biswas. Yet they are "nevertheless considered indispensable, and in arms races induced by panics, they are accumulated in ever-increasing numbers to provide a magical sense of impossible omnipotence that can overcome the paralysis."[25]

Preserving "national security" through nuclear deterrence is the main purported motivation for acquiring, possessing, and brandishing nuclear weapons, but in reality the nuclear weapon fetish seems to have much more to do with questions of national identity than security. Images of prestige and political power, coupled with domestic political dynamics, play a significant role in embedding nuclear weapons in the politics, economics, and culture of certain countries.[26]

A decision to deploy and maintain nuclear weapons is generated by an idea of the state as an important player on the world stage and an idea of nuclear weapons as a crucial element of being such a player. In this context, nuclear weapons are assigned particular meanings that must be strengthened and sustained in order to maintain a country's identity. In short, the thinking goes, if we want to be an important world power, we must have nuclear weapons as a representation of our power and as a means of enabling us to act in the world. This kind of national sense of identity reinforces the purported legitimacy and necessity of continued nuclear possession. Nuclear weapons have become signs of national power; the "preeminent national fetish"[27] designated as not just the "ultimate arbiter of state security"[28] but also as "the one true sign of 'superpower' status."[29]

In addition, competition between states within the imperial order drives states to accumulate such weapons. That is the logic that compelled the US to develop them in the first place—to prove their capacity to incinerate their rivals, beginning with Japan at the end of World War II, and to demonstrate "superiority" over the Soviet Union, initiating the Cold War. This logic has driven other states to pursue the obscenity of "mutually assured destruction." The same logic is driving relations among several nuclear-armed countries today, including the United States, Russia, and China as well India and Pakistan. Big and small players feel compelled by geopolitical competition to acquire nuclear weapons; it is the most grotesque expression of the drive to war and conquest rooted in the capitalist system.

States with imperial ambitions and a sense of invulnerable power also use nuclear weapons to coerce other states on matters of international relations. These bombs are not "hidden away in silos and subs awaiting a dreaded day of possible use, but instead are one of many tools used by imperial states to maintain global inequalities between states and within states."[30] Interviewing British nuclear policy-makers for his research, for example, Nick Ritchie found that "the possession of nuclear weapons imbues a subtle political confidence and has a quiet, implicit, intangible effect on the political decisions of other states, not as a crude, overt means of exercising influence, but as a deeply embedded, unstated form of political authority."[31]

This authority is used, among other ways, to protect economic interests and advance capitalist accumulation. Ironically, this strategy has perhaps most overtly played out under the pretense of preventing other countries from acquiring weapons of mass destruction—e.g., the United States and United Kingdom, two nuclear-armed states, using the pretense of Iraq developing weapons of mass destruction to invade, occupy, and secure oil resources for themselves, at the expense of millions of lives. This case also provides a stunning example of a core element of the nuclear weapon provenance and legacy: that of white supremacy.

Nuclear imperialism and radioactive racism

The projection of political authority offered by the bomb is built on what so many structures of violence are built upon—a white supremacist world order. The former UN Special Rapporteur on toxics, Baskut Tuncak, described nuclear weapon testing as "one of the cruellest examples of environmental injustice" that has left in its wake a "harmful legacy of racism that surrounds this tragic chapter of humanity."[32]

The history of nuclear weapons is a history of colonialism. If we look at testing in the Pacific alone, a clear pattern emerges. Between 1946 and 1996, France, the United Kingdom, and the United States tested over 315 nuclear weapons on largely remote, rural, and First Nations communities across the Pacific. These tests contaminated vast areas in the Marshall Islands (Bikini and Enewetak Atolls), Australia (Montebello, Emu Field, and Maralinga), French Polynesia (Moruroa and Fangataufa), and the Pacific islands of Kiritimati (Christmas Island), Malden Island, and Johnson Atoll (Kalama). As Nic Maclellan explains, "The deserts and islands of Australia and the Pacific were perceived as vast, 'empty' spaces." The choices of location for nuclear tests "promoted a 'nuclear racism' against Pacific Islanders, based on a racialized hierarchy of 'civilized' and 'primitive' peoples."[33]

This attitude extended beyond the Pacific. During this same period, the United States also dropped more than eight hundred nuclear bombs at the Nevada Test Site, which is located in the traditional land-use area of the Western Shoshone and Southern Paiute. The Western Shoshone are known as "the most bombed nation on earth."[34] The US government also detonated nuclear devices near the Aleutian island of Amchitka in southwest Alaska; Rulison and Rio Blanco, Colorado; Hattiesburg, Mississippi; and Alamogordo and Farmington, New Mexico.[35]

Meanwhile, the Soviet Union conducted about 715 tests, mostly at the Semipalatinsk Test Site in Kazakhstan. The United Kingdom conducted 45 tests in Australia on Indigenous territory, as well as in the Pacific and at the Nevada Test Site in the United States. France conducted 17 tests in Algeria and 193 tests in French Polynesia. China conducted 45 tests at the Lop Nor test site in Xinjiang. India conducted 6 tests at Pokhran, and Pakistan 6 at Ros Koh Hills and the Chagai District.

The common element throughout most nuclear testing, especially that done abroad, is the impact it had on the people living in those locations. "Governments and colonial forces exploded nuclear bombs on our sacred lands—upon which we depend for our lives and livelihoods, and which contain places of critical cultural and spiritual significance—believing they were worthless," said thirty-five Indigenous groups in a statement to the negotiations of the nuclear weapon ban treaty at the United Nations in July 2017. Delivered by Karina Lester, a Yankunytjatjara-Anangu woman from South Australia, the statement pointed out that Indigenous people "were never asked for, and we never gave, permission to poison our soil, food, rivers and oceans."[36]

The nuclear-armed states not only did not ask permission, in most cases they didn't even inform the people living in testing and fallout zones about the dangers of the detonations. Nor have they provided adequate (or in most cases, any) compensation, assistance, or remediation. In most cases they even failed to assess the damage to those living through the disaster, choosing instead to disseminate partial information or misinformation to evade accountability. For example, the key reference guide for radiation exposure is not adequate for measuring possible exposure among many populations. Throughout the nuclear age, radiation exposure has been measured based on the people primarily developing and testing nuclear weapons: adult white men. Nuclear regulators, including the International Commission on Radiological Protection, use what is called "Reference Man" to evaluate exposure. This model is based on adult white men—officially, "between 20 to 30 years of age, weighing 70 kg, is 170 cm in height, and lives in a climate with an average temperature of from 10°C to 20°C. He is a Caucasian and is a Western European or North American in habitat and custom."[37]

Due to differences in diet, activities, and housing, the radiation exposure of Native Americans is not well represented in the Department of Energy dose reconstructions. It leaves out exposure to radioactive iodine from eating small game, while exposures from drinking milk and eating vegetables have not yet been properly estimated for these communities.[38] Similarly, the references don't work for women and girls. Mary Olson, who leads the Gender and Radiation Impact Project, has found that sex and age are "potent factors influencing the outcome of radiation exposure."[39] Studies on women's health in the aftermath of the Hiroshima and Nagasaki bombings, nuclear testing in the Marshall Islands and in Kazakhstan, and the Chernobyl and Fukushima nuclear power disasters provide useful but incomplete analyses of ways in which women are uniquely impacted by radioactive violence. In particular, high rates of stillbirths, miscarriages, congenital birth defects, and reproductive issues (such as changes in menstrual cycles and the subsequent inability to conceive) have been recorded. A possible link between breast cancer in young women and women who were lactating at the time of exposure to nuclear radiation has also been found.[40]

In 2012, Calin Georgescu, the UN special rapporteur on toxics, visited the Marshall Islands to assess the impact on human rights of the nuclear testing conducted by the United States from 1946 to 1958. He found that the full effects of radiation on Marshallese women might have been underestimated. Among other factors, the bathing and eating habits of women potentially played a role in their higher rates of contamination.[41] Nuclear weapon testing and production has also had disproportionate impacts on Indigenous nations in the United States. The Diné/Navajo Nation saw cancer rates double from the 1970s to the 1990s due to nuclear weapon testing as well as uranium mining and milling in the southwestern US. Abandoned uranium mines in the region continue to pollute water supplies.[42] Uranium mining on Lakota lands in South Dakota is believed to have contributed to high levels of sterility, miscarriages, cancer, and other diseases on the Pine Ridge Reservation. Radioactive waste from the Sequoyah Fuels Nuclear Plant in Gore, Oklahoma, was spread on Cherokee lands. The list goes on.[43]

Other nuclear-armed states have treated nationals of their nuclear landscapes the same way. A recent study of declassified government documents by researchers at Princeton University's Program on Science and Global Security, the environmental justice research collective INTERPRT, and the investigative media Disclose revealed that the French government vastly "underestimated" the number of people exposed to the fallout from its tests in French Polynesia.[44] The study finds that over 110,000 people, almost the entire Polynesian population at the time, were exposed to significant amounts of ionizing radiation that would allow them today to seek compensation from the French government. This is ten times greater than the ten thousand people the French government has officially recognized as being significantly affected.[45] Further, French authorities concealed not only the number of those affected, but also the true impact of the nuclear tests on the health of Polynesians and the environment for more than fifty years. It also continues to severely restrict impacted persons' access to compensation, the process for which "has become equivalent to an unscalable wall," argue the investigators behind the

Moruroa Files. "The rejected applicants have no means of knowing why they were turned down, because the compensation committee provides no justification for its decisions, which are not made public."[46]

This is but one example. Each nuclear test has a similar story of devastation and deceit, a staggering lack of accountability for or even admission of the grave and persistent harms caused by nuclear weapon testing. The harms have lasted for generations, irradiating land and oceans, and scarring the bodies and minds of survivors and all who have come after. The secrecy of the nuclear age is matched only by the arrogance of its progenitors and patrons. "My belly is a crater empty of stories and answers," says poet Kathy Jetñil-Kijiner as she stands on top of the Runit Dome, the concrete structure housing radioactive waste from US nuclear testing in the Marshall Islands. "Only questions, hard as concrete. Who gave them this power? Who anointed them with the power to burn?"[47]

Resistance against radioactive racism

Despite all this suffering, those who have been subjected to nuclear testing and to the harms of nuclear weapon development have not been silent victims. Far from it. Almost immediately after the tests in the Marshall Islands, for example, Islanders were voicing concerns about their relocation and the effects of the testing. In 1954, after the devastation of the US government's Castle Bravo test that resulted in mass contamination, they presented a petition to the United Nations Trusteeship Council calling for the cessation of all nuclear tests on the islands. Since then, the country's advocacy has continued in a range of forms, including petitions, court cases, and lobbying through regional and international forums.

Reports of fallout across the Pacific led to some of the most sustained protests against nuclear testing in the world, particularly in the early 1970s when the French were still conducting atmospheric nuclear tests. Australia, New Zealand, and Fiji took a case to the International Court of Justice in 1973 and 74 to force France to end atmospheric testing.[48] Many Pacific nations created sanctions against French products and French airlines, which were picked up around the world. Algerians have also taken action against the French government for its testing there, with a major human rights organization in Algeria contacting the UN Human Rights Council in 2017 requesting it look into France's conduct of seventeen nuclear tests in the Algerian desert.[49]

African Americans organizing against nuclear weapons in the United States have frequently connected their work to both anti-racism initiatives at home and anti-colonial initiatives abroad. Coretta Scott King, Dr. Martin Luther King Jr., W.E.B. Du Bois, and other civil rights leaders elaborated on the inseparability of nuclear disarmament and the end of colonial empires. Bayard Rustin traveled to Algeria to help organize protests against French nuclear testing there with the US civil rights movement. "Black leftists held firm in their belief that the atomic bombings of Hiroshima and Nagasaki were inextricably linked to colonialism and racial equality," writes Vincent Intondi in his study of Black antinuclear activism.[50] They saw that colonialism, institutionalized racism, and segregation "each grew from the same seed and represented a form of violence," as Jacqueline Castledine noted.[51]

Indigenous activists in the United States have argued the same. "Colonization isn't just the theft and assimilation of our lands and people, today we're fighting against nuclear colonialism which is the theft of our future," remarked Leona Morgan of the Diné/Navajo Nation.[52] The Western Shoshone Nation, which has long protested the bombing of its lands at the Nevada Test Site, today continues its resistance against nuclear colonialism by fighting off a nuclear waste disposal site commissioned for Yucca Mountain in southwestern Nevada.[53] Indigenous activists have also commented on the connection between the struggles of Water Protectors fighting the construction of pipelines and those fighting to keep uranium in the ground.[54]

Persistent racism in nuclear weapon policy

The protests and legal actions taken by survivors of aggressive nuclear weapon activities by the colonial powers persist today. But so does the racist, colonial nuclear world order. It is one of the dominant paradigms present in discourses and practices around nonproliferation and nuclear disarmament today. Anthropologist Hugh Gusterson has well-documented the "nuclear Orientalism" commentary of Western governments and media about their racialized anxieties around "irrational" governments acquiring nuclear weapons.[55] This discourse continues to prevail in international diplomacy and national fearmongering.

The fact that some governments of the Global South or of non-Western countries possess nuclear weapons does not undermine these points. The value accorded to nuclear weapons by their possessors, described earlier, makes them desirable objects, situating nuclear weapons as objects of "white power." The driving force of nuclear weapon acquisition is the capitalist compulsion for states to compete for supremacy in the world system, regardless of the geography or racial composition of the state involved. The Indian government, for example, has argued that its acquisition of nuclear weapons proved equality with the "white nations" possessing the bomb and a rejection of racist, colonial nonproliferation efforts. But these weapons, as Arundhati Roy says, are "the ultimate colonizer."[56] Possession of nuclear weapons is not a postcolonial achievement of equity, but of a new form of subjugation—this time to the bomb. Those that buy into the idea that nuclear weapons provide security are perpetuating norms of violent power. They are deciding to take money away from the well-being of their populations to devote to the development of objects of obscene destruction. This is not independence; this is submission to constructs borne of white supremacy.

The racist underpinnings of nuclear policies extend not just to preventing proliferation of nuclear weapons to "non-white" countries but also to dismissing the legitimacy of their demands for nuclear abolition. During the recent process at the United Nations to ban nuclear weapons, for example, where diplomats primarily from the Global South together with those of a few European countries led the way,[57] the nuclear-armed states and their nuclear-supportive allies were quick to argue that these pro-ban countries had no relevant security interests that would entitle them to speak out on this subject.[58]

Thus, at the same time as the nuclear "powers" rode roughshod over the security interests of the inhabitants of the countries and Indigenous nations they bombed, leaving contamination of land, water, bodies, and politics for generations to come, they claim in international discussions that these same people had no grounds upon which to speak on the subject of nuclear weapons. This blatantly racist approach to nuclear weapon policy and practice has everything to do with colonial power and nothing to do with the lived reality of people around the world.

Patriarchy and the bomb

The denial of lived reality is a classic patriarchal technique, as is described below. Nuclearism itself is patriarchy: it is the dominance of a mindset that says violence equals power, that weapons equal security. Feminist scholars have long studied the connections between militarized masculinities, the quest for dominance in international relations, and nuclear weapons. Carol Cohn's "close encounter with nuclear strategic analysis" starting in 1984 led to illuminating articles in *Signs* and *Bulletin of the Atomic Scientists* about the gendered discourse on nuclear weapons.[59] These articles provided the foundations for a feminist analysis of nuclear war, nuclear strategy, and nuclear weapons themselves.

Cohn described the "sanitized abstraction and sexual imagery" used in US nuclear war planning, including metaphors that equate military and political power with sexual potency and masculinity—such as "vertical erector launchers, thrust-to-weight ratios, soft lay downs, deep penetration, the comparative advantages of protracted versus spasm attacks," and discussions about how "the Russians are a little harder than we are."[60] She and Sara Ruddick suggested that this type of highly sexualized language serves to "mobilize gendered associations and symbols in creating assent, excitement, support for, and identification with weapons."[61] It is also "a way of minimizing the seriousness of militarist endeavors, of denying their deadly consequences."[62]

In later years Cohn, along with Ruddick and Felicity Hill, expanded the inquiry into the sense of masculine strength afforded by nuclear weapons. After India's 1998 nuclear weapon tests, they listened to a Hindu nationalist leader who explained, "We had to prove that we are not eunuchs."[63] They argued that statements like this are meant to "elicit admiration for the wrathful manliness of the speaker" and to imply that being willing to employ nuclear weapons is to be "man enough" to "defend" your country. They also examined how disarmament is "feminized" and linked to disempowerment, weakness, and irrationality while militarism and attaining nuclear weapons are celebrated as signs of strength, power, and rationality.[64]

In her study on the valuation of nuclear weapons, Catherine Eschle illuminated the ways in which "the protector" is coded as masculine and "the protected" as feminine in discourses that defend nuclear weapons as necessary for security. She noted that these discourses reinforce and play into fantasies of "real men" and masculinity as defined by "invulnerability, invincibility, and impregnability."[65] She and Claire Duncanson further elaborated on how such gendered stereotypes guide the framework of security from a "realist" perspective on international relations and set the stage for a masculinized approach to security that accords status to nuclear weapons as markers of both masculine domination (capable of inflicting violence) and masculine protection (capable of deterring violence).[66]

Patriarchal techniques

This gender analysis of nuclear weapon possessions helps us decode much of the rhetoric around nuclear deterrence and the power of the bomb. It illuminates the rationale for all the efforts that the nuclear-armed states, and some of their allies, put into trying to discredit those who demand the abolition of nuclear weapons.

The process to develop the UN Treaty on the Prohibition of Nuclear Weapons (TPNW), for example, provides an excellent case study in patriarchal resistance to nuclear disarmament. Proponents of nuclear weapons sought to use a logic of rationalism and power to defend their possession of these weapons and to "feminize" opponents of nuclear weapons by claiming they are "emotional" and "irrational." The nuclear-armed and their allies ridiculed the TPNW supporters' perspectives on peace and security, accused them of threatening the world order, and suggested they were delusional. In one case, a Russian ambassador suggested that those wanting to prohibit nuclear weapons are "radical dreamers" who have "shot off to some other planet or outer space." In another, a UK ambassador said the security interests of ban proponents are either irrelevant or nonexistent. A US ambassador asserted that banning nuclear weapons might undermine international security so much it could even result in the use of nuclear weapons.[67]

These assertions are a study in patriarchy and patriarchal techniques—including victim-blaming and gaslighting. For example, the US government's suggestion that banning nuclear weapons could result in nuclear war is reminiscent of men who assert that women who have been victims of sexual assault must have been "asking for it" by acting or dressing a certain way. The message is clear: if you try to take away our toys of massive nuclear violence, we will have no choice but to use them, and it will be your fault.

Meanwhile, Russian and French representatives described the desire to prohibit nuclear weapons, and the focus on the humanitarian impacts of nuclear weapons, as being "emotional." The nuclear-armed states resist the conversation about the humanitarian impacts because this discourse focuses on what nuclear weapons actually do to human bodies and the planet. Looking at the physical and environmental impacts of nuclear weapons undermines the abstraction of these weapons as deterrents and refocuses attention on the fact that they are tools of genocide, slaughter, and extinction.

The assertion that the humanitarian impacts discourse is emotional is an easy way to dismiss and discredit those raising it. In effect, it is an act of gaslighting. This is the practice of denying lived reality, of questioning the capacity of an individual to understand what they are saying, given their emotional investment, and insisting on a truth that is fiction. It is an incredibly destabilizing technique, orchestrated through constant denial, misdirection and misinformation, and ridicule. Gaslighting in the realm of nuclear weapons has been practiced since the beginning of the atomic age. The discourse of deterrence denies the lived reality of those who have experienced the intergenerational harms of nuclear weapon use and testing. It insists that nuclear weapons are for security, not genocide. It claims that anyone who thinks otherwise is being emotional, overwrought, irrational, or impractical.

Privileging power through discourse

What is considered to be realistic, practical, and feasible is determined by those who hold power in a given situation. How these concepts are measured and used to describe reality relies exclusively on those who control the mainstream discourse or narrative. In the context of nuclear weapons, this control lies with men and women of incredible privilege: elites of their own societies and in the global community, such as politicians, government personnel, military commanders, and "national security" practitioners and academics. It is definitely not in the hands of the people affected by nuclear weapon development, testing, stockpiling, use, or threatened use.

Within the constructs of the "national security" elite, disarmament seems impossible—like a utopian vision of a world that cannot exist because, the argument goes, there will always be those who want to retain or develop the capacity to wield massive, unfathomable levels of violence over others. Therefore, the "rational" actors need to retain nuclear weapons for protection against the irrational others.

In a recent example, in 2018 the US government began asserting that all the past commitments it has made to nuclear disarmament are out of date and out of step with today's "international security environment"—as if the security environment is not directly related to the US government's own actions, including its buildup of its nuclear arsenal. The US administration has articulated a new approach to nuclear weapon policy, which is focused not on what the United States can do for nuclear disarmament but what the rest of the world can do for the United States in order to make it, as the most heavily militarized country in the world, feel "safer."[68]

This approach to international relations and disarmament insists upon the notion that states, as coherent units, must always be at odds with one another, rather than collectively pursuing a world in which mutual interdependence and cooperation could guide behavior through an integrated set of common interests, needs, and obligations—considerations that characterize human security. But "security can't be possessed or guaranteed by the state," argue Duncanson and Eschle. "It is a process, immanent in our relationships with others and always partial, elusive, and contested."[69]

Contesting security

Challenging mainstream, dogmatic conceptions of security is critical. The pursuit of "security" by elite factions within states lies at the heart of each of the structures of violence explored in this series. The justifications rendered for borders, for police forces, for the carceral system, for war and weapons all center on the ruthless quest for "security." The word itself must be contested, for its definition is fundamentally different depending on where its pursuer is situated.

Internationally, as well as nationally within most countries, security discourse and practice tend toward violence. As seen from the perspective of each state's political masters—its economic elite and the agencies built to police and preserve the unequal, extractive relations upon which many countries are built—security requires an arsenal of weapons, surveillance and carceral apparatus, and other technologies of violence, control, and coercion. Security, from this perspective, is about managing and enforcing the destruction of the commons—it is about maintaining the inequal distribution of wealth, power, and resources.

This framing of security is what is behind the United States' nuclear arsenal; its eight hundred military bases and its deployment of special forces and an alphabet soup of "intelligence" agencies around the globe; its military- and prison industrial complexes; its heavily armed police forces and border patrols. The dominance of militarized security is why the US government, regardless of which party or individual has the leadership, invests in weapons and war instead of the well-being of its own citizens, let alone its immigrants or people abroad.

This framing of security is also why so many other countries in the world invest in weapons and training for their military personnel instead of investing in the well-being of people. Rather than trying to prevent or mitigate the growing impacts of climate change, or investing in social safety nets that reduce inequalities, many governments follow the lead of the most heavily militarized countries in fortifying against unrest or migration by bolstering their capacity for violence.

These government choices of investing in perpetual war over peace are precisely why the majority of people in the world hold such a diametrically opposed view of "security." Security, for so many people, is about survival. It is about surviving the crumbling scaffolding holding up our world—surviving climate change, pandemic, famine, war. And it is about thriving, in a different world, in a different order, that is more equitable and fair.

For the majority of the world's population, security is not a weapon. It is not a prison. It is the direct opposite. It requires investments in completely opposing structures. Security means safe housing. Sustainable and healthy food, water, air, and energy. Equitable distribution of wealth and resources. Freedom from violence, fear, hunger. Freedom from the threats emanating from certain states—surveillance, incarceration, detainment, deportation, harassment, and murder. Security means not living under the constant threat of nuclear annihilation, police brutality, or systemic repression.

For most people, security means stability. Not "strategic stability," or other theoretical notions of equity among those capable of committing acts of monstrous violence against one another. But stability in terms of life and livelihood, of employment, access to health services, ability to care for family and community. Security, in this context, also means peace. Not some false "peace through terror" as professed by myths of nuclear deterrence, but the peace of promiscuous care, of nonviolent networks and mechanisms of solidarity and collective well-being.

Security is not an object or an achievement; it is a process that depends on the interactions of many moving parts. In this understanding, security cannot be reached through weaponization but through our relationships to one another and with our environment—and these are always changing, as are we. "*How* we live, *how* we organize, *how* we engage in the world—the process—not only frames the outcome, it is the transformation," writes Leanne Betasamosake Simpson.[70]

Thinking about security in this way and overturning the mainstream "security discourse" is part of the effort to build a different kind of world, a world that works for more people in more places. Changing narratives is a crucial part of changing minds, of overturning long-held beliefs about the way things work, the way things are, the way things "have to be." This deliberate shifting of mainstream consciousness was crucial to the suffrage movement, the civil rights movement, movements around labor and LGBTQ+ rights, for banning landmines, cluster bombs, and smoking, and any socially generated change.

Antinuclear organizers with the International Campaign to Abolish Nuclear Weapons (ICAN) built on the lessons of other social movements, intentionally refocusing international discussions toward the catastrophic humanitarian and environmental impacts of nuclear weapons. It might sound surprising, but for most of the last seventy-five years, this has not been the focus of intergovernmental discussion about nuclear weapons. At the United Nations, nuclear weapons have mostly been discussed by governments primarily in what Carol Cohn describes as "technostrategic" language—a language that helps nuclear war planners to rationalize their actions in planning the deaths of millions of people while disassociating themselves emotionally and morally from this task.[71] This affected the way even antinuclear governments spoke about nuclear weapons, primarily framing their opposition to the bomb in sanitized language about "international peace and security" and possible risks about use based on nuclear weapon policy details.

A key challenge for antinuclear activists and governments has been to disrupt this narrative and elevate in its place a discourse based on the realities of nuclear weapons: the death and destruction caused by their use and testing; the descriptions of what blast and heat from a nuclear detonation do to human bodies; the radioactive legacies and environmental degradation. Amplifying the testimonies of survivors over the theorizing of policymakers in boardrooms, and framing nuclear abolition as part of a broader pursuit of equity and justice, the diplomats and activists engaged in this work seek to stigmatize nuclear weapons in order to spur on their prohibition and abolition.

Banning the bomb

As a direct result of these efforts to change the discourse and to organize strategically for new pathways to disarmament, in 2017 the United Nations outlawed nuclear weapons.[72] Adopting the Treaty on the Prohibition of Nuclear Weapons on July 7, 2017, 122 governments voted to place nuclear weapons—along with chemical and biological weapons, blinding laser weapons, landmines, and cluster bombs—on the list of technologies that are unacceptable on the basis of their indiscriminate and horrifically devastating levels of violence.

You might not have heard about the ban. The nine nuclear-armed states did not participate in the negotiations. Nor did the countries that claim security from US nuclear weapons. The governments supporting the ban were largely those of the Global South. Most of the countries in Africa, Latin America and the Caribbean, and Southeast Asia participated actively. A cross-regional "core group" of countries, consisting of Austria, Brazil, Ireland, Mexico, Nigeria, and South Africa, together with a number of others such as Costa Rica, Jamaica, New Zealand, and Thailand, drove the process forward despite the opposition to it. And the opposition was great. The nuclear-armed governments of the world applied a lot of pressure—political and economic—against supporters of the ban to try to stop the process in its tracks. But they ultimately failed to prevent its negotiation and adoption, because the vast majority of the world's countries stood firm with the Red Cross, survivors of nuclear weapon use and testing, and nongovernmental organizations and activists from around the world to finally declare these weapons illegal.

Unlike the nuclear weapon governance agreements before it, the new instrument prohibits nuclear weapons for all countries and sets the stage for the elimination of these weapons. It offers various pathways for nuclear-armed states to comply with the treaty and eliminate their nuclear weapon programs, with verification and within set timeframes.

The treaty is also the first nuclear weapon agreement to recognize the disproportionate impacts that nuclear weapon activities have had on Indigenous communities, to recognize the gendered impacts of radiation, and to encourage gender diversity in discussions on nuclear weapons. It is also the first to include provisions on victim assistance and environmental remediation, recognizing the harms that have been caused and the needs of communities that have suffered.

The treaty officially entered into force on January 22, 2021. This means it is now legally binding on the countries that have joined it. Some have said that the treaty is irrelevant since none of the countries that have joined so far possess nuclear bombs. But for right now, that doesn't matter as much as you might think. The organizers and diplomats who worked on the treaty knew the nuclear-armed would reject it at first. The point was to create a new international tool to help us stigmatize nuclear weapons and start creating some economic and political barriers to their continued existence. Over time, the treaty will have a normative impact on the behavior of other countries, regardless of whether they join, and on financial institutions and other national and local actors. The changes that the nuclear ban brings to law, politics, and economics will help lead us to nuclear disarmament. As past social movements have taught us, change doesn't happen in an instant—it is iterative, contested, and must be constantly defended and built upon.

While the effort to ban nuclear weapons through an international agreement at the United Nations is a relatively recent effort, it builds on decades of antinuclear activism around the world. The 1960s and 1980s were particularly vibrant times for action against nuclear bombs and missiles, but those campaigning for nuclear abolition have been working all throughout the atomic age, demanding an end to the existential threat posed by these weapons of terror. Over these years, various agreements were reached among governments, largely due to the demands of people on the streets fighting for the future of their families and our planet. But all of these piecemeal arms control agreements are now under threat themselves, as the US government holds a lit match to the paper upon which various limitations to nuclear weapons were painstakingly written over decades.

Arms control as counterinsurgency

Until the Treaty on the Prohibition of Nuclear Weapons was adopted, the nuclear arms control agenda reigned supreme. Considered to be the only "practical," "feasible," and "realistic" approach to nuclear disarmament, for decade after decade the same "steps" were put forward by nuclear-armed states and their allies: ban nuclear testing, stop production of fissile material (uranium and plutonium) for nuclear bombs, be more transparent about nuclear arsenals and doctrines, reduce reliance on nuclear weapons for security, etc. These all sound like perfectly reasonable steps. Until you learn that the exact same measures have been talked about by governments since the 1950s without any concrete actions. Until you realize that during these decades of chats about what should be done, the nuclear-armed states have been investing billions of dollars a year into the modernization and expansion of their arsenals. Until you understand that for all the reductions of nuclear warheads undertaken by the United States and Russia since the end of the Cold War, they have merely dismantled the weapons and put the parts in storage, ready for reconstitution, rather than destroying them.

If we read the so-called nuclear arms control step-by-step process as reforms, we can hear the same cadence as reforms proposed to policing and prisons and immigration policy. Reformist agendas, as noted in the introduction, are counterinsurgency. In relation to police reforms, Dylan Rodríguez explains, "reform is best understood as a logic rather than an outcome:

an approach to institutional change that sustains existing social, economic, political, and/or legal systems."[73] Rather than contesting the legitimacy or morality of nuclear weapons, arms control reforms seek to reinforce the value of these weapons as deterrents, as necessary for security, and as instrumental for global stability. The step-by-step process does not advance disarmament, it stalls it indefinitely by constantly repackaging reforms that are never actually taken up by any of the governments proposing them.

Reforms "usually rest on the fundamental assumption that these systems must remain intact—even as they consistently produce asymmetrical misery, suffering, premature death, and violent life conditions for certain people and places," writes Rodríguez. Arms control—especially arms control measures that are never actually achieved—ensures that nuclear weapons live on indefinitely. The endless discussions about possible reforms provide an illusion of seriousness, of efforts made. But the reality falls far, far short of the rhetoric; while governments come up with different names and hold countless meetings about their latest "progressive agendas," nuclear weapons continue to put everyone in the world in peril. If counterinsurgency involves demoralization through propaganda, strategic misinformation, and psyops, then arms control fits the bill. Portraying themselves as reasonable and rational, as being (truly, really, honestly!) committed to nuclear disarmament, the nuclear-armed and their allies deny harms, defer action, avoid responsibility, and try to repress confrontation. They simultaneously assert that they desire nuclear abolition and prevent any meaningful action that could achieve it—and in fact, invest fully and unabashedly in armament instead. The Wizard of Oz is alive in well in nuclear policy, and it's past time to pull back the curtain.

The fraying remnants of nuclear arms control

In this context, it's important to note that even those arms control measures that have been adopted are coming apart at the seams. The doublespeak and obfuscation of nuclear counterinsurgency is not holding up to the pressures of reality.

A treaty aimed at preventing the proliferation of nuclear weapons, adopted in 1968, has been mostly successful in stopping the spread of nuclear weapons around the world. However, the nuclear-armed states that are party to that treaty have not complied with the legal obligation contained within to eliminate their nuclear weapons—which was part of the "grand bargain" in exchange for other countries never acquiring atomic bombs. More and more countries are expressing their discontent with this situation and uncomfortable whispers and literal walkouts have begun to happen in recent years at treaty meetings.

A treaty banning nuclear weapon tests, adopted in 1996, still hasn't entered into force. While most nuclear-armed states have exercised a moratorium on nuclear weapon testing in recent years, the Trump administration indicated that it might resume testing—a reminder that moratoriums will only hold if the government of the day chooses to abide by it.[74]

Throughout the Trump regime, the US government was determined to dismantle all the nuclear arms control architecture built over decades, withdrawing from and refusing to join or implement all the treaties that put any constraints on its nuclear arsenal. But even before Trump came to office, the United States was already initiating rhetoric claiming that the "international security environment" is no longer suitable for nuclear disarmament. It solidified this approach over the past few years, making it clear at the international level that the days of arms control were over.[75] Of course, this framing that nuclear disarmament is impossible because of the "security environment" glosses over the fact that US actions, above all else, determine the so-called security environment. It also ignores the fact that in the last seventy-five years, while the United States and Russia may have reduced their nuclear stockpiles, they have never pursued the elimination of their nuclear weapon arsenals. Finally, this position fails to acknowledge the fact that nuclear disarmament could, in fact, improve international security—even though most of the world's governments are clear that that is what they believe.

Minority rule

While it was initially the US government expounding this view that the world is not ready for nuclear disarmament, the other nuclear-armed states have all taken it up in various ways.[76] It provides a comfortable rhetoric to hide behind, i.e.: *We'd really like to do this thing we promised to do, but if we do it, it will hurt everyone, so . . . maybe later.* Yet despite the persistent gaslighting, most governments in the world reject the idea that the time is not "ripe" for nuclear disarmament. "Disarmament is a driver of security," the government of Ireland has argued, for example.[77] The international security environment "is not a pretext to shirk obligations or to defer progress on disarmament. Concrete progress on disarmament creates an enabling environment, enhances security and provides a reinforcing loop to allow further progress."[78]

Most countries have renounced nuclear weapons as tools of genocide and injustice. Criticizing the nuclear-armed states for their hypocrisy in asserting themselves as protectorates of "international security" while wielding weapons of unconscionable violence, many governments have acknowledged the global power disparity that is entrenched by nuclear weapon possession. South Africa's diplomats, for example, have drawn comparisons between the nuclear order and apartheid, arguing that it is another example of minority rule, in which "the will of the few will prevail, regardless of whether it makes moral sense."[79]

So far, the minority-ruling nine have all refused to join the Treaty on the Prohibition of Nuclear Weapons. So have the US allies that claim protection from nuclear weapons through their security agreements with the United States, which include the countries of the North Atlantic Treaty Organization, as well as Australia, Japan, and Republic of Korea. In contrast, it was the countries of Africa, Latin America and the Caribbean, Southeast Asia, and the Pacific, together with a few European countries, that championed the nuclear ban treaty.

These led the charge for a brilliant end run around the nuclear-armed states. Despite pressure and threats from several of the bullies with bombs, they stood their ground to say, enough. The normative impacts of this move cannot yet be measured, but the stigmatizing force is already being felt around the world. Financial institutions are divesting from nuclear weapon producers; political leaders and parliamentarians in nuclear-supportive countries are demanding a change to their governments' policies; city councils around the world are saying they do not want to be a target in a nuclear war.

. The nuclear landscape is changing, even as the nuclear-armed dig in their heels: the United Kingdom recently announced it will increase its nuclear arsenal (in breach of international law); the US, Russia, and all the others are continuing their nuclear weapon modernization programs, and they all continue to assert they'll never accept the prohibition on their bombs. Yet in the face of this intransigence, we can find hope, inspiration, and ideas in the broad spectrum of social movements, and in the knowledge that every step we gain in stigmatizing these weapons is a step toward their elimination.

Confronting the continuum of violence

Nuclear abolition is possible. The international law is in place. The technical capacity for dismantlement of nuclear bombs has been established. Most of the world is hungry for disarmament. But the nuclear-armed states are not ready—not ready to relinquish their self-perceived god-like power derived from "The Bomb." Not ready to join the rest of the world in cooperating for peace, instead asserting dominance and control over the order they created—the order from which they extract wealth and privilege.

Understanding the relationship between nuclear weapons and power, the role that the bomb plays in our current world—not as a relic of history but as an immediate and tangible threat to all life—is crucial to advancing toward abolition. This includes witnessing and renouncing nuclear weapons as part of the broader continuum of violence that so many of us confront every day: among other things, the systems of white supremacy behind nuclear weapon development and use; the patriarchal control possessors claim to derive from nuclear weapons; the economic tragedy of billions wasted on bombs at the expense of human well-being; the impacts a nuclear weapon detonation would have on our climate, food production, and environmental sustainability.

From here, we can oppose nuclear weapons not just as material objects in their own right, but as deadly cogs in a bigger system of violence and injustice. Our activism against the bomb is not "just" a demand for nuclear abolition, but for the disruption and dismantlement of the economic, political, and cultural systems that make nuclear weapons possible, that make them seem desirable, and that hold up other structures of violence that prevent us from developing equitable societies of care and nonviolence. There are many ways to connect nuclear weapons to other structures of violence that are considered in this series. At the heart of each is white supremacy, militarism, and capitalism.

Nuclear weapons and carceral systems

Beyond the embeddedness of white supremacy, nuclear weapon policy and activities also hold other similarities to carceral systems of policing and incarceration. As much as the bomb is a colonizer, it is also a prison. The justifications for nuclear weapon possession, told over and over to our populations and entrenched within our economies and politics, cage our imaginations along with our bodies and our futures.

Just as many people find it difficult to imagine security without police or prisons, many also find it difficult to imagine security without nuclear weapons. Yet, as Angela Davis notes, there is widespread "reluctance to face the realities hidden within [prisons], a fear of thinking about what happens inside them. Thus, the prison is present in our lives and at the same time, it is absent from our lives."[80] Likewise, many people acknowledge that nuclear weapons are horrible, yet claim they are a "necessary evil." They accept the abstract notion that nuclear weapons "keep us safe"—because the bomb is for them out of sight and out of mind, and not something they have ever experienced themselves. They exist, but we're told they are never meant to be used. Thousands of bombs have been detonated, but on Black and brown bodies, near poor communities, on Indigenous lands.

The persistence of the faith that nuclear weapons bring security, force-fed to us by the state as dogmatic Truth, is also similar to the faith in carceral systems to keep people safe. In both cases, we must ask, Whose security do they serve, and against what or whom do they offer protection? Much like police forces only bring stability and order to the capitalist class, to those with property and wealth that require "protecting" from the masses, nuclear weapons only bring stability and order to the warmongers who seek the capacity to destroy the world in order to preserve their dominance of it.

Responses to violence and inequalities that are witnessed are also similar. In the face of police brutality, some politicians or even activists suggest that the police can be reformed. Likewise, there are plenty of advocates for nuclear arms control, calling for reductions of nuclear arsenals down to a "reasonable" level, or the establishment of "no first use" policies or tweaks to the nuclear command and control structure. But as with police reforms, none of these adjustments gets to the heart of the problem—which is that carceral systems and nuclear weapons both are extremely violent tools to oppress, control, and kill human beings. The problem is not simply the way police or nuclear weapons are used but that each is *designed to cause harm*. You cannot reform away something when it is the fundamental nature of that thing.

Nuclear weapons and border imperialism

Police and prisons are also often justified on the basis that they deter crime. Yet even though "crime rates" in the United States have dropped since the 1990s, the prison population continues to increase. Theories of deterrence also relate to borders and nuclear bombs. Both rely on a theory of "deterrence" to justify their cruelty. The increasing global battlescape of "border security," described in chapter 4, is part the effort of wealthy

Western governments to work together to make sure that migrants, refugees, and asylum seekers have as difficult a time as possible entering their countries or even making it to their shores. But much like the theory of nuclear deterrence, deterring migration does not work. People still migrate but are exposed to more and more danger. But governments claim no responsibility for the deaths, treating the desert or the ocean as the perpetrator of violence rather than the policies that lead people to move in the first place.

The border zone is treated as a "state of exception," where human beings don't have rights, where they can be left to die in the desert, where they are blamed for their fate, says scholar Achille Mbembe. It is treated as a zone "where the violence of the state of exception is deemed to operate in the service of 'civilization.'"[81] Nuclear weapons are likewise treated as a state of exception, where the capacity and intent to commit genocide is treated as rational and necessary to protect so-called civilization. Further, as with nuclear policy, which refuses to acknowledge or listen to those who experience the harm from the producing, testing, and use of nuclear weapons, researcher Jason De León notes that "sovereign power produces migrants as excluded subjects to be dealt with violently while simultaneously neutralizing their ability to resist or protest."[82]

Nuclear weapons are about death, not deterrence; border imperialism and incarceration show callous indifference to human life. This can be seen in the abstract, technostrategic language that nuclear war planners use when they talk about casualties from atomic attacks,[83] just as it can be seen in the "closed door strategy meetings at Border Patrol headquarters in Tucson where new forms of 'deterrence' are plotted and schemed using euphemistic defense jargon and slick corporate promotional videos touting next season's line of unmanned aerial drones," says De León.[84]

Ultimately, nuclear weapons, borders, and carceral systems are about maintaining power and privilege for some at the expense of the lives of others—in the case of nuclear weapons, potentially everyone. They are about maintaining a political and economic world order built on, and reliant upon, extreme inequality and violence. Nuclear weapons are part of the toolkit for maintaining the inequitable privileged world order, a radio-active line between the "haves" and the "have-nots"—in terms of nuclear weapon possession, but even more acutely in terms of access to wealth and power. For the most part, nuclear weapon possessors and supporters are among the wealthiest countries in the world; most are located in the Global North. With the exception of Brazil and Mexico, the fifteen countries with the highest GDPs are all nuclear weapon possessors or support the US nuclear weapon program through alliance agreements.

These countries also are spending billions on "border security" to keep people out. As described in chapter 4, some of the same companies developing militarized surveillance apparatus for borders are also involved in weapons production, including nuclear weapons. For example, Leonardo, an Italian arms company, supplies drones to EU coast guard agencies. It is also involved in the production of medium-range air-to-surface missiles for France. Thales, a Dutch company, is also involved in building nuclear missiles and is currently developing border surveillance infrastructure for the European Border Surveillance System. The increasing militarization of borders is a boon to the military-industrial complex in the United States, Israel, and across Europe, creating new markets for weapons and other technologies of violent repression, coercion, and control.

Companies in the United States that manage the nuclear-industrial complex are also invested in the militarization of borders directly. Sandia National Laboratories in New Mexico, for example, has been part of the system for building and managing the US nuclear weapon arsenal since 1945; it was also commissioned in the early 1990s to draw up plans to militarize the US-Mexico border. It recommended militarized responses such as the construction of a triple-layer border wall, systematic checkpoints, and electronic surveillance, among others. Sandia was initially run by AT&T, then Lockheed Martin, and now by a subsidiary of Honeywell.[85]

Yet at the same time as the nuclear complex helps construct and enforce borders, nuclear weapons also trouble the concept of borders and the nation-state, as Joseph Masco notes. "They demonstrate the permeability, even irrelevance of national borders to nuclear technologies (to intercontinental missiles and radioactive fallout, for example)."[86] Nuclear war will know no borders. Radiation is transnational. The effects will be global. Yet borders are treated as essential to "defense" of the "nation" even as the nation stockpiles thousands of nuclear warheads, many of which are ready to fire at a moment's notice. This positioning is, indeed, gaslighting at its finest.

Overcoming the nuclear nightmare

The nuclear-industrial complex is largely responsible for the feat of magical realism surrounding mainstream nuclear weapon discourse and theory. It has actively worked to make sure its narratives about "strategic stability" and "mutually assured destruction" have held sway over nuclear weapon policies and investments all these years. Meanwhile, the cost of living for people everywhere has continued to rise—poverty, war, climate change; all have worked against a popular resistance to something as seemingly esoteric as the nuclear bomb.

But these weapons must not be considered "out of sight, out of mind" anymore. They are a living nightmare, to which those who have experienced them can attest. And they are critically bound up with so many of the other aspects of our societies we need to change in order to survive, and in order to thrive. They are embedded within the US political, economic, and cultural landscape, and seeing them as such could help us find new or innovative locations and strategies for our resistance and our efforts to build the structures of collective care we so desperately need.

In addition to the global work at the United Nations with governments of the world, antinuclear organizers are also already working locally[87] with city or municipal council members to divest public funds from nuclear weapon production. ICAN's Don't Bank on the Bomb initiative provides information about financial institutions around the world that invest in the companies contributing to the manufacture of nuclear weapon systems.[88] Local efforts in cities and towns across the United States and in other countries are helping to divest personal funds, as well as government pension funds and other public money, from these companies.[89] Activists are also encouraging their cities to comply with the Treaty on the Prohibition of Nuclear Weapons, and to call on their federal governments to join the treaty.[90]

Some activists situate their struggle at the sites of nuclear violence—sites of their use and testing, as well as their sites of production and manufacture, sites of uranium mining and waste dumping, sites of their assembly or their deployment. This work includes interrupting the daily work at the sites, distributing information about the humanitarian impacts of nuclear weapons and about the prohibition treaty, speaking with local communities and workers, and building connections among people. Others are working to disentangle their universities from nuclear weapon–related work, including the pipeline from science programs to the nuclear labs present in some schools.[91]

But more work is needed to integrate the nuclear abolition movement with other work for social change, and to support movements for broader social, economic, and environmental justice.

Seeking a continuum of activism to challenge the continuum of violence

Given the continuum of violence between and among various structures of violence in our societies, there are plenty of ways in which to connect, reinforce, and amplify social movements that stand against them. While the single-issue antinuclear organizing of the past may not be feasible or even desirable, the time is riper than ever for activism based on the fundamental redirection of security concepts and funding priorities, of which nuclear weapon issues are an important aspect.

The threat of nuclear war, the waste of resources on nuclear weapon modernization, maintenance, and deployment, and the risks to health and environment of nuclear weapon production are all very real, tangible costs of the atomic bomb that need to be considered within social movements looking to change how we can achieve safety, solidarity, and security as well as peace and justice. To address these concerns, it is imperative to incorporate feminist, queer, racial, and Indigenous justice and environmental perspectives in the actions we undertake.

Right now, there are calls in many countries to defund the police and prison industries and build alternative structures for preventing harm and for transformative justice. This incredible work is crucial toward building the type of communities in which we can all live and thrive. This work is about, among other things, disarming and demilitarizing; it is about divesting from weapons and violence and investing in peace and equality instead. Abolishing nuclear weapons is part of this work. Similarly, nuclear abolition is part of the work to prevent or mitigate the impacts of climate change. The environmental impacts of nuclear weapons, even in a single detonation, can be devastating; a nuclear war would lead to catastrophic impacts on the atmosphere, land, and water, leading to global famine and even mass extinction.

The bottom line, as Audre Lorde says, is that our activism can't be single issue, because we don't live single-issue lives. Integrating work against nuclear weapons into other movements, and supporting the work of movements for social justice and environmental preservation within the work against nuclear weapons, means recentering different perspectives and approaches in our work, as described above.

Queering antinuclearism

Queer theory and politics offer useful lessons here. As Gem Romuld of ICAN Australia notes, the Treaty on the Prohibition of Nuclear Weapons can be considered "queering nuclear disarmament" because it undermines the dominant patriarchal discourse around nuclear weapons and "prioritises, or at least amplifies, marginalised voices (countries and people impacted by nuclear testing)." This is helping change "security frameworks worldwide, putting nuclear-armed states and their allies on the defensive."[92]

Queer approaches to organizing and activism tend to push back against traditional power structures, methodologies, and spaces. For many queer activists, it is not sufficient for LGBTQ+ rights to be "recognized" or "tolerated" by heterosexist societies when queer lives are being destroyed and diminished in multifaceted ways. Some gay rights activists who do focus on "petitioning for rights and recognition before the law"—marriage equality or inclusion in the military, for example—have been described by others as collaborating with mainstream nationalist politics of identity, entitlement, inclusion, and personal responsibility.[93] Queer politics, in contrast, may offer an approach based not on integrating into dominant structures but on transforming "the basic fabric and hierarchies that allow systems of oppression to persist and operate efficiently."[94]

This may be why the fight against nuclear weapons tends to draw in queer activists, as Emma (Crunch) highlights. She points out that the nuclear-industrial complex is "a necessarily highly regulated, undemocratic industry with concentrated power," and queer-identified people "tend to try and break down some of these power structures in our lives and relationships, as well as power sources."[95] This alignment is also relevant for confronting the gender norms that associate weapons with power, as described above, including contesting and dismantling the connections between masculinity and weapons and instead building new understandings about violence and about more expansive possibilities for gender identities and relations.[96]

Queering antinuclearism relates to deconstructing gender, getting away from a binary of men/women, straight/gay, trans/cis. Binaries enable hierarchies. Gender binaries are accompanied by racial, religious, and other hierarchies. Deconstructing gender helps illuminate and undermine some of the foundations of state violence. This kind of deconstruction helps subvert the idea that "security" achieved through violence and "control" is necessary or desirable. Divesting from gender and other binaries means refusing to buy into notions of strong men and passive women, of states providing "protection" through the violence of nuclear weapons, war, and incarceration.

This work against the gender binary also helps illuminate nonbinary approaches to social ills—i.e., to "crime" and insecurity. It opens minds to alternative possibilities. Nonbinary approaches help us to see the connections between the underlying causes of harm in the world and help reveal solutions to violence and insecurity that will prevent future harm. Rather than looking at "crime" or "terrorism" or nuclear proliferation as something that requires punishment, nonbinary thinking can help us see the imperative of disarmament and demilitarization as credible options to prevent violence and explore options of transformative justice and new kinds of accountability, as explored further below.

Decolonizing antinuclearism

As with queer politics, Indigenous organizing often seeks to challenge the legitimacy of settler colonial institutions rather than applying to them for fulfillment of "rights and responsibilities." Some Indigenous organizers work for environmental protections and rights as citizens of First Nations, not of the states that continue to steal, rape, murder, and destroy their bodies, land, and water.[97] Nuclear weapons are part of settler states' quest for suppression and destruction of Indigenous peoples. In Algeria, Australia, the United States, and throughout the Pacific, colonial governments bombed the land, covering it with the black mist and white rain of radioactive fallout[98] and burying nuclear waste within it. As described above, from uranium mines to aboveground testing to radioactive waste storage, the production of nuclear weapons has predominantly been carried out on Indigenous land and bodies. Yet the nuclear-armed have rejected efforts of local communities to secure acknowledgement or compensation for these harms and they continue to reject the perspectives of survivors as relevant to policymaking.

Decolonization is instrumental to nuclear disarmament. The elimination of nuclear weapons must be part of the process of acknowledging the radioactive racism of the nuclear age and repairing this damage. The Treaty on the Prohibition of Nuclear Weapons recognizes this. Its negotiators listened to Indigenous appeals to include language on the disproportionate harms caused by nuclear weapon activities to Indigenous communities and to include victim assistance and environmental remediation in the treaty's provisions. While the damage can never be undone, naming it and working to address it are imperative to healing the wounds of nuclear colonialism and to preventing such acts from ever occurring again. Centering Indigenous experiences, perspectives, and voices in discussions about nuclear weapon policy is also crucial moving forward, given the disproportionate harms and the systemic suppression of such views in the past.

Dismantling power

Decolonizing and queering our approaches to nuclear weapons are key to challenging the dominant narratives—and thus policies—of nuclear-armed governments. After decades of appealing to the nuclear-armed states to comply with their legal and moral obligations to disarm, the majority of the world's governments finally rejected the structure of oppression imposed upon them through the established forums for discussion and negotiation and forged a new path. Utilizing the UN General Assembly, which gives each member state an equal vote, allowed the voices and interests of those not in control of massive world-destroying arsenals not only to be heard, but to dominate.

Consciously or not, the decision to turn to an alternative forum for action on nuclear weapons placed in the foreground a politics where the nonnormative and marginal position became the basis for progressive change. This is arguably a queering of process, in which those marginalized do not "search for opportunities to integrate into dominant institutions and normative social relationships, but instead pursue a political agenda that seeks to change values, definitions, and laws which make these institutions and relationships oppressive."[99] Learning from Indigenous knowledge, this type of shift also was a process that allowed participants to connect to the land, water, and sky through a renewed focus on the humanitarian and environmental impacts of nuclear weapons.

That said, the UN General Assembly is still an established forum. Of all the UN machinery, it may best maintain the spirit of the UN Charter's quest for international equality and cooperation, but at the end of the day it is still part of a broader architecture in which "power" rules. While the United Nations was founded to save succeeding generations from the scourge of war, its most militarized member states have used the system to prevent action that impedes their interests of capital accumulation through war, imperialism, and oppression.

"Power both inhabits and determines the structures of the system," writes Tim Hollo of the Green Institute in Australia. "Only by changing power can we change the system."[100] If we have some sense of what changing power means nationally or locally, in terms of building community resilience, mutual aid, and solidarity, what could it look like in relation to nuclear weapons? As we build alternatives to the other structures of violence and power we seek to undo—the carceral state, border imperialism, etc.—what are the lessons we can draw to effectively undermine the power structures that sustain nuclear weapons?

Transformative justice for nuclearism

For example, what would transformative justice look like in relation to nuclear weapons? Transformative justice processes, as described in chapter 2, are often used within communities to achieve accountability and healing without recourse to police and imprisonment. Such processes are about accountability, acknowledgement of harm, and apology for that harm. They are about reparations for the survivor and the survivor feeling heard and cared for by their community. They are about changing the behavior of the perpetrator, as well as preventing others from committing such harms and building the systems of care and accountability necessary for the future.

What does this mean in relation to nuclear weapons? Perhaps it means transnational solidarity of activists to listen to, acknowledge, and amplify experiences and perspectives of those harmed. Perhaps it means, as it did in the case of the Treaty on the Prohibition of Nuclear Weapons, *state actors* also doing the same—diplomats of non-nuclear countries working to create more inclusive spaces and methods of work. But it must go beyond this, to the creation of entirely new spaces and methodologies that do not mirror the structures of power we are working to circumvent and dismantle. Rather than embedding in the negotiations the idea that only states can make treaty law, there should be more experimentation with activists, survivors, and other members of civil society becoming directly engaged with negotiations in ways that are usually exclusively reserved for states. Such engagement has implications for transparency, access, and the diffusion of power to more levels of society and people, beyond our usual tried and tired methods of work.

Taking a transformative justice approach to nuclear weapons might also mean building community-type structures to help hold the experience of survivors but also to seek accountability from those who have perpetuated nuclear harm. This includes those within nuclear-armed governments, the nuclear-industrial complex, and the academia and think tank personnel who have built careers justifying nuclear violence. Creating space for them to own their participation in this system of extreme violence may be an important act to help transform and bring an end to nuclearism. In the case of sexual violence, for example, the very act of communities supporting survivors and calling out the violence for what it is helps shift the power dynamics within systems of abuse. While what we're talking about in relation to nuclear weapons may seem completely different, recognizing and naming the structures of violence that enable nuclear weapon possession and use can be a first step toward those engaged in that structure becoming increasingly uncomfortable and aware of their participation and complicity in what is ultimately the preparation for and justification of genocidal and ecocidal acts.

Toward abolition

These ideas are not meant to be presented as answers but as the beginning of a conversation about how antinuclearism—as a movement and a goal—can be more effective in strategy, more reflective and inclusive, and more supportive of other social justice work. Emerging from the (missile) silo of single-issue antinuclear organizing is imperative. While the work to bring into force, implement, and universalize the Treaty on the Prohibition of Nuclear Weapons must continue, we must simultaneously work to deconstruct and transform the structures that enable a select handful of governments and corporations to possess these weapons.

It is at the intersection of many abolitionist projects that we can find hope and inspiration for dismantling both the bomb and the political, economic, and cultural scaffolding that have facilitated its existence for seventy-five years. Viewing nuclear weapons as a metaphor and a grotesque physical manifestation of all the hate, fear, and violence in our world, we must place them within the spectrum of violence of which they are a blinding hot, radioactive part. To this end, understanding the relationship between nuclear weapons and capitalism is key. From the competitive driving forces of capitalism that spur arms races to the material ways nuclear weapons are bound up in the perpetual growth machine of the capitalist political economy, atomic bombs imperil our planet not just through their production and detonation but also through their capitalist underpinnings.

Chapter 7

‖‖

Demolishing Capitalism

This chapter was coauthored with Nela Porobić.

C apitalism is currently the predominant political and economic system on our planet. It was not inevitable that this would be so— nor is it inevitable that it will remain so. In fact, the survival of the planet depends upon us abolishing capitalism.

"You show me a capitalist and I'll show you a bloodsucker," said Malcolm X. Capitalism is a system of sheer brutality, established through slaughter and theft and sustained through destruction and commodification of life. It was built upon the death and dispossession of peasants who opposed the encloser of the commons in Europe, and of Indigenous and colonized people around the world whose wealth and resources were plundered and pillaged by Europeans. The "conquering" and occupation of foreign territory allowed capitalists to extract resources from territories all over the world to feed their coffers. Over the past century, neo-imperialism has enabled the continuation and expansion of this project, using economic power and influence through free trade agreements, international financial aid and assistance, as well as military power to coerce

215

governments across the world to adopt neoliberal economic policies that favor privatization and the "free reins" of the market.

Since the 1970s, the neoliberal brand of capitalism has had devastating effects around the world. Rejecting the "management" of capitalism by the state, neoliberal "free market" ideology and practice have demanded the decimation of the role the states play in regulating markets and social provisioning. According to neoliberalism, the only role the state should have is to secure private property rights and ensure the functioning of the markets—by force if needed. The rollback of the state's influence over the economy was to happen in favor of private actors, interests, and profits.

The mantra of capitalism is that capitalism means progress and that if you work hard you will be rewarded with freedom. Freedom in a capitalist world always comes from the individual's personal responsibility, entrepreneurial capacity, and hard work. If the markets are left unfettered, they will regulate themselves, rewarding "winners" and punishing "losers."[1] Inequalities are seen as a necessary part of any society, and the problem of poverty is portrayed not as a problem of the system but of the individual. Competitiveness is encouraged at every point. Economic "growth" is seen as the only measure of success of the system, which means perpetual plundering of the planet to continuously produce goods for consumption and disposal.

Neoliberal capitalism has also led to the elimination of progressive taxation and state ownership or control of principle industries and services. It incited the privatization of housing, industry, education, health care, and more, and the concentration of wealth, power, and privilege in the hands of the few. This has ravaged our world, as is laid bare in the data on the growth of wealth and its distribution. During the last thirty years, in which we saw a financial crisis[2] and a global pandemic damage the lives of billions, in the United States alone billionaires increased their wealth more than two hundred times more than the growth of the median wealth over the same period. At the same time, their tax obligations decreased by 79 percent.[3] Since as recently as March 2020 and the beginning of the COVID-19 pandemic, US billionaires increased their wealth by 34 percent, a staggering $1 trillion.[4] Across the world, the picture is no better. Trillions of dollars of wealth are in the hands of a few men, who have more money than 4.6 billion people. Barely 1 percent of the planet's population has more money than 60 percent of the rest.[5]

But it is not just about being in possession of more money than our brains can grasp. With money comes power and influence—over our social relations, decision-making structures, the rules put in place to regulate distribution, access to, and use of resources, our culture, emotions, the language we use to describe our realities and interactions, and so much more. With money comes power and influence over our very lives. From its very beginnings and throughout history, capitalism has been contested and opposed by the majority of those forced to suffer under its yoke. But opposition is met by the capitalists with incredible violence and repression in order to protect their profits and install accumulation of wealth as the guiding principle for economies the world over.

The complexities and disasters of capitalism are many, and this chapter does not intend to act as a guide to them. Instead, it focuses on one of the critical principles of capitalism, namely the "growth imperative" and the harm it causes to human beings as well as our animal, plant, land, air, and water relations. Capitalism, in its pursuit of endless growth, is patriarchal, racist, extractivist, environmentally devastating, and militarized. It excludes most people from the resources needed to lead decent, equal, and fulfilling lives. The "free market" fundamentalism of neoliberal capitalism leads to human rights abuses, social stratification, and extreme poverty and inequalities. This is always true, but even more with "disaster capitalism"—when capitalists use crisis to implement policies that increase their profits while increasing the suffering of ever more of the world's population. Militarism also plays a role in capitalism's growth and its perpetuation. From weapons production to war profiteering to the preservation of inequalities through policing, militarism helps to both generate and protect private wealth.

The capitalist system feels overwhelming. There's a common saying that it's easier to imagine the end of the world than the end of capitalism. But while it is hard, it is not impossible. People have always resisted the capitalist system and envisioned a different way of organizing care, justice, solidarity, and equality with each other and with our relations on this planet. Some countries have even tried to put in place a different economic, political, and social governance system. All these attempts to reimagine, good and bad, are important points of departure for us and they teach us that it is not impossible to work outside the capitalist box. Thinking about, organizing for, and building structures and mechanisms for degrowth, decolonization, and justice must guide our efforts away from the capitalist system toward a political economy that works for all people and the planet—one in which care and well-being are prioritized over profit.

The mechanics and horrors of the "growth imperative"

Capitalism is all about perpetual growth. To survive, it cannot stop growing—it always has to find new resources to extract, new avenues for investment, new things to produce. According to Karl Marx, who spent years studying the dynamics and the economic patterns underpinning the capitalist mode of production, the key driving motive of capitalism is the "valorization" of capital, i.e., the process of producing a commodity that is greater in value than the sum of the values used to produce it. The goal is not just to create something people can use or consume, but to ensure that it has "surplus value" beyond the expenses that were put into producing it.

In order for capital to be put in motion and turned into profit, the capitalist needs to have access to two things: labor power and the means of production. Labor power comes from the many people who have been dispossessed and deprived of access to the means of production, forced to sell their labor in order to survive. The means of production comes in the form of land, raw materials, machines, factories, infrastructure, and so forth. For this process to work, labor power must also be able to reproduce itself.[6] Those who work need to be fed, rested, clothed, and healthy to be able to return to work every day. Equally important is the biological reproduction of workers and their socialization into the capitalist political economy.[7]

Each time money (capital) is invested in the process of production, it generates a surplus, an increment in value. This is what motivates a capitalist to engage in the process of production and the main reason why capitalist production implies perpetual growth.[8] The process of valorization also means that the capitalist will reinvest some of the surplus value in order to continue and further develop the production of commodities and profits. The production process is thus a *reproduction process*. Capitalist production continues as long as capital is valorized. Surplus value is created through what Marx called the exploitation of labor power. Surplus value is the difference between the number of hours it takes for the worker to earn the wage (e.g., four hours of labor) and the amount of time the worker actually works (eight or more hours a day). The surplus value is thus created by capitalist exploitation of free labor of workers.[9]

Karl Marx studied and theorized about capitalism and what he called "the laws of motion of capital" in the context of the nineteenth century, but his findings are as valuable and relevant today as they were back then. David Harvey compares Marx's explanation of movement of capital to how H_2O circulates in nature by transforming itself to different forms and states at different rates before returning to the ocean. This behavior is similar to that of capital, which begins as money before taking on commodity form and then "passing through production systems and emerging as new commodities to be sold (monetised) in the market and distributed in different forms to different factions of claimants (in the form of wages, interests, rent, taxes, profits) before returning to the role of money capital once more."[10] The key difference between the hydrological cycle and the circulation of capital is that the latter is driven by a growth requirement and is a spiral in constant expansion.[11]

As capitalism is spiraling out of control, taking down with it not just the majority of people but the entire planet, Marx's explanation of growth seems particularly astute.

The (un)healthy economies

The "growth imperative" has come to dominate every aspect of our lives. It is presented to us as the natural order of things, a "common sense" to which there is no alternative. The bigger the growth, the better off we are—supposedly. But what the growth imperative does not measure, and in fact obscures, is the depletion of people and planetary resources as well as the conditions and levels of inequality and exploitation that are indispensable for the growth.

The growth imperative is articulated and performed daily by governments, international financial institutions, and neoliberal think tanks. Our economies are valued by how much they "grow," measured in the quantity and quality of the economic goods and services a society produces and consumes. According to the International Monetary Fund, gross domestic product (GDP) is a "reference point for the health of national and global economies."[12] The story goes that the bigger the GDP is, the better off we are. Measured like that, the United States, with its nominal GDP of $21 trillion, is the so-called healthiest economy in the world.[13]

Yet, during his official visit to "the healthiest" economy in the world, the United States, UN Special Rapporteur on extreme poverty and human rights Philip Alston found levels of inequality, incarceration, and houselessness disproportionate to the country's wealth.[14] Compared to other wealthy countries, the United States has fewer doctors and hospital beds, less access to water and sanitation, higher rates of disease and infections, and much lower economic mobility. His report also described how poverty in the United States is racialized and gendered, with Indigenous communities, people of color, and women facing the brunt of poverty's impacts, and how economic hardship is criminalized as a deliberate effort to conceal the problem. "At the end of the day," Alston wrote, "particularly in a rich country like the USA, the persistence of extreme poverty is a political choice made by those in power."

Thus, measuring how well we are doing in terms of GDP provides no context. It says nothing about how the "health" it captures is distributed; how well it takes care of our planet; or how many of us benefit from the wealth produced by all of our work combined. It speaks even less about the possible costs of, and limits to, consumption and growth. In a capitalist system, capital accumulation is everything and there is no such thing as growth limits.

The perpetual growth required by capitalism to sustain itself is not a natural order of things, but rather an inherent part to the dynamics of the capitalist system. The unimaginable wealth that it produces for some comes at a great cost for most of us, because the accumulated wealth does not "trickle down." In fact, it trickles up. Jeff Bezos's wealth of $200 billion, for example, is premised on labor power exploitation, tax evasions, and a complete disregard of the health of Amazon workers around the world.[15] Bezos's methods for accumulation of wealth are not a deviation from the system. Exploitation of workers and of the natural world is baked into capitalism.

Subjugation comes in many forms

Much like the reproduction of labor, capitalism also requires the reproduction of other systems of power relations that are "distinct from but deeply implicated in the capitalist system,"[16] such as patriarchy, racism, colonialism, and imperialism. It generates structural oppressions to divide and rule the working class, creating hierarchies among workers and the oppressed based on class, ethnicity/race, and gender—devaluing some while valuing others.[17]

Capitalism exploits, many times violently, the patriarchal norm of men's domination over women. It benefits from the subordination of women within what capitalism calls the productive, or "formal," economy, where women are disproportionately used as a cheap and undervalued workforce. It also benefits from the unpaid care work women do in homes and communities, the "informal" economy. Capitalism relies on structural subordination and oppression of women in its effort to control social reproduction, understood as a sum of all labor that goes into reproducing social life, including biological reproduction and unpaid care work.[18] The concept of social reproduction is a feminist adaptation of Marx's understanding of the process of reproduction of labor, an adaptation made in order to ensure that patriarchal forms and experiences of capitalist exploitation are captured.[19]

The patriarchy feminizes certain types of work, from the male perspective considered "natural" or "unskilled," and as such particularly "suitable" for women, such as care work.[20] The care work performed by mostly women (and some men from racialized communities) in the formal, "productive" economy is undervalued and poorly paid, while the care work performed by women in homes and communities—raising children, cooking food, providing emotional support, taking care of the elderly, etc.—is considered "unproductive" and is thus not paid or valued at all. Through this process of exploitation, capitalism also generates and perpetuates a gender binary, facilitating broader gender oppressions as well as homophobia and transphobia.

However, patriarchy is not the only system of exploitation from which capitalism benefits. The exploitation of labor power is also reliant on other systems of subordination. Capitalism is intimately linked with racism. It was built on white supremacy, on the colonial and imperialist projects that plundered, exploited, and exterminated people and resources on its quest to exert economic, political, and social dominance over countries, resources, peoples, and cultures. Capitalism continues to be built on marginalization and devaluation of the lives and labor of racialized communities and Indigenous people.

The plundering, the exploitation of people, and the extraction of so-called natural resources of conquered territories was part of capitalist policy to expand markets and profits, and it continues, constantly being shaped and reshaped through imperialist policies, backed up by military force, or disguised in financial aid, loans, or credits. As capitalism subordinates human beings and their labor to the pursuit of profit, so too does it subordinate other species and ecosystems, treating animals, plants, land, water, and air as means for value accumulation. The dominance over human relationships and the extraction of our other planetary relations go hand in hand.

Hoarding and the manufacturing of scarcity

Capitalism is "organised around the constant production of scarcity," notes Jason Hickel. It needs to keep people wanting or needing more—more food, more jobs, more land, etc. If people's needs are satisfied, they won't buy things, they won't labor as much, and the capitalist project will collapse on itself. "In a growth-oriented system, the objective is not to satisfy human needs, but to *avoid* satisfying human needs. It is irrational and ecologically violent" because it demands the constant extraction of resources and labor, and constant consumption, regardless of the impact on the planet or lives.[21]

The pursuit of constant growth is what makes capitalism so brutal. When it hits limits to growth—to what it can extract—the capitalist system "fixes" the situation by creating new markets. Nothing is safe from free market fundamentalism—education, housing, health care, our well-being—everything is subject to commodification. The methods used are many: privatizing goods and services, enclosing commons like water and seeds, colonizing countries, launching wars, forcing structural adjustment programs on governments, creating debt instruments, depleting public budgets, etc. The inherent competitiveness of capitalism drives its relentless expansion throughout the world, often leaving conflicts and environmental destruction in its wake.

Underscoring the growth imperative is capitalism's propensity for— or indeed, requirement of—hoarding. Hoarding wealth is a critical part of the capitalist system's functioning, not an anomaly or a side effect that can be "ironed out." It lies within the nature of capitalism to "overaccumulate." Overaccumulation is a structural crisis within capitalism that happens, as sociologist William I. Robinson explains, when the wealth produced exceeds the ability of the market to absorb it, because the inequalities created by capitalism are so great. Instead of seeking ways to redistribute wealth, capitalism, by its very nature, continues producing abundant wealth, driving the levels of inequality ever higher.[22]

When crisis hits and corporations cannot sell their commodities at high enough profit rates, the system tips into deep recessions and depressions. The only way the capitalist system can get out of such crises is by clearing out the overaccumulation, letting bankruptcies rip, and depressing the cost of labor, thereby setting the system in motion again. "If left unchecked, expanding social polarization results in crisis—in stagnation, recessions, depressions, social upheavals and war—just what we are experiencing right now" writes Robinson.[23]

Unleashing the free market system

Through this process, capitalism permeates all parts of our society. It is a system of governance, an idea, a systemic structure, built for one thing only: to extract maximum resources and profits with minimum investments. Everything in our societies is tuned into enabling this system of exploitation and inequality, including the state. Despite neoliberal assertions that the "free market" works best without state interference, the state has a key role to play. The state reproduces the growth imperative through its institutions and practices. A successful government is one that can make our economy "grow" by unleashing the full "potential of the market forces." The state enacts laws that enable capitalism, through for example (de)regulation of labor rights and markets. It polices the masses, exercises social control, and is also ultimately willing to engage in war on behalf of capitalist expansionist projects.

The state plays another crucial role: it bails out capitalists during crisis. For example, during the financial crisis in 2007 and 2008, an unimaginable amount of public money was committed to bailing out private banks.[24] The United States alone spent over \$1 trillion, while the United Kingdom's and Ireland's bailout programs reached \$718 billion and \$614 billion, respectively.[25] So, while the states around the world hurried to pick up the bill for the capitalists, the public sector suffered the consequences of these bailout programs. With massively depleted public budgets, the governments cut down further on investments into social infrastructure, thus in effect forcing billions of people to pay for the greed of the few.

Clearly, the state has an active role to play in enabling the exploitation and extractivism upon which capitalism thrives. Demolishing capitalism thus requires us to also think about the alternative models of governance, and to understand the functions and roles the current capitalist state has in the (re)production of the growth imperative and the capitalist political economy.

Private property, private fortunes

In order to achieve the levels of growth required to sustain their economic system and the profits it generates, the capitalist class requires as little interference into their business as possible and as much access to resources from which to extract profit as possible. Building on the idea of *free* trade on a *free* market, capitalists understand all too well that one cannot trade what one does not own, making private property rights the cornerstone of capitalism. There is nothing that cannot be owned and profited from: from land to housing, to goods and services, to ideas, and people.

This practice of commodification of everything has devastating implications for our lives. For example, as Leilani Farha, former UN special rapporteur on adequate housing, has noted, housing—one of the basic human rights—is commodified and used as yet another source of extraction.[26] Billionaires use housing or residential real estate as an extractive industry to park, grow, leverage, and hide big capital. This practice involves private equity firms as well as public pension funds. "The financialisation of housing by these actors has for years resulted in higher rents, evicting low-income tenants, failing to properly maintain housing in good repair and hoarding empty units in order to increase their profits," argue six current and former UN special rapporteurs.[27]

Efficiency and flexibilization in exchange
for marginalization and poverty

Alongside private property rights, unleashing and expanding the free market are key for capitalism. Everything can and needs to be put up for sale, to be privatized. Everything that is in the way must be removed, including the public sector. The smoke screen for the neoliberal onslaught against the public sector has been the claim about the inefficiency and inability of the public sector to provide the services demanded by the people. This "rigid" system had to be exchanged for private sector's "flexibility and efficiency." These terms, favorites in any capitalist's vocabulary, are just euphemisms for labor exploitation (temporary, part-time, nonunionized jobs with fewer benefits), decreased access to affordable and quality services for the many, and more profit for the few. As "vital public goods and services have been steadily outsourced to private companies," wrote six UN independent experts, "this has often resulted in inefficiency, corruption, dwindling quality, increasing costs and subsequent household debt, further marginalising poorer people and undermining the social value of basic needs like housing and water."[28]

Following the financial crisis of 2007–2008 and massive bailouts of the financial sector mentioned above, an onslaught on the public sector and public budgets became the standardized recipe to get out of the crisis. The most commonly prescribed measures to governments have been pension and social security reforms, which often result in tightening contribution requirements or raising workers' contribution rates while at the same time decreasing employers' social security contributions, prolonging the retirement age, and/or lowering benefits; flexibilization of labor rights, such as putting a cap on minimum wage, decentralizing collective bargaining, making it easier for companies to fire employees or to hire workers on temporary/atypical contracts; cutting wages, including of teachers and healthcare workers; reduction or elimination of subsidies, such as those on fuel, electricity, food, and agricultural inputs; strengthening the public-private partnership, frequently resulting in layoffs, tariff increases, and unaffordable and/or low-quality basic goods and services; increasing consumption taxes—e.g., increasing or expanding value-added tax rates; and healthcare reforms—e.g., raising fees for patients or introducing cost-saving measures in public healthcare centers.[29]

The International Monetary Fund was given a key role in ensuring that countries around the world adopt these policies in order to be considered "good" economic partners or financial aid recipients. The logic seemed to be that the public sector, public institutions, and laws that ensured labor protection, solidarity with people that needed support, and some redistributive effects were considered unaffordable and even burdensome, impeding competitiveness and discouraging growth.[30]

This situation is not compatible with states' human rights obligations. Governments are still accountable for their people's rights and well-being. Yet as states continue to reduce public spending and contract out public goods and services, governments are transforming their citizens "into the clients of private companies dedicated to profit maximization and accountable not to the public but to shareholders." The UN experts warn, "This affects the core of our democracies, contributes to exploding inequalities and generates unsustainable social segregation."[31]

Disaster capitalism—austerity to the people!

While inequality, segregation, and suffering are the inevitable result of the capitalist political economy, capitalists continue to double down in order to increase their profits as suffering worsens for more and more people. Over a decade ago, Canadian author Naomi Klein described the concept of "disaster capitalism" in her book *The Shock Doctrine*.[32] She exposed how neoliberal ideologues work with big corporations and other segments of the capitalist elite to use moments of crisis to ram through political and economic changes that benefit their accumulation of capital. In today's version of coronavirus capitalism, these efforts are well underway.[33]

The COVID-19 pandemic is not just a health crisis but also an economic one. As the pandemic spread around the world, a familiar and insidious neoliberal-shaped pattern spread along with it. While people were distracted and disoriented by what it will take to survive this virus—not just physically, but also economically, socially, and psychologically—the political and economic elite were actively seeking to implement agendas to ensure maximization of their profits and carrying out what former Australian Green Party Senator Scott Ludlam described as the "predatory rush to consolidate power in the midst of massive trauma."[34] Capitalists keep pushing beyond the boundaries of what is accepted in "normal" times, working relentlessly to impose ever more vicious policies to squeeze whatever they can out of the rest of the world for their own profit and power.

There are many ways in which disaster capitalists work to profit from the COVID-19 crisis and ensure their continued dominance once it is over.[35] From bailouts of corporations to protect their profit margins rather than workers' jobs,[36] to airlines making employees take unpaid leave while the executives receive billions in bailout cash,[37] to the dismantlement of social security mechanisms,[38] to profitmaking by big pharma and speculators[39]—capitalists are making the most of the crisis. Never mind that it was neoliberal economic policies that had decimated the public health sector in most countries, leaving them scrambling to contend with the overwhelming needs of the pandemic. The answer for those who have built this system is always more of the same, but worse.

International financial institutions, especially the World Bank and IMF, have played a key role in maintaining the given hegemonic order by propagating neoliberalism and its gospel of privatization. It is then no surprise that they facilitate disaster capitalism to profit from the COVID-19 pandemic. Oxfam International found that 84 percent of the IMF's COVID-19 loans encourage, and in some cases require, countries to adopt tough austerity measures in the aftermath of the health crisis.[40] Its investigations "found that 76 out of the 91 IMF loans negotiated with 81 countries since March 2020 push for belt-tightening that could result in cuts to public healthcare systems and pension schemes, wage freezes and cuts for public sector workers."[41] It also found that nine countries "are likely to introduce or increase the collection of value-added taxes (VAT), which apply to everyday products like food, clothing, and household supplies, and fall disproportionately on lowest income households, while 14 countries are likely to freeze or cut public sector wages and jobs."[42]

Oxfam also analyzed the full set of emergency health projects that are part of the World Bank's COVID-19 Strategic Preparedness and Response Program (SPRP) as of June 30, 2020, covering seventy-one countries. The organization found that "only 8 out of 71 projects make any move to eliminate or suspend fees that exclude people from life-saving health care."[43] This is despite fees being prohibitive in at least 80 percent of those countries. Oxfam also notes that "out-of-pocket healthcare expenses hit the poor and women the hardest and, prior to the pandemic, pushed 100 million people into poverty every year."[44] In their report "Global Austerity Alert" from April 2021, Isabel Ortiz and Matthew Cummins analyzed IMF fiscal projections finding that the projected average expenditure contractions in 2021 would be double the size of the contractions that took place during the financial crisis in 2007 and 2008.[45] This means that the governments will spend less money on public services than they did before the pandemic, which was already low. As much as 75 percent of the global population was affected in 2021, rising to 85 percent in 2022. By 2025, 6.3 billion people might be living under austerity.[46]

It doesn't have to be this way. Austerity is a choice, not a necessity. As the Indigenous activists behind the Red Deal explain, "Austerity is enforced scarcity." While the public is told that it is the only option to deal with "budget constraints," the reality is that neoliberal policies have "been a tax strike of the super wealthy, who have refused to pay their share of taxes and have locked away the world's wealth in tax havens and offshore accounts,"[47] leaving the rest of the population to suffer, after having labored to generate this wealth in the first place.

Militarism and capitalist bombs

Another sign that austerity is a choice is that in stark contrast to the devastating cuts in public spending on lifesaving systems such as health care, housing, and employment, governments around the world have not had any problem spending money on weapons. Increasing inequality, human suffering, and environmental destruction at the hands of capitalist exploitation and extraction gives birth to resistance, the capitalist response to which is, of course, violence. This brings us to militarism—the cause of and "solution" to so many of our world's problems.

Militarism is as an integral part of capitalism, for many reasons. The military-industrial complex and the wars it sustains provide a bottomless pit for the "valorization" of capital and profit-making. Military action is the go-to mechanism in response to the opposition to inequalities and social disintegration described above. It is also imperative for capitalism's colonial and neoimperial pursuit of "new markets," "cheap labor," and "natural resources"—and then for the response to the further inequalities and social disintegration and forced migration generated by this colonial and neoimperial violence and environmental destruction. The capitalist system's competitive nature also produces inter-state conflicts. States strive to protect their corporations' pieces of the pie and enforce their claims through arms races and, at certain points, war. It's an endless cycle of violence and harm from which war profiteers can gleefully reap vast fortunes.

Valorization through militarization

Military spending is used to valorize capital—to continuously grow the capitalist economy. Capital is sunk into war and occupations, arms production and trade, maintenance and modernization of nuclear weapon systems, research and developing of new technologies of violence, and deployments of military forces around the globe. Global military spending in 2020 reached almost $2 trillion—but as described in chapter 5, this figure does not even account for everything.[48]

There are different ways that investments in weapons and war generate profit. The standard circulation of capital and commodities applies to the international arms trade. It's extremely difficult to calculate the financial value of the international arms trade, though the Stockholm International Peace Research Institutes estimates that it amounts to at least $95 billion a year.[49] Then there is the "domestic consumption" of weapons—the bombs and bullets that fill a country's own arsenals. The more often the arsenal is depleted—that is, the more the state engages in violence—the more "need" there is for weapons development and production. War, then, becomes a lucrative, profit-generating industry for those in a position to benefit from it: the military corporations and their financiers.

Arms, more arms, and ever more arms

Whether they are produced for sale abroad or consumption by one's own military, weapons and ammunition have proven to be a "great" way to generate surplus value. Some critics have asserted that massive investments in militarism have harmed national economies. But studies of major arms producing countries, in particular the United States, have gone out of their way to show how these investments support the growth imperative—as long as governments don't let things like international law and human rights deter their arms sales or wars of aggression.

This is true for no country more than the United States. By the late 1940s, military production was viewed as the savior of the US economy. At that time, the US economy was sinking back into recession; the postwar consumption boom had been exhausted; unemployment was on the rise. State spending on military production was apparently deemed the best way to ensure continued valorization of capital, ensure full(er) employment, and increase aggregate demand.[50] As scholars Paul A. Baran and Paul M. Sweezy explain in *Monopoly Capitalism*, militarism provided capitalist societies "the answer to the 'on what' question: On what could the government spend enough to keep the system from sinking into the mire of stagnation? On arms, more arms, and ever more arms."[51]

This led, as C. Wright Mills argues in *The Power Elite*, to the US economy becoming both a permanent-war economy and a private-corporation economy. The merger of the capitalist economy and the military bureaucracy came into significance during World War II, he explains, after which US capitalism "is now in considerable part a military capitalism, and the most important relation of the big corporation to the state rests on the coincidence of interests between military and corporate needs, as defined by warlords and corporate rich."[52]

Jobs, jobs, jobs!

To justify this continued militarism, US capitalists argued that weapons production offered high employment rates. Many politicians try to steer arms manufacturers to their districts for this reason. However, the opposite is true. Even back in the 1980s, studies were showing that even the three largest military contractors, which accounted for over 40 percent of the Pentagon's total purchases from the private sector, created fewer jobs per dollar than the median manufacturing industry.[53]

One factor is the high level of technical expertise required for weapons-related jobs. The specialized nature of military production employment means that much of the new employment generated by a military buildup goes to people who need it least. The Los Alamos National Laboratory, for example, home to the Manhattan Project, which created nuclear weapons, is still touted as a regional "job creator" and generator of "economic growth" in the state of New Mexico. Yet as local activists point out, neither jobs nor sheer economic growth, "which is often concentrated in a relatively few hands," are reliable measures of broad economic benefit of military-industrial firms. Greg Mello of the Los Alamos Study Group notes that the claim of providing jobs "obscures more than it reveals. Crucial information omitted includes the answer to the question, jobs for whom?"[54] He also points out that it is possible that any given military facility "could drive away other jobs, perhaps many more than it provides.... So even while adding new jobs, it's quite possible Facility X could increase the number and worsen the plight of the poor in the area, or lead the region toward economic decline, even while adding 'jobs.'"[55]

The statistics for New Mexico demonstrate the relevance of these concerns. New Mexico's poverty rate in 2019 was 18.2 percent, making it one of the poorest states in the country.[56] Twenty-six percent of the state's children live below the poverty line, ranking New Mexico as forty-ninth nationwide, despite "improvements in the state's economy."[57] Yet Los Alamos, the town where the nuclear lab resides, is home to the highest concentration of millionaires in the United States. "Report findings state there are 885 millionaire households among the population of Los Alamos of around 18,000," giving the town an 11.7 percent concentration of millionaire households.[58]

War profiteering

But the relationship between capitalism and militarism isn't just about weapons production. Capitalism requires militarism and violence to expand to new markets and extract new "resources." The colonial and neo-imperialist projects of seizing land, plundering and extracting from it, subduing populations to labor and consume, all require weapons and war.

In turn, this perpetual violence requires ever more investment in the production of weapons and ammunition, and in the research and development of new methods and means by which to control, confine, and kill human beings. Thus, just as capitalism is said to "drive" technical innovation, so too does it drive innovations in the tools of death, injury, surveillance, and incarceration.

Meanwhile, as populations around the world grapple with the impacts of the use of bombs, guns, drones, and artillery in their cities, towns, and villages; as the incredible amounts of pollution and environmental degradation generated by armed conflict and military activities exacerbate climate change;[59] and as economic imperialism devastates communities and countries around the world—militarism is the "answer" of the capitalist class for dealing with it all. Already, we can see efforts to militarize against climate change, simultaneous with efforts to "greenwash" the military. Militarism is capitalism's "fixer," its cleanup crew, deployed to deal with the resistance of local populations as well as the migration of those fleeing violence, poverty, and environmental destruction.

Investments in the military-industrial complex are booming as people are increasingly on the move as a direct result of militarism, weapons, and war. The "national security industry" rakes in billions from "securing" borders, engaging in "counterterrorism," detaining and incarcerating those deemed to be "threatening," and training militaries and paramilitary forces to hunt, kill, and disappear human rights defenders and environmental activists. Many of the companies that manufacture weapons for war are the same as those receiving contracts for "border security," developing and selling technologies to keep out the people who are fleeing the violence created abroad.

In many cases they are also the same companies supplying police forces with weapons, used against civilians all over the world as the economic inequalities and poverty generated by capitalism destabilize societies or lead people to demand care and safety from their governments. Capitalists use police, who in turn use the weapons from which the capitalists profit, to protect those profits from the "surplus populations" suffering in cities around the world. Sociologist William I. Robinson describes this as "militarized accumulation" or "accumulation by repression," connecting the growth imperative of capitalism to the rise of the global police state.[60]

Then, there are the contractors that are granted multibillion dollar contracts for "reconstruction" after conflicts that the capitalists have initiated. Halliburton is one of the most profound examples of a corporation that has profited wildly from the US government's invasion and occupation of Iraq, but they are not the only ones.[61] DynCorp—also infamous for its role in trafficking women in the Balkans in the 1990s—has profited from training Iraqi police forces; Blackwater—infamous for among other things murdering Iraqi civilians—profited from providing "security" for contractors operating in the country; and the list goes on. As countries transit from war to peace, an "army" of private companies and contractors stand in line to "help" with the reconstruction, offering their services against a "small" profit. Private for-profit military and security is one of the fastest growing economic sectors, with private security agents outnumbering police officers in many countries and even outnumbering US soldiers at various points during the war in Afghanistan.[62]

Planetary destruction

While capitalism kills human beings wherever or whenever deemed necessary to extract a profit, it is also killing the planet, along with billions of species of animals, insects, and plants. The activities that result in this destruction, driven by the capitalist need for endless "growth," are active choices that are made every single day to drive the knife in further, to set yet another fire.

There is an abundance of clear evidence that we are destroying our world—from high-level scientific reports, documentation provided by environmental activists, academic research, journalistic coverage of environmental destruction, and not least our own experiences within our communities. We know that we are actively causing climate change and the degradation and death of countless living plants and animals. The destroyed rivers and wildlife in our vicinity; the mind-blowing immensity of the loss of biodiversity; the melting polar ice caps; the recurring flooding; the droughts; the polluted air—all of this reveals the grave and in many ways irreparable harm we are doing to our world and ourselves.

Capitalist activity is killing the planet, in particular through extractive industries; the political economy of oil and gas; the mega (and mini) power dams; the roadbuilding to support industrial transportation needs; the relentless deforestation; the invasion of tropical forests and wild landscapes; the treatment of animals and occupation of their habitats; the political economy of militarism, of nuclear bombs, of wars and the pollution they generate and leave in their wake; the industries that promote excessive consumerism; our use of energy.

The responsibility for this destruction, and the consequences of it, not surprisingly follow familiar patterns of domination and inequality that mark our world. The United States, for example, bears responsibility for 40 percent of "excess global carbon dioxide emissions."[63] The Global North as a whole—defined as the United States, Canada, Europe, Israel, Australia, New Zealand, and Japan—is responsible for 92 percent. In contrast, the Global South—which "is by far bearing the brunt of climate droughts, floods, famines, storms, sea level rise and deaths—is responsible for just 8% of excess global carbon dioxide emissions."[64]

Anti-environmentalist onslaught

The danger of organizing against the capitalist pursuit of endless growth and profit is also predominantly outsourced to the Global South and to Indigenous nations within settler colonial states. The environmental activists who dare to protest and stand up in defense of natural resources do so with great risk to their lives.[65] These are often women, Indigenous people, or other marginalized local communities. Capitalism does not tolerate anybody standing in the way of its pursuit of profit.

Capitalists are also loath to accept any legislation against their potential profit-making. The assault against environmental protection policies in the time of COVID-19 is a key aspect of the neoliberal agenda now that we are living in the age of climate change. Rising global concerns about the environment and the need to act urgently to have any hope of mitigating at least some of the impending climate disaster have started to impinge somewhat upon the profits of the oil, gas, and coal companies, and have begun to force all industries to consider their carbon emissions and other environmental impacts.

It is no wonder, then, that those who profit the most from these industries would seek to use moments of crisis to roll back environmental protections and to proceed with projects that otherwise would be facing public scrutiny and opposition.

Seizing the moment

Governments recognize the increase in environmental awareness among their constituencies, as well as the opportunity that lies in greenwashing their policies through good PR. Countless governments seized the COVID-19 pandemic as cover to drive forward environmentally devastating capitalist, extractivist projects in superb examples of disaster capitalism as described above.

Canada, a country that in 2017 called itself an international leader on environment and climate change,[66] is in conflict with several First Nations over the construction of a gas pipeline on unceded Wet'suwet'en land in British Columbia.[67] Before the coronavirus hit Turtle Island, the Wet'suwet'en had been blockading the Coastal GasLink project for months, building on their earlier blockades against oil and gas companies.[68] After the Trudeau administration sent in the Royal Canadian

Mounted Police (RCMP) in early 2020, Shut Down Canada actions sprang up across the country.[69]

Then, under cover of the measures to flatten the COVID-19 infection curve, TC Energy, the company responsible for the pipeline, moved ahead with the project under the protection of the RCMP. This put workers, who live and work in close quarters, at risk of contracting the coronavirus. It put Indigenous communities at risk of infection.[70] It will result in the environmental destruction that First Nations have been fighting to prevent. And, as if one pipeline project isn't enough, TC Energy then also announced that it would proceed with construction of the long-delayed and very controversial Keystone XL pipeline—with the help of a $1.1 billion "strategic investment" by the Alberta provincial government.[71] The Keystone XL pipeline was finally canceled in June 2021, thanks to persistent organizing against it.[72] But work by oil and gas industries to build pipelines on and through Indigenous land continues in both Canada and the United States—and continues to be faced with resistance by Indigenous and environmental organizers.[73]

It's not just oil and gas industries that take advantage of crisis to move forward with environmentally destructive projects. The nuclear industry sought to seize the moment, too. In Croatia, the government tried to move ahead with constructing a long-disputed radioactive waste dump near the border with Bosnia and Herzegovina.[74] After years of protest by both Croatian and Bosnian activists, the Croatian government used the shadow of both the coronavirus and an earthquake that had recently hit Zagreb to move the project along. In the United States, the Nuclear Regulatory Commission unleashed a proposal to dump radioactive waste in municipal landfills instead of a licensed facility.[75] And the Department of Energy sought a 49 percent increase in nuclear weapon activities at the Los Alamos National Laboratory, as well as increases and spending at other nuclear weapon labs around the country.[76]

In the United States, the government also ordered the Environmental Protection Agency to suspend its enforcement of environmental laws during the coronavirus crisis and lowered fuel emission standards for vehicles sold in the country.[77] The state-level governments of Kentucky, South Dakota, and West Virginia used the cover of COVID-19 to adopt laws imposing new criminal penalties on protests against fossil fuel infrastructure.[78]

The repression of environmental and other activists has also ramped up in other locations around the world. In Burkina Faso, for example, those sounding the alarm over the government's embezzlement of minerals in collusion with foreign mining companies were met with systematic bans on demonstrations and other more violent silencing of activists. "Covid-19 has contributed an 'additional' virus to a country already on its knees," writes Didier Kiendrebeogo of Organisation Démocratique de la Jeunesse.[79] Several US states also enacted laws during 2020 and 2021 aimed at rolling back rights of protestors and the right to protest, particularly in relation to land defenders and water protectors. As Indigenous activists highlight, "The state responds to water protectors—and those who care for and defend life—with an endless barrage of batons, felonies, shackles, and chemical weapons. If they weren't before, our eyes are now open: the police and the military, driven by settler and imperialist rage, are holding back the climate justice movement."[80]

The ecological limits of growth

At the heart of this colonialist, capitalist destruction of the world is capitalism's relation to "nature" and humans. Rather than seeing plants, land, water, animals, and other living things as being relations to, and living in relationship with, human beings, the capitalist system sees nature and humans are two separate things. Nature is merely a "resource" on which to capitalize. Something to put into its production line and spit out, for fast consumption and disposal. Profits are reinvested in new production, new consumer items, cheaper goods, systematic exploitation of workers through undervaluing of their labor, and extraction from nature—and so it goes on forever. Money, exploitation, money. Laying brick after brick into a house that has no foundation and is bound to crash.

But: "Ecological reality is making itself felt, with fire, flood and plague," writes Tim Pollo. The so-called common sense of capitalism, the idea "that the invisible hand of the market will take care of things if we all follow our own self-interest; that eternal growth on a finite planet is possible; that we are separate from and superior to the natural world; that we are all individuals and there is no such thing as society—cannot withstand that reality."[81]

Consuming energy as if there is no tomorrow

With endless economic growth as the "prime directive of capitalism,"[82] we need an endless supply of energy. But extraction and use of energy is killing our planet. Even if we switch to entirely renewable sources of energy, argues Jason Hickel, if we continue to try to grow economies by 2–3 percent per year, we will destroy the planet. "We will find ourselves plunging into ecological collapse well before we run into limits to growth," Hickel warns.[83]

Climate scientists have virtually all agreed that we need to stay under a temperature rise of 1.5 C in order to survive. To achieve this, we need to cut global emissions in half by 2030 and to zero by 2050. Transitioning to renewable energy is important, but it will not happen fast enough to meet these targets.

Moreover, switching to renewables itself requires *more* extraction of resources, for the minerals needed to build the infrastructure for solar, wind, and battery storage. Mining is a key driver of deforestation, ecosystem collapse, and biodiversity loss around the world. The mining industry is also infamous for its human rights abuses—from child labor, to brutal violence against the workers, extremely poor and dangerous working conditions, and destruction of homes and land.[84] As most of the key materials are in Latin America and Africa, these regions are likely to become the target of new colonial and neoimperial efforts to secure resources. The scramble for renewables could become violent, Hickel warns, and "clean energy firms could become as destructive as fossil fuel companies—buying off politicians, trashing ecosystems, lobbying against environmental regulations, even assassinating community leaders who stand in their way."[85]

Tech won't save us

Furthermore, as many climate activists warn, switching to renewables or improving energy efficiency, which are indeed essential to helping us reduce our impact on the climate, are frequently harnessed to advance the objectives of economic growth—"to pull ever-larger swathes of nature into circuits of extraction and production."[86] While energy-intensive industries, fossil fuel companies, and other major polluters turn to "corporate social responsibility" and greenwashing assertions that new technologies will save us from the climate nightmare to come, their claims not only exaggerate the benefits but also obscure the costs of this new tech.

Capitalism seeks to preempt any changes that would affect its unfettered pursuit of the accumulation of capital. It finds a way to co-opt environmental and ecological awareness and response, individualizing the responsibility for climate change. It is now possible to buy carbon offsets, energy-efficient lightbulbs, and expensive ecological food, to recycle, and adhere to a variety of useful and nature-friendly ways of living. While these are all important efforts to make, they obscure reality, and the reality is that the biggest polluters are not households but the military and the industrial sector.[87]

Meanwhile, these sectors claim that technological adjustments are all that's needed to save the planet and capitalism. But gains made in productivity and efficiency are "doing far more to enhance the profitability of big business than the sustainability of the earth," warns Peter Dauvergne. New technologies, such as artificial intelligence, are "accelerating natural resource extraction and the distancing of waste, casting dark shadows of harm across marginalized communities, fragile ecosystems, and future generations."[88] Artificial intelligence is, Dauvergne argues, "a tool of power, frequently deepening global inequities and the exploitation of natural resources."[89] As much as it may contribute to less waste or better renewable energy technologies, the profits from artificial intelligence "disproportionately enrich corporate billionaires, as productivity gains across global supply chains hide ecological costs, and as [transnational corporations] reinvest savings from cutting waste and optimizing operations into expanding production and consumption."[90]

The expanding use of technologies, and reliance upon them as saviors of economic growth, mean the perpetuation of a narrative of corporate responsibility that undermines efforts to reduce energy consumption and empowers transnational corporations to "lead" the climate change mitigation effort when they are the ones most responsible for this disaster. The belief in the technology as the answer to saving the planet also reproduces the dogma that our economic and other development can only be achieved through "economic growth" and ever-increasing consumption. Now that our lived realities are making it difficult to ignore the destructiveness of those narratives, the capitalist solution lies in repackaging and technically advancing our consumption so that we can grow and consume in perpetuity.

Technology cannot make capitalism sustainable. No source of energy can do this either. Not renewables on their own, and certainly not nuclear power, which unfortunately even some climate change activists believe should be included in the plan to reduce emissions. Due to the incredible expense, long planning cycles, carbon-intensive production, environmental destruction, and human health impacts from uranium mining and radioactive waste, risks of accidents and weaponization, nuclear energy is not the solution.[91] In a sense, nuclear power plants are a kind of "capitalism bomb," said US political prisoner Mumia Abu-Jamal in a statement in solidarity with those affected by the Fukushima disaster in 2011. "These structures are often built by government grants for private profits and then, when they fail, they destroy everything within miles, even at a molecular level."[92]

We need more than technical, formulaic solutions—we need systemic, radical changes. Taking care of the planet and stopping its destruction has to be about much more than changes in our individual behavior or in energy efficiency or even in switching to renewable sources of energy. Saving our planet—and all of our plant, animal, and water relations—depends on us rallying around ideas that have up until now been pushed outside of the mainstream political and economic thinking. For the sake of our future, we have to be able to imagine a world beyond endless pursuit of economic growth, where capitalism has been demolished. By transitioning away from capitalism to a degrowth economy, and by transforming institutions of capitalist accumulation into institutions of solidarity, care, and ecological well-being, we can achieve equality, justice, and a sustainable future for all.

A world beyond capitalism

Despite the odds stacked against our survival, there is hope. Throughout history and across continents, people have been imagining and reimagining a world beyond capitalism—and actively organizing to build it. The capitalist system depends on the labor of workers and those oppressed by the system. Without their labor, the system cannot function, as any major strike demonstrates.

We would not have an eight-hour working day or unionized jobs without collective efforts of the working class. The structural oppression of women and the gendered experiences of the capitalist political economy and of everyday life would have remained invisible without the invaluable work of feminists around the world. Our awareness about environmental destruction and climate change would not have been where it is today without the relentless struggle of Indigenous people and environmental activists. The militarization of our everyday lives, the production of weapons and vast expanse of the global arms trade, would not be questioned without the dedicated work of peace activists. White supremacy and structural racism would have gone unchallenged without a long history of anti-colonial and anti-racist struggles. Capitalism would have gone unchallenged and unchecked, becoming ever more exploitative, without all these collective efforts.

Collective organizing for change has, thus far, been successfully oppressed, or co-opted, or accommodated by the capitalist elite just enough to give the perception of change. But together, these different actors, movements, ideas, and struggles *can* put an end to capitalism, halt the ecological crisis, and get rid of the exploitative conditions under which we interact among ourselves and with the world we share. It is in our collective interest and power to abolish oppressive structures and ultimately get rid of capitalism.

Ecological sustainability and solidarity

We need to collectively embrace a new way of thinking about the economy and what we consider to be "development." We need to ground our societies in ecological sustainability and solidarity. Humanity, as a collective, has very little to gain from the endless pursuit of increasing GDP. Instead, our measurement of how well we are doing should be about the well-being of the planet and all life upon it.

We need to stop pursuing growth as the ultimate aim of the economy, and we need to downscale the overall use of our energy. We need to "degrow" the economy. This is not, of course, the only solution to capitalism or to climate change. Moreover, it must be done in such a way that recognizes the extreme imbalances in global contributions toward climate change and economic inequalities between the so-called Global North and Global South. But degrowth does offer a useful framework for moving toward a more equitable, just, and ecologically sound political economy.

The degrowth movement conceptualizes post-growth economies as based in radical reduction of total energy and material use. It aims to bring the economy in line with planetary boundaries and equal distribution of income and resources, ultimately leading to an improvement in people's lives. This might mean that GDP growth slows down or even declines, but that is acceptable because degrowth is about building a new political economy that is organized around human and ecological well-being rather than the accumulation of capital. Even in this process, some sectors might grow—such as clean energy, public health care, care, education, housing, regenerative agriculture, etc., while others decline, such as the fossil fuel industry, weapons production and military activities, and other environmentally and socially destructive aspects of the economy.

Degrowth is an important tool in building a world beyond capitalism. While capitalism is about expansion, occupation, extraction, and accumulation, explains Jason Hickel, degrowth is about release, recovery, and repair. It is about decolonizing our land and water, decolonizing communities, and decolonizing our minds. It is about de-enclosure of the commons, de-commodification of public goods, de-intensification of work and life, de-thingification of humans and nature, and de-escalation of ecological crisis.[93]

Decolonization and justice

In building societies that are equal and based on equitable political economy, we need to recognize and redress the unequal and unjust distribution of the violent consequences that the capitalist economic system leaves in its wake. We also need to recognize the unequal and unjust distribution of the impacts of climate change and the profits made from ecological destruction. We need to put justice at the center of our societies and our relations, addressing and redressing the role of colonialism in the destruction of the environment and the displacement and genocide of Indigenous populations. Changing our economic system is inseparable from ensuring an equal and just relationship with all the people and other living beings on the planet, starting with what some of the Indigenous activists have outlined in the Red Deal: Indigenous treaty rights, land restoration, sovereignty, self-determination, decolonization, and liberation.[94] "The path forward is simple," says the Red Nation. "It's decolonization or extinction. And that starts with land back."[95]

Land back is a political, social, and economic process. It means rebuilding "just relations between the human world and the other-than-human world" and restoring land, air, and water as essential for the return of humanity. It means demilitarizing relations between countries and "bringing in a new world based on peace and cooperation, not coercion and force."[96] Land back is not a slogan or a metaphor, it is a plan of action for changing the way we engage with others and our world, a plan which is intimately tied to the end of capitalism.

Justice and decolonization are critical to abolishing capitalism—they are both the "antidote" to the growth imperative and the key to solving the climate crisis. We need to decolonize our thoughts around economic development in order to allow different approaches to flourish. Rather than continuing to demand neoliberal reforms like privatization and to put the pursuit of accumulation of as much wealth as possible as the primary objective of our economic activities, we need to instead pursue economic activities that lead to equal societies and ecological well-being. As The Red Nation says, "Healing the planet is ultimately about creating infrastructures of caretaking that will replace infrastructures of capitalism."[97]

Challenging dominant frameworks

Decolonization of our minds is primary to all of this work. We need to challenge the hegemonic narratives about capitalism and economics, exposing how they are set up to benefit the privileged few. For example, those who want to accumulate as much wealth as possible by pursuing endless growth put us in the position of choosing between human welfare or ecological stability—but this is a false dichotomy. The choice is actually between living in a more equitable society and risking ecological disaster. But the dominant narrative is so entrenched in our minds and in public understandings of economics that we have a lot to undo in order to advance new objectives and methods to achieve them.

Movement building is imperative to shifting narratives. We can learn many lessons from Indigenous networks of care and relations with plants, animals, land, and water. We can also learn from the efforts to abolish slavery, achieve voting rights and other civil rights, ban weapons like cluster munitions, landmines, and nuclear bombs, and to end wars and occupations. We can learn from radical feminists' struggles to end domination and oppression, which have never been exclusively about women's position in the society but about overall equality, solidarity, and justice within and between nations and people. At their very core, social movements construct an alternative narrative that changes what is considered "common sense" or normative and works to spread these ideas throughout society, transforming institutions, creating new ones, and changing the landscape of what is possible.

In the context of degrowth, this means building ideas and structures that can provide alternatives to capitalist exploitation. Giacomo D'Alisa and Giorgos Kallis suggest that "alternative economies, say food cooperatives or community currencies, are new civil society institutions that nurture new common senses. As they expand, they undo the common sense of growth and make degrowth ideas potentially hegemonic, creating conditions for a social and political force to change political institutions in the same direction."[98] The state is not just politicians and bureaucrats and institutions but is itself a process—a dialectic between civil and political society as they contest each other's approaches and ideas, argue D'Alisa and Kallis. The state is affected as new ideas and common senses emerge and grow. It is through this process that degrowth can emerge as a new common sense. "A transition beyond growth would require an end to the ideological and institutional hegemony of growth—this means an abolition of growth institutions and a demise of taken-for-granted growth values."[99]

Ideas from other abolitionist movements are essential to degrowth. Among other lessons, they teach us how to think about change at the scale necessary to confront our current ecological and economic crises.[100] They also offer lessons in how to work with the state and against the state at the same time, how to apply pressure in certain areas to transform what already exists, while working with others to create alternatives. It's important to note here that, as with all other work to abolish structures of violence, we need to distinguish between reforms that strengthen the status quo and reforms that "fundamentally challenge the existing structure of power by prioritizing, organizing, and elevating the needs and demands of the masses."[101] As discussed elsewhere in this book, Ruth Wilson Gilmore and other prison abolitionists describe these as "non-reformist reforms." Understanding that the state protects capital and the ruling class, rather than the people, we cannot simply appeal to the state for changes it is willing to accept—we must compel deeper changes that lead to the dismantlement of the systems sustaining oppression and inequality.

Solidarity

This is why solidarity must be at the backbone of any movement aimed at abolishing capitalism. Solidarity is more than kindness. When we exercise solidarity, we are making a political statement. It is an act born out of an understanding that we live in a system of oppression and inequality. It is an act born out of an understanding that we, as individuals or as part of a collective, can help bring down that system.

As such, solidarity is subversive, and, unlike kindness, is dangerous for the establishment. An act of kindness is an emotional response and is fundamental to who we are as human beings. But in order to transform that kindness into more than an act of compassion, it needs to have an aim. Acts of kindness need to become political. When we turn our emotion into political action, aiming to remove the structures that create the injustices to which we are responding, our acts become a politically powerful tool—a tool of solidarity. As political theorist Hannah Arendt explains in her book *On Revolution*, when we act in solidarity, we don't do it out of pity, we do it because we understand we are all equal. It is in this assertion of equality where the subversive power of solidarity lies.

As the COVID-19 pandemic progressed throughout 2020, we saw different acts of solidarity. Young people formed groups to deliver food for the elderly or walk their dogs; people shared books and recipes; and other ordinary activities that in times of crisis become a testimony of our humanity, a testimony to the importance of the collective. From volunteers delivering groceries to high-risk groups in Canada,[102] to massive numbers of people offering their help to the National Health Service in the United

Kingdom,[103] to local grassroots networks organizing awareness-raising campaigns in Burkina Faso, Cameroon, and the Democratic Republic of the Congo,[104] around the world, people took care of each other.

All of this outreach testifies to the vast possibilities and alternatives beyond destruction and exploitation. But in order for this amazing demonstration of solidarity to continue, we need to create systems that can foster solidarity beyond crisis mode and place it at the very center of our economy, our political system, and our interactions with each other. We need to transform our systems of governance, at the local, regional, and international levels. We need to turn solidarity actions into policies, mechanisms, and functional institutions, so that solidarity becomes a matter of political choice. So that it becomes how we organize our societies—always, not just in times of crisis.

New systems and institutions

How do we begin this work? The answer requires an inherently political and ideological discussion. This conversation goes to the very core of our considerations of how we want to organize our societies; how we want to organize power relations and decision-making structures; and how we want to govern the access, use, and control over "resources" and common goods. Careful documentation, analysis, and sharing of our lived experiences across feminist, anti-racist, and anti-capitalist networks and movements will help us imagine contextualized local, regional, and global pathways that don't only reshape existing structures, but actively imagine new ones.

For example:

What if we redefined our abusive relationship with the planet and broke the myth of infinite resources that upholds the idea of perpetual growth? What if we decided to abandon the capitalist way of thinking that "what is worth investing in is what generates profits"? What if we decided that the way we evaluate our economy should not be based on indicators such as gross domestic product, but on the ability of governments to provide for people's and the planet's well-being and on governments' proactive decisions to expand and rebuild our social infrastructure, by, for example, shifting from investing in militarism to investing in healthcare, education, and ending poverty? What if we measured the health of the economy based on people's physical and mental health? To do that, we would need to reevaluate how our public sector—including care, health-care, education, transportation, water and sanitation, social protection, and energy—is designed, funded, and governed.

What if we invested in the Green New Deal and started boosting local production based on restoration and regeneration, putting sustainability of the ecosystem at the center? What would that look like locally, region-ally, and globally? What are the policies we need to make this happen? They could include offering strong incentives for those who shift toward greener production while making sure that the workers whose jobs would become obsolete are offered tools, knowledge, and work in green industries and production; building more resilient local food production and ending factory farming; reversing privatization of "natural resources" and putting them under public control and public interest, guided by a symbiosis with nature; demanding long-term (de)investment planning that is guided by gender and human rights impact assessments; introducing heavy regula-tions on gas and oil production, and nationalization of these industries; devising demilitarization programs and redirecting funds made available from it into creation of green jobs; decriminalizing caretaking, such as blockades, protests, and other activities undertaken by land defenders and water protectors aimed at providing safety for our planet and people. The possibilities are endless.

What if we capped resource and energy use now and ratcheted it back every year? What if we banned the planned obsolescence of products, which leads to incredible waste; established robust legal frameworks for reducing pollution and waste emissions; prohibited profit-making from "natural resources" and moved toward responsible use of resources within the realm of public and community needs? What would those policies look like, taking into consideration the disproportionate devastation and poverty that capitalism has created in the countries of the Global South?

What policies would need to be put in place to allow us, as a collective, to eliminate poverty globally while at the same time making the necessary adjustments to degrowth and sustainability?

What if we invested in the Red Deal alongside the Green New Deal, prioritizing decolonization and redistribution of land and ensuring an end to corporate land grabs? What if we worked to give land back to Indigenous nations and learned from their stewardship to remediate land, water, air, and animals? What if we enforced treaty rights and protected and restored sacred sites and respected traditional and sustainable agriculture practices? What if we worked to end the horror of ongoing Missing and Murdered Indigenous Women, Girls, and Two-Spirit people (MMI-WG2S)—and all gender, sexual, and domestic violence?

What if we reimagined what care is and who does the caring? What if we undo structures and norms that lead to women doing a disproportionate amount of the care, both paid and—mostly—unpaid, in our societies? What if we used that process to set in motion policies and public investment priorities that will take the unpaid and undervalued care work out of the realm of our homes and make it part of a collective effort? What would we need to do to reduce and redistribute the hours women spend on social reproductive work in their homes and in their communities? And what needs to happen for care to be valued according to its importance in society? What would systematic introduction of gender-responsive budgeting into our planning mean for equality? What if we designed, funded, delivered, and managed public service around our gender equality dreams?

What if we systematically rethought what type of labor is valued and how we value it? What if we cut down on working hours, from eight to say six hours, while simultaneously working toward guarantees for decent salaries and universal right to work? Or what if we introduced a universal basic income? What if we established a maximum wage policy that caps wage ratios between workers and executives? What if we erased the hierarchy between "workers" and "executives" and put in place mechanisms that would ensure that everybody is in control over their own labor? What effect would that have on us as persons and us as a collective?

What if we banned by law privatization of, and profiteering from, public sector services and made sure that the money in the public sector is always reinvested, constantly improving conditions and accessibility of those public services? What if we used this opportunity to turn our back on decades of austerity measures, and instead of saving money on public services, and public interest and rights, we looked for ways to expand the investments? What if we introduced free and sustainable housing, education, healthcare, public transportation, and healthy food? Imagine what all this would mean next time we faced a pandemic or natural disaster. Perhaps our schools and day care centers would have physical infrastructure and financial means to safely accommodate children whose parents cannot work from home; perhaps we would not have houseless people unable to "stay at home"; perhaps hospitals would be prepared to take on massive numbers of sick people so that medical staff would not have to choose between the younger people and those of age; perhaps fewer people would be at risk of getting sick at all. Perhaps. It is worth imagining.

What if we put in motion a substantive, long-term investment plan for our public healthcare systems? What if we centered those investments around our dream of universal healthcare coverage and investments into preventive healthcare, with mandatory sexual and reproductive services? What if we centered those investments around nonprofit-driven medical research, medical staff, and general healthcare infrastructure? What would this mean next time we are faced with a pandemic or something similar? Perhaps this essential segment of our society will then be as prepared as it can possibly be and we will not need to applaud their sacrifices but simply recognize their professionalism and service; perhaps access to vaccines would not be subject to big-pharma profitability calculations.

What if we recognized that our unemployment benefits and other social welfare provisioning are poorly conceptualized and equipped to deal with a situation where massive amounts of people lose jobs simultaneously, and used this understanding to rethink the whole social provisioning system? What if we used this opportunity to carefully look into how social provisioning, instead of treating people as "beneficiaries" of specific assistance programs, could be a mechanism that supports the delivery of social, economic, and cultural rights across the society, so that our systems reflect our societal commitment to everybody's right to a decent life, free from want?

What if we used our realization that a lot of the essential work and services in our societies is underpaid and precarious work, and that it is done by migrants and refugees, to restore our sense of solidarity and openness, and put in place mechanisms that radically transform our notion of "citizens" as exclusive rights holders within our countries? What if we changed the narrow concept of "citizenship" based on ethno-national and cultural identities and racialized borders? What if we accepted responsibility for people's displacement due to colonialism, imperialism, conflict, and climate change by extending and expanding care to all, irrespective of their legal status, while at the same time creating the necessary conditions for everybody to thrive?

What if we used the momentum to redefine the relationship between the Global North and the Global South (and everything in between), ensuring that the hundreds of years of exploitation and waging wars for profit is redressed and repaid? What if we reimagined racialized borders, and worked to abolish them?

Before we pose the question about where the money will come from, *what if* we demanded full demilitarization of our societies? What if we started with divestment from the military industry? What if we adopted a global ceasefire? What if we shut down arms manufacturing and stopped nuclear weapon modernization programs and divested from weapons research and development? What if we instead redirected the billions of dollars going to weapons and war toward social and environmental well-being? What if we invested in dialogue, nonviolent communication, cooperation, and reconciliation instead of settling conflicts through blood and destruction?

What if we shifted our thinking around taxation, as this is by far the most important revenue our governments have? What if we rethought how we collect taxes, from whom we collect taxes, and where and how we spend the money collected? What if we shut down tax evasion systems of corporations within countries and transnationally? What if we established a wealth tax?

What if we canceled all sovereign debt accumulated through exploitative relationships between the borrower and the lender? What if countries came together to help each other, financially or otherwise, based on a sense of interdependence and guided by the principle of care instead of profit and exploitation of those who are already in distress? What if we dismantled the International Monetary Fund and other exploitative international financial institutions and introduced democratic oversight of national and international markets and finances; what if we built new institutions that embody a relationship of trust and responsibility between the lenders and borrowers so that the money borrowed is contracted and spent under fair and transparent conditions?

What if we built a new governance model? Getting rid of the growth imperative and capitalism will inevitably put the capitalist state in the focus of our changes. The capitalist state is built around strategies meant to preserve and entrench capitalism, under which the so-called free market and the superiority of growth ideology is constantly reproduced. Our current model of governance is hierarchical and authoritarian where we need it to be collaborative; it is exploitative instead of redistributive; it is repressive instead of accountable; it is oppressive instead of caring; it is chauvinistic instead of feminist and intersectional; it is shortsighted instead of sustainable; and it prioritizes protecting the private and the individual instead of nurturing the public and the collective.

When conceptualizing new governance models, we have to make sure that we don't replace one oppressive model with another. What if we put in place anti-racist, feminist, de-colonial redistributive policies—locally, regionally, and internationally? What would they look like? What would the structures tasked with implementing them look like? What are intermediate steps that will help us overcome the tensions between the need for nonhierarchical models of governance and the immediate need for the state to act and implement these policies?

What if, as we undertake these reforms, we abolish the state itself? What if . . . ?

These ideas are by no means exhaustive. But this kind of imagining, this kind of decolonization of our thinking about what is possible, feasible, and desired, is imperative to abolishing capitalism and building a more just, equitable, and sustainable life for everyone and everything on the planet. Each and any of these ideas are about taking less from our planet, from each other, and sharing more. As Hickel writes, this shift could move us "from scarcity to abundance, from extraction to regenerations, from dominion to reciprocity, and from loneliness and separation to connection with a world that's fizzing with life."[105]

We are already seeing the growth of anti-capitalist movements around the world, from workers' strikes and unionization initiatives, to the actions of human rights, land, and water defenders, to protests against austerity, corruption, war, occupation, and police brutality—all of these have at their heart an opposition to the status quo, to rising inequality and poverty and planetary devastation. The world has been shaken by waves of revolt over the last decade by workers and the oppressed from the Arab Spring to the uprisings in Hong Kong, Thailand, Myanmar, and elsewhere, as well as the women's and climate strikes around the globe. In the United States, we've seen the uprisings from Occupy, Black Lives Matter, Chicago teachers' strikes, and most dramatically the 2020 revolts against police brutality, the largest in US history. Each of these is connected and provides opportunities to collaborate against capitalism, across borders, identities, and experiences.

The capitalist class has always sought to ensure alienation of workers from each other, based on race, gender, geography, or any other division they thought they could exploit. They understand that once we recognized the common cause among us all, the connections between our struggles and experiences and the solutions to these problems, we could revolt against the capitalist system together, disrupting their profits and threatening their wealth. It is through this commonality, discovered and strengthened through solidarity, that we as the majority—the abolitionist organizers, activists, workers, feminists, migrants, Indigenous nations, people of color, and more—can, and must, build a new world together.

Conclusion

Abolition as Movement

Abolishing state violence for global transformation has been the theme of this book. The critique has focused on systems, structures, and institutions that cause harm in our world, from police and prisons to borders and militarism to surveillance and capitalism—and how all of these are intertwined, feeding off each other to reproduce, self-perpetuate, and ultimately result in privilege and profit for the wealthy few and misery for the majority.

"The purpose of abolition is to expose and defeat all the relationships and policies that make the United States the world's top cop, war monger, and jailer," writes Ruth Wilson Gilmore.[1] This means that work to disarm, demilitarize, defund, disband, and demolish cannot focus exclusively on the police, or the military, or Immigration and Customs Enforcement, but on all of these systems and structures. Or rather, that while we critique and oppose each of these institutions, it should be as part of the bigger project of dismantling the foundations of them all, being attuned to their connections through budgets, weapons, tactics, training, and personnel; and centering opposition to each within the broader critique of racism, patriarchy, fascism, capitalism, colonialism, imperialism, and militarism that these institutions require to survive and thrive.

Abolishing these systems, however, is not just about eliminating them. It is about building something in their place, on the basis of justice, equality, and care. Replacing capitalism with degrowth and ecological sustainability; replacing police and prisons with structures of promiscuous care and transformative justice; and replacing weapons and war with nonviolence and cooperation. "Abolition is not just about closing the doors to violent institutions," write organizers Morgan Bassichis, Alexander Lee, and Dean Spade, "but also about building up and recovering institutions and practices and relationships that nurture wholeness, self-determination, and transformation."[2]

The divest-invest framework is essential to abolition. It means divesting money and support from institutions that cause harm—prisons, fossil fuels, nuclear weapons, militaries, etc.—and investing instead in care—in education, housing, jobs, food security, ecological sustainability, etc. Abolition can be read as having three main components: dismantling structures of harm, providing support to people targeted by the current system, and building the new systems we need to live in a world without police, prisons, borders, war, and other institutions of violence.[3] As Ruth Wilson Gilmore and Mariame Kaba and other prison abolitionists say again and again, we're not just out to dismantle prisons, we're working to dismantle the conditions that make prisons possible, under which prisons become the solution to problems. The same approach can be applied to borders, war, and all the other structures and institutions causing harm in our world.

Imagining and building our way out of destruction

For this work, we need feminist curiosity and imagination. We need to look beyond ourselves to what others need, to what our planet needs—not just to survive, but to heal and to thrive. "Feminism is a political project about what *could be*," explains writer Lola Olufemi. "It's always looking forward, invested in futures we can't quite grasp yet. It's a way of wishing, hoping, aiming at everything that has been deemed impossible. It's a task that has to be approached seriously—we must think about the limits of this world and the possibilities contained in the ones we could craft together."[4]

Abolition is about imagination, but it's also about facing the reality that we cannot continue the way that we've been going. It means understanding that the perpetual growth of capitalism is a myth. That the concept of nuclear deterrence is a theory. That the belief that violence makes one strong or that caging people makes others safe is detrimental to us all. The myths and misconceptions about our world are built deliberately by the select few who profit from them.

The reality of our history and current experience is rewritten, obscured, whited out, revised; institutions producing immense violence and suffering are whitewashed, pinkwashed, greenwashed by cosmetic reforms that preclude real change; and the truth of our present reality and the possibilities for our future are confined, limited, and curtailed by forces that often seem far greater than what we can muster in opposition. We are taught to wear blinders, which prevent us from becoming enraged about what has been done to us, to our planet, and from confronting those who have destroyed us and our future. Or we are told to accept the world for what it is: nasty, brutish, and, in the Anthropocene, increasingly short.

Unlearning the necessity of violence is essential to exploring what could be built in its place. This means turning on its head so much of what we are taught about what's necessary for safety and security in our world. It means learning to reject violence as a solution to all problems, interrogating and challenging systems of power that assert they exist to protect while instead they persecute and oppress. Abolition isn't radical, argues Indigenous organizer Robyn Oxley. "What is radical is living in a society where acts of violence are accepted because a blue uniform is worn or where racist legislation exists."[5] This is the mindset we need to grasp. Undoing state violence requires undoing the hold these institutions have on our imaginations, on our conceptions of what is normal, what we must live with, what is possible. While police, prisons, borders, and war uphold the world that is, "abolition fights for the world that should be."[6]

In this fight, we can't allow ourselves to be constrained by the institutions we oppose. Structures of violence and harm must not demarcate or limit what is credible or realistic or possible. Emancipatory politics and imaginings require us to revolt against what Tim Hollo of the Green Institute describes as "a supplicant politics, where we beg or demand of governments that they act."[7] We can instead learn from many Indigenous and queer activists who organize and build within spaces and with methods they have established in their own communities. For many First Nations, this is an existential imperative. "The genocidal intentions of settler states lie not only in the wide range of measures used to diminish, contain and destroy First Nations people, but in the suppression of Indigenous knowledge, ontologies and ways of living that are carried through and in the land," note scholars Brenna Bhandar and Rafeef Ziadah.[8] When the state is built to repress, appealing to it for equality or care is insufficient.

Organizing against state violence will mean not only contesting the institutions of the state but building alternatives. Doing an end run around power is entirely possible. Whether it's a bunch of countries outlawing nuclear weapons without the permission or participation of the nuclear-armed states, or the establishment of mutual aid groups, or the development of local transformative justice initiatives to deal with redress and restitution for harms caused within communities, or provision of humanitarian aid and safe havens along borders, there are countless ways in which people around the world are already engaged in the work of abolition.

Not everything will work. "Organizing is mostly about defeats," says leading abolitionist Mariame Kaba.[9] But abolition is not a zero-sum game. It's not about win-lose. It's about trying things out, building community and relations with others committed to change, and seeing what sticks. "Right now, all we're doing as organizers is creating the conditions that will allow our collective vision to take hold and grow," says Kaba. Abolition is not instantaneous; it's iterative, and it takes imagination.[10]

Decolonizing and decarcerating our minds

Challenging long-held narratives and fighting for our freedom to imagine are central to creating the conditions for change. We need to build movements of solidarity and care, rather than siloed and piecemeal corporate, private, or even nongovernmental initiatives that tinker at the edges while most of the world is dragged down below water. Radical organizing has been historically oppressed by the state, while the growth of the nonprofit sector has "professionalized" social movements, refocusing efforts on fundraising for specific projects deemed realistic or achievable, suggesting and appealing for reforms, rather than pursuing initiatives aimed at addressing the underlying causes of poverty, injustice, and inequality. This has "left significant sections of the radical left traumatized and decimated," warn Bassichis, Lee, and Spade, "shifting the terms of resistance from revolution and transformation to inclusion and reform, prioritizing state- and foundation-sanctioned legal reforms and social services over mass organizing and direct action."[11]

Nevertheless, ideas and actions for abolition are surging. In the wake of the growing nightmare created by imperialist governments for migrants around the world; the violent police crackdowns against Black, Indigenous, and other people of color in settler colonial states and against religious and ethnic minorities in many countries; the vast ecological destruction and economic inequalities generated by capitalist exploits and extraction; the impacts of wars and the "national security state"—in the wake of all these and more, people are looking for alternatives. While some turn to reform, pitched by the profiting and profiteering class as reasonable, realistic, and rational, many understand that reform is not going to save us—that we are so far gone that we need to engage in much more ambitious actions to protect people and planet.

The first step is decarcerating and decolonizing our minds from the violent institutions we are told are our protectors—including police, prisons, militaries, weapons, borders, surveillance systems, the capitalist economy—and recognizing that our freedom and well-being lie not with reforming that which oppresses us but with abolishing it altogether.

Abolition is about more than any one of these systems; it is about dismantling the underlying injustice, inequality, racism, militarism, colonialism, patriarchy, heteronormativity, ableism, etc. Being aware of the relationships among all the various structures of violence—which constitute, if you will, a war of the state against people and planet—enables us to mount more effective campaigns against each of the individual institutions and the collective war machine.

People experience oppression based on the intersections of their many identities and experiences. Thus, the opposition to the sources of oppression also needs to be reflective of these differences and allow these perspectives to inform crosscutting work for abolition. This includes building transnational activism that links anti-war, anti-militarism, and antinuclear work with the efforts of those campaigning for economic justice, environmental protection, open borders and migrant rights, anti-racism and anti-fascism, equality, and police and prison abolition. When the war system is considered as a whole, the relationship between these different sites of activism becomes clear.

This kind of thinking and work is already underway. The Abolitionist Platform toward Healthy Communities established by groups including Critical Resistance, Black Visions Collective, Survived and Punished, The Red Nation, and others calls for "the intersectional efforts of anti-imprisonment, anti-policing, and anti-imperialist struggles to coalesce concretely as a response to the COVID-crisis" and beyond.[12] Its demands include freedom for all imprisoned and detained people; resistance to surveillance, policing, and militarized responses to COVID-19; access to quality healthcare now and in the future; access to housing, food, and economic security; and international efforts to end US imperialism and militarism.

The Abolishing the War on Terror agenda, put forward by Justice for Muslims Collective, HEART Women & Girls, Vigilant Love, the Partnership to End Gendered Islamophobia, Project South, the Partnership for the Advancement of New Americans (PANA), and the US Campaign for Palestinian Rights (USCPR), draws inspiration from the movement demands to abolish ICE and defund the police.[13] Promoting a divest-and-invest framework of abolition, it asserts that the call to dismantle the military and the war on terror complex should be part of a broader discussion and organizing for global justice and transformation to provide care, protection, and repair for communities affected by the war on terror in the United States and abroad.

Many Indigenous activists see crosscutting opportunities with environmental activism, pointing out that many of the actions needed to mitigate climate change and protect land, water, and the environment are the same practices of preservation and respect that Indigenous communities have always honored. In response to the promotion of the Green New Deal by environmental and economic justice activists, The Red Nation has proposed a Red Deal[14] to ensure this kind of work also leads to decolonization, anti-imperialism, and an end to settler colonialism. Anti-war activists have also noted that the Green New Deal must have antimilitarism at its core, since war and the US military in particular "render impossible the aspirations contained in the Green New Deal."[15]

Meanwhile, the Poor People's Campaign's efforts to secure a cut to US military spending calls for an end to systemic racism, poverty and inequality, ecological devastation, and militarism and the war economy. Leaders of this campaign have recognized that as demands to demilitarize the police and redirect funds gain traction across the United States, the government needs to reimagine its approach to "national security." In particular, the Poor People's Campaign argues, "To create *real* security, we must slash the Pentagon budget, dismantle the war economy, and invest instead in meeting everyone's basic human needs."[16] Similarly, US peace group CODEPINK has articulated many of the connections between US wars abroad and at home and argued that defunding the police must be accompanied by defunding war.

There are also synergies in the movements to defund the military and police and those seeking open borders and the right for every person to have *the freedom to move or not to move*. Just as the Poor People's Campaign declares that everybody has the right to live, the no borders movement calls for the rights of being a person. In contrast to rights of property, consisting of the right to exclude others from enjoying that which has been privatized, the right of persons consists of the right not to be excluded. Joseph Nevins also describes this right in his appeal for "the right to the world"—a right to mobility and to share our planet's resources sustainably.[17] A no borders politics looks to dismantle the apparatus of border imperialism but is a broader emancipatory project that aligns well with movements to end the prison industrial complex, the surveillance state, and the institutions of weapons and war-making.

The recognition of the connections of these struggles for justice, equity, and well-being of people and planet of course goes back much further than our current time. Since the early days of resistance against settler colonialism, slavery, and segregation, Black and Indigenous organizers have identified the relationships between the violence committed against them and the institutions constructed by the state. They have also articulated and opposed the relationship between this violence at home and the wars of imperialism abroad. Feminists have long articulated the links between the violence of patriarchy and racism at home and abroad and have campaigned against war as the most violent expression of these systems. Since 1915, the Women's International League for Peace and Freedom (WILPF) has called for the abolition of war and war profiteering, identifying these as patriarchal institutions facilitating capitalist accumulation and global imperialism. WILPF demands that war be made illegal, rejecting armed conflict "as a means of settling differences between people" and calling for "the abolition of private manufacture of and traffic in munitions of war . . . as steps towards total international disarmament."[18] It has always connected these divesting from "the crushing burden of armaments" in order "to attack the social and economic problems created by large scale hunger, disease and illiteracy which have been among the prime causes of war."[19]

This history is important. It offers insights and inspirations into the collaborations that are possible and necessary to overcome the "sophisticated, high-tech system of militarized policing, caging, and borders" that has been built over hundreds of years. Constructing this system, argues

Dean Spade, "required changing society so that these ways of seeing and treating each other as disposable are acceptable and normal, producing whole new industries, producing whole new areas of research and knowledge production to support these activities, building the infrastructures of courts and administrative systems and laws, and of course the buildings and cages and fences and tanks and guns and tasers and paddy wagons and the rest."[20] But just as these systems were deliberately constructed, they can be deliberately deconstructed.

Working beyond hope

Drawing connections between oppressions, as well as between various sites of resistance to them, is imperative to the process of freeing our imaginations in preparation for building a new kind of world. Once we have imagined a different way of doing things, we must then act to achieve it. We must do this even if it feels like we can't, or like we won't make a difference, or that the system is too big, too entrenched, too powerful to ever be overcome.

In November 1940, during World War II, French philosopher Albert Camus wrote, "We can despair of existence, for we have no power over it, but not of history, where the individual can do everything. It is individuals who are killing us today. Why should not individuals manage to give the world peace? We must simply begin without thinking of such grandiose aims."[21] If the work of abolition and transformation seems too big, too grandiose, too impossible, just begin where you are, with the actions you can undertake. In your communities, your schools, your city councils. And when it's possible, look up, because you will see many others with you, working on different pieces of the same project, all over the world.

Our feelings of hopelessness or despair do not afford us the right to abdicate our individual and collective responsibility to at least try to make the world a better place. Instead, we need to work in solidarity with others that are pursuing the same ends. We don't have to be in relationship with everyone, we don't have to all do the same work or have the same skills or work against every injustice—but we can support each other and recognize that our efforts take place within a larger community of others working for abolition in a myriad of ways and places.

Hope, in this context, is not necessarily about us as individuals being able to achieve a specific end, but about the ability of us as a collective— including future generations—to drive forward the changes we need to bring justice, safety, and love to humankind and all relations with whom we share our lives on this planet. "Hope about the future and faith in the possibility of change is not something that comes easy," attests Spade; "it is an active practice based in our principles of winning deep, transformative change rather than system-affirming false victories."[22]

The dispossession and displacement created by the structures and systems of violence explored in this series are made through many different processes—settler colonialism, enslavement, occupation, wars, military bases, extraction, economic imperialism, and so much more. This is why solidarity among various abolitionist projects is imperative. As scholar Lisa Lowe argues, because we are working across different oppressions and experiences, "our analytic frames and organising practices likewise cannot be limited to a single logic, issue or national framework."[23] The scope of our vision benefits from a wider lens, even while our actions might be local.

Understanding this "big picture" doesn't mean we each as individuals need to solve every piece of it. But it does mean we need to recognize and support each other's efforts and reflect in our own work the analysis and organizing of various movements and projects. The sum of our whole is greater than our parts, and going up against the machine of capitalist violence can feel immense—unless we break it down and rebuild something else, together.

Ruth Wilson Gilmore has noted that so many people and groups are already part of abolitionist projects, many without even realizing it—faith organizations, neighborhood organizations, tenant organizations, artist organizations, prisoner organizations, libraries, environmental justice groups, legal aid providers, transit workers, rights advocates, public health advocates, bail funds, and so many more are actively working to "relieve the stress of organized abandonment" of neoliberal austerity and the capitalist political economy.[24] We can add to this list, we can all be a part of it. The work is only overwhelming if we are alone; as Kaba always says, everything worthwhile is done with other people.

It feels, most days, like we are reaching a crossroads. As the pandemic continues to devastate economies and exacerbate inequalities within and among countries; as people try to flee their homelands due to the ravages of climate change, colonialism, capitalism, and conflict, only to be met with border violence, walls, and weapons of detention and deportation; as we see white supremacists taking up their long-stockpiled arms against those standing up for Black lives; as we feel the surging pulse of fascism spread like a virus—as we face all this, we can either succumb to the violence, or we can stand to abolish the systems and structures that enable it. We have nothing to lose but our chains.

Acknowledgments

This book was created during a period of great suffering and incredible activism. The emergence of COVID-19 not only brought forth a global health pandemic but also compounded the already existing cruelties of our current world order. As people around the world have struggled with the virus and its economic and social consequences, the underlying pandemic of the capitalist world order has continued to wreak havoc on our ability to cope and survive. Simultaneously, the murders of yet more Black people in the United States by police; the cruelty against migrants in detention centers around the world; the ongoing bombings and occupations of so many towns, cities, and countries; and the lasting and contemporary impacts of settler colonialism on Indigenous communities have forced, in many places, a reckoning with past and current oppression and violence.

This book is not meant to be a comprehensive accounting or analysis of all the harms caused in our world but is rather an effort to bring together some critical strands of nonviolent confrontations and oppositions to racism, militarism, capitalism, and patriarchy. I am incredibly grateful to all the authors and activists whose work I reference throughout these chapters. Generations of thought and organizing have gone into confronting the systems of violence that oppress and harm people and the planet; every day there are new inspirations and sources for action, study, and struggle. While this collection does not cover everything, it tries to amplify some of the past and ongoing work across a range of abolitionist efforts. Thank you to all the organizers, activists, academics, and others who work for abolition.

I am so appreciative to my colleagues and friends at the Women's International League for Peace and Freedom (WILPF) who helped transform some of my thoughts about abolition into this book. Thank you to Nina Maria Mørk Hansen for the idea of turning essays I was writing in mid-2020 into a long-read series for WILPF and then into an e-publication, which then led to the creation of this book. Thanks to Emily Dontsos for help with copyediting the e-pub, which was very useful when it came to preparing the first draft of the book. And, as always, thanks to Ashish Mahajan for fixing all the things and making so much possible.

I have worlds of gratitude for those who read the first drafts of these essays, providing thoughts and comments and ideas for additional resources. Thank you to Nela Porobić, Dean Peacock, and Madeleine Rees for all your time and brilliant insights. Extra huge thanks to Madeleine for always giving me the space and courage to write ambitiously and creatively, and to Nela for not only coauthoring the chapter on capitalism with me while trying to meet her own writing deadlines, but also for being a true comrade through thick and thin.

Thanks to Liz O'Sullivan, Jack Poulson, Allison Pytlak, and Felicity Ruby for feedback on the surveillance chapter and to Zia Mian for reading through it all. Extra hat tip to Allison, with whom I get to work daily, for sharing my gallows humor about the insidious, relentless development of technologies that human beings craft to kill each other more "efficiently." Without camaraderie, so much of the work we do would be so much more difficult. In this spirit, endless thanks to Amy Brown and Alicia Godsberg for the refuge, Dimity Hawkins for encouragement across oceans, Chris Moore for the many stoop hangs through a long, cold winter, and Tim Wright for always being up for abolishing everything.

Thanks to all the other organizers, activists, and writers who have taught me along the way, especially those working to build something better, disrupting business as usual with direct action, advocating outside of the "credibility trap," collaborating across borders and identities, and more. Many of these I am fortunate to work with and learn from directly; many I do not know personally but have influenced my thinking and shaped my actions. The work of people from both categories is reflected throughout this book in references and the further resources section. Creating a list here of people to thank for my political education would be too long and would inevitably, unintentionally, leave people out. But a few quick shout-outs are warranted, including to Robert Croonquist for being a Direct-Action Hero, always setting an example with legendary organizing and vegan cookies, including during a pandemic; to Kathleen Sullivan and Blaise Dupuy for bringing people together and valuing community; and to Gem Romuld and the rest of the queer Australian antinuclear crew for being a touchstone of fierceness, creativity, and compassion in organizing and action.

From Haymarket Books, enormous thanks go to Rory Fanning for seeing this series of essays for what it could be and taking it forward with confidence. Endless thanks also to Nisha Bolsey for incredible guidance, advice, and encouragement, and for answering so many of my novice questions with grace. Thanks to Julie Fain for stepping in to bring it to fruition. Thank you to Ashley Smith for the extremely thoughtful suggestions that helped deepen this book, and to Lillian Duggan for the careful copyediting that helped this book become a better version of itself. It's been a lifelong dream of mine to write for Haymarket, and I'm honored and humbled to have been able to share this experience with such a dedicated, friendly team.

Most of all, thank you to everyone who engages in struggle for a better world. This is about and for all of you.

Further Resources

The resources provided here are by no means comprehensive. They are meant to highlight important tools for learning and organizing across a range of abolitionist efforts covered by this book. The resources listed are predominantly situated within or developed by those situated in the United States, Canada, and Europe. A global list of resources would be much more expansive and inclusive.

Organizations, coalitions, and campaigns

#8toAbolition
www.8toabolition.com

Abolish Frontex
www.abolishfrontex.org

About Face: Veterans Against the War
www.aboutfaceveterans.org

Algorithmic Justice League
www.ajl.org

Amnesty Tech
www.amnesty.org/en/tech

Beyond Prisons
www.beyond-prisons.com

Black & Pink
www.blackandpink.org

Black Lives Matter
www.blacklivesmatter.com

Black Visions Collective
www.blackvisionsmn.org

Black Youth Project 100
www.byp100.org

Border Violence Monitoring Network
www.borderviolence.eu

Campaign Against Arms Trade
www.caat.org.uk

Care Not Cops
www.carenotcops.org

The Citizen Lab
www.citizenlab.ca

Coalition Against Stalkerware
www.stopstalkerware.org

CODEPINK
www.codepink.org

Conflict and Environment Observatory
www.ceobs.org

CorpWatch
www.corpwatch.org

Costs of War
www.watson.brown.edu/costsofwar

Critical Resistance
www.criticalresistance.org

Defund the Police
www.defundpolice.org

Detention Watch Network
www.detentionwatchnetwork.org

Electronic Frontier Foundation
www.eff.org

Fight for the Future
www.fightforthefuture.org

Gays Against Guns
www.gaysagainstguns.net

Gidimt'en Checkpoint
www.yintahaccess.com

Global Detention Project
www.globaldetentionproject.org

Idle No More
www.idlenomore.ca

INCITE! Women, Gender Non-conforming, and Trans People of Color Against Violence
www.incite-national.org

International Campaign to Abolish Nuclear Weapons
www.icanw.org

Justice for Muslims Collective
www.justiceformuslims.org

Mapping Police Violence
www.mappingpoliceviolence.org

MPD150
www.mpd150.com

Ni Una Menos
www.niunamenos.org.ar

No More Deaths/No Más Muertes
www.nomoredeaths.org

No Name Kitchen
www.nonamekitchen.org

Prison Abolition Resource Guide
www.micahherskind.com/abolition-resource-guide

Prison Culture
www.usprisonculture.com/blog

Prison Policy Initiative
www.prisonpolicy.org

Privacy International
www.privacyinternational.org

Project Nia
www.project-nia.org

Project South
www.projectsouth.org

Reclaim the Block
www.reclaimtheblock.org

The Red Nation
www.therednation.org

Rise and Resist
www.riseandresist.org

School of the Americas Watch
www.soaw.org

Stop Killer Robots
www.stopkillerrobots.org

Stop LAPD Spying
www.stoplapdspying.org

Stop Line 3
www.stopline3.org

Stop the Arms Fair
www.stopthearmsfair.org.uk

Surveillance & Society
www.surveillance-and-society.org

Surveillance Technology Oversight Project
www.stopspying.org

Survived and Punished
www.survivedandpunished.org

Tech Workers Coalition
www.techworkerscoalition.org

Transbalkanska Solidarnost
www.transbalkanskasolidarnost.
home.blog

TransformHarm
www.transformharm.org

Veterans for Peace
www.veteransforpeace.org

War Resisters' International
www.wri-irg.org

Women's International League for Peace and Freedom
www.wilpf.org

Books, articles, and Internet publications

Abu Saif, Atef. *The Drone Eats with Me: A Gaza Diary.* Boston: Beacon Press, 2014.

Acheson, Ray. *Banning the Bomb, Smashing the Patriarchy.* London: Rowman and Littlefield, 2021.

Ahmed, Kaamil and Lorenzo Tondo. "Fortress Europe: the millions spent on military-grade tech to deter refugees." *The Guardian*, December 6, 2021.

Alexander, Michelle. *The New Jim Crow: Mass Incarceration in the Age of Colorblindness.* New York: The New Press, 2012.

Anderson, Bridget, Nandita Sharma, and Cynthia Wright. "Editorial: Why No Borders?"

Refuge: Canada's Journal on Refugees 26, no. 2 (2009): 5–18.

Are You Syrious? (daily news digest). areyousyrious.medium.com.

Arruzza, Cinzia, Tithi Bhattacharya, and Nancy Fraser. *Feminism for the 99%: A Manifesto.* London: Verso, 2019.

Asaro, Peter. "Will #BlackLivesMatter to Robocop?" University of Miami School of Law, 2016.

Baran, Paul and Paul Sweezy. *Monopoly Capital: An Essay on the American Economic and Social Order.* New York: New York University Press, 1968.

Benjamin, Ruha. *Race After Technology: Abolitionist Tools for the New Jim Code.* Boston: Polity, 2019.

Bennis, Phyllis. "A Green New Deal Needs to Fight US Militarism." *Jacobin*, March 8, 2019.

Berger, Dan. *The Struggle Within: Prisons, Political Prisoners, and Mass Movements in the United States.* San Francisco: PM Press, 2014.

Berger, Dan and Emily K. Hobson. *Remaking Radicalism: A Grassroots Documentary Reader of the United States, 1973–2001.* Athens: University of Georgia Press, 2020.

Bhandar, Brenna and Rafeef Ziadah, eds. *Revolutionary Feminisms: Conversations on Collective Action and Radical*

Thought. London: Verso, 2020.

Biswas, Shampa. *Nuclear Desire: Power and the Postcolonial Nuclear Order.* Minneapolis: University of Minnesota Press, 2014.

Blitzer, Jonathan. "Is It Time to Defund the Department of Homeland Security?" *New Yorker*, July 24, 2020.

The Border Chronicle. https://theborderchronicle.substack.com.

Brockway, Fenner and Frederic Mullally. *Death Pays a Dividend.* London: Victor Gollancz Ltd, 1944.

Brown, Kate. *Plutopia: Nuclear Families, Atomic Cities, and the Great Soviet and American Plutonium Disasters.* Oxford: Oxford University Press, 2013.

Buolamwini, Joy, Aaina Agarwal, Nicole Hughes, and Sasha Costanza-Chock. "We Must Fight Face Surveillance to Protect Black Lives." Medium, June 3, 2020.

Camp, Jordan T. and Christina Heatherton. *Policing the Planet: Why the Policing Crisis Led to Black Lives Matter.* New York: Verso Books, 2016.

Cantú, Francisco. *The Line Becomes a River: Dispatches from the Border.* New York: Riverhead Books, 2018.

The Care Collective. *The Care Manifesto: The Politics of Interdependence.*

London: Verso, 2020.

Chacón, Justin Akers. *The Border Crossed Us: The Case for Opening the US-Mexico Border.* Chicago: Haymarket Books, 2021.

Chamayou, Grégoire. *A Theory of the Drone.* New York: The New Press, 2015.

Chengeta, Thompson. "Accountability Gap: Autonomous Weapon Systems and Modes of Responsibility in International Law." *Denver Journal of International Law* 45, no. 1 (2016): 1–50.

———. "Dignity, ubuntu, humanity and autonomous weapon systems (AWS) debate: an African perspective." *Brazilian Journal of International Law* 13, no. 2 (2016): 461–502.

Chomsky, Noam. *Hegemony or Survival: America's Quest for Global Dominance.* New York: Metropolitan Books, 2003.

———. "The Pentagon System." *Z Magazine*, February 1993.

Cockburn, Cynthia. *Antimilitarism: Political and Gender Dynamics of Peace Movements.* London: Palgrave Macmillan, 2012.

———. *From Where We Stand: War, Women's Activism, and Feminist Analysis.* London: Zed Books, 2007.

Cohen, Cathy J. "Punks, Bulldaggers, and Welfare Queens: The Radical Potential of Queer Politics?" *GLQ* 3 (1997): 437–85.

Cohn, Carol. "Sex and Death in the Rational World of Defense Intellectuals." *Signs* 12, no. 4 (1987): 687–718.

———. "Wars, Wimps, and Women: Talking Gender and Thinking War." In *Gendering War Talk*, edited by Miriame Cooke and Angela Woollacott, 227–46. Princeton: Princeton University Press, 1993.

Cohn, Carol and Sara Ruddick. "A Feminist Ethical Perspective on Weapons of Mass Destruction." In *Ethics and Weapons of Mass Destruction: Religious and Secular Perspectives,* edited by Sohail H. Hashmi and Steven P. Lee, 405–35. Cambridge: Cambridge University Press, 2004.

Cook-Lynn, Elizabeth. *New Indians, Old Wars.* Chicago: University of Illinois Press, 2007.

CopsAreFlops. "Re-imagining Justice in South Africa Beyond Policing— New info pack on policing and abolition." 2020. https://drive. google.com/file/d/1krNcg_ saPFABqjuFkQvtVKUpIjivd8Es/ view.

Crawford, Neta C. "Pentagon Fuel Use, Climate Change, and the Costs of War." In "Costs of War." Watson Institute for International and Public Affairs at Brown University,

July 1, 2019, https://watson.brown.edu/research/2019/pentagon-fuel-use-climate-change-and-costs-war.

———. "United States Budgetary Costs and Obligations of Post-9/11 Wars through FY2020: $6.4 Trillion." In "Costs of War." Watson Institute for International and Public Affairs at Brown University, 2019.

Crawford, Neta C. and Catherine Lutz. "Too much military spending got us into this mess." *Boston Globe*, June 7, 2020.

Crenshaw, Kimberlé. "Demarginalizing the Intersection of Race and Sex: A Black Feminist Critique of Antidiscrimination Doctrine, Feministy Theory and Antiracist Politics." *University of Chicago Legal Forum* 1989, no. 1 (1989): 139–67.

Critical Resistance. *Abolition Now!* Oakland, CA: AK Press, 2008.

———. "Abolitionist Platform Toward Healthy Communities Now and Beyond COVID-19." April 2020. http://criticalresistance.org/abolitionist-platform-toward-healthy-communities-now-and-onward.

D'Alisa, Giacomo, Federico Demaria, and Giorgos Kallis, eds. *Degrowth: A Vocabulary for a New Era*. London and New York: Routledge, 2015.

D'Alisa, Giacomo and Giorgos Kallis. "Degrowth and the State." *Ecological Economics* 169 (2020): 1–9.

Das, Runa. "Colonial legacies, post-colonial (in)securities, and gender(ed) representations in South Asia's nuclear policies." *Social Identities* 16, no. 6 (2010): 717–40.

Davis, Angela. *Abolition Democracy: Beyond Empire, Prisons, and Torture*. New York: Seven Stories Press, 2005.

———. *Are Prisons Obsolete?* New York: Seven Stories Press, 2003.

———. *Freedom Is a Constant Struggle: Ferguson, Palestine, and the Foundations of a Movement*. Chicago: Haymarket Books, 2015.

———. "Masked Racism: Reflections on the Prison Industrial Complex." Colorlines, September 10, 1998.

Davis, Angela and Gina Dent. "Prison as a Border: A Conversation on Gender, Globalization, and Punishment." *Signs* 26, no. 4 (Summer 2001): 1235–41.

Davis, Angela, Gina Dent, Erica R. Meiners, and Beth E. Richie, *Abolition. Feminism. Now.* Chicago: Haymarket Books, 2022.

Davis, Mike. "Hell factories in the field: a prison-industrial complex." *The Nation*, February 20, 1995.

DeGrasse, Robert W. *Military Expansion, Economic Decline*. New York: Council on

Economic Priorities, 1983.

De León, Jason. *The Land of Open Graves: Living and Dying on the Migrant Trail*. Oakland, CA: University of California Press, 2015.

Dixon, Ejeris and Leah Lakshmi Piepzna-Samarasinha, eds. *Beyond Survival: Strategies and Stories from the Transformative Justice Movement*. Oakland, CA: AK Press, 2020.

Du Bois, W.E.B. *Black Reconstruction in America: An Essay Toward the History of the Part Which Black Folk Played in the Attempt to Reconstruct Democracy in America, 1860–1880*. New York: The Free Press, 1998 [1935].

Dubrofsky, Rachel E. and Shoshana Amielle Magnet, eds. *Feminist Surveillance Studies*. Durham, NC: Duke University Press, 2015.

Ellsberg, Daniel. *The Doomsday Machine: Confessions of a Nuclear War Planner*. New York: Bloomsbury, 2017.

Enloe, Cynthia. *Bananas, Beaches and Bases: Making Feminist Sense of International Politics*. Berkeley, CA: University of California Press, 2014.

———. "Beyond 'Rambo': women and the varieties of militarized masculinity." In *Women and the Military System*, edited by Eva Isaakson, 71–93. New York:

St. Martin's Press, 1988.

———. *Globalization and Militarism: Feminists Make the Link*. London: Rowman and Littlefield, 2016.

Estes, Nick. *Our History is the Future: Standing Rock versus the Dakota Access Pipeline, and the Long Tradition of Indigenous Resistance*. New York: Verso, 2019.

Fakier, Khayaat, Diana Mulinari, and Nora Räthzel, eds. *Marxist-Feminist Theories and Struggles Today*. London: Zed Books, 2020.

Frey, John Carlos. *Sand and Blood: America's Stealth War on the Mexico Border*. New York: Bold Type Books, 2019.

Gago, Verónica. *Feminist International: How to Change Everything*. London: Verso, 2020.

Galeano, Eduardo. *Open Veins of Latin America: Five Centuries of the Pillage of a Continent*. New York: Monthly Review Press, 1973.

Gamal, Fanna. "The Racial Politics of Protection: A Critical Race Examination of Police Militarization." *California Law Review* 104, no. 4 (2016): 979–1008.

Gilmore, Ruth Wilson. *Change Everything: Racial Capitalism and the Case for Abolition*. Chicago: Haymarket Books, 2022.

———. "Globalisation and US

prison growth: from military Keynesianism to post-Keynesian militarism." *Race and Class* 40, no. 2-3 (1998–1999): 171–87.

———. *Golden Gulag: Prisons, Surplus, Crisis, and Opposition in Globalizing California*. Berkeley and Los Angeles: University of California Press, 2007.

Gusterson, Hugh. "Nuclear Weapons and the Other in the Western Imagination." *Cultural Anthropology* 14, no. 1 (1999): 111–43.

Halper, Jeff. *War Against the People*. London: Pluto Press, 2015.

Hamaji, Kate, Kumar Rao, Marbre Stahly-Butts, Janaé Bonsu, Charlene Carruthers, Roselyn Berry, and Denzel McCampbell. "Freedom to Thrive: Reimagining Safety & Security in our Communities." Center for Popular Democracy, Law for Black Lives, Black Youth Project 100, 2017.

Hamid, Sarah T. "Community Defense: Sarah T. Hamid on Abolishing Carceral Technologies." *Logic Magazine* 11, August 31, 2020.

Harrington de Santana, Anne. "Nuclear Weapons as the Currency of Power: Deconstructing the Fetishism of Force." *Nonproliferation Review* 16, no. 3 (2009): 325–345.

Harvey, David. *A Brief History of Neoliberalism*. Oxford: Oxford University Press, 2005.

———. *Marx, Capital, and the Madness of Economic Reason*. London: Profile Books, 2017.

Hersey, John. "Hiroshima." *New Yorker*, August 23, 1946.

Herskind, Micah. "Three Reasons Advocates Must Move Beyond Demanding Release for 'Nonviolent Offenders.'" Medium, April 14, 2020.

Herzing, Rachel. "Standing Up for Our Communities: Why We Need a Police-Free Future." Truthout, March 7, 2017.

Hickel, Jason. *Less is More: How Degrowth Will Save the World*. London: William Heinemann, 2020.

Hilton, Elizabeth. *From the War on Poverty to the War on Crime: The Making of Mass Incarceration in America*. Cambridge, MA: Harvard University Press, 2017.

Holland Michel, Arthur. *Eyes in the Sky: The Secret Rise of Gorgon Stare and How It Will Watch Us All*. Boston: Houghton Mifflin Harcourt, 2019.

Hollo, Tim. "There's No Time Left Not to Do Everything." *Arena Quarterly* 3, September 2020.

hooks, bell. "Feminism and Militarism: A Comment." *Women's Studies Quarterly* 23, no. 3/4 (1995): 58–64.

Horgan, John. "Let's Defund the Pentagon, Too." *Scientific*

American, July 8, 2020.

Hussain, Murtaza. "War on the World: Industrialized Militaries Are a Bigger Part of Climate Change Than You Know." The Intercept, September 15, 2019.

The Intercept. "The Drone Papers." https://theintercept.com/drone-papers.

———. "Oil and Water" investigative series. https://theintercept.com/series/oil-and-water.

———. "Policing the Pipeline" investigative series. https://theintercept.com/series/policing-the-pipeline.

Intondi, Vincent J. *African Americans Against the Bomb*. Stanford, CA: Stanford University Press, 2015.

Jackson, George. *Blood in My Eye*. New York: Random House, 1972.

Johnson, Taylor N. "'The most bombed nation on Earth': Western Shoshone resistance to the Nevada National Security Site." *Atlantic Journal of Communication* 26, no. 4 (2018): 224–39.

Jones, Reece. *Violent Borders*. New York: Verso, 2017.

———. *White Borders: The History of Race and Immigration in the United States from Chinese Exclusion to the Border Wall*.

Boston: Beacon Press, 2021.

Justice for Muslims Collective, HEART Women & Girls, Vigilant Love, the Partnership to End Gendered Islamophobia, Project South, the Partnership for the Advancement of New Americans, and the US Campaign for Palestinian Rights. "Abolishing the War on Terror, Building Communities of Care: A Grassroots Policy Agenda." March 2021. https://www.justiceformuslims.org/grassroots-policy-agenda.

Kaba, Mariame. "Against Punishment: A Resource." Project Nia and Interrupting Criminalization, 2020. https://issuu.com/projectnia/docs/against_punishment_curriculum_final.

———. *We Do This 'Til We Free Us: Abolitionist Organizing and Transforming Justice*. Chicago: Haymarket Books, 2021.

Kaepernick, Colin, ed. *Abolition for the People: The Movement for a Future Without Policing & Prisons*. New York: Kaepernick Publishing, 2021.

Kallis, Giorgos, Susan Paulson, Giacomo D'Alisa, and Federico Demaria. *The Case for Degrowth*. Cambridge, MA: Polity, 2020.

Kim, Mimi E. "From carceral feminism to transformative justice: Women of color feminism and alternatives to incarceration." *Journal of Ethnic & Cultural Diversity in Social Work* 27, no. 3 (2018): 219–33.

Klein, Naomi. *The Shock Doctrine: The Rise of Disaster Capitalism*. Toronto: Knopf Canada, 2007.

Kohso, Sabu. *Radiation and Revolution*. Durham, NC: Duke University Press, 2020.

Kwet, Michael. "Digital colonialism: US empire and the New Imperialism in the Global South." *Race & Class* 40, no. 4 (2019): 3–26.

Law, Victoria. "Prisons Make Us Safer": And 20 Other Myths about Mass Incarceration. Boston: Beacon Press, 2021.

——. *Resistance Behind Bars: The Struggles of Incarcerated Women*. San Francisco: PM Press, 2009.

Lazare, Sarah. "As the World Economy Grinds to a Halt, the U.S. War Machine Churns On." *In These Times*, April 6, 2020.

——. "'Colonizing the Atmosphere': How Rich, Western Nations Drive the Climate Crisis." *In These Times*, September 14, 2020.

Lifton, Robert J. and Richard Falk. *Indefensible Weapons: The Political and Psychological Case Against Nuclearism*. New York: Basic Books, 1982.

Lorde, Audre. "Age, Race, Class, and Sex: Women Redefining Difference." In *Sister Outsider: Essays and Speeches*, 114–23. Berkeley, CA: Crossing Press, 1984.

Lovato, Roberto. "The Age of Intersectional Empire Is Upon Us." *The Nation*, May 10, 2020.

Loyd, Jenna M. and Alison Mountz. *Boats, Borders, and Bases: Race, the Cold War, and the Rise of Migration Detention in the United States*. Berkeley, CA: University of California Press, 2018.

Lyon, David, ed. *Surveillance as Social Sorting: Privacy, Risk and Digital Discrimination*. London: Routledge, 2003.

MacKenzie, Megan and Nicole Wegner, eds. *Feminist Solutions for Ending War*. London: Pluto Press, 2021.

Maclellan, Nic. "Nuclear Testing and Racism in the Pacific Islands." In *The Palgrave Handbook of Ethnicity*. Singapore: Palgrave Macmillan, 2019, 1–21.

Magnet, Shoshana. *When Biometrics Fail: Gender, Race, and the Technology of Identity*. Durham, NC: Duke University Press, 2011.

Masco, Joseph. *The Nuclear Borderlands: The Manhattan Project in Post–Cold War New Mexico*. Princeton, NJ: Princeton University Press, 2006.

McCoy, Alfred W. *Policing America's*

Empire. Madison, WI: University of Wisconsin Press, 2009.

Melamed, Jodi. "Racial Capitalism." *Critical Ethnic Studies* 1, no. 1 (2015): 76–85.

Miller, Todd. *Border Patrol Nation.* San Francisco: City Lights Books, 2014.

———. *Build Bridges, Not Walls: A Journey to a World Without Borders.* San Francisco: City Lights Books, 2021.

———. *Empire of Borders: The Expansion of the U.S. Border Around the World.* New York: Verso, 2019.

Miller, Todd and Nick Buxton. "Biden's Border: The industry, the Democrats and the 2020 elections." Transnational Institute, February 17, 2021. https://www.tni.org/en/bidensborder.

Mills, C. W. *The Power Elite.* New York: Oxford University Press, 2000.

Mlinarević, Gorana and Nela Porobić. "The Peace That Is Not: Feminist Critique of Neoliberal Approaches to Peacebuilding." Women's International League for Peace and Freedom, 2021. https://www.wilpf.org/wp-content/uploads/2022/01/WILPF_The-Peace-That-is-Not_final.pdf.

Murakawa, Naomi. *The First Civil Right: How Liberals Built Prison America.* New York: Oxford

University Press, 2014.

Mystal, Elie. "Trump's Secret Police Have Never Been a Secret to Brown People." *The Nation*, July 27, 2020.

Nevins, Joseph. "The Right to the World." *Antipode* 49, no. 5 (2017): 1349–67.

New Left Review, ed. *Exterminism and Cold War.* London: Verso, 1982.

Nuwer, Rachel. "Environmental Activists Have Higher Death Rates Than Some Soldiers." *Scientific American*, August 5, 2019.

Olufemi, Lola. "Why imagination is the most powerful tool that feminists have at our disposal." *gal-dem*, March 26, 2020.

Peltier, Heidi. "The Growth of the "Camo Economy" and the Commercialization of the Post-9/11 Wars." In "Costs of War." Watson Institute for International and Public Affairs at Brown University, 2020. https://watson.brown.edu/costsofwar/files/cow/imce/papers/2020/Peltier%202020%20-%20Growth%20of%20Camo%20Economy%20-%20June%2030%20 2020%20-%20FINAL.pdf.

Perlroth, Nicole. *This Is How They Tell Me the World Ends: The Cyber-Weapons Arms Race.* London: Bloomsbury Publishing, 2021.

Peterson, V. Spike. *A Critical Rewriting of Global Political*

Economy: Integrating reproductive, productive, and virtual economies. London: Routledge, 2003.

———. "How (the Meaning of) Gender Matters in Political Economy." *New Political Economy* 10, no. 4 (2005): 499–521.

Philippe, Sébastien and Tomas Statius. *Toxic: Investigation into French Nuclear Tests in Polynesia.* Paris: Puf, 2021.

Prison Research Education Action Project. *Instead of Prisons: A Handbook for Abolitionists.* Syracuse: Prison Research Education Action Project, 1976.

Purnell, Derecka. *Becoming Abolitionists: Police, Protests, and the Pursuit of Freedom.* New York: Verso, 2021.

The Red Nation. *The Red Deal: Indigenous Action to Save Our Earth.* Brooklyn: Common Notions, 2021.

Richards, Neil M. "The Dangers of Surveillance." *Harvard Law Review* 126, no. 7 (2013): 1934–1965.

Richie, Beth E. *Arrested Justice: Black Women, Violence, and America's Prison Nation.* New York: New York University Press, 2016.

Ritchie, Andrea. *Invisible No More: Police Violence Against Black Women and Women of Color.*

Boston: Beacon Press, 2017.

Ritchie, Andrea J. and Joey L. Mogul. "In the Shadows of the War on Terror: Persistent Police Brutality and Abuse of People of Color in the United States." *DePaul Journal for Social Justice* 1, no. 2 (2008): 175–250.

Ritchie, Nick. "Valuing and Devaluing Nuclear Weapons." *Contemporary Security Policy* 34 no. 1 (2013): 155–59.

Ritchie, Nick and Kjølv Egeland. "The diplomacy of resistance: power, hegemony and nuclear disarmament." *Global Change, Peace and Security*, April 27, 2018, 1–21.

Robinson, Cedric J. *Black Marxism: The Making of the Black Radical Tradition.* Durham, NC: University of North Carolina Press, 1983.

Robinson, William I. *The Global Police State: Militarization, Repression and Capitalism in the US.* London: Pluto Press, 2020.

———. "What are the real reasons behind the New Cold War?" *ROAR*, May 6, 2021.

Rodríguez, Dylan. "Reformism Isn't Liberation, It's Counterinsurgency." In *Abolition for the People: The Movement for a Future Without Policing & Prisons*, edited by Colin Kaepernick. New York: Kaepernick Publishing, 2021. Also published by LEVEL at https://level.medium.com/reformism-isnt-liberation-it-s-counterinsurgency-7ea0a1ce11eb, October 20, 2020.

Sangari, Kumkum, Neeraj Malik, Sheba Chhachhi, and Tanika Sarkar. "Why Women Must Reject the Bomb." In *Out of Nuclear Darkness: The Indian Case for Disarmament.* New Delhi: Movement in India for Nuclear Disarmament, 1998.

Scahill, Jeremy. *Blackwater: The Rise of the World's Most Powerful Mercenary Army.* New York: Nation Books, 2007.

———. *Dirty Wars: The World is a Battlefield.* New York: Nation Books, 2013.

Schenwar, Maya and Victoria Law. *Prison By Any Other Name: The Harmful Consequences of Popular Reforms.* New York: The New Press, 2020.

Schlosser, Eric. "The Prison-Industrial Complex." *The Atlantic*, December 1998.

Schrader, Stuart. *Badges Without Borders: How Global Counterinsurgency Transformed American Policing.* Berkeley, CA: University of California Press, 2019.

Schwarz, Elke. *Death Machines.* Manchester: Manchester University Press, 2018.

Shamas, Diala and Nermeen Arastu. "Mapping Muslims: NYPD Spying and its Impact on American Muslims." The Muslim American Civil Liberties Coalition (MACLC), Creating Law Enforcement Accountability & Responsibility (CLEAR), and the Asian American Legal Defense and Education Fund (AALDEF), March 2013.

Shaw, Ian G. R. *Predator Empire.* Minneapolis: University of Minnesota Press, 2016.

Simpson, Leanne Betasamosake. *As We Have Always Done: Indigenous Freedom Through Radical Resistance.* Minneapolis: The University of Minnesota, 2017.

Spade, Dean. *Mutual Aid: Building Solidarity During This Crisis (And The Next).* London: Verso, 2020.

Spade, Dean and Aaron Belkin. "Queer Militarism?! The Politics of Military Inclusion Advocacy in Authoritarian Times." *GLQ* 27, no. 2 (2021): 281–307.

Stanley, Eric A. and Nat Smith, eds. *Captive Genders: Trans Embodiment and the Prison Industrial Complex.* Oakland, CA: AK Press, 2011.

Stanley, Eric A., Dean Spade, and Queer (In)Justice, "Queering Prison Abolition, Now?" *American Quarterly* 64, no.1 (2012): 115–127.

Sudbury, Julia, ed. *Global Lockdown: Race, Gender, and the Prison-Industrial Complex.*

London: Routledge, 2005.

———"A World Without Prisons: Resisting Militarism, Globalized Punishment, and Empire." *Social Justice* 31, no. 1 (2004): 9–30.

Taylor, Keeanga-Yamahtta. "The Emerging Movement for Police and Prison Abolition." *New Yorker*, May 7, 2021.

———, ed. *How We Get Free: Black Feminism and the Combahee River Collective.* Chicago: Haymarket Books, 2017.

———. "We Should Still Defund the Police." *New Yorker*, August 14, 2020.

Thompson, Heather. *Blood in the Water: The Attica Prison Uprising of 1971 and Its Legacy.* New York: Pantheon, 2016.

Turse, Nick. "America's Secret War in 134 Countries." *The Nation*, January 16, 2014.

———. *The Changing Face of Empire: Special Ops, Drones, Spies, Proxy Fighters, Secret Bases, and Cyberwarfare.* Chicago: Haymarket Books, 2012.

Valencia, Sayak. *Gore Capitalism.* Translated by John Pluecker. South Pasadena, CA: Semiotext(e), 2018.

Vine, David. *Base Nation: How U.S. Military Bases Abroad Harm America and The World.* New York: Metropolitan Books, 2015.

Vitale, Alex S. *The End of Policing.* Brooklyn: Verso, 2018.

Walia, Harsha. *Border & Rule: Global Migration, Capitalism, and the Rise of Racist Nationalism.* Chicago: Haymarket Books, 2021.

———. *Undoing Border Imperialism.* Oakland, CA: AK Press, 2013.

Wang, Jackie. *Carceral Capitalism.* Los Angeles: Semiotext(e), 2018.

Washington, John. *The Dispossessed: A Story of Asylum at the US-Mexican Border and Beyond.* New York: Verso, 2019.

———. "Is the US Border Patrol Committing Crimes Against Humanity?" *Guernica*, May 2, 2018.

———. "'Kick Ass, Ask Questions Later': A Border Patrol Whistleblower Speaks Out About Culture of Abuse Against Migrants." The Intercept, September 20, 2018.

Washington Post. "The Black Budget" investigative series. https://www.washingtonpost.com/wp-srv/special/national/black-budget.

Wilcox, Lauren. "Embodying algorithmic war: Gender, race, and the posthuman in drone warfare." *Security Dialogue* 48, no. 1 (2017): 11–28.

Wittner, Lawrence S. Confronting the Bomb: A Short History of the World Nuclear Disarmament Movement. Stanford, CA: Stanford University Press, 2009.

Woodly, Deva. Reckoning: Black Lives Matter and the Democratic Necessity of Social Movements. Oxford: Oxford University Press, 2021.

Zabarte, Ian. "Indigenous Peoples Condemn Nuclear Colonialism on 'Columbus' Day." PopularResistance. org, October 10, 2016.

Zuboff, Shoshana. *The Age of Surveillance Capitalism.* London: Profile Books, 2019.

Webinars, videos, and podcasts

Center for Constitutional Rights. "Episode 12: Transformative justice in an era of mass criminalization, Mariame Kaba and Victoria Law." Podcast, March 14, 2019.

CODEPINK. "Policing & Militarism: Connecting the Struggles." YouTube video, July 9, 2020.

Democracy Now! "Angela Davis on Abolition, Calls to Defund the Police, Toppled Racist Statues, and Voting in 2020 Election." Video, June 12, 2020.

For The Wild. "Mariame Kaba on Moving Past Punishment." Podcast, December 27, 2019.

Gays Against Guns. "Guns and Nuclear Weapons: The Continuum of Violence from Handguns to Nuclear

Weapons." Podcast, March 2, 2021.

Haymarket Books. "Abolish ICE is Not Just a Slogan," YouTube video, May 19, 2020.

———. "Abolition Can't Wait." YouTube video, June 25, 2020.

———. "Black and Indigenous Liberation through Abolition." YouTube video, October 1, 2020.

———. "Covid 19, Decarceration, and Abolition," YouTube video, April 17, 2020.

———. "Indigenous Resistance Against Oil Pipelines During a Pandemic," YouTube video, June 3, 2020.

———. "On the Road with Abolition: Assessing Our Steps Along the Way." YouTube video, June 12, 2020.

———. "PIC Abolition, the War on Terror, and the Deportation Machine." YouTube video, May 25, 2021.

———. "Ruth Wilson Gilmore on Covid-19, Decarceration, and Abolition." YouTube video, April 17, 2020.

Intercepted. "Ruth Wilson Gilmore Makes the Case for Abolition." Podcast, June 10, 2020.

Lin, Dan and Kathy Jetñil-Kijiner. "Anointed." Video poem, April 2018.

Material Girl$. "Episode 10: Feminist

Peace." Podcast, October 2021.

NBC News. "Thinking about how to abolish prisons with Mariame Kaba." Podcast, April 10, 2019.

On AiR: IR in the age of AI. "AI, Technology, and Patriarchy." Podcast, July 4, 2021.

Surveillance and the City podcast series. www. surveillanceandthecity.com.

WBEZ 91.5 Chicago. "Women Now At Top of Military-Industrial Complex. A Feminist Reaction from Cynthia Enloe." Radio interview, January 8, 2019.

Notes

Introduction

1. Dan Berger and David Stein, "What Is & What Could Be: The Policies of Abolition," in *Abolition for the People: The Movement for a Future Without Policing & Prisons*, Colin Kaepernick, ed. (New York: Kaepernick Publishing, 2021). Also published by LEVEL at https://level.medium.com/what-is-and-what-could-be-the-policies-of-abolition-9c1b49eb5a1f, October 29, 2020.

2. Angela Davis, "Why Arguments Against Abolition Inevitably Fail," in *Abolition for the People: The Movement for a Future Without Policing & Prisons*, Colin Kaepernick, ed. (New York: Kaepernick Publishing, 2021). Also published by LEVEL at https://level.medium.com/why-arguments-against-abolition-inevitably-fail-991342b8d042, October 6, 2020.

3. Keeanga-Yamahtta Taylor, "The Emerging Movement for Police and Prison Abolition," *New Yorker*, May 7, 2021.

4. Andreas Chatzidakis et al., "COVID-19 pandemic: A Crisis of Care," Verso Books (blog), March 26, 2020.

5. bell hooks, "Understanding Patriarchy" (Louisville, KY: Louisville Anarchist Federation, 2010), 1.

6. Lisa Wade, "Tough Guise 2: The ongoing crisis of violent masculinity," Society Pages, October 15, 2013; and Maya Eichler, "Militarized Masculinities in International Relations," *Brown Journal of World Affairs* XXI, no. 1 (2014).

7. The Red Nation, *The Red Deal: Indigenous Action to Save Our Earth* (Brooklyn, NY: Common Notions, 2021), 44.

8. Haymarket Books, "PIC Abolition, the War on Terror, and the Deportation Machine," YouTube video, May 25, 2021, https://youtu.be/o2IER14CyMA.

9. Haymarket Books, "PIC Abolition."

10. Harsha Walia, Border & Rule: Global Migration, Capitalism, and the Rise of Racist Nationalism (Chicago: Haymarket Books, 2021), 11.

11. Walia, *Border & Rule*, 35–36.

12. Timothy Pachirat, Every Twelve Seconds: Industrialized Slaughter and the Politics of Sight (New Haven: Yale University Press, 2013), 14.

13. Judith Butler, *Precarious Life: The Powers of Mourning and Violence* (London: Verso Books, 2004), 37–38.

14. Jason De León, *The Land of Open Graves: Living and Dying on the Migrant Trail* (Oakland, CA: University of California Press, 2015), 214.

15. Ruth Wilson Gilmore, Change Everything: Racial Capitalism and the Case for Abolition (Chicago: Haymarket Books, 2022).

16. George Jackson, *Blood in My Eye* (New York: Random House, 1972), 118.

17. Dylan Rodríguez, "Reformism Isn't Liberation, It's Counterinsurgency," in *Abolition for the People: The Movement for a Future Without Policing & Prisons*, Colin Kaepernick, ed. (New York: Kaepernick Publishing, 2021). Also published by LEVEL at https://level.medium.com/reformism-isnt-liberation-it-s-counterinsurgency-7ea0a1ce11eb, October 20, 2020.

18. Rodríguez, "Reformism Isn't Liberation."

19. Dean Spade and Aaron Belkin, "Queer Militarism?! The Politics of Military Inclusion Advocacy in Authoritarian Times," *GLQ* 27, no. 2 (2021): 297.

20. Mariame Kaba, "Moving Past Punishment," interview by Ayana Young, For the Wild podcast, December 27, 2019, https://forthewild.world/listen/mariame-kaba-on-moving-past-punishment-151. Transcript in Mariame Kaba, "Moving Past Punishment," in *We Do This 'Til We Free Us: Abolitionist Organizing and Transforming Justice*, ed. Tamara K. Nopper (Chicago: Haymarket Books, 2021), 155.

21. Todd Miller, *Build Bridges, Not Walls: A Journey to a World Without Borders* (San Francisco: City Lights Books, 2021), 146.

22. Mariame Kaba and Kelly Hayes, "A Jailbreak of the Imagination: Seeing Prisons for What They Are and Demanding Transformation," Truthout, May 3, 2018.

23. Angela Davis, "Angela Davis on Abolition, Calls to Defund Police, Toppled Racist Statues & Voting in 2020 Election," interview with Amy Goodman, Democracy Now!, June 12, 2020.

24. For more on intersectionality, see Kimberle Crenshaw, "Demarginalizing the Intersection of Race and Sex: A Black Feminist Critique of Antidiscrimination Doctrine, Feminist Theory and Antiracist Politics," *University of Chicago Legal Forum* 1989, no. 1 (1989): 139–67; also Jane Coaston, "The intersectionality wars," Vox, May 28, 2019.

25. Davis, "Angela Davis on Abolition."

26. Dan Berger, *The Struggle Within: Prisons, Political Prisoners, and Mass Movements in the United States* (Oakland, CA: PM Press/Kersplebedeb, 2014).

27. Critical Resistance, *Abolition Now!* (Oakland, CA: AK Press, 2008), 145.

Chapter 1: Disbanding Police

1. Laurie Penny (@PennyRed), "The police are rioting across America tonight . . .," Twitter, May 31, 2020, https://twitter.com/PennyRed/status/1266980991454703617.

2. Matthew Dessem, "Police Erupt in Violence Nationwide," Slate, May 31, 2020.

3. Dan Lamothe and Missy Ryan, "Trump pulls military into political fray of Minneapolis unrest but is unlikely to follow through on threat," *Washington Post,* May 29, 2020.

4. Robert Mackey, "Racist History Behind Trump's Threat to Shoot Minneapolis Protesters Spurs Twitter to Act," The Intercept, May 29, 2020.

5. The enclosure of the commons refers to the capitalist process beginning in thirteenth-century England of consolidating land and restricting access to it, which disenfranchised people from having access to common land for communal use and benefited the capitalist elite landowning class. This process continued throughout history, with the capitalist economic system building from the fifteenth to the seventeenth century.

6. Mark Neocleous, *War Power, Police Power* (Edinburgh: Edinburgh University Press, 2014).

7. Ian G. R. Shaw, *Predator Empire: Drone Warfare and Full Spectrum Dominance* (Minneapolis: University of Minnesota Press, 2016), 205.

8. The Red Nation (@The_Red_Nation), "The origin of police in the US is rooted in systemic racism . . .," Twitter, June 15, 2020, https://twitter.com/The_Red_Nation/status/1272559425501487106.

9. Angela Davis, "Why Arguments Against Abolition Inevitably Fail," in "Abolition for the People: The Movement for a Future Without Policing & Prisons," Kaepernick Publishing and LEVEL, October 6, 2020, https://level.medium.com/why-arguments-against-abolition-inevitably-fail-991342b8d042.

10. Stokely Carmichael and Charles V. Hamilton, *Black Power: The Politics of Liberation* (New York: Random House, 1967).

11. Keeanga-Yamahtta Taylor, "We Should Still Defund the Police," *New Yorker,* August 14, 2020.

12. Keeanga-Yamahtta Taylor, "The Emerging Movement for Police and Prison Abolition," *New Yorker,* May 7, 2021.

13. The "broken windows" theory of policing posits that cleaning up visible signs of vandalism, "crime," or disorder in a community, such as graffiti and littering, can prevent more serious "crimes" from taking place.

14. Richard C. Auxier, "What Police Spending Data Can (and Cannot) Explain amid Calls to Defund the Police," Urban Wire, June 9, 2020; also see Kate Hamaji et al., "Freedom to Thrive: Reimagining Safety & Security in our Communities," Center for Popular Democracy, Law for Black Lives, Black Youth Project 100, 2017, https://www.nfg.org/resources/freedom-thrive-reimagining-safety-security-our-communities.

15. Alice Speri, "New York City and Los Angeles slash budgets—but not for police," The Intercept, May 22, 2020.

16. Phillip Francis, "The NYPD Is One of the World's Strongest Militarities," CheatSheet, April 8, 2018.

17. Speri, "New York City and Los Angeles."

18. See for example "'Nothing to Lose': Colombians Protest 'Fascist Mafia Regime' Amid Deadly Police & Military Crackdown," Democracy Now!, May 6, 2021.

19. Nir Hasson and Jack Khoury, "Tensions Over Jerusalem Day March, Temple Mount Clashes Culminate in Rocket Fire From Gaza," Haaretz, May 10, 2021.

20. See for example "Nigeria: Crackdown on Police Brutality Protests," Human Rights Watch, October 16, 2020.

21. See Laurène Dufayet, Nicolas Soussy, and Charlotte Giorgard, "French protests: why defensive bullet launchers should be banned," The Lancet 396, no. 10253 (2020): 757–58; Aurore Chauvin et al., "Ocular injuries occurred by less-lethal weapons in France," The Lancet 394, no. 10209 (2019): 1616–7; and "Maintaining public order and freedom of assembly in the context of the 'yellow vest' movement: recommendations by the Council of Europe Commissioner for Human Rights," Council of Europe Commissioner for Human Rights, February 26, 2019.

22. Chris Fox and Brian Aguilar, "Protestors in downtown Toronto demand answers in death of Regis Korchinski-Paquet," CP24, May 30, 2020; Lauren O'Neil, "Toronto police accused of pushing black woman from balcony to her death," blogTO, May 2020.

23. Nick Boisvert, "Black people 'grossly overrepresented' in violent police interactions, Ontario human rights report says," CBC, December 10, 2018.

24. Sean Carleton, "Might is not right: A historical perspective on coercion as a colonial strategy," Canadian Dimension, February 21, 2020.

25. Jaskiran Dhillon and Will Parrish, "Exclusive: Canada police prepared to shoot Indigenous activists, documents show," The Guardian, December 20, 2019.

26. See for example Brooke Fryer, Douglas Smith, and Jack Latimore, "Aggressive police upending Aboriginal lives," The Point, February 20, 2019; Lorena Allam, Calla Wahlquist, and Nick Evershed, "Indigenous deaths in custody worsen in year of tracking by Deaths Inside project," The Guardian, August 22, 2019; Giovanni Torre, "Protests across Australia as police officer charged with murdering 19-year-old Aboriginal man," The Telegraph, November 14, 2019; and Michael McGowan, "NSW police put children as young as nine, many of them Indigenous under surveillance," The Guardian, February 13, 2020.

27. Robyn Oxley, "Defunding the police and abolishing prisons in Australia are not radical ideas," The Guardian, September 17, 2020.

28. Yassine Boubout, "In Europe, We Also Can't Breathe," Politico, June 3, 2020.

29. "Roma Register: State guilty of ethnic discrimination," Radio Sweden, June 10, 2016.

30. Fatima Naib, "Social media and research: Swedes tackle police racism," Al Jazeera, February 4, 2018.

31. Alisha Ebrahimji, "These controversial statues have been removed following protests over George Floyd's death," CNN, June 7, 2020.

32. Fadel Allassan, "Confederate monuments become flashpoints in protests against racism," Axios, June 7, 2020.

33. Ebrahimji, "These controversial statues."

34. Leah Asmelash, "Statues of Christopher Columbus are being dismounted across the country," CNN, June 11, 2020.

35. Che (@cruisingatopia), "Tear down all the monuments to slavery," June 7, 2020, Twitter, https://twitter.com/cruisingatopia/status/1269675166998630400.

36. John Eligon and Shawn Hubler, "Throughout Trial Over George Floyd's Death, Killings by Police Mount," New York Times, April 17, 2021; Taylor, "The Emerging Movement."

37. Mapping Police Violence, https://mappingpoliceviolence.org.

3838. Mapping Police Violence, "2021 Police Violence Report," January 2022, www.policeviolencereport.org.

39. Mapping Police Violence, https://mappingpoliceviolence.org.

40. Mapping Police Violence, https://mappingpoliceviolence.org.

41. Ryan Devereaux, "Police attacks on protesters are rooted in violent ideology of reactionary grievance," The Intercept, June 6, 2020.

42. Alfred W. McCoy, Policing America's Empire (Madison, WI: University of Wisconsin Press, 2009).

43. Shaw, Predator Empire.

44. Shaw, Predator Empire, 212.

45.   Dexter Filkins, "'Do Not Resist' and the crisis of police militarization," *New Yorker,* May 13, 2016.

46.   "1033 Program FAQs," Defense Logistics Agency, https://www.dla.mil/DispositionServices/Offers/Reutilization/LawEnforcement/ProgramFAQs.aspx.

47.   Alex S. Vitale, *The End of Policing* (Brooklyn, NY: Verso, 2018), 25.

48.   "War Comes Home: The Excessive Militarization of American Policing," American Civil Liberties Union, 2014, https://www.aclu.org/issues/criminal-law-reform/reforming-police/war-comes-home.

49.   Kanya Bennett, "365 Days and 605 Armored Military Vehicles Later: Police Militarization a Year After Ferguson," American Civil Liberties Union, August 7, 2015, https://www.aclu.org/blog/criminal-law-reform/reforming-police/365-days-and-605-armored-military-vehicles-later-police.

50.   Deadly Exchange, https://deadlyexchange.org/about-deadly-exchange.

51.   Jonathan Mummolo, "Militarization fails to enhance police safety or reduce crime but may harm police reputation," *National Academy of Sciences* 115, no. 37 (2018): 9181.

52.   Casey Delehanty et. al., "Militarization and police violence: The case of the 1033 program," *Research and Politics* 4, no. 2 (2017).

53.   Rashmee Kumar, "Envisioning an America free from police violence and control," The Intercept, October 15, 2017.

54.   Officer A. Cab, "Confessions of a Former Bastard Cop," Medium, June 6, 2020.

55.   Critical Resistance (@C_Resistance), "Many reforms & strategies . . .," Twitter, June 4, 2020, https://twitter.com/C_Resistance/status/1268712313634209794.

56.   Joe Biden, "Biden: We must urgently root out systemic racism, from policing to housing to opportunity," *USA Today,* June 10, 2020.

57.   Haymarket Books, "On the Road with Abolition: Assessing Our Steps Along the Way," YouTube video, 2:07:54, June 12, 2020, https://www.youtube.com/watch?v=GHdg4dqBMyk.

58.   Micah Herskind (@micahherskind), "Something the history of criminalization shows is that . . .," Twitter, June 22, 2020, https://twitter.com/MicahHerskind/status/1275265266411339776.

59.   Taylor, "The Emerging Movement."

60.   Angela Davis, "Why Arguments Against Abolition."

61.   Ben Kesslen, "Calls to reform, defund, dismantle and abolish the police, explained," NBC News, June 8, 2020.

62.   Haymarket Books, "On the Road."

63. Mariame Kaba, "Moving Past Punishment," interview by Ayana Young, For the Wild podcast, December 27, 2019, https://forthewild.world/listen/mariame-kaba-on-moving-past-punishment-151. Transcript in Mariame Kaba, "Moving Past Punishment," in *We Do This 'Til We Free Us: Abolitionist Organizing and Transforming Justice*, ed. Tamara K. Nopper (Chicago: Haymarket Books, 2021), 148–156.

64. Cab, "Confessions."

65. Cab, "Confessions."

66. "What is the PIC? What is abolition?" Critical Resistance, 2020, http://criticalresistance.org/about/not-so-common-language.

67. "Angela Davis on Abolition, Calls to Defund Police, Toppled Racist Statues & Voting in 2020 Election," Democracy Now!, July 3, 2020.

68. Haymarket Books, "On the Road."

69. Madison Pauly, "What a World Without Cops Would Look Like," *Mother Jones*, June 2, 2020.

70. Dan Berger and David Stein, "What Is and What Could Be: The Policies of Abolition," in "Abolition for the People: The Movement for a Future Without Policing & Prisons," Kaepernick Publishing, and LEVEL, October 29, 2020, https://level.medium.com/what-is-and-what-could-be-the-policies-of-abolition-9c1b49eb5a1f.

71. Naomi Klein, "Coronavirus capitalism—and how to beat it," The Intercept, March 16, 2020.

72. Astead W. Herndon, "How a Pledge to Dismantle the Minneapolis Police Collapsed," *New York Times*, September 26, 2020.

73. Alice Speri, "The defund police movement takes aim at fusion centers and mass surveillance," The Intercept, April 21, 2021.

74. Steve Eder, Michael H. Keller, and Blacki Migliozzi, "As New Police Reform Laws Sweep Across the U.S., Some Ask: Are They Enough?" *New York Times*, April 18, 2021.

75. Defund the Police, defundpolice.org. Statistics current as of May 2021.

76. Rachel Herzing, "Standing Up for Our Communities: Why We Need a Police-Free Future," Truthout, March 7, 2017.

77. Mariame Kaba, "Thinking about how to abolish prisons with Mariame Kaba," interview by Chris Hayes, NBC News, April 10, 2019.

78. Dakota Smith, "LAPD union decries Garcetti's 'killers' comment. He says he wasn't talking about police," *LA Times*, June 5, 2020.

79. Gregory Pratt, "In wake of looting, Chicago to spend $1.2 million on private security firms to help protect businesses," *Chicago Tribune*, June 6, 2020.

80. Kenyon Farrow (@kenyonfarrow), "I was a member and eventually staff of . . .," Twitter, June 7, 2020, https://twitter.com/kenyonfarrow/status/1269683590167756802?s=20.

Chapter 2: Dismantling Prisons

1. Michel Foucault, *Discipline and Punish: The Birth of the Prison*), Alan Sheridan, trans. (New York: Pantheon Books, 1977).
2. Wendy Sawyer and Peter Wanger, "Mass Incarceration: The Whole Pie 2020," Prison Policy Initiative, March 24, 2020, https://www.prisonpolicy.org/reports/pie2020.html.
3. Sawyer and Wanger, "Mass Incarceration."
4. NAACP, "Criminal Justice Fact Sheet," https://www.naacp.org/criminal-justice-fact-sheet.
5. Lorraine Stutzman Amstutz, "Indigenous peoples in the United States and mass incarceration," Intersections, August 27, 2018.
6. "Native Lives Matter," Lakota People's Law Project, February 2015, https://s3-us-west-1.amazonaws.com/lakota-peoples-law/uploads/Native-Lives-Matter-PDF.pdf.
7. Harsha Walia, *Undoing Border Imperialism* (Oakland, CA: AK Press, 2013), 55.
8. Angela Y. Davis, *Are Prisons Obsolete?* (New York: Seven Stories Press, 2003), 49.
9. Michelle Alexander, *The New Jim Crow: Mass Incarceration in the Age of Colorblindness* (New York: The New Press, 2012).
10. Naomi Murakawa, *The First Civil Right: How Liberals Built Prison America* (New York: Oxford University Press, 2014), 3.
11. Murakawa, *First Civil Right*.
12. Robert Nichols, "The Colonialism of Incarceration," *Radical Philosophy Review* 17, no. 2 (2014): 446.
13. Eric A. Stanley, Dean Spade, and Queer (In)Justice, "Queering Prison Abolition, Now?" *American Quarterly* 64, no.1 (2012): 115–127.
14. Stanley, Spade, and Queer (In)Justice, "Queering Prison Abolition," 116.
15. Morgan Bassichis, Alexander Lee, and Dean Spade, "Building an abolitionist trans and queer movement with everything we've got," in *Captive Genders: Trans Embodiment and the Prison Industrial Complex,* Eric A. Stanley and Nat Smith, eds. (Oakland, CA: AK Press, 2011), 24.
16. Bassichis, Lee, and Spade, "Building an abolitionist."
17. "World military spending rises to almost $2 trillion in 2020," Stockholm International Peace Research Institute, April 26, 2021.

18. Hans M. Kristensen and Matt Korda, "United States nuclear forces, 2020," *Bulletin of the Atomic Sciences* 76, no. 1 (2020): 46–60.

19. Greg Mello and Trish Williams-Mello, "United States," in "Assuring destruction forever: 2022 edition," Allison Pytlak and Ray Acheson, eds., Reaching Critical Will of the Women's International League for Peace and Freedom, 2022, 112–34.

20. Dan Berger (@dnbrgr), "Where does the phrase . . .," Twitter, December 6, 2018, https://twitter.com/dnbrgr/status/1070749158947008512.

21. Mike Davis, "Hell factories in the field: a prison-industrial complex," *The Nation*, February 20, 1995.

22. Sawyer and Wanger, "Mass Incarceration."

23. Ruth Wilson Gilmore, *Golden Gulag: Prisons, Surplus, Crisis, and Opposition in Globalizing California* (Berkeley and Los Angeles: University of California Press, 2007).

24. Gilmore, *Golden Gulag*.

25. NAACP, "Criminal Justice."

26. Angela Davis, "Masked Racism: Reflections on the Prison Industrial Complex," Colorlines, September 10, 1998.

27. Christian Parenti, *Lockdown America: Police and Prisons in the Age of Crisis* (London and New York: Verso, 1999).

28. George L. Jackson, *Blood in My Eye* (New York: Random House, 1972), 106.

29. Gilmore, *Golden Gulag*, 24–25.

30. Gilmore, *Golden Gulag*, 26.

31. Keeanga-Yamahtta Taylor, "We Should Still Defund the Police," *New Yorker*, August 14, 2020.

32. Keeanga-Yamahtta Taylor, "The Emerging Movement for Police and Prison Abolition," *New Yorker*, May 7, 2021.

33. Bernadette Rabuy and Daniel Kopf, "Prisons of Poverty," Prison Policy Initiative, July 9, 2015, https://www.prisonpolicy.org/reports/income.html.

34. "The Relationship between Poverty & Mass Incarceration," Center for Community Change, https://www.masslegalservices.org/system/files/library/The_Relationship_between_Poverty_and_Mass_Incarceration.pdf.

35. Alexi Jones, "Correctional Control 2018," Prison Policy Initiative, December 2018, https://www.prisonpolicy.org/reports/correctionalcontrol2018.html.

36. Julia Sudbury, "A World Without Prisons: Resisting Militarism, Globalized Punishment, and Empire," *Social Justice* 31, no. 1 (2004): 95–96.

37. Eric Schlosser, "The Prison-Industrial Complex," *The Atlantic*, December 1998.

38. Dwight D. Eisenhower, "President Dwight D. Eisenhower's Farewell Address," January 17, 1961, https://www.ourdocuments.gov/doc.php?flash=true&doc=90.

39. "Mass Incarceration Costs $182 Billion Every Year, Without Adding Much to Public Safety," Equal Justice Initiative, February 6, 2017, https://eji.org/news/mass-incarceration-costs-182-billion-annually/.

40. Peter Wagner and Bernadette Rabuy, "Following the Money of Mass Incarceration," Prison Policy Initiative, January 25, 2017, https://www.prisonpolicy.org/reports/money.html.

41. Davis, *Are Prisons Obsolete?*

42. Schlosser, "The Prison-Industrial Complex."

43. Wagner and Rabuy, "Following the Money."

44. Haymarket Books, "Covid 19, Decarceration, and Abolition," YouTube video, 1:37:28, April 17, 2020, https://www.youtube.com/watch?v=hf3f5i9vJNM&feature=emb_logo.

45. US Department of Education, Policy and Program Studies Service, *State and Local Expenditures on Corrections and Education* (2016).

46. Department of Education, *State and Local Expenditures.*

47. Jackie Wang, *Carceral Capitalism* (Los Angeles: Semiotext(e), 2018), 84.

48. Taylor, "The Emerging Movement."

49. Yesim Yaprak Yildiz, "The Paradox of Tear Gas," *Jacobin*, May 4, 2018.

50. Daniel Moattar, "Prisons Are Using Military-Grade Tear Gas to Punish People," *The Nation*, April 28, 2016.

51. Moattar, "Prisons Are Using."

52. Dana Liebelson, "The Shooting Gallery," Huffington Post, 2017, https://highline.huffingtonpost.com/articles/en/the-shooting-gallery.

53. "Inmate Abuse by Corrections Officers and the Legal Recourse Available," FogelLaw, https://www.nsfogel.com/articles/inmate-abuse-by-corrections-officers-and-the-legal-recourse-available/.

54. Parenti, *Lockdown America.*

55. Ian G. R. Shaw, *Predator Empire* (Minneapolis: University of Minnesota Press, 2016), 207.

56. Shaw, *Predator Empire.*

57. For more details, see "Demands," Beyond Prisons, https://www.beyond-prisons.com/demands.

58. Micah Herskind, "Three Reasons Advocates Must Move Beyond Demanding Release for 'Nonviolent Offenders,'" Medium, April 14, 2020.

59. Kameelah Janan Rasheed, "The Carceral State," *New Inquiry*, November 12, 2014.

60. Sudbury, "A World Without Prisons."

61. Gilmore, *Golden Gulag*, 11.

62. Gilmore, *Golden Gulag*, 14.

63. Amanda Aguilar Shank, "Beyond Firing: How do we create community-wide accountability for sexual harassment in our movements," in *Beyond Survival: Strategies and Stories from the Transformative Justice Movement*, Ejeris Dixon and Leah Lakshmi Piepzna-Samarasinha, eds. (Oakland, CA: AK Press, 2020), 38.

64. Haymarket Books, "Abolition Can't Wait," YouTube video, 1:32:54, June 25, 2020, https://www.youtube.com/watch?v=QfSm7JDhGL4&feature=youtu.be.

65. As quoted in Davis, *Are Prisons Obsolete?*, 45.

66. Care Not Cops, carenotcops.org.

67. Lincoln Larson and S. Scott Ogletree, "Can Parks Help Cities Fight Crime?" The Conversation, June 25, 2019.

68. "7. Provide safe housing for everyone," 8toAbolition, https://www.8toabolition.com/provide-safe-housing-for-everyone.

69. "6. Invest in community self-governance," 8toAbolition, https://www.8toabolition.com/invest-in-community-self-governance.

70. Davis, *Are Prisons Obsolete?*, 107.

71. Davis, *Are Prisons Obsolete?*, 107.

72. Essie Justice Group, "#BecauseShesPowerful Pledge," YouTube video, 0:53, December 19, 2018, https://www.youtube.com/watch?v=nnw5TH1hJ7M.

73. "Crime Survivors Speak: The First-Ever National Survey on Victims' Views on Safety and Justice," Alliance for Safety and Justice, 2018, https://allianceforsafetyandjustice.org/crimesurvivorsspeak/.

74. Mariame Kaba and Shira Hassan, "From 'Me Too' to 'All of Us': Organizing to End Sexual Violence," interview by Sarah Jaffe, *In These Times*, January 2017.

75. Mariame Kaba and Andrea J. Ritchie, "We Want More Justice for Breonna Taylor Than the System That Killed Her Can Deliver," *Essence*, July 16, 2020.

76. Shank, "Beyond Firing," 60.

77. "The Criminal Justice System: Statistics," RAINN, https://www.rainn.org/statistics/criminal-justice-system.

78. Joshua Bote, "Two NYPD detectives accused of raping teen in their custody won't get jail time," *USA Today*, August 30, 2019.

79. Conor Friedersdorf, "Police Have a Much Bigger Domestic-Violence Problem Than the NFL," *The Atlantic*, September 19, 2014.

80. Kaba and Hassan, "From 'Me Too.'"

81. Stanley, Spade, and Queer (In)Justice, "Queering Prison Abolition," 121.

82. Kaba and Ritchie, "We Want More Justice."

83. Mariame Kaba, "Against Punishment: A Resource," Project Nia and Interrupting Criminalization, 2020, 3, https://issuu.com/projectnia/docs/against_punishment_curriculum_final.

84. Race Forward, "Building a Movement," Facebook Live video, 1:53:32, June 18, 2020, https://www.facebook.com/watch/live/?v=209147303485329.

85. Ann Russo, "Locking people up won't help combat sexual violence," *Red Pepper*, May 15, 2019.

86. "Ending Child Sexual Abuse: A Transformative Justice Handbook," generationFIVE, 2017, http://www.generationfive.org/wp-content/uploads/2017/06/Transformative-Justice-Handbook.pdf.

87. Kai Cheng Thom, "What to do when you've been abusive," in *Beyond Survival: Strategies and Stories from the Transformative Justice Movement*, Ejeris Dixon and Leah Lakshmi Piepzna-Samarasinha, eds. (Oakland, CA: AK Press, 2020), 113.

88. Ejeris Dixon, "Building Community Safety: Practical steps towards liberatory transformation," in *Beyond Survival: Strategies and Stories from the Transformative Justice Movement*, Ejeris Dixon and Leah Lakshmi Piepzna-Samarasinha, eds. (Oakland, CA: AK Press, 2020), 21.

89. Janaé E. Bonsu, "Excerpt from 'Black Queer Feminism as Praxis: Building an Organization and a Movement,'" in *Beyond Survival: Strategies and Stories from the Transformative Justice Movement*, Ejeris Dixon and Leah Lakshmi Piepzna-Samarasinha, eds. (Oakland, CA: AK Press, 2020), 74.

90. Shank, "Beyond Firing," 58.

91. Philly Stands Up! "A Portrait of Praxis, an Anatomy of Accountability," in *Beyond Survival: Strategies and Stories from the Transformative Justice Movement*, Ejeris Dixon and Leah Lakshmi Piepzna-Samarasinha, eds. (Oakland, CA: AK Press, 2020), 136–149.

92. Elisabeth Long, "Vent Diagrams as Healing Practice: TJ tips from the overlap," in *Beyond Survival: Strategies and Stories from the Transformative Justice Movement*, Ejeris Dixon and Leah Lakshmi Piepzna-Samarasinha, eds. (Oakland, CA: AK Press, 2020), 309.

93. Mariame Kaba, "The Practices We Need: #MeToo and Transformative Justice," interview by Autumn Brown and adrienne maree brown, *How to Survive the End of the World*, November 7, 2018.

94. Mariame Kaba and Rachel Herzing, "Transforming Punishment: What Is Accountability without Punishment?" in *We Do This 'Til We Free Us: Abolitionist Organizing and Transforming Justice*, Tamara K. Nopper, ed. (Chicago: Haymarket Books, 2021), 132–138.

95. Mariame Kaba, "Toward the Horizon of Abolition," interview by John Duda, *Next System Project*, November 9, 2017; Mariame Kaba, "Thinking about how to abolish prisons with Mariame Kaba," interview by Chris Hayes, NBC News, April 10, 2019.

96. Mariame Kaba and Kelly Hayes, "The Sentencing of Larry Nassar Was Not 'Transformative Justice.' Here's Why," The Appeal, February 5, 2018.
97. Davis, *Are Prisons Obsolete?*, 15.
98. Stanley, Spade, and Queer (In)Justice, "Queering Prison Abolition," 121.
99. Haymarket Books, "Abolition Can't Wait."

Chapter 3: Decoding Surveillance

1. David Lyon, "Introduction," in *Surveillance as Social Sorting: Privacy, Risk and Digital Discrimination*, David Lyon, ed. (London: Routledge, 2003).
2. Lewis West, "Jasbir Puar: Regimes of Surveillance," Cosmologics, December 4, 2014.
3. Neil M. Richards, "The Dangers of Surveillance," *Harvard Law Review* 126, no. 7 (2013).
4. See for example Juan Hourcade, "The perils of next-gen surveillance technology," *ACM Interactions* XXVI, no. 4 (July–August 2019); and Aziz Choudry, ed., *Activists and the Surveillance State: Learning from Repression* (London: Pluto Press, 2019).
5. Anja Kovacs, "Reading Surveillance through a Gendered Lens: Some Theory," Gendering Surveillance, February 2017, https://genderingsurveillance.internetdemocracy.in/theory.
6. See for example Eduardo Galeano, *Open Veins of Latin America: Five Centuries of the Pillage of a Continent* (New York: Monthly Review Press, 1973).
7. Jackie Wang, *Carceral Capitalism* (Los Angeles: Semiotext(e), 2018), 40.
8. For details see "Plus D: Public Library of US Diplomacy," WikiLeaks, https://search.wikileaks.org/plusd.
9. Richards, "The Dangers of Surveillance."
10. For details see Felicity Ruby, "Five Eyes," https://felicityruby.com/five-eyes.
11. Sneha Khale, "Felicity Ruby on STEM, Edward Snowden, and Threats in the Digital Age," Women Love Tech, 2018, https://womenlovetech.com/felicity-ruby-stem-edward-snowden-digital-age.
12. John Naughton, "'The goal is to automate us': welcome to the age of surveillance capitalism," *The Guardian*, January 20, 2019; also see Shoshana Zuboff, *The Age of Surveillance Capitalism* (London: Profile Books, 2019).
13. Naughton, "'The goal is to automate us,'" and Zuboff, *The Age of Surveillance Capitalism*.
14. The "Internet of things" is a term used for the collection of network-enabled devices—items that can be connected to the Internet and to other connected devices—that collect and share data about the way they are used and the environment around them.

15. Donell Holloway, "Explainer: what is surveillance capitalism and how does it shape our economy?," *The Conversation*, June 24, 2019.

16. Richards, "The Dangers of Surveillance," 1938.

17. Chris Jay Hoofnagle et al., "Behavioral Advertising: The Offer You Cannot Refuse," *Harvard Law & Policy Review* 6 (2012): 279.

18. Stuart A. Thompson and Carlie Warzel, "Twelve Million Phones, One Dataset, Zero Privacy," *New York Times*, December 19, 2019.

19. Garfield Benjamin, "Amazon Echo's privacy issues go way beyond voice recordings," *The Conversation*, January 21, 2020.

20. Dorian Lynskey, "'Alexa, are you invading my privacy?'—the dark side of our voice assistants," *The Guardian*, October 9, 2019.

21. See for example Tom Warren, "Facebook has been collecting call history and SMS data from Android devices," The Verge, March 25, 2018.

22. Amnesty International, "Facebook and Google's pervasive surveillance poses an unprecedented danger to human rights," November 21, 2019, https://www.amnesty.org/en/latest/news/2019/11/google-facebook-surveillance-privacy/.

23. See for example Joe Westby, "'The Great Hack': Cambridge Analytica is just the tip of the iceberg," Amnesty International, July 24, 2019, https://www.amnesty.org/en/latest/news/2019/07/the-great-hack-facebook-cambridge-analytica/.

24. Privacy International, "Investigating Apps interactions with Facebook on Android," December 2018 (updated March 2019), https://privacyinternational.org/appdata.

25. Sarah Joseph, "Why the business model of social media giants like Facebook is incompatible with human rights," The Conversation, April 2, 2018.

26. Gilad Edelman, "Social Media CEOs Can't Defend Their Business Model," *Wired*, March 25, 2021.

27. Jack Linchuan Qui, *Goodbye iSlave: A Manifesto for Digital Abolition* (Chicago: University of Illinois Press, 2016). Also see Jenny Chan, Pun Ngai, and Mark Selden, *Dying for an iPhone: Apple, Foxconn, and The Lives of China's Workers* (Chicago: Haymarket Books, 2020).

28. Richards, "The Dangers of Surveillance," 1941.

29. Christine Chinkin and Madeleine Rees, "How new technologies are violating women's rights in Saudi Arabia," London School of Economics, *Women, Peace and Security* (blog), March 21, 2019; Maya Oppenheim, "Google refuses to remove Saudi government app that lets men track and control women," Independent, March 5, 2019.

30. Corrine Mason and Shoshana Magnet, "Surveillance Studies and Violence Against Women," *Surveillance & Society* 10, no. 2 (2012): 105–106.

31. Nandini Chami and Tanvi Kanchan, "Podcast Series | A Feminist Social Media Future: How Do We Get There?" GenderIT.org: Feminist Reflection on Internet Policies, March 29, 2021. Also see this source for podcasts and other resources on gender and technology.

32. "Technology and gender-based violence," YWCA, September 2017, https://www.ywca.org/wp-content/uploads/WWV-Technology-and-GBV-Fact-Sheet.pdf.

33. Ronald J. Deibert et al., "Submission of the Citizen Lab (Munk School of Global Affairs, University of Toronto) to the United Nations Special Rapporteur on violence against women, its causes and consequences, Ms. Dubravka Šimonović," 2 November 2017, 16.

34. Deibert et al., "Submission of the Citizen Lab," 16.

35. Deibert et al., "Submission of the Citizen Lab," 15.

36. Deibert et al., "Submission of the Citizen Lab," 16.

37. Shmyla Khan, "Surveillance as a Feminist Issue," Privacy International, November 21, 2017.

38. Khan, "Surveillance."

39. Allison Pytlak and Deborah Brown, "Why Gender Matters in International Cyber Security," Women's International League for Peace and Freedom and the Association for Progressive Communications, April 2020, https://www.apc.org/en/pubs/why-gender-matters-international-cyber-security; also see Chami and Kanchan, "Podcast Series."

40. See for example Gemma Fox, "Egypt police 'using dating apps' to find and imprison LGBT+ people," Independent, October 1, 2020.

41. For an overview, see for example Rachel E. Dubrofsky and Shoshana Amielle Magnet, eds., *Feminist Surveillance Studies* (Durham, NC: Duke University Press, 2015).

42. Torin Monahan, "Dreams of Control at a Distance: Gender, Surveillance, and Social Control," *Cultural Studies* ↔ *Critical Methodologies* 9, no. 2 (2009): 286.

43. Monahan, "Dreams of Control," 294.

44. Toby Beauchamp, "Artful Concealment and Strategic Visibility: Transgender Bodies and U.S. State Surveillance After 9/11," *Surveillance & Society* 6(4): 356–366.

45. Gary Kafer and Daniel Grinberg, "Editorial: Queer Surveillance," *Surveillance & Society* 17, no. 5 (2019): 593. Also see Os Keyes, "The Misgendering Machines: Trans/HCI Implications of Automatic Gender Recognition," *Proceedings of the ACM on Human-Computer Interaction* 2, no. CSCW (2018): Article 88; and Shoshana Magnet, *When Biometrics Fail:*

Gender, Race, and the Technology of Identity (Durham, NC: Duke University Press, 2011).

46.   Kovacs, "Reading Surveillance."

47.   "Challenging Patriarchy Through the Lens of Privacy," Privacy International, December 1, 2017.

48.   Khan, "Surveillance."

49.   Joel Bakan, The Corporation: The Pathological Pursuit of Profit and Power (New York, NY: Free Press, 2005).

50.   Michael Kwet, "Digital colonialism: US empire and the New Imperialism in the Global South," *Race & Class* 40, no. 4 (2019): 6.

51.   Kwet, "Digital colonialism," 7.

52.   Simon Lambert and Robert Henry, "Surveilling Indigenous Communities in a Time of Pandemic," *Surveillance & Society* 18, no. 3 (2020): 422–25.

53.   Fabian Rogers, "For Indigenous Peoples, Surveillance Is Nothing New," Surveillance Technology Oversight Project, October 12, 2020.

54.   See for example "Being Aware of Visible (and Invisible) Surveillance at Protests," Melbourne Activist Legal Support, July 10, 2020, https://melbactivistlegal.org.au/2020/07/10/being-aware-of-visible-and-invisible-surveillance-at-protests.

55.   Alleen Brown, Will Parrish, and Alice Speri, "Police used private security aircraft for surveillance in Standing Rock no-fly zone," The Intercept, September 29, 2017.

56.   Alleen Brown, Will Parrish, and Alice Speri, "Standing Rock documents expose inner workings of 'surveillance-industrial complex,'" The Intercept, June 3, 2017.

57.   Alleen Brown, Will Parrish, and Alice Speri, "As Standing Rock camps cleared out, TigerSwan expanded surveillance to array of progressive causes," The Intercept, June 21, 2017.

58.   George Joseph, "Exclusive: Feds regularly monitored Black Lives Matter since Ferguson," The Intercept, July 24, 2015.

59.   Alfred W. McCoy, *Policing America's Empire* (Madison: University of Wisconsin Press, 2009).

60.   Kwet, "Digital colonialism."

61.   Malak Shalabi, "America's Hyper-Surveillance of Muslims Targets Our Religious Identity," Politics Today, March 24, 2021.

62.   See for example American Civil Liberties Union, "Factsheet: The NYPD Muslim Surveillance Program," https://www.aclu.org/other/factsheet-nypd-muslim-surveillance-program; Diala Shamas and Nermeen Arastu, "Mapping Muslims: NYPD Spying and its Impact on American Muslims," The Muslim American Civil Liberties Coalition (MACLC), Creating Law

Enforcement Accountability & Responsibility (CLEAR), and the Asian American Legal Defense and Education Fund (AALDEF), March 2013; and Rose Hackman, "American, Muslim, and under constant watch: the emotional toll of surveillance," *The Guardian*, March 27, 2016.

63. Joseph Cox, "How the U.S. Military Buys Location Data from Ordinary Apps," *VICE*, November 16, 2020.

64. See for example Elizabeth Hilton, *From the War on Poverty to the War on Crime: The Making of Mass Incarceration in America* (Cambridge, MA: Harvard University Press, 2017); Katy Sian, "Countering racism in counter-terrorism and surveillance discourse," *Palgrave Communications* 3, no. 1 (December 2017): 1–3; and Fanna Gamal, "The Racial Politics of Protection: A Critical Race Examination of Police Militarization," *California Law Review* 104, no. 4 (2016): 979–1008.

65. Sahil Chinoy, "The Racist History Behind Facial Recognition," *New York Times*, July 10, 2019.

66. Tim Perkins, "'It's techno-racism': Detroit is quietly using facial recognition to make arrests," *The Guardian*, August 17, 2019.

67. Karen Hao, "A US government study confirms most recognition systems are racist," *MIT Technology Review*, December 20, 2019.

68. Joy Buolamwini et al., "We Must Fight Face Surveillance to Protect Black Lives: An urgent letter from the Algorithmic Justice League," Medium, June 3, 2020.

69. Inioluwa Deborah Raji and Joy Buolamwini, "Actionable Auditing: Investigating the Impact of Publicly Naming Biased Performance Results of Commercial AI Products," *AIES '19: Proceedings of the 2019 AAAI/ ACM Conference on AI, Ethics, and Society* (January 2019): 429–35; and Joy Buolamwini and Timnit Gebru, "Gender Shades: Intersectional Accuracy Disparities in Commercial Gender Classification," *Proceedings of Machine Learning* 81 (2018): 1–15; also see gendershades.org.

70. Joy Buolamwini, "Response: Racial and Gender bias in Amazon Rekognition—Commercial AI System for Analyzing Faces," Medium, January 25, 2019.

71. Naomi Ishisaka, "Is Surveillance Tech Widening America's Racial Divide?" *Seattle Times*, October 28, 2019.

72. Caroline Haskins, "How Ring Went From 'Shark Tank' Reject to America's Scariest Surveillance Company," *VICE*, December 3, 2019; also see Caroline Haskins, "US Cities Are Helping People Buy Amazon Surveillance Cameras Using Taxpayer Money," *VICE*, August 2, 2019.

73. Caroline Haskins, "Amazon Provided Police with 'Heat Maps' of Package Theft for Sting Operation," *VICE*, July 9, 2019; Caroline Haskins, "Amazon

is Coaching Cops on How to Obtain Surveillance Footage Without a Warrant," *VICE*, August 5, 2019; and Caroline Haskins, "Police Promised Witnesses Free Ring Surveillance Cameras If They Testified Against Neighbors," *VICE*, August 15, 2019.

74. "MediaJustice responds to report on Amazon Ring's racist culture and police partnerships," MediaJustice, December 9, 2019.

75. Matthew Guariglia, "Police Will Pilot a Program to Live-Stream Amazon Ring Cameras," Electronic Frontier Foundation, November 3, 2020.

76. Jason Kelley and Matthew Guariglia, "Amazon Ring Must End Its Dangerous Partnerships With Police," Electronic Frontier Foundation, June 10, 2020.

77. Alex Brook Lynn, "Episode 7: BBB: Big Brother Buildings," *Surveillance and the City*, Podcast audio, October 2, 2020.

78. "University of Miami Reportedly Used Facial Recognition to Discipline Student Protestors," Democracy Now!, October 16, 2020.

79. Kari Paul, "'Ban this technology': students protest US universities' use of facial recognition," *The Guardian*, March 2, 2020.

80. Lauren Kaori Gurley, "Students and Maintenance Staff Protest Surveillance at Wesleyan University," *VICE*, March 5, 2020.

81. Drew Harwell, "Cheating-detection companies made millions during the pandemic. Now students are fighting back," *Washington Post*, November 12, 2020; Joe Mullin, "Student Surveillance Vendor Proctorio Files SLAPP Lawsuit to Silence a Critic," Electronic Frontier Foundation, February 23, 2021.

82. Tim Lau, "Predictive Policing Explained," Brennan Center for Justice, April 1, 2020.

83. Wang, Carceral Capitalism, 43.

84. Micah Herskind, "Three Reasons Advocates Must Move Beyond Demanding Release for 'Nonviolent Offenders,'" Medium, April 14, 2020.

85. Liz O'Sullivan, Email to author, April 21, 2021.

86. Sarah T. Hamid, "Community Defense: Sarah T. Hamid on Abolishing Carceral Technologies," interview with *Logic Magazine* 11, August 31, 2020.

87. Wang, *Carceral Capitalism*, 251.

88. Morgan Meaker and Gogi Kamushadze, "Marseille's fight against AI surveillance," Coda Story, March 26, 2020.

89. "Netherlands: End dangerous mass surveillance policing experiments," Amnesty International, September 29, 2020, https://www.amnesty.org/en/latest/news/2020/09/netherlands-end-mass-surveillance-predictive-policing/.

90. UN Office of the High Commissioner for Human Rights, "UN Committee issues recommendations to combat racial profiling," November 26, 2020.

91. Caroline Haskins, "Scars, Tattoos, And License Plates: This Is What Palantir and The LAPD Know About You," BuzzFeed News, September 29, 2020.

92. Laura Nolan, "The Moral Vacuum that is Palantir CEO Alex Karp's S-1 Letter," *Responsible Computing* (blog), August 29, 2020.

93. Sam Biddle, "Police surveilled George Floyd protests with help from Twitter-affiliated startup Dataminr," The Intercept, July 9, 2020.

94. Sam Biddle, "Twitter surveillance startup targets communities of color for police," The Intercept, October 21, 2020.

95. Kashmir Hill, "The Secretive Company That Might End Privacy as We Know It," *New York Times*, January 18, 2020.

96. Ryan Mac et al., "Surveillance Nation," BuzzFeed News, April 6, 2021.

97. Louise Matsakis, "Scraping the Web Is a Powerful Tool. Clearview AI Abused It," *Wired*, January 25, 2020.

98. Johana Bhuiyan, "Civil Rights Activists Sue to Stop Clearview AI Data Scraping," Government Technology, March 10, 2021.

99. Richards, "The Dangers of Surveillance," 1937–38.

100. Richards, "The Dangers of Surveillance," 1937–38.

101. MEE Staff, "Israel: Lawyers call on Shin Bet to halt text message threats targeting Palestinians," Middle East Eye, May 13, 2021.

102. Richards, "The Dangers of Surveillance," 1937–38.

103. Allison Pytlak and Brandon Valeriano, "The Frontlines of Cyber Repression: Thailand and the Crop Top King," Niskanen Center, August 4, 2017, https://www.niskanencenter.org/frontlines-cyber-repression-thailand-crop-top-king/.

104. Hannah Ellis-Petersen, "Censorship and silence: south-east Asia suffers under press crackdown," *The Guardian*, February 24, 2019.

105. Patrick Howell O'Neill, "How WeChat censors private conversations, automatically in real time," *MIT Technology Review*, July 15, 2019.

106. Danny O'Brien, "China's Global Reach: Surveillance and Censorship Beyond the Great Firewall," Electronic Frontier Foundation, October 10, 2019.

107. Isobel Cockerell, "The Uyghur women fighting China's surveillance state," Coda Story, May 9, 2019.

108. Chris Buckley and Paul Mozur, "How China Uses High-Tech Surveillance to Subdue Minorities," *New York Times*, May 22, 2019.

109. Chris Buckley, "China Is Detaining Muslims in Vast Numbers. The Goal: 'Transformation,'" *New York Times*, September 8, 2018; Nick Cumming-Bruce, "U.S. Steps Up Criticism of China for Detentions in Xinjiang," *New York Times*, March 13, 2019.

110. Cooper Quintin and Mona Wang, "Watering Holes and Million Dollar Dissidents: the Changing Economics of Digital Surveillance," Electronic Frontier Foundation, September 9, 2019.

111. Philip Dorling, "Spies eye green protestors," *Sydney Morning Herald*, January 7, 2012; Clive Hamilton, "Is spying on anti-coal activists just the tip of the iceberg?" The Conversation, June 4, 2014.

112. Cait Kelly, "Young climate activists 'most at risk' of being spied on by AFP," *New Daily*, July 16, 2019.

113. Jim Bronskill, "'This isn't about national security': Civil liberties group publishes CSIS reports related to alleged spying," CBC, July 8, 2019.

114. Jim Bronskill, "Here's a look at how protests have been policed across Canada," Global News, March 4, 2020.

115. Lynn Desjardins, "Privacy watchdog warns facial recognition tools endanger human rights," Radio Canada International, May 10, 2021.

116. Algeria, Bahrain, Bangladesh, Brazil, Canada, Cote d'Ivoire, Egypt, France, Greece, India, Iraq, Israel, Jordan, Kazakhstan, Kenya, Kuwait, Kyrgyzstan, Latvia, Lebanon, Libya, Mexico, Morocco, the Netherlands, Oman, Pakistan, Palestine, Poland, Qatar, Rwanda, Saudi Arabia, Singapore, South Africa, Switzerland, Tajikistan, Thailand, Togo, Tunisia, Turkey, the UAE, Uganda, the United Kingdom, the United States, Uzbekistan, Yemen, and Zambia.

117. Bill Marczak et al., "Hide and Seek: Tracking NSO Group's Pegasus Spyware to Operations in 45 Countries," The Citizen Lab, September 18, 2018.

118. Bill Marczak et al., "Champing at the Cyberbit: Ethiopian Dissidents Targeted with New Commercial Spyware," The Citizen Lab, December 6, 2017.

119. Alex Hern, "Hacking Team hacked: firm sold spying tools to repressive regimes, documents claim," *The Guardian*, July 6, 2015.

120. United Nations Security Council Resolution 2396 (2017), S/RES/2396 (2017)*, December 21, 2017.

121. Krisztina Huszti-Orbán and Fionnuala Ní Aoláin, "Use of Biometric Data to Identify Terrorists: Best Practice or Risky Business?," University of Minnesota Law School's Human Rights Center, 2020.

122. Ian G. R. Shaw, *Predator Empire: Drone Warfare and Full Spectrum Dominance* (Minneapolis: University of Minnesota Press, 2016), 240.

123. Will Parrish (@willparrishca), "Reminder that Customs and Border Protection also used this drone for surveillance at Standing Rock, 2016," Twitter, May 31, 2020, https://twitter.com/willparrishca/status/1267236072087404546.

124. Associated Press, "Baltimore board OKs surveillance planes amid opposition," ABC News, April 2, 2020.

125. Conor Friedersdorf, "Eyes Over Compton: How Police Spied on a Whole City," *The Atlantic*, April 21, 2014. For more on Gorgon Stare and potential domestic use, see Arthur Holland Michel, *Eyes in the Sky: The Secret Rise*

of Gorgon Stare and How It Will Watch Us All (Boston: Houghton Mifflin Harcourt, 2019).

126. Jennifer Lynch, "Drone Surveillance of Border Far Greater Than Previously Known," Common Dreams, January 15, 2014.

127. Kevin Rector, "LAPD gets approval to begin recording, storing aerial footage of protests," *Los Angeles Times*, October 27, 2020.

128. Ali Winston (@awinston), "Yet one more way in which protests are treated with counter-insurgency tactics," Twitter, October 27, 2020, https://twitter.com/awinston/status/1321248987505188864.

129. For example, Project Raven, in which former US National Security Agency operatives were employed by the United Arab Emirates to profile, hack, and collect data on the government's "enemies"—mostly journalists, dissidents, human rights defenders, and rival political leaders. See Christopher Bing and Joel Schectman, "Inside the UAE's Secret Hacking Team of American Mercenaries," Reuters, January 30, 2019, and Nicole Perlroth, *This Is How They Tell Me the World Ends: The Cyber-Weapons Arms Race* (London: Bloomsbury Publishing, 2021).

130. Cora Currier, "The Kill Chain: The Lethal Bureaucracy Behind Obama's Drone War," The Drone Papers 3, The Intercept, October 15, 2015, https://theintercept.com/drone-papers/the-kill-chain.

131. Kevin Jon Heller, "'One Hell of a Killing Machine': Signature Strikes and International Law," *Journal of International Criminal Justice* 11, no. 1 (2013): 89–119.

132. Ashley S. Deeks, "Predicting Enemies," *Virginia Law Review* 104, no. 8 (2018): 1529–92.

133. Lauren Wilcox, "Embodying algorithmic war: Gender, race, and the posthuman in drone warfare," *Security Dialogue,* 48, no. 1 (2017): 6.

134. Robin D. G. Kelley, "Thug Nation: On State Violence and Disposability," in *Policing the Planet: Why the Policing Crisis Led to Black Lives Matter*, Jordan T. Camp and Christina Heatherton, eds. (New York: Verso Books, 2016), 47.

135. Micah Herskind, "Three Reasons Advocates Must Move Beyond Demanding Release for 'Nonviolent Offenders,'" Medium, April 14, 2020.

136. Jennifer Rhee, *The Robotic Imaginary: The Human and the Price of Dehumanized Labor* (Minneapolis: Minnesota University Press, 2018), 164.

137. Thomas Gregory, "Drones, Targeted Killings, and the Limitations of International Law," *International Political Sociology* 9, no. 3 (2015): 197–212.

138. Jeremy Scahill and Glenn Greenwald, "The NSA's role in the U.S. assassination program," The Intercept, February 10, 2014.

139. Jordan Pearson, "The Problem With Using Metadata to Justify Drone Strikes," *VICE*, October 15, 2015.

140. See "Drone Warfare," Bureau of Investigative Journalism, https://www.thebureauinvestigates.com/projects/drone-war.

141. Sidney Fussell, "A New York Lawmaker Wants to Ban Police Use of Armed Robots," *Wired*, March 18, 2021; Emma Bowman, "'Creepy' Robot Dog Loses Job With New York Police Department," NPR, April 30, 2021.

142. For more information about these technologies, see the Campaign to Stop Killer Robots at stopkillerrobots.org.

143. Richard Moyes, "Target profiles: An initial consideration of 'target profiles' as a basis for rule-making in the context of discussions on autonomy in weapons systems," Article 36, August 2019, 1, https://article36.org/wp-content/uploads/2019/08/Target-profiles.pdf.

144. Article 36, "Killing by machine: Key issues for understanding meaningful human control," April 2015, https://article36.org/wp-content/uploads/2013/06/KILLING_BY_MACHINE_6.4.15.pdf.

145. Jo Becker and Scott Shane, "Secret 'Kill List' Proves a Test of Obama's Principles and Will," *New York Times*, May 29, 2012.

146. Ray Acheson, "Autonomous weapons and gender-based violence," Reaching Critical Will of the Women's International League for Peace and Freedom, October 2020, https://reachingcriticalwill.org/images/documents/Publications/aws-and-gbv.pdf.

147. Mattha Busby, "Killer robots: pressure builds for ban as governments meet," *The Guardian*, April 9, 2018.

148. Julia Carrie Wong, "'We won't be war profiteers': Microsoft workers protest $480m army contract," *The Guardian*, February 22, 2019.

149. Preston Gralla, "Should Microsoft help the Pentagon 'increase lethality?'" Computerworld, November 5, 2018.

150. Ray Acheson, "Autonomous weapons and patriarchy," Women's International League for Peace and Freedom and Campaign to Stop Killer Robots, October 2020, https://reachingcriticalwill.org/images/documents/Publications/aws-and-patriarchy.pdf.

151. Peter Asaro, "Will #BlackLivesMatter to Robocop?" University of Miami School of Law, March 28, 2016, http://robots.law.miami.edu/2016/wp-content/uploads/2015/07/Asaro_Will-BlackLivesMatter-to-Robocop_Revised_DRAFT.pdf.

152. See for example Tom Simonite, "Algorithms Were Supposed to Fix the Bail System. They Haven't," *Wired*, February 19, 2020.

153. Jacob Snow, "Amazon's Face Recognition Falsely Matched 28 Members of Congress With Mugshots," American Civil Liberties Union, July 26, 2018, https://www.aclu.org/blog/privacy-technology/surveillance-technologies/amazons-face-recognition-falsely-matched-28.

154. Sidney Fussel, "An Algorithm That 'Predicts' Criminality Based on a Face Sparks a Furor," *Wired*, June 24, 2020.

155. Perlroth, *This Is How*.

156. Isabelle Jibilian and Katie Canales, "The US is readying sanctions against Russia over the SolarWinds cyber attack. Here's a simple explanation of how the massive hack happened and why it's such a big deal," *Business Insider*, April 15, 2021.

157. United Nations General Assembly, Report of the Group of Governmental Experts on Developments in the Field of Information and Telecommunications in the Context of International Security, A/70/174, July 22, 2015.

158. For reporting and analysis of UN discussions on cyber issues, see the work of Allison Pytlak in the *Cyber Peace & Security Monitor* at the Reaching Critical Will program of the Women's International League for Peace and Freedom, https://reachingcriticalwill.org/disarmament-fora/ict/oewg/cyber-monitor.

159. Frank Pasquale, "'Machines set loose to slaughter': the dangerous rise of military AI," *The Guardian*, October 15, 2020.

160. See https://www.stopspying.org.

161. See https://www.stoplapdspying.org.

162. See https://www.fightforthefuture.org.

163. See https://www.techworkerscoalition.org.

164. See https://www.eff.org.

165. See https://www.stopkillerrobots.org.

166. See https://www.reachingcriticalwill.org/disarmament-fora/ict.

167. See https://www.amnesty.org and https://www.amnesty.org/en/tech.

168. See https://decoders.amnesty.org.

169. See https://www.aclu.org/issues/national-security/privacy-and-surveillance.

170. Chris Mills Rodrigo, "New coalition launches against 'surveillance advertising,'" MSN News, March 22, 2021.

171. See https://ooni.org.

172. See https://stopstalkerware.org.

173. Kwet, "Digital colonialism," 21.

174. See for example Sebastian Eb, "Fighting for a fairer Internet," DW Akademie, February 18, 2019; Carla Jancz, Helena Prado, and Thais Jussim, *Imagery About Community Networks in Comics*, Instituto Bem Ester (IBE) Brasil, 2019; and Mélanie Dulong de Rosnay and Félix Tréguer, eds., *Telecommunications Reclaimed: A Hands-On Guide to Networking Communities* (Internet Society, Association for Progressive Communications, and netCommons, 2020).

Chapter 4: Deconstructing Borders

1.   Esyllt W. Jones, *Influenza 1918: Disease, Death, and Struggle in Winnipeg* (Toronto: University of Toronto Press, 2007).

2.   The Peace of Westphalia refers to two peace treaties, one ending the Thirty Years' War (1618–48) and the other ending the Eighty Years' War (1568–1648), which combined killed approximately eight million people in Europe.

3.   Harsha Walia, *Border & Rule: Global Migration, Capitalism, and the Rise of Racist Nationalism* (Chicago: Haymarket Books, 2021), 6.

4.   At the Berlin Conference in 1884, European governments set out regulations for colonization of and trade in Africa. Some bilateral agreements had been reached earlier, but this conference is widely seen as the solidification of the colonial partitioning of Africa.

5.   Reece Jones, *Violent Borders* (New York: Verso, 2017).

6.   Jeff Halper, *War Against the People* (London: Pluto Press, 2015).

7.   Halper, *War Against the People*.

8.   Todd Miller, *Build Bridges, Not Walls: A Journey to a World Without Borders* (San Francisco: City Lights Books, 2021), 33.

9.   See for example Justin Akers Chacón, "Opening the border through class struggle and solidarity," puntorojo, January 13, 2020, and Harsha Walia, *Undoing Border Imperialism* (Oakland, CA: AK Press, 2013).

10. Jones, *Violent Borders*, 138.

11. William Robinson, "Globalization and the Struggle for Immigrant Rights in the United States," ZNET, March 10, 2007.

12. Walia, *Border & Rule*, 73.

13. Kate Lyons, "Climate refugees can't be returned home, says landmark UN human rights ruling," *The Guardian*, January 20, 2020.

14. Sebastian Rees, "A Massive Proxy Military Escalation is Taking Place in Libya," albawaba, May 28, 2020.

15. "UN chief calls for Libya mass grave investigation," UN News, June 13, 2020, https://news.un.org/en/story/2020/06/1066272.

16. UNHCR, "Operational portal: Refugee situations (Libya)," last updated June 30, 2020, https://data2.unhcr.org/en/country/lby.

17. UNHCR, "Operational portal: Refugee situations (Yemen)," last updated December 31, 2020, https://data2.unhcr.org/en/country/yem.

18. UNHCR, "Operational portal: Refugee situations (Syria)," last updated May 5, 2021, https://data2.unhcr.org/en/situations/syria.

19. See for example Jennifer Dathan, "The Reverberating Effects of Explosive Weapon Use in Syria," Action on Armed Violence, 2019, https://www.inew.org/wp-content/uploads/2019/02/Reverberating-effects-of-explosive-weapons-in-Syria.V5.pdf; "'Targeting Life in Idlib'": Syrian and Russian

Strikes on Civilian Infrastructure," Human Rights Watch, October 15, 2020, https://www.hrw.org/report/2020/10/15/targeting-life-idlib/syrian-and-russian-strikes-civilian-infrastructure.

20. Meaghan Beatley, "America's Guns Fuel Mexico's Domestic Violence Epidemic," *Foreign Policy,* May 27, 2020.

21. The Western Hemisphere Institute for Security Cooperation, formerly known as the School of the Americas, is a US military training school based in Fort Benning, Georgia. Previously operated by the US Army, it is now an institute of the US Department of Defense. It has trained officers from a variety of Latin American countries, many of which have been implicated in serious human rights abuses, including torture and forced disappearances. See School of the Americas Watch at www.soaw.org for more information.

22. John Washington, *The Dispossessed* (New York: Verso, 2019).

23. Walia, *Border & Rule,* 2.

24. Haymarket Books, "Abolish ICE is Not Just a Slogan," YouTube video, 1:41:08, May 19, 2020, https://www.youtube.com/watch?time_continue=454&v=3Z7SKGTgYqQ&feature=emb_logo.

25. Todd Miller, "5 Book Plan: The Politics of Borders," Verso blog, September 13, 2019.

26. Rebecca Berke Galemba, *Contraband Corridor* (Stanford, CA: Stanford University Press, 2017).

27. Todd Miller, Empire of Borders: The Expansion of the U.S. Border Around the World (New York: Verso, 2019).

28. Jenna M. Loyd and Alison Mountz, *Boats, Borders, and Bases: Race, the Cold War, and the Rise of Migration Detention in the United States* (Berkeley, CA: University of California Press, 2018).

29. Jones, *Violent Borders,* 39.

30. Jones, *Violent Borders,* 40.

31. "Border militarisation," War Resisters International, https://www.wri-irg.org/en/pm-themes/border-militarisation.

32. John Carlos Frey, *Sand and Blood: America's Stealth War on the Mexico Border* (New York: Bold Type Books, 2019), 79.

33. Frey, *Sand and Blood,* 79.

34. Todd Miller reports in *Empire of Borders* that an Israeli brigadier general publicly described Gaza as a laboratory, plainly acknowledging that oppression of Palestinians has helped them develop weapons and surveillance technology for export.

35. Will Parrish, "The U.S. Border Patrol and an Israeli military contractor are putting a Native American reservation under 'persistent surveillance,'" The

Intercept, August 25, 2019; also see Todd Miller, *Border Patrol Nation* (San Francisco: City Lights Books, 2014).

36.   Lee Fang and Sam Biddle, "Google AI Tech will be used for virtual border wall, CBP contract shows," The Intercept, October 21, 2020.

37.   "Report of the Special Rapporteur on contemporary forms of racism, racial discrimination, xenophobia and related intolerance," UN Office of the High Commissioner on Human Rights, A/75/590, November 10, 2020, 16.

38.   "Report of the Special Rapporteur," 6.

39.   James W. E. Sheptycki, "The global cops cometh: reflections on transationalization, knowledge work and policing subculture," *British Journal of Sociology* 49, no. 1 (1998): 70.

40.   Dean Wilson and Leanne Weber, "Surveillance, Risk and Preemption on the Australian Border," *Surveillance and Society* 5, no. 2 (2002): 124.

41.   "Report of the Special Rapporteur," 1.

42.   "Report of the Special Rapporteur," 1.

43.   "Report of the Special Rapporteur," 10.

44.   "Report of the Special Rapporteur," 13.

45.   "Report of the Special Rapporteur," 15.

46.   "Palantir technology contracts raise human rights concerns before NYSE direct listing," Amnesty International, September 28, 2020, https://www.amnestyusa.org/press-releases/palantirs-contracts-with-ice-raise-human-rights-concerns-around-direct-listing/.

47.   Petra Molnar and Lex Gill, "Bots at the Gate: A Human Rights Analysis of Automated Decision-Making in Canada's Immigration and Refugee System," Citizen Lab and International Human Rights Program (Faculty of Law, University of Toronto), Research Report No. 114, September 2018, 6.

48.   Molnar and Gill, "Bots at the Gate," 18.

49.   Molnar and Gill, "Bots at the Gate," 18–19.

50.   Wilson and Weber, "Surveillance, Risk and Preemption," 126.

51.   Wilson and Weber, "Surveillance, Risk and Preemption," 128.

52.   Associated Press, "In post-pandemic Europe, migrants will face digital fortress," *Daily Mail*, May 31, 2021.

53.   "The Cost of Immigration Enforcement and Border Security," American Immigration Council, July 7, 2020, https://www.americanimmigrationcouncil.org/research/the-cost-of-immigration-enforcement-and-border-security.

54.   Miller, *Empire of Borders*.

55.   Todd Miller and Nick Buxton, "Biden's Border: The industry, the Democrats and the 2020 elections," Transnational Institute, February 17, 2021, https://www.tni.org/en/bidensborder.

56. Miller and Buxton, "Biden's Border."

57. Miller, *Empire of Borders*, 83.

58. Mark Akkerman, "The Business of Building Walls," Transnational Institute, Stop Wapenhandel, Centre Delàs, 2019, https://www.tni.org/files/ publication-downloads/business_of_building_walls_-_full_report.pdf.

59. Charlotte Gifford, "The true cost of the EU's border security boom," *World Finance*, January 21, 2020.

60. Apostolis Fotiadis, "Why are we letting the defence industry hijack the EU?" *The Guardian*, December 11, 2019.

61. "Border security, military industry and EU militarisation," Stop Wapenhandel, April 14, 2019, https://stopwapenhandel.org/node/2271.

62. Samuel Stolton, "EU signs contract for large-scale biometric database to protect borders," Euractiv, June 4, 2020.

63. Fotiadis, "Why are we."

64. See for example Francisco Cantú, *The Line Becomes a River: Dispatches from the Border* (New York: Riverhead Books, 2018); Jason De León, *The Land of Open Graves: Living and Dying on the Migrant Trail* (Oakland, CA: University of California Press, 2015); John Washington, "Is the US Border Patrol Committing Crimes Against Humanity?" Guernica, May 2, 2018; Caitlin Dickerson, "A Rare Look Inside Trump's Immigration Crackdown Draws Legal Threats," *New York Times*, July 23, 2020; John Carlos Frey, *Sand and Blood: America's Stealth War on the Mexico Border* (New York: Bold Type Books, 2019); Miller, *Build Bridges*.

65. De León, *Land of Open Graves*, 8.

66. Zack Campbell and Lorenzo D'Agostino, "Friends of the Traffickers: Italy's Anti-Mafia Directorate and the 'Dirty Campaign' to Criminalize Migration," The Intercept, April 30, 2021.

67. Washington, *The Dispossessed*.

68. "Migrant deaths and disappearance," Migration Data Portal, https:// migrationdataportal.org/themes/migrant-deaths-and-disappearances.

69. Gifford, "The true cost."

70. Washington, *The Dispossessed*.

71. For regularly updated accounts, see *Are You Syrious?* at https:// areyousyrious.medium.com and Transbalkanska Solidarnost at https:// transbalkanskasolidarnost.home.blog/eng. Also see Amnesty International, "Croatia: EU complicit in violence and abuse by police against refugees and migrants," March 13, 2019, https://www.amnesty.org/en/latest/ news/2019/03/croatia-eu-complicit-in-violence-and-abuse-by-police-against-refugees-and-migrants/.

72.   Oxfam, Belgrade Centre for Human Rights, and Macedonian Young Lawyers Association, "A Dangerous 'Game': The pushback of migrants, including refugees, at Europe's borders," Oxfam International, April 2017, 4.

73.   Oxfam, Belgrade Centre, and Macedonian Young Lawyers, "A Dangerous 'Game,'" 4.

74.   Border Violence Monitoring Network, https://www.borderviolence.eu/statistics.

75.   Raja Abdulrahim, "Greek Police Are Rounding Up Asylum Seekers and Forcing Them Into Turkey, Migrants Say," *Wall Street Journal*, May 20, 2020.

76.   War Resisters League, "Greek authorities use range of tear gas against migrants," March 6, 2020.

77.   John Washington, "'I Didn't Exist': A Syrian Asylum-Seeker's Case Reframes Migrant Abuses as Enforced Disappearances," The Intercept, February 28, 2021.

78.   "Immigration Policing & Border Violence," INCITE!, https://incite-national.org/immigration-policing-border-violence.

79.   Katharina Buchholz, "Number of Immigrant Detainees Rises Quickly," statista, January 3, 2020.

80.   "Europe," Global Detention Project, https://www.globaldetentionproject.org/regions-subregions/europe.

81.   "Australia," Global Detention Project, https://www.globaldetentionproject.org/countries/asia-pacific/australia.

82.   Washington, *The Dispossessed*, 187.

83.   Are You Syrious? "AYS Special from Lesvos: COVID-19 and an island bursting at the seams," Medium, March 29, 2020.

84.   Are You Syrious? "AYS Special."

85.   "Moria nightmare," Refugee Support Aegean, January 24, 2020, https://rsaegean.org/en/moria-nightmare. See also Chico Harlan, "'We are living like animals': Migrants wait up to eight hours for meals as tourists dine on octopus in Greece," Independent, February 24, 2020.

86.   Are You Syrius? "AYS Daily Digest 19/5/20: Maltese offshore prisons," Medium, May 20, 2020.

87.   "Inspections of Australia's immigration detention facilities 2019 Report," Australian Human Rights Commission, December 2020, https://humanrights.gov.au/our-work/asylum-seekers-and-refugees/publications/inspections-australias-immigration-detention.

88.   Damien Cave, "A Timeline of Despair in Australia's Offshore Detention Centres," *New York Times*, June 26, 2019.

89.   Behrouz Boochani, *No Friend But the Mountains: Writing from Manus Prison*, Omid Tofighian, trans. (Sydney, NSW: Picador Australia, 2018).

90.   Justin Akers Chacón, "Close the Concentration Camps," REBEL, July 11, 2019.

91. John Washington, "Family Separations at the Border Constitute Torture, New Report Claims," The Intercept, February 25, 2020.

92. José Olivares and John Washington, "'He Just Empties You All Out': Whistleblower Reports High Number of Hysterectomies at ICE Detention Facility," The Intercept, September 15, 2020.

93. John Washington, "ICE Threatened to Expose Asylum-Seekers to COVID-19 If They Did Not Accept Deportation," The Intercept, February 6, 2021.

94. John Washington, "ICE Mismanagement Created Coronavirus 'Hotbeds of Infection' In and Around Detention Centers," The Intercept, December 9, 2020.

95. Washington, *The Dispossessed*.

96. See "Mapping U.S. Immigration Detention," Freedom for Immigrants, https://www.freedomforimmigrants.org/map.

97. Washington, *The Dispossessed*.

98. Asylum Insight, "Private contractors at onshore and offshore processing centres," last updated April 4, 2021, https://www.asyluminsight.com/private-contractors#.XtlLilB7nu0.

99. Paul Farrell, "Immigration department suppressed detention contractor's name due to boycotts," *The Guardian*, March 28, 2017.

100. Bill MacKeith, "Private companies that run detention centres in the UK," Melting Pot, February 23, 2005, https://www.meltingpot.org/2005/02/private-companies-that-run-detention-centres-in-the-uk/.

101. Elisabetta Poveloda, "Italy's Migrant Detention Centers Are Cruel, Rights Groups Say," *New York Times*, June 5, 2013.

102. Admir Skodo, "How immigration detention compares around the world," The Conversation, April 19, 2017.

103. Sally Hayden, "The U.N. Is Leaving Migrants to Die in Libya," *Foreign Policy*, October 10, 2019.

104. Transbalkan Solidarity, "Call to Action: Stop Funding Violence Now!," May 2020, https://transbalkanskasolidarnost.home.blog/stop-funding-violence-now.

105. Border Violence Monitoring Network, "Special Report: COVID-19 and Border Violence along the Balkan Route," April 2020, 6, https://www.borderviolence.eu/wp-content/uploads/COVID-19-Report.pdf.

106. Iida Käyhkö and Laura Schack, "Policing the pandemic: 'security' for whom?," ROAR, April 2, 2020.

107. No Name Kitchen, "The Impact of COVID-19 on the Balkans Route," Webinar, May 26, 2020, https://www.youtube.com/watch?v=AOMGX5NiGA&feature=youtu.be.

108. No Name Kitchen, "The Impact of COVID-19."

109. Border Violence Monitoring Network, "Special Report."

110. See for example https://www.detentionwatchnetwork.org/covid-19 and https://freethemall4publichealth.org.

111. De León, *Land of Open Graves*, 3–4.

112. Bridget Anderson, Nandita Sharma, and Cynthia Wright, "Editorial: Why No Borders?" *Refuge: Canada's Journal on Refugees* 26, no. 2 (2009): 8.

113. Anderson, Sharma, and Wright, "Editorial," 9.

114. Miller, *Empire of Borders*.

115. Joseph Nevins, "The Right to the World," *Antipode* 49, no. 5 (2017).

116. Haymarket Books, "Abolish ICE."

117. Gustav Landauer, *Revolution and Other Writings: A Political Reader*, Gabriel Kuhn, ed. and trans. (Oakland, CA: PM Press, 2010), 214.

118. Harsha Walia, *Undoing Border Imperialism* (Oakland, CA: AK Press, 2013), 265.

119. Washington, *The Dispossessed*, 325.

120. Andreas Chatzidakis et al., "COVID-19 pandemic: A Crisis of Care," Verso Books (blog), March 26, 2020.

121. Miller, *Build Bridges*, 25.

Chapter 5: Demobilizing War

1. Hannah Arendt, *On Violence* (New York City: Harvest Books, 1970), 80.

2. Amanda Macias, "America has spent $6.4 trillion on wars in the Middle East and Asia since 2001, a new study says," CNBC, November 20, 2019.

3. Neta C. Crawford et al., "Detention," in "Costs of War," Watson Institute of International & Public Affairs at Brown University, https://watson.brown.edu/costsofwar/costs/social/rights/detention.

4. See the International Network on Explosive Weapons at inew.org for information and resources.

5. "Explosive Weapons Devastating for Civilians," Human Rights Watch, February 6, 2020, https://www.hrw.org/news/2020/02/06/explosive-weapons-devastating-civilians.

6. Christina Wille, "The Implications of the Reverberating Effects of Explosive Weapons Use in Populated Areas for Implementing the Sustainable Development Goals," United Nations Institute for Disarmament Research, 2016.

7. "Waiting to declare famine 'will be too late for Yemenis on brink of starvation,'" UN News, July 10, 2020, https://news.un.org/en/story/2020/07/1068101.

8. Rasha Jarhum and Alice Bonfatti, "We Are Still Here: Mosulite Women 500 Days After the Conclusion of the Coalition Military Operation," Women's

International League for Peace and Freedom, 2019, https://www.wilpf.org/wp-content/uploads/2019/08/ENG_We-Are-Still-Here_Mosulite-Women.pdf.

9. Medea Benjamin and Nicolas J. S. Davies, "Trump & Biden's Secret Bombing Wars," Common Dreams, March 4, 2021.

10. Jennifer Dathan, "'Blast Injury': a report on the reverberating health impacts from the use of explosive weapons," Action on Armed Violence, 2020.

11. See for example Keyan Salarkia et al., "Stop the War on Children," Save the Children, 2020, https://www.stopwaronchildren.org/.

12. See the Conflict and Environment Observatory at https://ceobs.org for more information.

13. Roos Boer and Wim Zwijnenburg, "Exploring environmental harm from explosive weapons in populated areas," PAX, May 28, 2020, https://paxforpeace.nl/news/blogs/exploring-environmental-harm-from-explosive-weapons-in-populated-areas.

14. See Melissa Chan, "They Survived Mass Shootings. Years Later, The Bullets Are Still Trying to Kill Them," Time, May 31, 2019; and Alex Yablon, "Gun Ranges Produce Thousands of Tons of Toxic Pollution Every Year," The Trace, April 17, 2016.

15. Wim Zwijnenburg, "Laid to Waste: depleted uranium contaminated military scrap in Iraq," PAX, June 2014, https://ceobs.org/wp-content/uploads/2018/03/PAX_Laid_to_Waste.pdf.

16. David Thorpe, "Extracting a disaster," The Guardian, December 5, 2008.

17. Baskut Tuncak, "75th anniversary of the Trinity nuclear tests, 16 July 2020," United Nations Human Rights Office of the High Commissioner, July 16, 2020.

18. Nic Maclellan, "Nuclear Testing and Racism in the Pacific Islands," The Palgrave Handbook of Ethnicity (Singapore: Palgrave Macmillan, 2019): 1–21.

19. Neta C. Crawford, "Pentagon Fuel Use, Climate Change, and the Costs of War," in "Costs of War," Watson Institute for International and Public Affairs at Brown University, July 1, 2019, https://watson.brown.edu/research/2019/pentagon-fuel-use-climate-change-and-costs-war.

20. Crawford, "Pentagon Fuel Use."

21. Murtaza Hussain, "War on the World," The Intercept, September 15, 2019.

22. Elizabeth Cook-Lynn, New Indians, Old Wars (Chicago: University of Illinois Press, 2007), 72.

23. Alexa Liautaud, "White House acknowledges the U.S. is at war in seven countries," VICE, March 15, 2018.

24. Nick Turse, "Pentagon's Own Map of U.S. Bases in Africa Contradicts Its Claim of 'Light' Footprint," The Intercept, February 27, 2020.

25. David Vine, Base Nation: How U.S. Military Bases Abroad Harm America and the World (New York: Metropolitan Books, 2015).

26. Timothy McGrath, "The US is now involved in 134 wars or none, depending on your definition of 'war,'" *The World*, September 16, 2014. Also see Nick Turse, "America's Secret War in 134 Countries," *The Nation*, January 16, 2014.

27. Dan Lamothe and Missy Ryan, "Trump pulls military into political fray of Minneapolis unrest but is unlikely to follow through on threat," *Washington Post*, May 29, 2020.

28. Stuart Schrader, "Trump Has Brought America's Dirty Wars Home," *New Republic*, July 21, 2020.

29. About Face: Veterans Against the War (@VetsAboutFace), "People are so stressed . . .," Twitter, June 8, 2020, https://twitter.com/VetsAboutFace/status/1269883998463037440.

30. Justin Jackson (@J_ManPrime21), "I know that a lot of people . . .," Twitter, June 5, 2020, https://twitter.com/J_ManPrime21/status/1268961287406366721.

31. CODEPINK, "Policing & Militarism: Connecting the Struggles," YouTube webinar, July 9, 2020, 44:31, https://www.youtube.com/watch?v=-gVI3ywZoJo.

32. Kanya Bennett, "365 Days and 605 Armored Military Vehicles Later: Police Militarization a Year After Ferguson," American Civil Liberties Union, August 7, 2015, https://www.aclu.org/blog/criminal-law-reform/reforming-police/365-days-and-605-armored-military-vehicles-later-police.

33. Haymarket Books, "Indigenous Resistance Against Oil Pipelines During a Pandemic," YouTube webinar, June 3, 2020, 1:38:22, https://youtu.be/W5zp8SonR8o.

34. "World military spending increases to almost $2 trillion in 2020," Stockholm International Peace Research Institute, April 26, 2021.

35. "Global military expenditure sees largest annual increase in a decade—says SIPRI—reaching $1917 billion in 2019," Stockholm International Peace Research Institute, April 27, 2020.

36. Neta C. Crawford, "United States Budgetary Costs and Obligations of Post-9/11 Wars through FY2020: $6.4 Trillion," in "Costs of War," Watson Institute for International and Public Affairs at Brown University, 2019, https://watson.brown.edu/costsofwar/papers/2019/united-states-budgetary-costs-and-obligations-post-911-wars-through-fy2020-64-trillion.

37. See for example Congressional Budget Office, "The Cost of Supporting Military Bases," November 2019, and Overseas Base Realignment and Closure Coalition, "U.S. Military Bases Overseas: The Facts," 2018.

38. Hans M. Kristensen and Matt Korda, "United States nuclear forces, 2020," *Bulletin of the Atomic Sciences* 76, no. 1 (2020): 46–60.

39. Greg Mello and Trish Williams-Mello, "United States," in "Assuring destruction forever: 2020 edition," Allison Pytlak and Ray Acheson, eds., Reaching Critical Will of the Women's International League for Peace and Freedom, 2020, 109–125.

40. Federation of American Scientists, "Intelligence Budget Data," Intelligence Resource Program, https://fas.org/irp/budget.

41. "The Black Budget," *Washington Post*, https://www.washingtonpost.com/wp-srv/special/national/black-budget/.

42. "Border Security: 2020 Budget Fact Sheet," Executive Office of the President of the United States, March 2019, https://www.whitehouse.gov/wp-content/uploads/2019/03/FY20-Fact-Sheet_Immigration-Border-Security_FINAL.pdf.

43. Kate Hamaji et al., "Freedom to Thrive: Reimagining Safety & Security in our Communities," Center for Popular Democracy, Law for Black Lives, Black Youth Project 100, 2017, https://www.nfg.org/resources/freedom-thrive-reimagining-safety-security-our-communities.

44. Public Citizen (@Public_Citizen), "The NYPD's $6,000,000,000 budget would . . .," Twitter, June 10, 2020, https://twitter.com/Public_Citizen/status/1270741042069934083.

45. "Following the Money of Mass Incarceration," Prison Policy Initiative, January 25, 2017, https://www.prisonpolicy.org/reports/money.html.

46. Heidi Peltier, "The Growth of the 'Camo Economy' and the Commercialization of the Post-9/11 Wars," in "Costs of War," Watson Institute for International & Public Affairs of Brown University, 2020, https://watson.brown.edu/costsofwar/files/cow/imce/papers/2020/Peltier%202020%20-%20Growth%20of%20Camo%20Economy%20-%20June%2030%202020%20-%20FINAL.pdf.

47. Alex Horton and Aaron Gregg, "Use of military contractors shrouds true costs of war. Washington wants it that way, study says," *Washington Post*, June 30, 2020.

48. Brett Murphy, Nick Penzenstadler, and Gina Barton, "The Pulse nightclub shooting and other G4S scandals," *USA Today*, October 30, 2019.

49. Women's International League for Peace and Freedom, "IV. International Cooperation," in "WILPF Resolutions," 1st Congress, April 1915, 3, https://wilpf.org/wp-content/uploads/2012/08/WILPF_triennial_congress_1915.pdf.

50. Fenner Brockway and Frederic Mullally, *Death Pays a Dividend* (London: Victor Gollancz Ltd, 1944), 60.

51. William I. Robinson, "What are the real reasons behind the New Cold War?" ROAR, May 6, 2021.

52. Niall McCarthy, "The World's Biggest Arms-Producing Companies," statista, December 9, 2019.

53. Pieter D. Wezeman, Alexandria Kuimova, and Siemon T. Wezean, "Trends in International Arms Transfers, 2020," Stockholm International Peace Research Institute, March 2021.

54. Wezeman, Kuimova, and Wezean, "Trends in International Arms"; also see "USA and France dramatically increase major arms exports; Saudia Arabia is largest arms importer, says SIPRI," Stockholm International Peace Research Institute, March 9, 2020.

55. Andrew Tangel and Doug Cameron, "Boeing to Emerge as Big Stimulus Winner," *Wall Street Journal*, March 27, 2020.

56. Sarah Lazare, "As the World Economy Grinds to a Halt, the U.S. War Machine Churns On," *In These Times*, April 6, 2020.

57. António Guterres, "The fury of the virus illustrates the folly of war," United Nations, March 23, 2020, https://www.un.org/en/un-coronavirus-communications-team/fury-virus-illustrates-folly-war.

58. See for example Steven Chase, "Canada to resume approving military-goods exports to Saudi Arabia," *Globe and Mail*, April 9, 2020.

59. Naomi Klein, *The Shock Doctrine* (Toronto: Knopf Canada, 2007).

60. Katie Rabinowitze and Kevin Uhrmacher, "What Trump proposed in his 2020 budget," *Washington Post*, March 12, 2019.

61. Senator Bernie Sanders, "The Trump Budget for 2021," United States Senate Budget Committee, https://www.budget.senate.gov/imo/media/doc/SBC%20Trump%20Budget%20Reaction%202-11-20%20REVISED.pdf.

62. Matt Hourihan, "AAAS Guide to the President's Budget: Research & Development FY 2021," American Association for the Advancement of Science, April 2020, https://www.aaas.org/news/guide-presidents-budget-research-development-fy-2021.

63. John Horgan, "Let's Defund the Pentagon, Too," *Scientific American*, July 8, 2020.

64. Neta C. Crawford and Catherine Lutz, "Too much military spending got us into this mess," *Boston Globe*, June 7, 2020.

65. Jessica Semega et al., "Income and Poverty in the United States: 2018," United States Census Bureau, revised June 2020, https://www.census.gov/content/dam/Census/library/publications/2019/demo/p60-266.pdf#page=20.

66. "Study says domestic, not military spending, fuels job growth," Brown University, May 25, 2017, https://www.brown.edu/news/2017-05-25/jobscow.

67. "Study says domestic."

68. Philip Alston, "Statement on Visit to the USA," United Nations Human Rights Office of the High Commissioner, December 15, 2017, https://www.ohchr.org/EN/NewsEvents/Pages/DisplayNews.aspx?NewsID=22533.

69. Alston, "Statement on Visit."

70. Connor Bradbury, "4 Facts About Poverty in Iraq," Borgen Project, June 22, 2020.

71. "The World Bank in Afghanistan," The World Bank, https://www.worldbank.org/en/country/afghanistan/overview.

72. "Global military expenditure."

73. "Global military expenditure"; also see Michael Birnbaum, "NATO members increase defense spending for fourth year in a row following Trump pressure," *Washington Post*, March 14, 2019.

74. "Global military expenditure."

75. See for example International Organization for Migration, "Information on the implementation of the projects related to Emergency Response to the Migrant and Refugee Situation in Bosnia and Herzegovina funded by the European Union," January 13, 2021; International Organization for Migration, "Saopštenje Za Medije / Press Release," October 11, 2019; Delegation of the European Union to Bosnia and Herzegovina & European Union Special Representative in Bosnia and Herzegovina, "EU donated valuable equipment to the Ministry of Interior of Una-Sana Canton," September 27, 2019; and Delegation of the European Union to Bosnia and Herzegovina & European Union Special Representative in Bosnia and Herzegovina, "European Union's donation to increase the mobility and protection of police officers in Una-Sana Canton," October 10, 2019.

76. Bidemi Badmus, "Military Expenditure versus Structural Adjustment Programmes: Implications and Alternatives," *Afro Asian Journal of Social Studies* VIII, no. II (2017): 1–15.

77. Angela Davis, "Masked Racism: Reflections on the Prison Industrial Complex," History Is a Weapon, https://www.historyisaweapon.com/defcon1/davisprison.html.

78. Michel Foucault, *Discipline and Punish: The Birth of the Prison*, Alan Sheridan, trans. (New York: Pantheon Books, 1977).

79. Frank J. Barrett, "The Organizational Construction of Hegemonic Masculinity: The Case of the US Navy," *Gender, Work & Organization* 3, no. 3 (1996): 130.

80. See for example Carol Cohn with Felicity Hill and Sara Ruddick, "The Relevance of Gender for Eliminating Weapons of Mass Destruction," The Weapons of Mass Destruction Commission, No. 38 (2006); and Carol Cohn, "Sex and Death in the Rational World of Defense Intellectuals," *Signs* 12, no. 4 (1987): 687–718.

81. William Arkin and Lynne R. Dobrofsky, "Military Socialization and Masculinity," *Journal of Social Issues* 34, no.1 (2010): 151–68.

82. Judy Wajcman, *Feminism Confronts Technology* (University Park, PA: The Pennsylvania State University Press, 1991), 146.

83. Cynthia Enloe, *Bananas, Beaches and Bases: Making Feminist Sense of International Politics* (Berkeley, CA: University of California Press, 2014).

84. See for example Carol Cohn, "Wars, Wimps, and Women: Talking Gender and Thinking War," in *Gendering War Talk*, Miriame Cooke and Angela Woollacott, eds. (Princeton, NJ: Princeton University Press, 1993), 227–46.

85. Cynthia Enloe, "Beyond 'Rambo': women and the varieties of militarized masculinity," in *Women and the Military System*, Eva Isaakson, ed. (New York: St. Martin's Press, 1988), 71–93.

86. See for example Kirby Dick, dir., *The Invisible War*, https://www.pbs.org/independentlens/films/invisible-war.

87. See for example Sitaji Gurung et al., "Prevalence of Military Sexual Trauma and Sexual Orientation Discrimination Among Lesbian, Gay, Bisexual, and Transgender Military Personnel: a Descriptive Study," *Sex Res Social Policy* 15, no. 1 (2018): 74–82.

88. Heather Ley, "Team Minot wonder women," Minot Air Force Base, March 12, 2019, https://www.minot.af.mil/News/Article-Display/Article/1782779/team-minot-wonder-women/.

89. Roberto Lovato, "The Age of Intersectional Empire Is Upon Us," *The Nation*, May 10, 2020.

90. For more on this subject, see Ray Acheson, "Abolish Nuclear Weapons: Feminist, Queer, and Indigenous Knowledge for Ending Nuclear Weapons," in *Feminist Solutions for Ending War*, Megan Mackenzie, ed. (London: Pluto Press, 2021).

91. Cynthia Enloe, "Women Now at Top of Military-Industrial Complex: A Feminist Reaction," interview with Julian Hayda, WBEZ 91.5 Chicago, January 8, 2019.

92. Heather Hurlburt et al., "The 'Consensual Straitjacket': Four Decades of Women in Nuclear Security," New America, 2019, https://www.newamerica.org/political-reform/reports/the-consensual-straitjacket-four-decades-of-women-in-nuclear-security/.

93. David Brown, "How women took over the military-industrial complex," Politico, January 2, 2019.

94. Nancy Fraser, Cinzia Arruzza, and Tithi Bhattacharya, "Notes for a Feminist Manifesto," *New Left Review* 114 (Nov–Dec 2018): 117.

95. Dean Spade and Aaron Belkin, "Queer Militarism?! The Politics of Military Inclusion Advocacy in Authoritarian Times," *GLQ* 27, no. 2 (2021): 298.

96. Spade and Belkin, "Queer Militarism?!," 301.

97. Ta-Nehisi Coates, "Ta-Nehisi Coates on *Vanity Fair*'s September Issue, The Great Fire," *Vanity Fair,* August 24, 2020.

98. Jonathan Blitzer, "Is It Time to Defund the Department of Homeland Security?" *New Yorker,* July 24, 2020.

99. John Washington, "'Kick Ass, Ask Questions Later': A Border Patrol Whistleblower Speaks Out About Culture of Abuse Against Migrants," The Intercept, September 20, 2018.

100. John Washington, "Is the US Border Patrol Committing Crimes Against Humanity?" Guernica, May 2, 2018; also see John Carlos Frey, *Sand and Blood: America's Stealth War on the Mexico Border* (New York: Bold Type Books: 2019).

101. Caitlin Dickerson, "A Rare Look Inside Trump's Immigration Crackdown Draws Legal Threats," *New York Times,* July 23, 2020.

102. Elie Mystal, "Trump's Secret Police Have Never Been a Secret to Brown People," *The Nation,* July 27, 2020.

103. Tina Vaquez (@TheTinaVasquez), "Yes, I'm deeply alarmed . . .," Twitter, July 26, 2020, https://twitter.com/TheTinaVasquez/status/1287403413555290124.

104. Ryan Devereaux, "Amnesty International condemns U.S. attacks on border journalists and human rights defenders," The Intercept, July 2, 2019.

105. "Military style raid: border patrol detains 30+ people receiving care at humanitarian aid station," No More Deaths/No Más Muertes, August 1, 2020.

106. Justice for Muslims Collective et al., "Abolishing the War on Terror, Building Communities of Care: A Grassroots Policy Agenda," March 2021, 3. https://www.justiceformuslims.org/grassroots-policy-agenda.

107. Reece Jones, *Violent Borders* (New York: Verso, 2017), 35.

108. Sarah Stillman, "The Invisible Army," *New Yorker,* June 6, 2011.

109. Harsha Walia, Border & Rule: Global Migration, Capitalism, and the Rise of Racist Nationalism (Chicago: Haymarket Books, 2021), 60.

110. Amira Jarmakani, *An Imperialist Love Story: Desert Romances and the War on Terror* (New York: New York University Press, 2015), 46.

111. Jarmakani, *Imperialist Love Story,* 47.

112. Ian G. R. Shaw, *Predator Empire: Drone Warfare and Full Spectrum Dominance* (Minneapolis: University of Minnesota Press, 2016).

113. Ray Acheson, "Autonomous weapons and patriarchy," Women's International League for Peace and Freedom and Campaign to Stop Killer Robots, October 2020, https://reachingcriticalwill.org/images/documents/Publications/aws-and-patriarchy.pdf.

114. Harsha Walia, *Undoing Border Imperialism* (Oakland, CA: AK Press, 2013), 61.

115. Shaw, *Predator Empire,* 128.

116.   Elke Schwarz, *Death Machines* (Manchester: Manchester University Press, 2018), 119.

117.   Schwarz, *Death Machines*, 14.

118.   Mariame Kaba and Kelly Hayes, "A Jailbreak of the Imagination," Truthout, May 2018.

119.   "GDAMS Healthcare Not Warfare Infographic," Global Campaign on Military Spending, May 2020, http://demilitarize.org/resources/gdams-healthcare-not-warfare-infographic/.

120.   "Nuclear Spending vs. Healthcare," International Campaign to Abolish Nuclear Weapons, https://www.icanw.org/healthcare_costs.

121.   Mikhail Gorbachev, "Mikhail Gorbachev: When the Pandemic Is Over, The World Must Come Together," Center for Citizen Initiatives, April 15, 2020.

Chapter 6: Decommissioning Nuclear Weapons

1.   Laurie Patton, trans., *The Bhagavad Gita* (New York: Penguin, 2008).

2.   "These are our stories," International Campaign to Abolish Nuclear Weapons, https://rise.icanw.org/updates.

3.   See Beatrice Fihn, ed., "Unspeakable Suffering: The Humanitarian Impacts of Nuclear Weapons," Reaching Critical Will of the Women's International League for Peace and Freedom, 2013.

4.   Joseph Masco, *The Nuclear Borderlands: The Manhattan Project in Post-Cold War New Mexico* (Princeton, NJ: Princeton University Press, 2006), 8.

5.   Hans M. Kristensen and Matt Korda, "Status of World Nuclear Forces," Federation of American Scientists, https://fas.org/issues/nuclear-weapons/status-world-nuclear-forces.

6.   "Complicit: nuclear weapon spending increased by $1.4 billion in 2020," International Campaign to Abolish Nuclear Weapons, https://www.icanw.org/complicit_nuclear_weapons_spending_increased_by_1_4_billion_in_2020.

7.   Allison Pytlak and Ray Acheson, eds., "Assuring destruction forever: 2022 edition," Reaching Critical Will of the Women's International League for Peace and Freedom, 2022.

8.   "Shorting our security: Financing the companies that make nuclear weapons," PAX and International Campaign to Abolish Nuclear Weapons, 2019, https://www.dontbankonthebomb.com/wp-content/uploads/2019/06/2019_HOS_web.pdf. Also see divest.icanw.org.

9.   See for example Ward Wilson, *Five Myths About Nuclear Weapons* (Boston: Houghton Mifflin Harcourt, 2013).

10. See for example Nick Ritchie, "Deterrence dogma: Challenging the relevance of British nuclear weapons," *International Affairs* 85, no. 1 (2009): 81–98; Daniel Ellsberg, *The Doomsday Machine: Confessions of a Nuclear War Planner* (New York: Bloomsbury, 2017); Eric Schlosser, *Command and Control: Nuclear Weapons, the Damascus Accident, and the Illusion of Safety* (New York: Penguin Books, 2013); Joseph Gerson, *Empire and the Bomb: How the U.S. Uses Nuclear Weapons to Dominate the World* (London: Pluto Press, 2007); and David P. Barash, "Nuclear deterrence is a myth. And a lethal one at that," *The Guardian*, January 14, 2018.

11. Robert J. Lifton and Richard Falk, Indefensible Weapons: The Political and Psychological Case Against Nuclearism (New York: Basic Books, 1982), ix.

12. Masco, *Nuclear Borderlands*, 4–5.

1313. Masco, *Nuclear Borderlands*.

14. Masco, *Nuclear Borderlands*, 34.

15. The Red Nation, *The Red Deal: Indigenous Action to Save Our Earth* (Brooklyn, NY: Common Notions, 2021), 11.

16. Amira Jarmakani, *An Imperialist Love Story: Desert Romances and the War on Terror* (New York: New York University Press, 2015), 25.

17. Jarmakani, *An Imperialist Love Story*.

18. Kate Brown, Plutopia: *Nuclear Families, Atomic Cities, and the Great Soviet and American Plutonium Disasters* (Oxford: Oxford University Press, 2013), 7.

19. Masco, *Nuclear Borderlands*, 77.

20. Masco, *Nuclear Borderlands*, 12.

21. See as an example Carol Cohn, "Sex and Death in the Rational World of Defense Intellectuals," *Signs* 12, no. 4 (Summer 1987), 687–718.

22. Edward Thompson, "Notes on Exterminism, the Last Stage of Civilization," in *Exterminism and Cold War*, New Left Review, ed. (London: Verso, 1982), 7.

23. Anne Harrington de Santana, "Nuclear Weapons as the Currency of Power: Deconstructing the Fetishism of Force," *Nonproliferation Review* 16, no. 3 (2009): 327.

24. Nick Ritchie, "Relinquishing nuclear weapons: identities, networks and the British bomb," *International Affairs* 86, no. 2 (2010): 466.

25. Shampa Biswas, *Nuclear Desire: Power and the Postcolonial Nuclear Order* (Minneapolis: University of Minnesota Press, 2014), 124–25.

26. See, for example, Peter Lavoy, "Nuclear myths and the causes of nuclear proliferation," *Security Studies* 2, no. 3 (1993): 192–212; Scott Sagan, "Why do states build nuclear weapons? Three models in search of a bomb," *International Security* 21, no. 3 (Winter 1996/1997): 54–86; Stephen Meyer, *The dynamics of nuclear proliferation* (Chicago: University of Chicago Press, 1984); Jacques Hymans, *The psychology of nuclear proliferation* (Cambridge:

Cambridge University Press, 2006); and Nick Ritchie, "Valuing and Devaluing Nuclear Weapons," *Contemporary Security Policy* 34 no. 1 (2013): 155–59.

27. Bryan C. Taylor and Judith Hendry, "Insisting on Persisting: The Nuclear Rhetoric of Stockpile Stewardship," *Rhetoric and Public Affairs* 11, no. 2 (2008): 314.

28. Biswas, *Nuclear Desire*, 131.

29. Carol Cohn and Sara Ruddick, "A Feminist Ethical Perspective on Weapons of Mass Destruction," in *Ethics and Weapons of Mass Destruction: Religious and Secular Perspectives,* Sohail H. Hashmi and Steven P. Lee, eds. (Cambridge: Cambridge University Press, 2004), 19.

30. Darwin BondGraham et al., "Rhetoric vs. reality: the political economy of nuclear weapons and their elimination," in *Beyond arms control: challenges and choices for nuclear disarmament*, Ray Acheson, ed. (New York: Women's International League for Peace and Freedom, 2010), 9–10.

31. Ritchie, "Valuing and Devaluing," 157.

32. Baskut Tuncak, "75th anniversary of the Trinity nuclear tests, 16 July 2020," United Nations Human Rights Office of the High Commissioner, July 16, 2020.

33. Nic Maclellan, "Nuclear Testing and Racism in the Pacific Islands," *The Palgrave Handbook of Ethnicity* (Singapore: Palgrave Macmillan, 2019), 1–21.

34. Taylor N. Johnson, "'The most bombed nation on Earth': Western Shoshone resistance to the Nevada National Security Site," *Atlantic Journal of Communication* 26, no. 4 (2018): 224–39.

35. Kyle Mizokami, "America Has Dropped 1,032 Nuclear Weapons (On Itself)," *National Interest*, August 30, 2018.

36. "Indigenous Statement to the U.N. Nuclear Weapons Ban Treaty Negotiations," July 2017, https://reachingcriticalwill.org/images/documents/Disarmament-fora/nuclear-weapon-ban/statements/IndigenousStatement.pdf.

37. "Report of the Task Group on Reference Man," International Commission on Radiological Protection, No. 23, Pergamon Press, 1975, 4.

38. Eric Frohmberg et al., "The Assessment of Radiation Exposures in Native American Communities from Nuclear Weapons Testing in Nevada," *Risk Analysis* 20, no. 1 (March 2000): 101–111.

39. Mary Olson, "Human consequences of radiation: A gender factor in atomic harm," in *Civil Society Engagement in Disarmament Processes: The Case for a Nuclear Weapon Ban* (New York: United Nations Office for Disarmament Affairs, 2016), 32.

40. See, for example, Sebastian Pflugbei et al., *Health Effects of Chernobyl: 25 years after the reactor catastrophe* (Berlin: German Affiliate of the International Physicians for the Prevention of Nuclear War, April 2011); Reiko Watanuki,

Yuko Yoshida, and Kiyoko Futagami, "Radioactive Contamination and the Health of Women and post-Chernobyl Children," Chernobyl Health Survey and Healthcare for the Victims—Japan Women's Network, 2006; and Whitney Graham and Elena I. Nicklasson, "Maternal Meltdown: From Chernobyl to Fukushima," Inter Press Service, April 16, 2011.

41. Calin Georgescu, "Report of the Special Rapporteur on the implications for Human Rights of the Environmentally Sound Management and Disposal of Hazardous Substances and Wastes," UN Human Rights Council, Twenty-First Session, Agenda Item 3: Promotion and protection of all human rights, civil, political, economic, social and cultural rights, including the right to development, 2013.

42. Laicie Heeley, "To make and maintain America's nukes, some communities pay the price," *The World,* January 30, 2018.

43. "Nuclear War: Uranium Mining and Nuclear Tests on Indigenous Land," *Cultural Survival Quarterly Magazine*, September 1993.

44. See the Moruroa Files available at moruroa-files.org; also see Sébastien Philippe and Tomas Statius, *Toxique: Enquête sur les essais nucléaires français en Polynésie* (Paris: Puf, 2021).

45. Sébastien Philippe, Sonya Schoenberger, and Nabil Ahmed, "Radiation Exposures and Compensation of Victims of French Atmospheric Nuclear Tests in Polynesia," arXiv:2103.06128 [physics.med-ph], March 9, 2021; Adrian Cho, "France grossly underestimated radioactive fallout from atom bomb tests, study finds," *Science*, March 11, 2021.

46. Moruroa Files, "The compensation trap," https://moruroa-files.org/en/investigation/battle-for-compensation.

47. Dan Lin and Kathy Jetñil-Kijiner, *Anointed*, April 2018, https://vimeo.com/264867214.

48. Gough Whitlam, *The Whitlam Government 1972–1975* (Ringwood, Victoria: Viking Press, 1985), 611–13.

49. "Algerians take steps to prosecute France for nuclear tests," Middle East Monitor, February 15, 2017.

50. Vincent J. Intondi, *African Americans Against the Bomb* (Stanford, CA: Stanford University Press, 2015).

51. Jacqueline Castledine, Cold War Progressives: Women's Interracial Organizing for Peace and Freedom (Urbana, IL: University of Illinois Press, 2012), 17.

52. Ian Zabarte, "Indigenous Peoples Condemn Nuclear Colonialism on 'Columbus' Day," PopularResistance.org, October 10, 2016.

53. Matthew Neisius, "Western Shoshone Nation Opposes Yucca Mountain Nuclear Repository," Commodities, Conflict, and Cooperation program at Evergreen State College (Fall 2016 and Winter 2017).

54. Zabarte, "Indigenous Peoples."

55. Hugh Gusterson, "Nuclear Weapons and the Other in the Western Imagination," *Cultural Anthropology* 14, no. 1 (1999): 111–43.

56. Arundhati Roy, *The Cost of Living* (New York: Modern Library, 1999), 101.

57. Ray Acheson, "Resisting Nuclear Weapons Means Resisting Injustice and Oppression," *The Nation*, February 2, 2018.

58. Ray Acheson, "The nuclear ban and the patriarchy: a feminist analysis of opposition to prohibiting nuclear weapons," *Critical Studies on Security* 7, no. 1 (2018): 78–82.

59. Carol Cohn, "Sex and Death in the Rational World of Defense Intellectuals," *Signs* 12, no. 4 (Summer 1987), 687–718; and Carol Cohn, "Slick 'Ems, Glick 'Ems, Christmas Trees, and Cookie Cutters: Nuclear Language and How We Learned to Pat the Bomb," *Bulletin of the Atomic Scientists* (June 1987): 17–24.

60. Cohn, "Sex and Death," 693.

61. Cohn and Ruddick, "Feminist Ethical Perspective," 19.

62. Cohn, "Sex and Death," 696.

63. Carol Cohn with Felicity Hill and Sara Ruddick, "The Relevance of Gender for Eliminating Weapons of Mass Destruction," The Weapons of Mass Destruction Commission, No. 38 (2006), 3.

64. Cohn, Hill, and Ruddick, "Relevance of Gender," 6.

65. Catherine Eschle, "Gender and Valuing Nuclear Weapons," Working Paper for Devaluing Nuclear Weapons: Concepts and Challenges, University of York Department of Politics, March 20–21, 2012.

66. Claire Duncanson and Catherine Eschle, "Gender and the Nuclear Weapons State: A Feminist Critique of the UK Government's White Paper on Trident," *New Political Scientist* 30, no. 4 (2008): 545–563.

67. See Ray Acheson, "Patriarchy and the bomb: banning nuclear weapons against the opposition of militarist masculinities," in *The Gender Imperative: Human Security vs State Security*, Betty A. Reardon and Asha Hans, eds. (New York: Routledge, 2019), 392–409; and Acheson, "Nuclear ban," 1–5.

68. Ray Acheson, "Moving the nuclear football, from 1946 to 2019," *NPT News in Review* 16, no. 2 (May 2, 2019): 1–2.

69. Duncanson and Eschle, "Gender and the Nuclear Weapons State," 15.

70. Leanne Betasamosake Simpson, *As We Have Always Done: Indigenous Freedom Through Radical Resistance* (Minneapolis: University of Minnesota, 2017), 19.

71. Cohn, "Sex and death," 690.

72. For a detailed overview of the process of achieving the nuclear weapon ban treaty, see Ray Acheson, *Banning the Bomb, Smashing the Patriarchy* (London: Rowman and Littlefield, 2021).

73. Dylan Rodríguez, "Reformism Isn't Liberation, It's Counterinsurgency," in *Abolition for the People: The Movement for a Future Without Policing & Prisons*, Colin Kaepernick, ed. (New York: Kaepernick Publishing, 2021). Also published by LEVEL at https://level.medium.com/reformism-isnt-liberation-it-s-counterinsurgency-7ea0a1ce11eb, October 20, 2020.

74. John Hudson, "Trump administration discussed conducting first nuclear test in decades," *Washington Post*, May 22, 2020.

75. See, for example, "Creating the conditions for nuclear disarmament," Working paper submitted by the United States of America, Second Session of the Preparatory Committee for the 2020 Review Conference of Parties to the Treaty on the Non-Proliferation of Nuclear Weapons, NPT/CONF.2020/PC.II/WP.30, April 18, 2018; and "Operationalizing the Creating an Environment for Nuclear Disarmament (CEND) Initiative," Working paper submitted by the United States of America, Third Session of the Preparatory Committee for the 2020 Review Conference of Parties to the Treaty on the Non-Proliferation of Nuclear Weapons, NPT/CONF.2020/PC.III/WP.43, April 26, 2019.

76. See for example Acheson, "Moving the nuclear football."

77. Statement by Permanent Mission of Ireland to the United Nations to the UN General Assembly First Committee on Disarmament and International Security, New York, October 16, 2019, https://reachingcriticalwill.org/images/documents/Disarmament-fora/1com/1com19/statements/16Oct_Ireland.pdf.

78. Statement by Permanent Mission of Ireland.

79. Ray Acheson, "Uprising," *NPT News in Review* 13, no. 17 (25 May 2015), 2.

80. Angela Davis, *Are Prisons Obsolete?* (New York: Seven Stories Press, 2003), 15.

81. Achille Mbembe, "Necropolitics," *Public Culture* 15, no. 1 (2003), 24.

82. Jason De León, *The Land of Open Graves: Living and Dying on the Migrant Trail* (Oakland, CA: University of California Press, 2015), 28.

83. See for example Ellsberg, *Doomsday Machine*; Cohn, "Sex and Death."

84. De León, *Land of Open Graves*, 9.

85. John Carlos Frey, *Sand and Blood: America's Stealth War on the Mexico Border* (New York: Bold Type Books: 2019).

86. Masco, *Nuclear Borderlands*, 12.

87. Ray Acheson et al., "Rebuilding the Antinuclear Movement," *The Nation*, June 1, 2018.

88.   Don't Bank on the Bomb, https://www.dontbankonthebomb.com. Also see divest.icanw.org.

89.   See for example "New York Banking on the Bomb? Fuggedaboutit!," Don't Bank on the Bomb, https://www.dontbankonthebomb.com/nyc.

90.   ICAN Cities Appeal, cities.icanw.org.

91.   Schools of Mass Destruction, universities.icanw.org.

92.   Jessie Boylan, "This Is Not Nowhere," Curve, September 14, 2018.

93.   See for example David L. Eng, Judith Halberstam, and José Esteban Muñoz, "What's Queer About Queer Studies Now?," *Social Text* 84–85, Vol. 23, Nos. 3–4 (Fall–Winter 2005): 2–17; and Lisa Duggan, *The Twilight of Equality? Neoliberalism, Cultural Politics, and the Attack on Democracy* (Boston: Beacon, 2003).

94.   Cathy J. Cohen, "Punks, Bulldaggers, and Welfare Queens: The Radical Potential of Queer Politics?," *GLQ* 3 (1997): 437.

95.   Boylan, "This Is Not Nowhere."

96.   Ray Acheson, "Guns and Nuclear Weapons: The Continuum of Violence from Handguns to Nuclear Weapons," interview with Tricia Cooke and Paul Rowley, *Radio GAG*, Gays Against Guns, March 2, 2021.

97.   See for example Nick Estes, *Our History is the Future: Standing Rock versus the Dakota Access Pipeline, and the Long Tradition of Indigenous Resistance* (New York: Verso, 2019); and Qwo-Li Driskill et al., eds., *Queer Indigenous Studies: Critical Interventions in Theory, Politics, and Literature* (Tucson, AZ: University of Arizona Press, 2011).

98.   See Black Mist Burnt Country at https://blackmistburntcountry.com.au.

99.   Cohen, "Punks, Bulldaggers," 444–45.

100. Tim Hollo, "There's No Time Left Not to Do Everything," *Arena Quarterly* 3, September 2020.

Chapter 7: Demolishing Capitalism

1.   Robert Kuttner, "Neoliberalism: Political Success, Economic Failure," *American Prospect*, June 25, 2019.

2.   Gautam Mukunda, "The Social and Political Costs of the Financial Crisis, 10 Years Later," *Harvard Business Review*, September 25, 2018.

3.   Chuck Collins, Omar Ocampo, and Sophia Paslaski, "Billionaire Bonanza 2020: Wealth Windfalls, Tumbling Taxes, and Pandemic Profiteers," Institute for Policy Studies, 2020.

4.   Chuck Collins, "Updates: Billionaire Wealth, U.S. Job Losses and Pandemic Profiteers," Inequality.org, December 9, 2020, https://inequality.org/great-divide/updates-billionaire-pandemic.

5. "5 shocking facts about extreme global inequality and how to even it up," Oxfam International, https://www.oxfam.org/en/5-shocking-facts-about-extreme-global-inequality-and-how-even-it.

6. David Harvey, *Marx, Capital and the Madness of Economic Reason* (London: Profile Books, 2017), 7.

7. Alena Heitlinger, Women and State Socialism: Sex Inequality in the Soviet Union & Czechoslovakia (London: Palgrave Macmillan, 1979), 24.

8. Harvey, *Marx, Capital*, 11.

9. Harvey, *Marx, Capital*.

10. Harvey, *Marx, Capital*, 3–4.

11. Harvey, Marx, *Capital*, 4.

12. Tim Gallen, "Gross Domestic Product: An Economy's All," International Monetary Fund, February 24, 2020, https://www.imf.org/external/pubs/ft/fandd/basics/gdp.htm.

13. See "GPD, current prices," International Monetary Fund, https://www.imf.org/external/datamapper/NGDPD@WEO/OEMDC/ADVEC/WEOWORLD.

14. Philip Alston, "Statement on Visit to the USA," United Nations Human Rights Office of the High Commissioner, December 15, 2017, https://www.ohchr.org/EN/NewsEvents/Pages/DisplayNews.aspx?NewsID=22533.

15. See for example Lauren Kaori Gurley, "Amazon Workers to Stage Coordinated Black Friday Protests in 15 Countries," *VICE*, November 26, 2020; and Kenya Evelyn, "Amazon workers walk out over lack of protective gear amid coronavirus," *The Guardian*, March 30, 2020.

16. Cynthia Cockburn, "Standpoint theory," in *Marxist-Feminist Theories and Struggles Today*, Khayaat Fakier, Diana Mulinari, and Nora Räthzel, eds. (London: Zed Books, 2020), 13.

17. See for example Justin Akers Chacón, *Radicals in the Barrio: Magonistas, Socialists, Wobblies, and Communists in the Mexican American Working Class* (Chicago: Haymarket Books, 2018).

18. Shirin M. Rai, Jacqui True, and Maria Tanyag, "From Depletion to Regeneration: Addressing Structural and Physical Violence in Post-Conflict Economies," *Social Politics: International Studies in Gender, State & Society* 26, no. 4 (2019): 561–85.

19. Tine Haubner, "Reading Marx Against the Grain: Rethinking the Exploitation of care work beyond profit-seeking," in *Marxist-Feminist Theories and Struggles Today*, Khayaat Fakier, Diana Mulinari, and Nora Räthzel, eds. (London: Zed Books, 2020), 88–99.

20. V. Spike Peterson, "How (the Meaning of) Gender Matters in Political Economy," *New Political Economy* 10, no. 4 (2005): 499–521.

21. Jason Hickel, *Less is More: How Degrowth Will Save the World* (London: William Heinemann, 2020), 233.

22. William I. Robinson, "What are the real reasons behind the New Cold War?" ROAR, May 6, 2021.

23. Robinson, "What are the real reasons?"

24. James Petras and Henry Veltmeyer, "The Global Capitalist Crisis: Whose Crisis, Who Profits?," *International Review of Modern Sociology* 38, no. 2 (2012): 199–219.

25. Emiliano Grossman and Cornelia Woll, "Saving the Banks: The Political Economy of Bailouts," *Comparative Political Studies* 47, no.4 (2013): 574–600.

26. "Enough is Enough: Privatisation and public services, a conversation," Webinar streamed live on October 19, 2020, https://www.youtube.com/watch?v=2zXjzgOOyCY.

27. Leilani Farha et al., "Covid-19 has exposed the catastrophic impact of privatising vital services," *The Guardian*, October 19, 2020.

28. Farha et al., "Covid-19."

29. Isabel Ortiz and Matthew Cummins, "Austerity: The New Normal: A Renewed Washington Consensus 2010–24," working paper for Initiative for Policy Dialogue et al., 2019.

30. Ortiz and Cummins, "Austerity," 20.

31. Farha et al., "Covid-19."

32. Naomi Klein, *The Shock Doctrine: The Rise of Disaster Capitalism* (Toronto: Vintage Canada, 2008).

33. See for example Marie Solis, "Coronavirus Is the Perfect Disaster for 'Disaster Capitalism,'" *VICE*, March 13, 2020; and "'Coronavirus Capitalism': Naomi Klein's Case for Transformative Change Amid Coronavirus Pandemic," Democracy Now!, March 19, 2020.

34. Scott Ludlam (@Scottludlam), "the predatory rush to consolidate power in the midst of massive trauma," Twitter, 18 March 2020, https://twitter.com/Scottludlam/status/1240419908602609664.

35. See for example "#CoronaCapitalism," Corporate Watch, April 2, 2020, https://corporatewatch.org/understanding-coronacapitalism.

36. Alison Pennington, "In the Middle of a Pandemic, the Australian State Is Pummeling Workers," *Jacobin*, March 24, 2020.

37. "#CoronaCapitalism: Companies cashing in part 2—airline bailouts, Travelodge, Blackstone, Goldman Sachs, Wren Kitchens . . .," Corporate Watch, March 30, 2020.

38. Jim Tankersley, "Trump's Payroll Tax Cut Would Dwarf the 2008 Bank Bailout," *New York Times*, March 12, 2020.

39. "Corona Capitalism: Some of the companies cashing in on the crisis, from Bezos to Big Pharma . . .," Corporate Watch, March 24, 2020.

40. "Spending, Accountability, and Recovery Measures included in IMF COVID-19 loans," Oxfam International, September 2020, https://www.oxfam.org/en/international-financial-institutions/ imf-covid-19-financing-and-fiscal-tracker.

41. Nadia Daar and Nona Tamale, "A Virus of Austerity? The COVID-19 spending, accountability, and recovery measures agreed between the IMF and your government," Oxfam International, October 12, 2020.

42. Daar and Tamale, "Virus of Austerity?"

43. Anna Marriott and Katie Malouf Bous, "People can't afford to pay for health care in a pandemic. Why isn't the World Bank doing more to help?" Oxfam International, October 12, 2020.

44. Marriott and Bous, "People can't afford."

45. Isabel Ortiz and Matthew Cummins, "Global Austerity Alert: Looming Budget Cuts in 2021–2025 and Alternative Pathways," working paper for Initiative for Policy Dialogue et al., 2021.

46. Ortiz and Cummins, "Global Austerity Alert."

47. The Red Nation, *The Red Deal: Indigenous Action to Save Our Earth* (Brooklyn, NY: Common Notions, 2021), 22.

48. "World military spending rises to almost $2 trillion in 2020," Stockholm International Peace Research Institute, April 26, 2021. See chapter 5 in this book for details about the broader scope of US military spending.

49. "Financial value of the global arms trade," Stockholm International Peace Research Institute, https://www.sipri.org/databases/ financial-value-global-arms-trade.

50. Noam Chomsky, "The Pentagon System," *Z Magazine*, February 1993, http://www.thirdworldtraveler.com/Chomsky/PentagonSystem_Chom.html.

51. Paul Baran and Paul Sweezy, *Monopoly Capital: An Essay on the American Economic and Social Order* (New York: NYU Press, 1968), 213.

52. C. Wright Mills, *The Power Elite* (New York: Oxford University Press, 2000), 276.

53. Robert W. DeGrasse, *Military Expansion, Economic Decline* (New York: Council on Economic Priorities, 1983).

54. Greg Mello, "Does Los Alamos National Lab Help or Hurt the New Mexico Economy?" Los Alamos Study Group, July 2006, http://www.lasg.org/ LANLecon_impact.pdf, 1.

55. Mello, "Does Los Alamos?," 1.

56. "Poverty rate in New Mexico from 2000 to 2019," statista, September 2020, https://www.statista.com/statistics/205493/poverty-rate-in-new-mexico.

57. Russell Contreras, "New Mexico child poverty ranking back to 49th in nation, Kids Count report finds," *Las Cruces Sun News*, January 15, 2020.

58. Chris Parsons, "Millionaire meltdown in Los Alamos: Nuke lab town has highest concentration of rich in America," *Daily Mail*, November 4, 2011.

59. Neta C. Crawford, "Pentagon Fuel Use, Climate Change, and the Costs of War," in "Costs of War," Watson Institute for International and Public Affairs at Brown University, July 1, 2019, https://watson.brown.edu/research/2019/pentagon-fuel-use-climate-change-and-costs-war. For more details on climate change and other environmental impacts of armed conflict, see the Conflict and Environment Observatory at https://ceobs.org.

60. William I. Robinson, *The Global Police State: Militarization, Repression and Capitalism in the US* (London: Pluto Press, 2020).

61. See for example Pratap Chatterjee, "Halliburton Makes a Killing on Iraq War," CorpWatch, March 20, 2003.

62. Robinson, "What are the real reasons?"

63. Jason Hickel, "Quantifying national responsibility for climate breakdown: an equality-based attribution approach for carbon dioxide emissions in excess of the planetary boundary," *The Lancet* 4, no. 9 (2020): 399–404.

64. Sarah Lazare, "'Colonizing the Atmosphere': How Rich, Western Nations Drive the Climate Crisis," *In These Times*, September 14, 2020.

65. Rachel Nuwer, "Environmental Activists Have Higher Death Rates Than Some Soldiers," *Scientific American*, August 5, 2019.

66. Government of Canada, "Canada demonstrates international leadership on environment and climate change," News Release from Environment and Climate Change Canada, June 7, 2017.

67. Declan Keogh, "Canada versus First Nations: Whose land is it anyway?" *NOW Magazine*, January 19, 2019.

68. See Unist'ot'en Camp, https://unistoten.camp.

69. See for example Dylan Penner (@DylanPenner), "After Tyendinaga raid, 7+ new blockades," Twitter, February 24, 2020, https://twitter.com/DylanPenner/status/1232094337913249792.

70. Erin Rubin, "Pipeline Builders Exploit the Moment on Wet'suwet'en Frontlines," *Nonprofit Quarterly*, March 25, 2020.

71. Geoffrey Morgan, "'Critical for our economic future': Keystone XL surprise go-ahead to energize struggling oilpatch," *Financial Post*, March 31, 2020. Also see "Keystone XL pipeline: Why is it so disputed?" BBC, January 24, 2017.

72. Matt Egan, "Developer pulls the plug on Keystone XL oil pipeline," CNN Business, June 10, 2021.

73. See for example Gidimt'en Checkpoint, www.yintahaccess.com; The Intercept, "Policing the Pipeline," www.theintercept.com/series/policing-the-pipeline.

74. Maja Isović Dobrijević, "SAZNAJEMO Preuzeta kasarna Čerkezovac. Nuklearni otpad sve bliži BiH," buka, April 1, 2020.

75. Rachel Frazin, "Advocates raise questions about proposal to allow some nuclear waste to be disposed in landfills," The Hill, April 3, 2020.

76. Greg Mello, "Administration seeks 49% increase in Los Alamos nuclear weapons activities, 33% plus-up for LANL overall," Los Alamos Study Group, February 23, 2020, http://www.lasg.org/press/2020/press_release_23Feb2020.html.

77. Alexander C. Kaufman and Chris D'Angelo, "Trump Moves Forward on Biggest Environmental Rollback to Date Amidst Pandemic Chaos," Huffington Post, March 31, 2020.

78. Alexander C. Kaufman, "States Quietly Pass Laws Criminalizing Fossil Fuel Protests Amid Coronavirus Chaos," Huffington Post, March 27, 2020; Burak Bir, "US, petchem firms practicing 'disaster capitalism,'" AA, March 30, 2020.

79. ROAPE, "Out of Control: Crisis, Covid-19 and Capitalism in Africa," *Review of African Political Economy*, March 26, 2020.

80. Red Nation, *Red Deal*, 8.

81. Tim Pollo, "There's no time left not to do everything," *Arena Quarterly 3*, September 2020, https://arena.org.au/theres-no-time-left-not-to-do-everything.

82. Hickel, *Less is More*, 20.

83. Hickel, *Less is More*, 123.

84. Amnesty International, "South Africa: Mining gathering must confront human rights violations," February 3, 2020, https://www.amnesty.org/en/latest/news/2020/02/south-africa-mining-gathering-must-confront-human-rights-violations/.

85. Hickel, *Less is More*, 142.

86. Hickel, *Less is More*, 23.

87. George Monbiot, "The big polluters' masterstroke was to blame the crisis on you and me," *The Guardian*, October 9, 2019.

88. Peter Dauvergne, "Is artificial intelligence greening global supply chains? Exposing the political economy of environmental costs," *Review of International Political Economy* (2020): 1.

89. Dauvergne, "Is artificial intelligence?," 2.

90. Dauvergne, "Is artificial intelligence?," 3.

91. See Sabu Kohso, *Radiation and Revolution* (Durham, NC: Duke University Press, 2020); M. V. Ramana, "Second Life or Half-Life? The Contested Future of Nuclear Power and Its Potential Role in a Sustainable Energy Transition," in *The Palgrave Handbook of the International Political Economy of Energy*, Thijs Van de Graaf et al., eds. (New York: Palgrave Macmillan, 2016), 363–396; and Ray Acheson, ed., *Costs, myths, and risks of nuclear power: NGO world-wide study on the implications of the catastrophe at the Fukushima Dai-ichi Nuclear Power Station* (New York: Women's International League for Peace and Freedom, 2011).

92. Mumia Abu-Jamal, "Against Japan's Nuclear Dangers," *Prison Radio*, July 27, 2011.

93. Hickel, *Less is More*, 251, 287.

94. Nick Estes, "A Red Deal," *Jacobin*, August 6, 2019.

95. Red Nation, *Red Deal*, 7.

96. Red Nation, *Red Deal*, 29–30.

97. Red Nation, *Red Deal*, 108.

98. Giacomo D'Alisa and Giorgos Kallis, "Degrowth and the State," *Ecological Economics* 169 (2020): 6.

99. D'Alisa and Kallis, "Degrowth and the State," 7.

100. Andy Battle, "Hope against Hope: An interview with Out of the Woods on COVID-19, Climate Crisis, and Disaster Communism," *Common Notions* (blog), May 13, 2020.

101. Red Nation, *Red Deal*, 37.

102. St. John Alexander, "Volunteers deliver groceries and prescriptions to isolated Vancouverites for free," CTV News, April 2, 2020.

103. "Coronavirus: Thousands volunteer to help NHS with vulnerable," BBC, March 25, 2020.

104. Genevieve Riccoboni, "WILPF Sections Mobilising to Prevent Pandemic in Africa," Women's International League for Peace and Freedom, April 16, 2020.

105. Hickel, *Less is More*, 287–88.

Conclusion: Abolition as Movement

1. Dan Berger, *The Struggle Within* (Oakland, CA: PM Press, 2014).

2. Morgan Bassichis, Alexander Lee, and Dean Spade, "Building an Abolitionist Trans and Queer Movement with Everything We've Got," in *Captive Genders: Trans Embodiment and the Prison Industrial Complex*, Eric A. Stanley and Nat Smith, eds. (Oakland, CA: AK Press, 2011), 36.

3. Dean Spade and Aaron Belkin, "Queer Militarism?! The Politics of Military Inclusion Advocacy in Authoritarian Times," *GLQ* 27, no. 2 (2021).

4. Lola Olufemi, "Why imagination is the most powerful tool that feminists have at our disposal," *gal-dem*, March 26, 2020.

5. Robyn Oxley, "Defunding the police and abolishing prisons in Australia are not radical ideas," *The Guardian*, September 17, 2020.

6. Dan Berger and David Stein, "What Is and What Could Be: The Policies of Abolition," in "Abolition for the People: The Movement for a Future Without Policing & Prisons," Kaepernick Publishing and LEVEL, October 29, 2020, https://level.medium.com/what-is-and-what-could-be-the-policies-of-abolition-9c1b49eb5a1f.

7. Tim Hollo, "There's No Time Left Not to Do Everything," *Arena Quarterly* 3, September 2020.

8. Brenna Bhandar and Rafeef Ziadah, eds., *Revolutionary Feminisms: Conversations on Collective Action and Radical Thought* (London and New York: Verso, 2020), 59.

9. Mariame Kaba, "A Love Letter to the #NoCopAcademy Organizers from Those of Us on the Freedom Side . . .," *Prison Culture*, March 13, 2019.

10. Mariame Kaba, "Everything Worthwhile Is Done with Other People," interview with Eve L. Ewing, Adi Magazine, Fall 2019.

11. Bassichis, Lee, and Spade, "Building an Abolitionist," 15-40.

12. "Abolitionist Platform toward Healthy Communities Now and beyond COVID-19," http://criticalresistance.org/abolitionist-platform-toward-healthy-communities-now-and-onward.

13. "Abolishing the War on Terror, Building Communities of Care Grassroots Policy Agenda," https://www.justiceformuslims.org/grassroots-policy-agenda.

14. The Red Nation, *The Red Deal: Indigenous Action to Save Our Earth* (Brooklyn, NY: Common Notions, 2021).

15. Phyllis Bennis, "A Green New Deal Needs to Fight US Militarism," *Jacobin*, March 8, 2019.

16. Liz Theoharis, "Dismantle the war economy," openDemocracy, July 19, 2020.

17. Joseph Nevins, "The Right to the World," *Antipode* 49, no. 5 (2017): 1349–67.

18. Women's International League for Peace and Freedom, "WILPF Resolutions," 2nd Congress, Zurich, Switzerland, 1919, https://wilpf.org/wp-content/uploads/2012/08/WILPF_triennial_congress_1919.pdf.

19. Women's International League for Peace and Freedom, "WILPF Resolutions," 12th Congress, Paris, France, August 4–8, 1953, https://wilpf.org/wp-content/uploads/2012/08/WILPF_triennial_congress_1953.pdf.

20. Spade and Belkin, "Queer Militarism?!," 296–97.

21. Maria Popova, "A Life Worth Living: Albert Camus on Our Search for Meaning and Why Happiness Is Our Moral Obligation," themarginalian (formerly brainpickings), September 22, 2014.
22. Spade and Belkin, "Queer Militarism?!," 301.
23. Lisa Lowe, "Afterword: Revolutionary Feminisms in a Time of Monsters," in *Revolutionary Feminisms: Conversations on Collective Action and Radical Thought*, Brenna Bhandar and Rafeef Ziadah, eds. (Brooklyn: Verso, 2020), 576.
24. Todd Miller, *Build Bridges, Not Walls: A Journey to a World Without Borders* (San Francisco: City Light Books, 2021), 141.

Index

About the Author

Photo by Tim Wright

Ray Acheson is director of disarmament at the Women's International League for Peace and Freedom and a steering group member of the International Campaign to Abolish Nuclear Weapons, which was awarded the Nobel Peace Prize in 2017 for its work to highlight the humanitarian impacts of nuclear weapons and work with governments to develop the Treaty on the Prohibition of Nuclear Weapons. Acheson is the author of *Banning the Bomb, Smashing the Patriarchy*.

About Haymarket Books

Haymarket Books is a radical, independent, nonprofit book publisher based in Chicago. Our mission is to publish books that contribute to struggles for social and economic justice. We strive to make our books a vibrant and organic part of social movements and the education and development of a critical, engaged, international left.

We take inspiration and courage from our namesakes, the Haymarket martyrs, who gave their lives fighting for a better world. Their 1886 struggle for the eight-hour day—which gave us May Day, the international workers' holiday—reminds workers around the world that ordinary people can organize and struggle for their own liberation. These struggles continue today across the globe—struggles against oppression, exploitation, poverty, and war.

Since our founding in 2001, Haymarket Books has published more than five hundred titles. Radically independent, we seek to drive a wedge into the risk-averse world of corporate book publishing. Our authors include Noam Chomsky, Arundhati Roy, Rebecca Solnit, Angela Y. Davis, Howard Zinn, Amy Goodman, Wallace Shawn, Mike Davis, Winona LaDuke, Ilan Pappé, Richard Wolff, Dave Zirin, Keeanga-Yamahtta Taylor, Nick Turse, Dahr Jamail, David Barsamian, Elizabeth Laird, Amira Hass, Mark Steel, Avi Lewis, Naomi Klein, and Neil Davidson. We are also the trade publishers of the acclaimed Historical Materialism Book Series and of Dispatch Books.